ACRL PUBLICATIONS IN LIBRARIANSHIP NO. 56

The Changing Academic Library

Operations, Culture, Environments

John M. Budd

Association of College and Research Libraries
A DIVISION OF THE
American Library Association
Chicago   2005

The paper used in this publication meets the minimum requirements of American National Standard for Information Sciences—Permanence of Paper for Printed Library Materials, ANSI Z39.48-1992. ∞

Library of Congress Cataloging-in-Publication Data

Budd, John M., 1953

   The changing academic library : operations, cultures, environments / John M. Budd.
     p.   cm. — (Publications in librarianship ; no. 56)
   Rev. ed. of: The academic library. Englewood, Colo. : Libraries Unlimited, 1998.
   Includes bibliographical references and index.
   ISBN 0-8389-8318-9 (alk. paper)
   1. Academic libraries—United States. I. Budd, John M., 1953– Academic library. II. Title.
III. Series: ACRL publications in librarianship ; no. 56.

Z674.A75 no. 56
[Z675.U5]
027.7'0973—dc22 2005005851

Printed in the United States of America

09 08 07 06 05   5 4 3 2 1

CONTENTS

ACKNOWLEDGMENTS

M y first thanks go out to all those people who have inquired into so many aspects of academic libraries. Most of what I've done here is to cumulate their work. I also want to thank Tony Schwartz, editor of *PIL*, for all the work he put into this book. Most of all, I want to express enormous gratitude to Tony, Stanley Wilder, and Diane Zabel. These three people are the highest exemplars of manuscript reviewers I've ever seen. Their close readings of the work have made this a much better book. Of course, all errors are entirely my responsibility.

Chapter 1

Introduction and a Little History

WHY STUDY ACADEMIC LIBRARIES?

The question that heads this chapter is not a rhetorical one. In fact, the entirety of this text is based on an assumption that is relevant to an answer to the question—the need for the discipline of library and information science (LIS) and, perhaps more particularly, the profession of librarianship to be more reflexive, to take a more critical look at underlying purposes. Some may question the need for type-of-library courses in LIS programs, given the pervasive sensitivity to information throughout all of society. This is not a trivial concern; it is important to think about the place of information in our world—its technology, economics, politics, and so on. The existence of a text such as this one depends on the realization of shared ground among types of libraries and information agencies and, more important, the unique features of the academic library that warrant a course of study devoted to it. This initial chapter explores the rationale for such study and sets the stage for the rest of the text.

As was just stated, there are commonalities among types of libraries. For instance, all information agencies must be aware of the means of production of information. This entails knowledge about authorship, the business of publishing, decisions regarding dissemination (including media), and pricing. Beyond these considerations are the matters of local storage and retrieval, issues of access, the space within the library devoted to specific functions, and delivery mechanisms (including remote delivery of electronic or physical forms of information). Naturally, local aspects will be the most likely determinants of any library's response to the challenges inherent in the aforementioned elements of information. Nonetheless, each library, regardless of its environment, must incorporate the features of the information landscape into its decision making. The production and dissemination of information is largely external to the library at the present time (although some have suggested that academic libraries become more active in production and dissemination, and some, such as Johns Hopkins University, Cornell University, and the University of Virginia, have taken up this call). It probably has to be acknowledged that libraries may not be in the strongest position to exert influence over much of the world of information, although academic libraries can have a voice in the direction of scholarly communication. Libraries of all types have been reactive to the decisions, frequently market driven, of those who have control over the economics of the information business. As we will see, however, libraries are definitely not satisfied with a passive role and are trying to influence policy and practice.

To a greater or lesser extent, libraries in all environments constitute a relatively small proportion of the market. I am not referring solely to the market for published materials, although the observation holds for that as well. When a library must buy, for instance, office desks and chairs, the supplier with whom the library negotiates probably sells to a broad audience and does not depend only on library trade for its livelihood. The same is true when the library purchases computer hardware, peripherals, and some software. The market also is broad for many office supplies and other products. On the other hand, libraries do constitute a substantial market for some products, such as shelving for books and periodicals, materials storage cabinets, and carrels. The market clout that libraries can exert may enable them to influence product design and, to some degree perhaps, price. For example, the automation vendors that are most responsive to the library market in terms of both system capabilities and cost tend to be those that thrive. Even with some materials the library market is extremely important to producers. Reference works such as indexes are purchased or licensed principally by libraries. In general, the market influence that libraries have tends to cross environmental lines, with all types of libraries sharing it, even if disproportionately.

Beyond products and markets, libraries share some internal similarities. Libraries of a certain size tend to exhibit few variations in organizational structure. In most libraries with more than a few staff members, the lines of authority and decision-making responsibilities are usually clearly defined and, more often than not, follow a hierarchical pattern. Ultimate authority rests with the director, and the amount of authority and responsibility vested in other individuals tends to vary from one library to the next, but independently of library type. Moreover, most libraries tend to organize along functional lines. That is, libraries separate functions such as public services and technical services, and decisions are frequently made within the sphere of a particular functional specialization (e.g., the reference department), with decision parameters defined by the needs and activities of that specialization. It is true that functional specializations may very somewhat from one type of library to another, but the concept of functional division crosses environmental lines. Staffing patterns also follow the functional organization, with professional staff holding certain positions and support staff performing duties within a fairly specific, and constrained, set of guidelines. Organizational communication follows the basic organizational pattern, in many libraries being primarily vertical in direction. (This observation pertains more frequently to formal communication; informal communication may take many different forms and is influenced by both social and organizational factors.) It should be noted that the description of vast generalizations is not intended to depict the organizational structure of any specific library but, rather, to illustrate broad tendencies. Also, the mention of these tendencies does not imply approval of the general organizational pattern. Much more is said about organization later.

THE ACADEMIC LIBRARY AND ITS ENVIRONMENT

To understand the functioning of the academic library—the content of its collections, the mechanisms of access, the purposes of services, the qualifications and character of personnel—it is essential that the college and the university be understood. This is not a simple task; the academic institution is not any one single thing. Although there is some consistency of mission (all recognize an educational imperative), there is a considerable degree of diversity in higher education. The research university and the community college are, in some ways, worlds apart. As we move through each chapter and each topic of this book, we explore the distinctions as they affect every aspect of libraries—their collections, their services, and their staffs. With that said, it is still helpful to describe the academic institution, at least in the abstract. Although they focus their attention on the university, Louis Round Wilson and Maurice Tauber summed up the functions of higher education several decades ago. They wrote that "it may be noted that the university is concerned with (1) conservation of knowledge and ideas, (2) teaching, (3) research, (4) publication, (5) extension and services, and (6) interpretation" (Wilson and Tauber 1945, 17). Although the order and the extent of emphasis on those elements differ among the various kinds of institutions, there are similarities as well. As is true of all organizations, the college and the university have their own political structures, their own cultures. Further, they have their own ways of responding to the outside world. The academic library is part of the politics, part of the culture, and part of the response of its parent institution. Whatever affects higher education affects the academic library. Part of the shared impact is obvious: changes in financial support, upward or downward, determine the ability of the institution or the library to accomplish its goals; a sensitivity to market pressures has an impact on curricula and programs, as well as on collections and services; demographic changes affect the institution's delivery of education and the library's delivery of service. Derek Bok observed that one reality for American higher education is the competition among institutions for students, funding, and favor. He asked, "How does competition affect the process of education and the development of academic programs" (Bok 1986, 34)? For some time, institutional competition has included libraries. The dominant thinking has been that bigger is better—bigger budgets, more holdings and subscriptions, larger staffs. It is doubtful that the measures of the past will carry the same weight in the future. This is not to say that they will be forsaken but, rather, the external and internal factors that affect teaching (including not only the lesson plans, but also the means of delivery), finance, and knowledge growth will work to alter the definition of success in libraries. It is time to outline some of the principal challenges faced by higher education, which are explored in greater depth in later chapters.

THE CHANGING FACE OF HIGHER EDUCATION

Because the library is an integral component of the mission of every college or university, it is incumbent upon academic librarians to understand the changes that are taking place in higher education. Some of the changes have a direct impact on the library and its services. These include alterations in institutions' curricula, demographic changes in student bodies, and additions to the media used in the classroom (and beyond) and in support of research. Other changes to higher education have equally broad and deep implications. The first, and most important, of these changes is in the realm of financial support. The very simple explanation of the problem is that support from public or other external sources has dwindled as the costs of running colleges and universities have increased. But there are more facets to the problem than this. In chapter 7, finances are dealt with in much greater depth, but some initial presentation of the dilemma is necessary here to provide a context for all that is to follow. One of the first things to realize is that there are differences between privately and publicly supported institutions. (To complicate matters, there is now a small, but growing, number of for-profit universities. A discussion of these institutions may fit best within the topic of distance education in chapter 10.)

Private colleges and universities, though varying considerably, share some common concerns with regard to financial support. These schools rely heavily on income from tuition and donations from without, ideally contributions to endowment funds. The importance of endowments is clear; they provide an ongoing base of financial resources. Endowments, however, are subject to the fluctuation, upward or downward, of financial markets, because they are invested in any of a number of ways. Because of the fluctuation that certainly cannot be controlled completely by the institution, the return on the college or university's investment will vary from year to year. If this seems to be a disadvantage, remember that no investment yields no return. Private institutions of all sizes and missions seek to attract substantial donations in order to, first, meet the immediate needs of the school and, second, to provide for future growth and development. The number of existing institutions means that there is competition for private and corporate support. There also is competition for students. At the risk of oversimplifying, two factors, more than any other, influence the recruitment of students—quality and cost. The colleges and universities of highest-perceived quality tend to be able to recruit from a national base. Many other colleges have to focus on recruiting in a more narrowly defined geographic region. Those colleges, then, become subject to demographic shifts that affect some areas of the United States. As might be expected, private colleges and universities have practical limits on the amounts they can charge for tuition, but the limits vary greatly from one institution to another.

Public schools also must recruit students and also are engaged in competition for qualified students. Moreover, public schools are sensitive to the limits to the amount they can charge for tuition, but these limits are greatly affected by the amounts of public support they receive. William Friday, long-time president of the University of North Carolina, noted, "Increases that reflect rising costs of living are appropriate, but our quick and ready turn to tuition as the way out of our difficulties is now bringing us face to face with a new danger: We may make the ability to pay the primary condition of admission to higher education" (1994, 32). The "public" in public colleges and universities most frequently refers to the state because state governments are usually the principal sources of support. The common lament of colleges and universities is that government support has not kept pace with the cost of education and the demands placed on it. The diminishing proportion of many colleges' and universities' budgets coming from the state has led some institutions to refer to themselves as "state assisted," rather than state supported. Direct federal support for many institutions has been minimal in the recent past, and there is no indication that the federal government sees direct support for higher education as a priority. In response to constrained avenues of public support, public institutions also have begun to create or enhance endowments from private sources. Such action prompted Bok to state that "the differences between public and private universities have steadily narrowed; many private colleges now receive assistance from their state governments, while public institutions have raised tuitions and have grown increasingly aggressive in seeking private gifts" (1986, 11). In addition to private donations, some institutions seek out corporate donations or relationships. Corporate donations may carry some implications that colleges and universities will want to be wary of, however.

For a complex set of reasons, certainly not exclusive of financial matters, colleges and universities are coming under increasing criticism. The sources of the criticism reside both without and within academe. Further, the criticism comes from both liberal and conservative sources. Cary Nelson and Michael Bérubé offered a litany of some of the common complaints against higher education:

> teachers don't teach; scholars fritter away their time and your tax dollars on studies of music videos; campus regulations thwart free speech; the Western cultural heritage is besieged by tenured radicals; heterosexual white men are under attack from feminist, multiculturalist, and gay and lesbian groups; universities are buying luxury yachts with federal research dollars; academic standards of all kinds are in tatters; undergraduates lack both reading skills and moral foundations; and, in the midst of all this, to add financial insult to intellectual injury, college tuitions are skyrocketing (1995, 1).

The complaints are so numerous and so varied, and so likely to affect academic libraries and their place within institutions, we are obliged to examine them in much more detail in chapter 4.

Another extremely important recent change in higher education reflects larger societal shifts that impinge upon people's ability to take advantage of traditional college and university offerings. Reasons for the shift include pressures on individuals to join the workforce before they have the opportunity to attend a college or university, relatively inflexible work schedules, and the need for many to attain new knowledge and skills. The primary effect of these factors has been, over the last couple of decades, to change the makeup of the student bodies at many institutions. Undergraduate students are no longer only in the 18- to 22-year-old range. More people want to attend on a part-time basis. The initial responses of colleges and universities have been to add a larger number and greater variety of evening classes and, in some instances, weekend classes. (Quite a while ago, some institutions offered weekend classes.) The trend of such course offerings appears to be cyclical, though the reasons for the offerings change over time. For instance, a number of schools have a long-standing commitment to extension teaching, that is, offering courses at sites other than the home of the institution. Many such efforts have been located in publicly supported schools and motivated by a goal of serving the needs of the tax-paying populace. Although this goal certainly has not disappeared, more colleges and universities, including private institutions, are building their extension offerings as a means of enhancing their income.

One particular response to the demand for offerings aimed at part-time, nonresident students is a specific articulation of distance learning. Although traditional extension efforts have entailed an individual in the classroom to teach and lead the class, more institutions are employing technology to transmit the teacher's presentation to several sites simultaneously. Some such transmissions are still "one-way," which is to say that the lecturer's image and/or voice, along with some graphic images, are transmitted to the receiving sites, but the people at the sites cannot communicate with the lecturer. However, technological advances have made interactive transmission much more feasible. Web-based courses using commercially available courseware are becoming quite common in both public and private institutions. And some are using Internet video. This kind of distance learning still can be seen to be at an emerging stage. Colleges and universities are grappling with a number of vital questions: What are the institutional costs of establishing a distance learning initiative? What are the costs to the sites (and who pays)? What pedagogical skills are needed in such an environment? Do the educational benefits equal those of a class on the home campus? Are there unique compensation issues (for instance, if a teacher's classes are videotaped for later use)? There is another set of important questions of concern to libraries: What are the information needs of the remote sites? How can they be met, and at what cost? These are definitely not trivial questions and, at most colleges and universities, they have yet to be fully resolved.

ELECTRONIC INFORMATION

The entire library community and the entirety of higher education are deeply concerned about the state of information today and in the future. For many decades, both the library and the university (and to a somewhat lesser extent, the college) have resigned themselves to growth of the graphic record. Over that time period, the number of books published grew at a substantial rate as scholars and researchers sought to communicate their work with colleagues. (It should be noted that the future of the scholarly monograph is not certain; finances and emerging technologies will have an impact on both the medium of production and the number of titles produced.) Over the same period, the amount of periodical literature has grown at a much faster rate. This growth has taken a couple of forms. The number of journals published has increased greatly; each year, new journals are established in just about every discipline. The growth has been especially pronounced in science, technology, and medicine (STM), where both the numbers of journals published and the prices of those journals have created serious problems for academic libraries. In addition to increasing in number, journals have increased in size. Again, this is most prominent in STM, where many journals have increased their frequency of publication over the years and where each issue has grown in number of pages. It has not been unusual for the increases in frequency and size of a title to lead the publisher to split that single title into two (and sometimes more) titles, each appearing frequently and growing in size over time.

CHANGE AND ORGANIZATIONAL STRUCTURE

Throughout the twentieth century, higher education has grown in size and complexity. This growth has been pronounced over the most recent three decades in particular. As the United States began to perceive competitive importance in education, there came more "official" attention to the role higher education could play in advancing national interests in science, technology, and other areas. Vast increases in funding from government sources (principally states, but federal support as well) enabled public colleges and universities especially to add to their faculties and their physical plants in order to deal with the rise in the number of students. Throughout the 1960s, the growth of every facet of higher education was enormous. This period marked growth not only in size, but also in the diversity of course offerings, programs of study, and opportunities for research. The focus on campuses in the early days of the growth spurt was decidedly on short-term matters, such as constructing classroom buildings and dormitories and hiring faculty. The pressure felt by academic administrators was tied to the immediate needs of educating and housing increasing numbers of students. Little time was available for examination of the organizational structure of the institution. Because such time was at a premium, traditional structures continued to dominate in higher education.

What are these traditional structures? Colleges and universities had been influenced by the modes of organizing that dominated the corporate world and public institutions. These, in turn, had been outgrowths of the evolution of organization observed by Max Weber. As companies, governments, and others grew ever more complex, the organizational structures reflected specialization in knowledge and expertise and, more important, in authority and decision making. The work these institutions were engaged in became too diverse for individuals to be able to have a large sphere of authority. As it grew, higher education took on organizational characteristics of these other institutions because there was increasing complexity in fiscal responsibility, personnel management, and disciplinary administration. Colleges and universities were affected by the factors recognized by Jerald Hage and Michael Aiken (1967): (1) organizational complexity, that is, the level of knowledge and expertise in an organization;

(2) centralization, defined as the degree of participation in decision making; (3) formalization, or the number of rules and the degree of job codification; and (4) stratification, referring to the distribution of rewards. Given these elements, it is not surprising that academic institutions have adopted a bureaucratic form of organization.

The academic library, as it likewise grew in size and complexity (marked by increases in staff sizes, budgets, numbers of material formats, and so on), emulated its parent organization's organizational patterns. Whether the emulation was conscious is moot, the library organized itself according to functions and sometimes media. The traditional bifurcation of the library into public and technical services seemed to be the logical scheme because there were clearly perceivable differences in the kinds of work and knowledge embodied in those functions. Over time, additional functions were added to the original ones, notably collection development and library automation. As some libraries grew even larger, the organizational divisions began to take on the character of academic disciplines. With this came the rise of chemistry libraries, music libraries, business libraries, and so forth. In addition, the divisions were based on perceptions of needed knowledge and expertise. In time, dissatisfaction with this mode of organization began to transcend single institutions and become a part of the discourse of academic librarianship. The result has been some different conceptions of the basis of organization, as well as some conscious changes founded on those reconceptions.

THE ACADEMIC LIBRARY USER

For much of the twentieth century, the typical college student was between 18 and 22 years old and attending school full-time. As we have already seen, with the economic downturns of the 1970s came a revision of the model for the "typical" student. This is not to say that all students prior to 1970 were resident students in their late teens and early twenties. At an accelerated rate, however, more women began attending colleges and universities, as did more nonwhite and older students. Campuses began to reflect the racial, ethnic, cultural, and age diversity of the general population. In part, the student body was transformed by increasing opportunities: governments were supporting financial aid packages in various forms, more institutions (especially two-year schools) were opening, and a number of four-year institutions were adjusting schedules to be more amenable to a part-time, working student body. There has been a particular responsiveness on the parts of two-year colleges founded since 1970 (and two-year colleges that existed in 1970 became more responsive) to a potential student body that may be coming to college later in life and may not have the economic wherewithal to attend school on a full-time basis. These institutions are generally designed to serve such a population.

What can we say about the nontraditional student? One thing that becomes evident is that many individuals who are classified in the "nontraditional" category are first-generation attendees of higher education. Their backgrounds may be different from the academic world, which usually requires both individual and institutional adjustment if the students are to succeed. Colette Wagner and Augusta Kappner (1988) offer some characteristics of nontraditional students that still apply today:

> *academically*, they are at high risk in the traditional college classroom due to insufficient preparation at lower levels of the educational system;
>
> *economically*, they are struggling for survival and require financial assistance in order to undertake college study;
>
> *socially*, they are predominantly members of minority groups and first generation college students;
>
> *experientially*, they are likely to be older and more accustomed to bearing the wage-earning, child-rearing, and other responsibilities of a mature adult;
>
> *attitudinally*, they are less likely to take college for granted, skeptical of authority, interested in exerting some "ownership" rights over their own education, and highly motivated (1988, 44–45).

The colleges and universities of today are in a position to cease viewing these individuals as nontraditional. Most institutions have two decades or more of experience serving a diverse student body. It now is incumbent upon the schools to come to a full realization of the myriad purposes people have for seeking higher education and to alter former models of success for students.

Change for colleges and universities is not restricted to students. Faculty and their academic disciplines also have seen transformation since 1970. For some, there has been an increased emphasis on scholarly productivity, as defined principally by numbers of publications. As might be expected, the pressure on faculty to publish began at research universities but has spread to many four-year institutions. Pressures to publish are not quite as simple and straightforward as they might at first seem. In part, the source of pressure results from some institutional insistence on accountability of faculty. Publications, especially in respected journals or by prestigious presses, are easily measured gauges by which faculty can be judged. One potential criticism of this means of evaluation is that the assessment of quality is removed from the institution and placed into the hands of editors, referees, and publishers. The assumptions by the college or university is that if a faculty member is able to get a paper accepted by a highly selective journal, the paper is, de facto, of high quality.

The dynamic is more complicated than such a single scenario might suggest. Since the 1970s, there has been an oversupply of doctorates; that is, there are more people earning doctorates in some disciplines than there are faculty positions coming open. Academic institutions are in the position of being very selective when they hire a new faculty member. They can afford to look for those individuals whose accomplishments, such as publications, will accrue favorably to the prestige and notoriety of the institution. In this sense, there is an objective measure that academic administrators can use when hiring or making tenure decisions. If we add to numbers of publications the attraction of external funding for research, we see an emerging algorithm that might be used to help with personnel assessment. As we will see, there are many without and within academe who are critical of such an objective approach to hiring, tenure, and promotion. The criticisms take several forms and focus on different manifestations of the perceived problems, and offer different solutions to the dilemma.

Beyond t is the area of cognitive science. Cognitive science is not the property of any single department; work in the discipline traverses the fields of psychology, neuroscience, artificial intelligence, philosophy, and linguistics. Individual scholars are transcending traditional bounds with work on specific research questions. One effect of this phenomenon is a broadeninhe pressure to produce more, faculty are taking upon themselves some revisions of the foundations of inquiry. As notions are shifting regarding the appropriate models for research in all disciplines, many faculty are looking beyond potentially restrictive departmental designations for opportunities to delve into persistent questions. One example of the interaction of various academic disciplinesg of the basis for collaboration. To an extent, such efforts have been facilitated by institutions through the establishment of research centers and/or areas studies units (such as American studies or women's studies).

Naturally, these changes also have affected academic libraries. The latter, interdisciplinary study and research, has necessitated a more holistic view of services, including reference and collection development. A structure based on subject specialists who have responsibility for discreet subject areas or academic departments may not be the most effective means of supporting inquiry that crosses disciplinary lines. At the least, the library's subject specialists should be willing to communicate with one another, both at the time of occurrence and in anticipation of any cross-disciplinary collaboration. Regarding the former development (pressure to publish), the increases in publication by faculty—articles submitted to journals, books published—has resulted in more than the library can, and possibly should, acquire. An offshoot of faculty's activities has been the expansion of existing journals, the creation of new journals, and the publication of more books. It must be said, though, that the publishing outlets for scholarly books are not as plentiful as they were just a few years ago. (This situation is explored in greater detail in a later chapter.) In the midst of the increasing size of the record of scholarship (publications) and the need to provide new sources of data and communication, many scholars are arguing for the need to maintain traditional library functions. The disparate demands of faculty tug at libraries' financial and personnel resources in ways that certainly are not diminishing.

WHAT IS A LIBRARY?

The foregoing suggests an open question: What is an academic library? This book probably will not provide a definitive answer to the question, but, if successful, it will provide a framework for an examination of the purpose of the library in the environment of higher education. Such an examination will likely last throughout a career. Integral to the project is the context, the world of the academy. That context defines the purpose of the library, even if it cannot define how that purpose is to be fulfilled. The library of yesterday, today, and tomorrow has elements that transcend time. To the extent that there is instruction, the library offers a supplement and complement to the curriculum. It offers content essential to the acts of teaching and learning. It provides content that is integral to inquiry, whether the inquirer is a freshman or the most respected professor. Note the word "content." In some senses, it does not matter if the content is in print or virtual. That is, if the most effective means of transmitting the information is through one medium in particular, the library will—and should—handle that medium.

With that said, there are what some would term challenges (others might refer to them as problems) to providing content in the environment of the colleges and universities. Although instruction is likely to remain at the heart of the academy, we are seeing new developments in the means by which instruction occurs. The most dramatic change is in distance learning. We will look at this phenomenon more closely, but for now it should be realized that there is considerable impetus, from a number of sources, to deliver instruction to the student without the student being at the site of the institution. Interactive video and audio transmission and Web-based tools can make such a desire a reality. But what about information resources? If the student is many miles from the college, he or she is many miles from the college library. How might the needs of such a student be met? What would be the cost of the various alternatives that may meet this challenge? These questions have many elements. For one thing, it must be decided what set of assumptions will guide decision making in the instance of distance learning. It will have to be determined if the essential need is access to course-related information, to a wide array of supplementary resources, or to the mediation that is part of reference services. It also must be determined what it takes—money, materials, telecommunications, personnel— to provide the essential service.

It is certain that the academic library is a multifarious being and subject to evolution. It may be that the defining feature of the library will become service, and perhaps that is as it should be. The library is not merely an agglomeration of "stuff" that is open to all potential users. It is, assuredly, a collection, but it also is an access mechanism. Access is provided by formal means, such as the library's catalog (and we will have to examine the construction of the library's catalog later) and user instruction. It also is provided by more flexible means, such as reference services. The most critical element of the academic library, or any library, is the user (and the use to which he or she will put the library). The user is interested principally in content, in something that genuinely informs him or her. The medium by which the content is transmitted depends on the nature of the content (some kinds of content are more amenable to particular media), the cost of transmission, and the needs of the user. These principles will govern our exploration as we delve into the nature and structure of higher education (which defines use), the means by which the library works with users and content, and the ways libraries structure work to accomplish their missions.

At this point, we have a context for the study of academic libraries. Academic libraries are different from other types of libraries, primarily because their environments are different. As was just stated, we study these organizations because, for the academic library to be effective, we must understand all that surrounds it. That means coming to grips with the purpose of higher education in rhetoric and in fact, the strictures imposed on higher education, the information base that is integral to the work of the academy, the structure of the library that supports the college or university, and the diversity of the library's users. The context can be enriched by some historical background.

A BRIEF HISTORY OF HIGHER EDUCATION AND ACADEMIC LIBRARIES IN THE UNITED STATES

We should explore, at least cursorily, how the American college and university came to be as they are today. Along the way, we will see how the libraries attached to these institutions have evolved. One may ask why we would want to study the history of higher education and libraries. Can't we learn everything we need to know by looking at things as they are now? To be sure, we do have to examine the present state if we are to understand at all how these organizations function, what drives them, and what challenges they face. However, just as each of us is a product of all that has happened to him or her, of the experiences, events, and thoughts of an individual past, so, too, are colleges and universities (and their libraries) shaped by all that has gone before. As we will see, the history of higher education was not a journey taken in isolation. Education has been a product of many of the aims and ambitions of humans, and it has not been separate from the religious, political, social, and economic lives of the people who have helped to shape it and those who have, themselves, been shaped by it.

Origins

As an institution, the university is younger than the library by a couple of millennia or so. The earliest Western university dates back to the twelfth century, so this institution has been with us for a little more than 800 years. Paris and Bologna were the homes of the first universities; by the year 1400, fifty-six were scattered around Western Europe. The two universities at Paris and Bologna distinguished themselves from other schools (such as the one at Salerno, which was almost exclusively a school of medicine) by offering students a broader education to students. The medieval university was characterized by a couple of important features: its organization and its curriculum. The earliest universities were organized principally by students. The structure was influenced by existing guilds of artisans and craftsmen. The students were responsible for the founding of some of these early universities, for their organization, for the establishment of rules and regulations, and for the hiring of faculty. The university was, in some senses, a collective bargaining unit. Originally, faculty salaries came from the fees that the students established and levied upon themselves. Further, the students devised a set of rules for the faculty. For example, there was to be no unexcused absence: if a professor left town, he paid a deposit to ensure his return. If the professor did not get an audience of at least five students for a lecture, he was fined as though he were absent. The lecture had to begin with the class bell and could extend no longer than one minute past the ending bell. Further, the professor had to cover the subject systematically and thoroughly, and he served at the students' pleasure.

The foundation of education was fairly simple. Everything rested on the seven liberal arts: the quadrivium (based on form), which included mathematics, astronomy, geometry, and music; and the trivium (based on interpretation of form), which included grammar, rhetoric, and logic. To these, eventually, was added specialized study, for instance, in medicine, law, or theology. Instruction consisted largely of lecture and recitation. The professor spoke on the subject and, to demonstrate a command of what was taught, the student would repeat. To earn the degree, the student had to be able to present a disputation of the lecture's content. Because the early universities predated printing, it would be expected that there were few textbooks. At some universities, though, the professor's lectures were turned over for copying so that students could have access to them. This book trade was carefully regulated by the university to ensure availability and control pricing. Customarily, the students rented the textbooks (to reduce the amount of copying needed) and were charged on the basis of length, for instance, a fixed price per quire (25 leaves).

Librarians were likewise something of a rarity at the beginning of the university. Little recorded information was available, except on materials of a religious nature. As Charles Homer Haskins observed, "In course of time, however, books were given for the use of students, chiefly in the form of bequests to the colleges, where they could be borrowed or consulted on the spot. By 1338 the oldest extant catalogue of the Sorbonne, the chief (University of) Paris library, lists 1722 volumes" (1957, 39). From the sixteenth century on, libraries grew in holdings and importance to the universities. The business of printing not only ensured that more copies of books were readily available, but it also spurred growth in the numbers of individuals writing on many subjects, including secular subjects. Printing enabled the widespread communication of ideas that would be of interest to faculty and students. Moreover, greater numbers of titles were being printed than could be included in the curriculum, so the library became more important as the source of supplementary reading and individual study.

The proliferation of printed books prompted some benefactors of universities to take it upon themselves to promote the growth of libraries. One example of the beneficence of an individual is the rebirth of the library at Oxford (which had fallen into disrepair in the course of the sixteenth century), due almost entirely to Thomas Bodley. Under his auspices, its collection grew sufficiently for the library to be reopened in renovated quarters in 1602. The library's catalog of 1605, compiled by the keeper of the books, Thomas James, listed 5,611 entries, including both printed and manuscript books. This was a modest beginning, but almost all of those books had been acquired by Bodley. For his efforts the library was named for him. Oxford's library got a huge boost in 1610 because of an agreement with the Stationers Company (the official copyright registration body in Great Britain), whereby one copy of every book registered by the company was deposited in the library. The libraries of the universities at Cambridge, Dublin, and Edinburgh likewise benefited from the Stationers Company's action.

By the seventeenth century, the universities of Europe were expanding their curriculum, reflecting the growing interest in breadth of learning and rising levels of literacy. The burgeoning interest in scholarship was certainly aided by the business of printing, which, by then, was a widespread and thriving enterprise. The established universities of Europe, and especially of England, would provide a model for the first steps toward higher education in colonial America.

Colonial Colleges and Their Libraries

As stated above, the universities of England provided the models for the first colleges in the British colonies. By an act of the Massachusetts General Court in 1636, Harvard College was founded and named for its first notable benefactor, John Harvard. (It should be noted that Harvard was not the first such institution in the New World; that honor belongs to the University of Santiago in what is now the Dominican Republic, founded in 1538.) Because many of the Massachusetts colonists were graduates of Cambridge University, Harvard was modeled after Emmanuel College, Cambridge. The initial intention behind the founding of Harvard was to provide the Bay Colony with a supply of clergymen. Also in the minds of the founders was the provision of new generations of political leaders.

Harvard was founded early in the development of the Massachusetts colony, and its early years mirror that of the colony itself in growing from immediate religious needs to the secular needs of the body politic, especially the need for educated leaders. Harvard's early success, and perhaps that of the Bay Colony, may have been due, in part, to the concentration of the colony's population. Settlement centered on Boston and Cambridge to such an extent that there was an immediate and constant supply of students, as well as a concentrated source of financial and political support.

Before too lofty an impression of the early days of Harvard is engendered, it has to be said that the college was small during the entirety of the colonial period. Only a tiny portion of the population was of sufficient upbringing, status, and financial wherewithal to attend Harvard. And we cannot forget that higher education was then closed to women and would be for some time to come. Harvard was at a comparative disadvantage to its European counterparts. Because it was new and small in the seventeenth century, it was not an easy matter to find educated individuals to take faculty positions. The possibility didn't exist to recruit professors who had been educated at universities not too far away. But then the colony's population didn't grow so rapidly that Harvard required a large faculty for an increasing number of students. Also, in the pre-Revolutionary years, the curriculum of Harvard was narrow and prescribed. With virtually no choice regarding subjects of study, there was little need for an expansive faculty or a large physical plant.

In 1667, the first librarian, Solomon Stoddard, was appointed. That same year, the first set of library regulations was implemented. These rules dictated who might borrow books from the library, the penalty for abusing those privileges, the care of the library, and the acceptance of gifts. The limitations on use of the library were quite severe; only senior members of the college community were allowed to borrow books, and the daily hours of operation were eleven o'-clock in the morning until one in the afternoon. Although these regulations seem restrictive, it is important to remember that the early collection was neither large nor especially distinguished and that the mode of instruction was lecture and recitation, so undergraduate students had little need of the library's collection. Moreover, access was limited in that no catalog existed until 1723. It was not until 1764, just prior to the Revolutionary War and nearly 130 years after its founding, that Harvard's library collection numbered 5,000 volumes.

Only one other colonial college was founded in the seventeenth century: the College of William and Mary in Virginia in 1693. Whereas Harvard was modeled after Emmanuel College, Cambridge, William and Mary was based on Queen's College, Oxford, because more of the settlers of Virginia were graduates of Oxford. However, the mode of instruction was similar to that at Harvard: lecture and recitation. The College of William and Mary grew slowly; one reason for the difficulty of building a student body was the economic structure of the colony. Virginia was built on farming, so the population was more dispersed than it was in Massachusetts. One necessity of farming or plantation management was having the male children at home to help with work and supervision. Further, the tendency was stronger in Virginia to send sons to Europe for their higher education. As with Harvard, an initial mission of William and Mary was the education of clergy, but its mission soon expanded to include public service.

Seven more colleges were founded prior to the Revolutionary War. Rather than recount the particulars of their founding (which could become a bit tedious), table 1.1 presents the nine pre-Revolutionary colleges along with their dates of founding. The circumstances surrounding the founding of these colleges are not so dissimilar that they warrant more detailed treatment here. All of the colonial colleges were founded by members of Protestant sects, but all quickly became much more than church schools. Early in the history of each of the colleges,

TABLE 1.1   Colonial U.S. Colleges

College	Date of Founding
Harvard College	1636
College of William and Mary	1693
Collegiate School on Connecticut (Yale)	1701
College of Philadelphia (U. of Pennsylvania)	1740
College of New Jersey (Princeton)	1746
King's College (Columbia)	1754
College of Rhode Island (Brown)	1764
Queen's College (Rutgers)	1766
Dartmouth College	1769

the need for a broader mission became evident and each embraced the expanded mission. Also, in each case support came principally from private funds, although some public money was appropriated. Today, two of the nine, William and Mary and Rutgers, are publicly supported.

The histories of the libraries of all nine colleges have similarities as well. In each instance, the donation of books by a generous benefactor provided the foundation of the library collection. The library at each college was a single room in the college's main (or only) building. Of course, not a great deal of space was needed; each collection was small. Prior to the war, Yale's collection was second in size to Harvard's, with about 4,000 volumes in 1766. One departure in terms of support for the library occurred at the College of Philadelphia (the University of Pennsylvania). Students were charged library fines, but fees also were levied for degrees and a portion of the fees collected went to the library. It cost a student fifteen shillings to receive a bachelor's degree and one pound for a master's. Library fees, then, are not such a new phenomenon. Also, the library was administered by a faculty committee, so faculty generally have long been accustomed to having a proprietary attitude toward the library.

The colleges and their libraries suffered greatly during the Revolutionary War. One devastating effect was the toll on potential students. Able-bodied young men put aside higher learning in the cause of independence. Harvard graduated sixty-three students in 1771; it would be another forty years before Harvard would have a graduating class of that size again. The burning or destruction of college building was not uncommon. For example, though it wasn't destroyed, Nassau Hall, the main and largest building (and the building housing the library) of the College of New Jersey (Princeton University), was occupied in turn by American, then British, then American troops. Furniture and some books were used to fuel fireplaces; other books were carted away by Cornwallis's troops. When the war ended, Dr. Ashbel Green entered Nassau Hall and observed that "what was left, did not deserve the name of a library" (Shores 1966, 31). At King's College (Columbia University), much of the collection was literally lost. Many books were removed from the library for safekeeping but eventually found in 1802 in St. Paul's Chapel. Of the nine colleges, only Dartmouth was spared, primarily because Hanover, New Hampshire, was sufficiently out of the way of fighting and troop movement. For the other eight, their institutional lives had to begin anew.

Life after the Revolution

Shortly after the Revolutionary War ended, the process of recovery began. Perhaps the most notable development of this era was the infusion of public funds for the support of higher education. Even the colonial colleges were able to get into the act. In 1792, the New York legislature appropriated £1,500 to help rebuild the Columbia University library. Some states founded their own public universities. The University of Georgia was chartered in 1785 and opened in 1795; the University of North Carolina was chartered in 1789 and opened in 1793. Both of these institutions still claim bragging rights as the first public university in the U.S. As the population of the newly formed United States began to grow and as people began to move westward, the founding of colleges became a favorite participant sport. Many of these new colleges were founded by religious sects and the foundings, to an extent, followed the westward expansion. At times, competing sects founded their own colleges in the same locales. The majority of these colleges were very small and poorly funded. Not surprisingly, most closed not long after they opened.

Another phenomenon in the immediate aftermath of the war was a change in the curriculum of many institutions. Because the early colleges based themselves on the British model, their curricula centered on classical learning, not all that far removed from the *trivium* and *quadrivium.* Some notable individuals who were shapers of the new republic *and* of the new universities, such as Benjamin Franklin and Thomas Jefferson, were influenced by Enlightenment thought that swept through Europe in the eighteenth century. This mode of thinking was characterized by an intellectual skepticism, the belief in the perfectibility of humankind (and all of the secular implications that came along with such a belief), and an openness to science and its attendant potential for progress. Instead of studying the teachings of Aristotle, Plato, and others of the classical world, the movers and shapers of many of the New World universities were reading David Hume and Adam Smith and influenced by the physics of Isaac Newton. The secular was not utterly replacing the religious by a long shot, but the entire tenor of higher education was undergoing a transformation. At some universities, courses in modern literature and language were initiated, as well as in medicine and agriculture. The transformation was far from total, but the debate over the curriculum had begun in earnest.

There remained considerable support for the traditional, the orthodox, in curricular matters. The most vigorous statement in favor of the old way was the Yale Report of 1828. This statement would not have been nearly so influential had it not come from a university of Yale's stature and size. Yale's faculty was joined in its zealous defense of classical learning by Princeton's faculty. Why did these two institutions make such a difference in curricula of higher education across the country and its territories? A missionary attitude prevailed at both Yale and Princeton that didn't exist at other notable universities, such as Harvard. Frederick Rudolph summed up the situation: "By sending out enthusiastic young graduates to found colleges in the barbaric West and South and by training clergymen to become college presidents, Yale and Princeton, in a way that the University of Virginia was not, were in a position to define what the American college would be" (1962, 131). In a nutshell, the Yale Report outlined the ideal of the faculty—a curriculum uncluttered by the frills of modernity. The cornerstones of the curriculum were the balanced aims of rigorous development of reason through the likes of mathematics and the nurturing of taste and discrimination through the classics. The report's influence was overwhelming but could hold off those who advocated a progressive curriculum for only so long.

From the foregoing, one might surmise that higher education was a substantial growth industry during the first half of the nineteenth century, but that is not exactly the case. Although there were lively exchanges regarding curricular matters, and increasing involvement on the parts of state governments and religious sects in the founding and development of institutions, the colleges and universities remained small. The largest antebellum university was Yale, and its student body numbered only 400. Attendance at college was still out of reach for the majority of the U.S. citizenry. For one thing, women were largely excluded from higher education. Prior to 1860, very few women's colleges or coeducational institutions existed. Rudolph offered an assessment of the exclusion women faced:

> The failure of coeducation and of separate women's colleges to make much headway before 1860 should be viewed in the context of those other educational reforms which also remained essentially blocked until after the war. . . . (T)he movement for higher education of women . . . would suffer from the essential poverty of the collegiate foundations and from the widespread suspicion of the class- and sectarian-conscious colleges (1962, 312).

The institutional limitations Rudolph mentioned also precluded a college career for many young men. As a result, colleges and universities of the time remained small and somewhat limited in significance.

Given the above, it should come as no surprise that the libraries of colleges and universities also were small through the first half of the nineteenth century. In 1800, Harvard's library collection (the largest in the country) contained about 13,000 volumes. The principal criticism by the faculty and students of most schools was that the libraries were largely useless. The collections were too small to supplement learning effectively and contained many irrelevant materials as a result of accepting whatever donations happened to be offered. Harvard's library, at least, continued to grow, though; by 1849, it had 56,000 volumes. No other university's library had half that many books. Even though Harvard's collection was sizable, it was still housed in a building that included other functions. The first building used solely as a library was built in 1840 at the University of South Carolina. Also, the librarians of the colleges and universities tended to be recent graduates, young men biding time until a suitable position became available. The position of librarian was not considered worthy of anyone with intelligence and ambition. When Daniel Coit Gilman (who would have an illustrious career in higher education) resigned as librarian at Yale, President Woolsey said to him,

> In regard to your leaving your place my thoughts have shaped themselves thus: the place does not possess that importance which a man of active mind would naturally seek; and the college cannot, now or hereafter, while its circumstances remain as they are, give it greater prominence. With the facilities you possess . . . you can in all probability secure for yourself . . . a more lucrative, a more prominent and a more varied, as well as stirring employment. I feel sure that you will not long content yourself . . . in your present vocation, and therefore I regard it better, if you must leave, to leave now, better I mean for yourself (Hamlin 1981, 26).

There are some fairly clear indications of the inadequacy of libraries to the work of the students and faculty of the colleges and universities. One indicator is the hours of opening of the libraries. In 1849, Yale's were far and away the most liberal; the library was open about thirty hours a week. This compares with the University of Virginia at nine hours a week, Columbia University at four hours a week, and Bowdoin College at three hours a week. Of course, some practical concerns limited opening hours. There was a strong reluctance to use gas or other forms of flame lighting amidst materials as flammable as books, so opening hours were frequently limited to those during which natural lighting could be employed. Another indicator of inadequacy is the phenomenon of literary societies and their libraries. Students frequently created these debating and social societies to further their own educations. They tended to assess membership fees and use some of the proceeds to build book collections for the members' use. They could control what was acquired and offer much freer access to the society's library than they had to the college or university's library. One example serves to illustrate the impact of these literary society libraries: the Dialectic and Philanthropic Society of the University of North Carolina built such a substantial collection that, in 1849, it had 8,800 books, compared to 3,500 in the university library (Harding 1971). The world of higher education, though, was about to change drastically, just as the fabric of American society was about to be transformed irrevocably.

Postwar Growth

For the second time in less than a hundred years the nation was ravaged by war. The political and strategic implications of the Civil War did not bypass higher education. For one thing, because much of the fighting occurred in the Southern states, the destruction there was of huge proportions and colleges and universities were unable to escape it. Some campuses were destroyed completely. The libraries at the University of Alabama and the newly established Louisiana State University (whose first president was William Tecumseh Sherman) were wiped out. Perhaps of more importance to higher education at that time was the loss of the existing and potential student body. Casualties were great on both sides, and the losses were naturally heaviest among college-age men. Moreover, even after the war had ended, it would be some time before colleges and universities could begin to grow. Able-bodied young men were needed at home, and the economic devastation of some areas meant that many who formerly had the financial wherewithal to send sons to college were no longer able to do so. The process of rebuilding would be a slow one in many instances.

One action, actually taken during the war, would have considerable effect of the future of higher education on many fronts. In 1857, Justin Morrill, congressman from Vermont, introduced a bill aimed at providing a formal legislative impetus for agricultural and mechanical education. There was strong opposition to the bill from the Southern states, whose representatives questioned the constitutionality of the proposed legislation. Also, a skepticism of higher education that transcended geography proved to be formidable obstacle. After the South left the Union, the way was a bit clearer for the legislation to be enacted and, in 1862, it was. The Morrill Act, known officially as the Land Grant College Act of 1862, made specific provisions for agricultural education and lands to be used for that purpose. Each state was given public lands or script equaling 30,000 acres for each senator and representative according to the apportionment of 1860. One complaint was that the more populous and less agrarian Northern states would benefit disproportionately. In any event, millions of acres of public lands were sold and the monies given to colleges and universities for the establishment (in most cases) or continued development of agricultural and mechanical programs.

States handled the provisions of the new legislation in various ways. In some instances, new A&M colleges were created and added to existing institutions. Some, such as Wisconsin, Minnesota, North Carolina, and Missouri, gave the land-grant responsibilities to existing state universities. A few—Oklahoma, Texas, South Dakota, and Washington—established new colleges that would immediately be competitors with the existing universities for state funding. Four states—Ohio, California, Arkansas, and West Virginia—founded state universities and attached A&M colleges to them. The land-grant movement was aided by the passage of a second Morrill Act in 1890, which provided for on-going, annual appropriations for land-grant colleges. A provision of the 1890 act still has repercussions today: it was stipulated the no student could be denied admission to a land-grant institution on the basis of race. The alternative offered was the establishment of separate, but equal, facilities. Seventeen states decided to go that route.

The worlds of higher education and libraries were affected by events in one watershed year—1876. That was the founding year of the American Library Association (ALA), at which time a large step was taken toward the professionalization of librarianship. In part, the founding of ALA was a realization of the growing need for librarians. In 1876, the U. S. Office of Education published the monumental *Public Libraries in the United States of America: Their History, Condition, and Management.* This huge survey was not limited to what we now know as public libraries but, rather, attempted to investigate the state of all publicly supported libraries in the U.S. Among other things, the report illustrated the growth in both the number and size of libraries during the third quarter of the nineteenth century. As a supplement, it included Charles Ammi Cutter's *Rules for a Dictionary Catalog.* Higher education and libraries (or at least their contents) were brought together in a chapter entitled "Professorships of Books and Reading." Although ambitious in its quest for the elevation of the study of literature, the chapter embodies the influences of nineteenth-century scientism (that is, the belief that the best model of truth and the best strategy for examination are provided by the natural sciences). It was a time in which science was on the rise as an ideal of learning and in prestige. According to the chapter, the new professor will find a different discipline of literature and reading: "It might be compared with the calculus in applied mathematics; it is a means of following up swiftly and thoroughly the best researches in any direction and of then pushing them further; it seeks to give a last and highest training for enlarging any desired department of recorded human knowledge. It is the science and art of reading for a purpose; it is a calculus of applied literature" (Perkins 1876, 231).

Perhaps the most important event in higher education in 1876 was the founding of Johns Hopkins University. That university was definitely a product of the heightened attention to research. Originally intended to be solely a graduate school, the conduct of research was, from the first, the driving force behind Johns Hopkins. The most profound influence on Johns Hopkins was the German university. The place of science and the model of the German university are inextricably linked. In the abstract, this model focused on two central tenets—*lehrfreiheit* (the freedom to teach) and *lernfreiheit* (the freedom to learn). In the German model, and at Johns Hopkins, these ideals of freedom were best realized through individual freedom of inquiry. Less emphasis was placed on the lecture and the teacher and more on the personal investigation of the learner (including both student and professor). Johns Hopkins itself was successful in its early days largely because of Daniel Coit Gilman (mentioned above) who was able to attract faculty and facilitate their research.

In the latter part of the nineteenth century, the university often was the product of the vision, mind, and personality of a single man—its president. During this period when growth was possible at some institutions, the universities were transformed by such strong-willed individuals. Such was certainly the case at Harvard with Charles Eliot. Eliot had definite notions of what higher education should be and how the goals should be attained, and he set about reshaping Harvard into a university that reflected his vision. At Columbia, Nicholas Murray Butler imposed his will, which differed considerably from that of Eliot. Butler was more conservative, both personally and educationally, and strove to maintain the preeminence of the liberal arts and to fight against the elective system. With Eliot and Butler, the challenge was to shape an institution that had considerable histories into universities fitted to personal goals. In other instances the opportunity existed to begin from scratch. New (or newer) universities, such as the University of Michigan, Johns Hopkins, and the University of Chicago, presented the possibility of creating something anew. Respectively, James B. Angell, Daniel Coit Gilman, and William Rainey Harper embraced the challenge at those three universities. Each man had a unique vision for his institution and set about realizing that vision with an almost single-minded purpose. One thing they all shared in common was the overseeing of a growth in the administration of the university; substantial bureaucratic organizations grew up in those universities that also were experiencing growth in faculty and student size, physical plant, and prestige. This was not a phenomenon that was universally looked upon with favor. In his book *The Higher Learning in America,* Thorstein Veblen (1957) accused universities of adopting a business model of organization and behavior that, he believed, was in opposition to the ideal of learning that had formerly been the rhetorical foundation of higher education. This, too, is a tension that is still with us.

The institutions mentioned above, along with a few others, took the lead in establishing the university as not just the locus of teaching and learning, but also as a burgeoning social force in America. This transformation was just beginning in the late nineteenth century, and the lead taken by the most aggressive of the presidents was not followed by all educational administrators. Many were complacent and content with the educational world as it had been. Moreover, the public was not quite ready to ascribe to higher education the respect and acceptance as an integral force in many people's lives that would come later. The sizes of library collections at the end of the century reflect both the growth of some universities and the discrepancy between them and the majority of higher education. By 1900, some library collections were reaching impressive sizes: Harvard had 976,000 volumes; Columbia, 345,000; Yale, 309,000; Chicago (which had only been founded less than a decade before), 303,000; Cornell, 268,000; and Pennsylvania, 260,000. On the other hand, the library collections at many universities were small and inadequate: Wisconsin had 81,000 volumes; Virginia, 50,000; Illinois, 47,000; Ohio State and Texas, 45,000; and North Carolina, 43,000. The discrepancy is further reflective of some changes to the faculties of universities. Transformation and altered vision meant a new breed of faculty with different ideas about education and their place in it.

The Twentieth Century

By 1900, the world of higher education was poised for a thorough transformation. What had begun at a few select universities would soon influence all of higher education. The most subtle element of the transformation was the increasing bureaucratic organization of colleges and universities. The institution at the beginning of the twentieth century was not merely the teacher and the student; it was the infrastructure, the physical plant, the laboratory, and the budget. Faculty more and more frequently held the doctorate, and more and more institutions were establishing doctoral programs to feed the Ph.D.-hungry colleges and universities. Some complained that learning was giving way to degree granting. William James (1903) fired perhaps the most famous salvo at the evolved university in his article, "The Ph.D. Octopus." The doctorate, said James, was a vanity; it was a symbol of the overspecialization of the student, who would then carry that excess into a faculty post—and be applauded for it. The Ph.D. was also, to some, a symbol of the bureaucracy that higher education had become. At its founding, Johns Hopkins was intended to be a reaction against the strictures and constraints of conventional practice, but it, too, turned to the standardized program of the doctorate. One account tells why Johns Hopkins made such a turn:E3

> We must offer something to keep these students in line. The Ph.D. degree was the next thing after the A.B. degree, and we recognized that we must offer this in order to keep that body of workers in line, and that, in order to secure the results we wanted, it was also necessary to require a piece of research as a requisite for that degree. That is the machinery we used. We thought, at first, that we might avoid it, but we found that we must adopt it (Veysey 1965, 313–14).

Most telling is the equation of the students with a "body of workers." The inescapable implication is that, in some minds at least, the purpose of the university is its own existence and growth, and only tangentially the education of inquiring students.

A characteristic of the twentieth-century institution came to be research. Professionals, as academics were becoming, needed to lend legitimacy to their expertise; what better way than through research? A very important step toward professionalization was establishment of the learned society. Just as the founding of the ALA marked a giant step on the way to the professionalization of librarianship, so, too, did the founding of the American Association for the Advancement of Science, the American Historical Association, the Modern Language Association, the American Chemical Society, and others move the disciplines closer to that professional ideal. What's more, these associations established official journals intended to communicate both within and without the discipline the advances made as a result of research. The research activities required resources; in addition to the growing amount of money raised by the universities themselves for research, the U.S. government got into the act. In 1900, the federal government appropriated $11 million to research activities. From that time on, higher education has depended on government support for a substantial portion of the funding for faculty research.

The professional scholar (essentially a twentieth-century phenomenon) was one who not only taught, but also engaged in formal research and inquiry. These activities had some important implications for the institutions that employed the scholars. If these faculty were eager to, and expected to, conduct research, they had to have all the necessary tools to succeed, including lessened teaching responsibilities. Of course, an essential resource to the research endeavor was—and still is—money. The universities that initially were able to succeed at research were those that had ample financial resources. Research was a high priority at a minority of institutions, but those that did have such an emphasis depended on sufficient funding. Given that money was the requisite tool, Roger Geiger noted that

> This is not to deny that hard choices were often involved—that some universities were more willing than others to sacrifice campus amenities to the goal of the advancement of knowledge. Rather, it is simply to highlight the inescapable fact that low teaching loads, space for faculty research, up-to-date laboratories, and large libraries first required the availability of ample institutional resources, and only then decisions about deployment (1986, 67).

For much of the inquiry engaged in by faculty, a strong library collection was invaluable.

Along with the expansion of the research initiative of universities and the growth of their assets, including library collections, came diversity in their curricular offerings. In the twentieth century, Eliot's concept of offering students elective choices gained favor, at least to some extent, at a majority of colleges and universities. There were more possibilities for major areas of study and for individual courses. Institutional offerings extended beyond the traditional arts and sciences; a number of universities initiated a variety of professional programs (beyond law and medicine), necessitating more faculty while presenting students with greater choice. The most vocal critic of what perhaps may be called the modern American university was Abraham Flexner (1930). He tended to paint with a sweeping brush, but critics of higher education still invoke the name of Flexner when they want to question the efficacy of specific university offerings. The dilemma in Flexner's time and now is that many subject areas are covered inconsistently by universities, with some providing a rigorous intellectual base and others falling short of that goal.

The transformation of American higher education was slowed a bit during the 1930s, as colleges and universities suffered some ill effects of the Depression. The devastation of this time was not so severe at many institutions, particularly those that had been on sound financial footing in the 1920s. Research universities especially were able to ride out a downturn and then return to prosperity. As Geiger noted, the cost of living was lower in the 1930s, which helped to offset, somewhat, the budget rescissions and endowment losses of institutions (1986, 246–47). The production of information did not really diminish during this time, and library acquisitions, though curtailed a bit, still continued. If we take a broader view and examine the state of libraries over the first four decades of the twentieth century, we see an overall pattern of growth that has been a source of some alarm to a number of observers. In the early 1940s, Fremont Rider undertook a longitudinal study of academic library growth. In the aftermath of his investigation, he concluded that "every scrap of statistical evidence that we can gather shows that, as far back as we can reach, the story is exactly the same. It seems . . . to be a mathematical fact that, ever since college and university libraries started in this country, they have, on the average, doubled in size every sixteen years" (1944, 8). Extrapolating from his hypothesis of exponential growth, he suggested that:

> the Yale Library will, in 2040, have approximately 200,000,000 volumes, which will occupy over 6,000 miles of shelves. Its card catalog file— if it then has a card catalog—will consist of nearly three-quarters of a million catalog drawers, which will of themselves occupy not less than eight acres of floor space. New material will be coming in at the rate of 12,000,000 volumes a year; and the cataloging of this new material will require a cataloging staff of over six thousand persons (1944, 12).

These projections sound fantastic, and, in fact, for many reasons (not the least of which is the extreme unlikelihood of 12,000,000 new books being published in the year 2040) they are a fantasy. Rider tried to solidify his stance by saying that the librarian of two hundred years before would have been skeptical of the state of affairs of 1940, but that skepticism does not alter the reality of the situation. It may be easy for us to dismiss Rider's vision of the future, but on what grounds? Robert Molyneux delved deeply into both Rider's hypothesis and the phenomenon of growth and he offered, not only a perceptive assessment of the work done by Rider, but also an insightful examination of collection growth (Molyneux, 1986a; Molyneux, 1986b; Molyneux, 1994). His work epitomizes the best of both conceptual and quantitative study in our field. However, the reality remains that library collections are dynamic, and their expansion, coupled with the proliferation of published work, is a sore predicament (this is a time to eschew the euphemism "challenge") for libraries dealing with matters of finances, space, selection, and so on.

Beyond World War Two

After the Second World War, higher education experienced more change than in any half-century period before. A substantial amount of the impetus for change came from outside the educational world. In 1948, the G. I. Bill of Rights created the financial wherewithal for, eventually, millions who served in the armed forces to attend colleges and universities. This is one instance of the federal government's involvement in higher education. Greater involvement was to come. The G. I. Bill led to gradual increases in enrollment through the 1950s. In the later fifties, though, the global climate was such that the United States felt its sense of educational superiority eroding. Although a number of phenomena converged at that time to cause concern, one event captured the spirit of the time better than any other. On July 1, 1957, the Soviet Union launched a satellite, Sputnik I, into orbit around the earth. The most immediate fear felt by the U.S. government was one of becoming strategically unready to answer any potential challenge to global security. This translated quickly into a concern for academic preparedness and competitiveness. The result was an infusion of federal funds into education at all levels. Some of the funding went into institutions directly so that they could initiate some reforms. The funding push coalesced into the Higher Education Act (HEA) in the 1960s. HEA provided for curricular development, scholarships, fellowships, and improvements to libraries. Research funding increased dramatically through departments and agencies such as the Department of Defense, the National Institutes of Health, and the National Science Foundation.

Throughout the 1960s, there was an increased emphasis on education, including increased opportunities for financial assistance. The various factors influencing enrollment had tremendous effects. Enrollment in higher education in the decade of the sixties increased from just over 3,000,000 to about 8,000,000. As might be expected, this enrollment surge put pressure on the institutions. New buildings had to be constructed—dormitories, classroom and office buildings, additions to libraries, or new library buildings. In addition, there was the need for faculty to educate the increasing number of students. More doctoral programs were instituted at more universities. In a short period of time, a generation of faculty was educated, hired, and tenured. By no means did all of these faculty have a strong commitment to research. The complexity of the institutions of the 1960s prompted Clark Kerr to refer to them as "multiversities." He observed that, unlike the medieval university, there is no single, unified group of students that share intellectual and academic goals for the eventual use of their educations (Kerr 2001).

The complexity has continued since Kerr coined the word. Economic recessions have forced educational administrators to revisit some of the creations of the 1960s and 1970s, such as area studies centers and research institutes. The economic constraints of the recent past has forced those within colleges and universities to realize that public, especially state, funding for higher education is limited, that the deep pockets of three decades ago no longer exist. Institutions have altered their thinking to look at their own competitive stances in the educational world. There is competition for students, for faculty, and for money from a variety of sources. There also is increasing demand for the provision of services never before offered or for traditional services offered via new means. As state, and even endowment, funding has come to be seen as less than adequate to support the ambitions of individual schools, other sources of money have to be explored. One source is the research funding provided by government and foundation sources. To be able to compete for these pots of money, the institutions have to be competitive when it comes to research. One result of this competitiveness that will only be mentioned briefly at this point is that many more institutions have come to adopt research missions, whether or not that is in concert with the rest of their institutional mission.

Of course, libraries have been caught in the midst of the changes occurring around them. Academic libraries have had to grow in order to serve the increasing numbers of students and faculty. They have had to adopt strategies first to acquire and then to provide access to the rapidly growing amount of information being produced. They also have had to adjust to the constriction of funds, which has made choices of services and acquisitions more difficult. Moreover, libraries have had to react to, and help to create, technological innovations that have affected information production, storage, and retrieval.

As electronic information has proliferated, libraries have had to incorporate the technology (and funding for it) into all they have done traditionally. Moreover, they have looked to large-scale automation efforts that have transformed their organization, services, staffs, and users. Given the financial states of institutions in the recent past, libraries have done an admirable job of opening up to new possibilities. However, this is not to say that everything libraries have done has been successful. In chapters to come, much more attention is paid to the current state of higher education and academic libraries and the challenges they face.

SOME QUESTIONS TO PONDER

Given the purpose for studying academic libraries and the history of higher education and libraries, certain things come to mind and deserve some contemplation. These considerations can become a part of discussion about where higher education came from and how it reached its present state. They also can provide a basis for thinking about the place academic libraries occupied and how the changes they have faced have paralleled their home institutions. To that end, the following questions are suggested as probes for discussion:

> Are libraries merely reactive pawns in the hands of academic administrators?
>
> Is the community of the academic library genuinely different from that of other libraries?
>
> To what extent does information technology influence information content?
>
> Does the internal organization of the library matter?
>
> Is there such a thing as a typical user of the academic library?
>
> Why did the Western world decide that an institution such as the university was necessary to its health and well-being?
>
> In the centuries before printing, how could knowledge be considered a growing thing?
>
> What good were the colonial colleges?
>
> Was an increasing bureaucratic organization of colleges and universities inevitable?
>
> Were Thorstein Veblen, William James, and Abraham Flexner correct in their criticisms?

Chapter 2

Organizational Culture and Higher Education

As is evident from even a casual reading of management literature, there are many different ways to look at organizations. A number of these varying schools of thought make their way into basic management courses in colleges of business and elsewhere. The variances among the schools of thought are fundamental and focus on different aspects or elements of the organization. The one thing they share is the goal of understanding human organizations—why they exist, how they are structured, what facilitates decision making, how they can be impediments to progress, and what kinds of communication they allow. Although the goal is common, the means of accomplishing it can be very different. This chapter focuses on one specific school of thought—organizational culture. Organizational culture's "theories are based upon assumptions about organizations and people that depart radically from those of the 'mainline' school of organization theory. Secondly, the organizational culture school does not believe that quantitative, experimental-type, 'scientific' research is especially useful for studying organizations" (Shafritz and Ott 1987, 373). In short, this particular way of looking at organizations is founded on the recognition that humans act according to complex cognitive, social, political, and emotional motivations, and not simply as physical entities without minds or wills. Inherent in this approach is the belief that humans do not necessarily behave in individually predictable ways but, rather, gravitate toward some socially influenced states. This approach is more fruitful especially for the examination of complex organizations composed of self-determining professionals, such as colleges and universities and their libraries.

The organizational culture school is intended to apply generally to all human organizations, while relying on examinations of the particulars of a specific environment, the people in it, and the nature of their work. Because of its flexibility, it seems to be a particularly conducive means of studying all aspects of higher education. Colleges and universities are complicated environments, incorporating a variety of very different kinds of work. No mechanistic method can encompass the diversity of activities and of individuals operating in such an environment. For these reasons, we use the guidelines of the organizational culture approach to peer into the workings of higher education in order to investigate the complexities of its politics, policies, decisions, disciplines, and purposes. Although there are several conceptions of organizational culture, some of the consistent points, according to Joanne Martin and Caren Siehl (1983), are: organizational cultures exist; each organizational culture is relatively unique; organizational culture is a socially constructed concept; organizational culture provides organizational members with a way of understanding and making sense of events and symbols; and organizational culture is a powerful lever for guiding organizational behavior. To accomplish such an investigation, it is necessary first to take a glimpse at some other theories of organization and why they fall short. It is true that this is not a management textbook, but it is impossible to ignore the administration of colleges and universities and of their libraries.

APPROACHES TO THE STUDY OF ORGANIZATIONS

Early in this century, a number of thoughtful individuals turned their attention to human organization. Some of these people were students of the human condition and were looking at the structures of organizations to gain insight into something in which human beings spent a great amount of their time. The interest in organizations came at a time when the Industrial Revolution was completed, when there was considerable movement from rural to urban settings, and when businesses were growing in both size and their influence in people's lives. With manufacturing being heavily mechanized, fewer individuals were able to sustain themselves by operating family shops; the large industries could produce more goods and produce them more cheaply. As individuals were less able to be self-sustaining, more people gravitated to the large manufacturing plants to seek employment. It is important to remember that in the early part of the twentieth century, the machine was more than just a tool. It was a metaphor for progress because, through industrialization, people were able to purchase affordable automobiles, appliances, and other amenities for the home. The machine signified a new age of convenience and prosperity. Beyond this, it also signified a way of looking at human society and human organization. If the parts of the machine could work together toward the ends of production, so, too, could the human elements of the organizations—or so some people tended to believe.

The machine represented a rational structure, and the idea of a governing rationality was extended to the organization as a whole. There is no doubt that this is a deterministic approach; it signals a belief that the means of organizing determines the outcome. An outgrowth of such a belief is that the initial focus is on the desired outcome and then an organization is designed to produce that outcome, in much the same way that a machine is designed and built to execute a particular function. The early days of organization theory constitute a period commonly known as the classical school of thought. The fundamental ideas of the classical school, though formally expressed in the twentieth century, have their roots in the later eighteenth-century beginnings of the Industrial Revolution. Jay Shafritz and Steven Ott noted that the fundamental ideas of the classical school include the following:

1. Organizations exist to accomplish production-related and economic goals.
2. There is one best way to organize for production, and that way can be found through systematic, scientific inquiry.
3. Production is maximized through specialization and division of labor.
4. People and organizations act in accordance with rational economic principles (1987, 21).

The last of the tenets is probably the most important. The thinking about organizations at that time was characterized by faith in rationality. Such faith was not unique to industry or organization theory; it was quite pervasive throughout academic and popular belief.

We have to begin a cursory look at the classical school with Max Weber. Weber's interests were far-reaching and he devoted a good bit of time and thought to human organization. We will not engage in a detailed examination of Weber's ideas here, but some of what he was stating many decades ago remains influential today. Weber certainly did not create bureaucracies, but he was the first to study them seriously as a rational form of human organization. In examining the organizations of his day (early twentieth century), he noticed some differences between them and the organizations of the past. The latter-day organizations were likely to be characterized by division of labor (not a new phenomenon, but specialization was being carried to extremes not before seen), centralization of authority, a rational program of personnel administration (marked by a close match of job descriptions with applicants' abilities), clearly articulated and exhaustive rules and regulations, and the keeping of detailed written records to ensure uniformity of action in the future. A principal aim of the bureaucratic organization was—and is—control of all levels of operation.

Control is achieved through the rational application of accounting (for fiscal control) and of hierarchy (for control of personnel).

Weber's ideas were expanded on by a contemporary of his, Henri Fayol. Fayol broke down what he saw as the essential organizational imperatives of planning, organizing, coordination, and control. He detailed the most important principles of management as the following:

1. Division of work.
2. Authority.
3. Discipline.
4. Unity of command.
5. Unity of direction.
6. Subordination of individual interests to the general interest.
7. Remuneration.
8. Centralization.
9. Scalar chain (line of authority).
10. Order.
11. Equity.
12. Stability of tenure of personnel.
13. Initiative.
14. Esprit de corps (1971, 101–2).

Two things are particularly striking about Fayol's principles: he obviously concurs with Weber's vision of a top-down path of authority and responsibility, and he believes that incentives can play a role in productivity. A belief in incentives is one particular articulation of a mechanistic view of humans in human organization, one that assumes that additional remuneration will, eventually, be advantageous to the organization.

Scientific Management

Also contemporary with some of the notions of Weber, and also beginning during the early part of this century, was scientific management. The best-known proponent of scientific management was Frederick Taylor (1987). At the heart of scientific management is the goal of bringing the aims of managers and workers together by ensuring productivity (and, thus, higher pay) for the workers and higher profits for the managers through increases in productivity. Taylor's theory is opposed to incentives; rather, it focuses attention on analysis of the work to be done and selection of the workers in order to achieve a heightened state of productivity without adding to the workforce. The idea is that higher productivity, along with control of expenditures, will result in a larger profit margin. All in the organization can then share in the surplus of profits. On the basis of this utopian ideal, Taylor founded his organizational ideal:

> The new outlook that comes under scientific management is this: The workmen, after many object lessons, come to see and the management come to see that this surplus can be made so great, providing both sides will stop their pulling apart, will stop their fighting and will push as hard as they can to get as cheap an output as possible, that there is no occasion to quarrel. Each side can get more than ever before. The acknowledgement of this fact represents a complete mental revolution (1987, 70–71).

Over the years, scientific management has not been limited to industrial organizations nor is it an idea that has disappeared completely. To illustrate this assertion, we can look to one example of the persuasiveness and longevity of scientific management. It so happens that the example is in the field of librarianship. Richard M. Dougherty and Fred Heinritz were advocates of this particular school of thought and made their stance clear at the outset of their book on the subject: "The scientific manager applies the principles of science to problems of administration. Most of us are aware of these principles, even if we cannot recite them. The scientific method is little more than the use of common sense and strategy to solve problems: one formulates a hypothesis, gathers data, evaluates the data, implements a solution, and evaluates the solution" (1982, 3). They especially see applicability of scientific management in handling the routine, repetitive tasks common in most libraries. It quickly becomes evident that, as did the classical theorists before them, Dougherty and Heinritz emphasize control as integral to the efficient operation of libraries.

Through the first half of this century, the classical school *was* organization theory. Eventually, there came some observers of human organization who were critical of the classical theorists. A number of writers noted that the rationalist view of organizations was inadequate to see the impact of the environment on business, industry, government offices, and so on. These individuals, many of whom were sociologists, stressed that there are nonrational elements of human behavior that cannot be explained by any rationalist approach. Such elements can subvert the utopian ideals of the classical school, leading to dysfunction within the organization. Managers see any dysfunction as antithetical to productivity and methods to combat it must be employed. The observers of organizations have noted that, where the cooperative ideal does not exist, other strategies, such as cooptation (trying to subsume disputatious elements into the dominant group), are employed to minimize dysfunction. There are some consistent aspects of the newer generation of theorists. Less faith is placed in the efficacy of a scientific approach to organizing, such as that espoused by Dougherty and Heinritz. Related to the foregoing, there has been a more prominent recognition that organizations, regardless of managerial intent, are not purely mechanistic entities; rather, they are social in nature, with all of the dynamics of any social grouping. When the domination of the classical school was broken, theorists felt freer to offer different conceptions of organizations.

The Classical School

One perspective that grew out of the freedom to transcend the thinking of the classical school is the structural approach. Adherents of this way of thinking owe a debt to the likes of Weber and Fayol, who provided a context for examination of the structure of organizations. Structural theory examines the traditional bureaucracy in terms of authority, coordination, function, and product. Given this, what is the difference between the classical and structural approaches? The primary difference is that, in structural theory, it is not assumed that there is a single organizational type that suits all purposes. For instance, Amitai Etzioni (1987) stated that organizations have different goals (which he labels "order," "economics," and "culture") and, of necessity, different means of compliance ("coercive," "utilitarian," "normative"). An organization such as a prison, which has mainly order-based goals, achieves them through coercion. A religious organization, on the other hand, has culture-based goals and achieves them by normative means.

According to Lee Bolman and Terrence Deal, the assumptions underlying the structural approach are:

1. Organizations exist to achieve established goals and objectives.
2. Organizations work best when rationality prevails over personal preferences and external pressures.
3. Structures must be designed to fit an organization's circumstances (including its goals, technology, and environment).
4. Organizations increase efficiency and enhance performance through specialization and division of labor.
5. Appropriate forms of coordination and control are essential to ensuring that individuals and units work together in the service of organizational goals.
6. Problems and performance gaps arise from structural deficiencies and can be remedied through restructuring (2003, 40).

These assumptions suggest that organizations are akin to puzzles. To an extent, they are inscrutable, but there is a key to their solution. When the key is found, the fundamental problems of the organization are soluble. The solution in one instance might be a mechanistic structure characterized by a rigid hierarchy. In another instance a very different structure, perhaps one sensitive to creativity and innovation, would be suitable. In any case, there is some rigidity of thought in the structural approach; one answer exists for each individual organization and success depends on finding that answer and adhering to it.

The Systems Approach

Another school of thought has adapted the work done in systems theory, with the particular aim of searching for order in the interaction of complex variables. This approach relies somewhat on the groundbreaking thought of Norbert Wiener and Ludwig von Bertalanffy. One feature of the systems approach is the realization that, because of the multitude of complex interactions in any organization, a change or alteration in one aspect leads to change in other aspects. Theorists of this school tend to focus their attention on interconnections, both within the organization and between the organization and the environment. Perhaps the most influential work that can be classified as the systems approach is that of Daniel Katz and Robert Kahn. They articulated an open systems theory, which posits that organizations must be constantly adapting to a constantly changing environment. The organization is thus likened to the biological organism, which adapts at cellular, organic, and system levels to changes of varying magnitudes. As Katz and Kahn stated,

> Organizations as a special class of open systems have properties of their own, but they share other properties in common with all open systems. These include the importation of energy from the environment, the through-put or transformation of the imported energy into some product form which is characteristic of the system, the exporting of that product into the environment, and the re-energizing of the system from sources in the environment (1987, 261).

The theory of Katz and Kahn has been applied explicitly to academic libraries. Maurice Marchant examined each of the elements of an open system, as enumerated by Katz and Kahn, as it might have relevance to the academic library. However, Marchant betrayed a misunderstanding of their work. For instance, he said that "a library in a steady state retains the same service at the same level operating in the same way" (1985, 163). This is not what Katz and Kahn intended in their description of the phenomenon of the steady state. A more accurate interpretation would be the recognition that if a library aims at offering more (or enhanced) services that require more resources, the energy would have to be imported from outside. Stated another way, if a library wants to offer a new service that requires, say, two full-time professional librarians, it will have to attract enough money to hire two new librarians or move the two librarians from existing functions in the library. This and other problems with Marchant's analysis illustrate the need for informed, critical assessment of the thought of other disciplines prior to adoption of that thought to librarianship.

The majority of organization theorists would probably fit in one (or a variation) of the aforementioned schools. I do not say this to denigrate any individual theorist or approach. Elements of each of the approaches discussed here can be seen in today's organizations, including libraries. One drawback of some schools of thought is that the tenets of the approaches are not intended solely as elements for observation. In some cases, the theories set forth are prescriptive; that is, they are intended as recipes for effective organization. It has become increasingly clear that organizations are too dynamic (and exist in too dynamic a world) for any prescription to apply fully or to apply for the long term. The shortcomings of the classical school, and to some extent the structural approach, have been pointed out. In addition, both the structural and system schools embrace a set of conditional assumptions that render their programs questionable. Karl Weick (1982) stated these assumptions: a self-correcting system of interdependent people; consensus on objectives and methods; coordination achieved through sharing information; and predictable organizational problems and solutions. So where does this leave us? Well, we are left with an analytical tool that does not pretend to be prescriptive. This tool enables us to examine and reach an understanding about organizations, in part as categorical types, but more as individual instances of human organization. This tool is the organizational culture approach.

Perhaps the most complete and most useful examination of organizational structures is that offered by Bolman and Deal. Their book, *Reframing Organizations,* presents a thorough investigation of four major frames ("windows on the world and lenses that bring the world into focus" [2003, 12]): structural, human resources, political, and symbolic. Along with the frames come metaphors, concepts, images of leadership, and leadership challenges. Each of these items is manifested differently in each of the four frames. Further, the four frames differ when it comes to some major process, such as strategic planning, decision making, reorganizing, evaluating, approaching conflict, goal setting, communication, meetings, and motivation (Bolman and Deal 2003, 267–68). For example, if the structural frame is in place, motivation is attempted through economic incentives. On the other hand, within the political frame, coercion, manipulation, and seduction may be used to motivate. A central point made by Bolman and Deal is that situations differ among and within organizations. This means that leaders have to be very sensitive to the challenges facing the organization, personnel on hand, external factors, and other things. Given these variables, the leader needs to engage in some questioning in order to determine what frame best applies and how to proceed. One example Bolman and

Deal provide is that if the answer to the question "Is the technical quality of the decision important?" is yes, the structural frame may be most appropriate. What their recommendations boil down to is a clear understanding that the *organization* shouldn't adopt a frame, frames should be adopted for particular situations. If students or professionals were to read only one book about organizations, this probably should be the one.

WHAT IS ORGANIZATIONAL CULTURE?

There are at least a couple of ways to answer this question. One response addresses organizational culture from a theoretical point of view; another takes the question literally. The former answer is predicated on the recognition, stated previously, that the organizational culture approach is not predictive; it is not a blueprint for the ideal organization. As we have seen, the other schools of thought are somewhat lacking as means to understanding the diverse aspects of human organization. Although the organizational culture approach is not perfect (no single theoretical perspective on organizations is), it has the advantage of formally allowing for the investigation of many of the nondeterministic, nonmechanistic elements and activities of organizations. Examination of an organization's culture necessitates that the observer be cognizant of the complexities of human behavior and of the reality that an organization does not (and cannot) fully regulate that behavior, despite the intentions of some in its upper echelon. That said, one purpose of the approach is to ascertain those organizational aspects that exhibit some consistency, some pervasiveness, and how these aspects either guide or reflect behavior within the organization. The standpoint of the observer includes the recognition that human organization is essentially social. Granted, the interaction of the members may not always be by choice, but the foundations are social. Because of the social nature of organizations, study of them should incorporate this foundational element in order to arrive at the fullest understanding of the dynamics of any organization.

The literal answer to the question means defining organizational culture. Although this approach is a relatively new one in organization theory, some writers have taken stabs at coming up with an adequate definition. Edgar Schein, for instance, began by stating that organizational culture is encompassing in nature; it is a part of every phase of organizational life. It includes the members' behavioral regularities, the norms that are somehow established for how the work is done and the output of the individuals, the values that are embraced by those in the organization, and the atmosphere that results from the total organizational climate (Schein 1987, 384). The assertion that an organization has a culture does not mean that within any organization there is uniformity of belief and action. As is true of any culture, there are inevitably going to be disputes, disagreements, and even contradictions. Nonetheless, an organization is characterized by a fundamental sharing of a set of beliefs and assumptions that are, at some level, a part of the belief system of the organization's members. A word that has been commonly used to illustrate the active role that each individual plays in the construction and maintenance of the culture is "enactment." The term refers to the interpretive devices we all employ in order to understand and create reality. As Gareth Morgan stated,

> In recognizing that we accomplish or enact the reality of our everyday world, we have a powerful way of thinking about culture. For this means that we must attempt to understand culture as an ongoing, proactive process of reality construction. This brings the whole phenomenon of culture alive. When understood in this way, culture can no longer just be viewed as a simple variable that societies or organizations possess. Rather, it must be understood as an active, living phenomenon through which people create and recreate the worlds in which they live (1986, 131).

Schein expanded on his definition of culture: "Culture manifests itself at three levels: the level of deep tacit assumptions that are the essence of the culture, the level of espoused values that often reflect what a group wishes ideally to be and the way it wants to present itself publicly, and the day-to-day behavior that represents a complex compromise among the espoused values, the deeper assumptions, and the immediate requirements of the situation" (1996, 12). The three-tiered nature of culture is an important concept. As we examine first the academy and then the library, we can appreciate the workings of each level. A question that arises is, Which came first? It seems evident that if the deep assumptions are tacit, something must have existed earlier so that those assumptions could form. The stated values (and articulated values are a concern at this time; witness the ALA's effort to arrive at a statement of values; see http://www.ala.org/congress/corevalues/index.html) can be either a formal expression of day-to-day action or a reaction against mundane action so as to change an existing culture. The three levels are not independent; rather, they simultaneously shape and are shaped by one another. This means that an organizational culture is both conscious and tacit. As all three levels become manifest, the culture becomes a deep, even profound, way of life.

The enactment with the context of an organization is not solely an individual phenomenon. To emphasize a point, the organization is a construction, a tool, of society. It serves purposes that fit in the larger society, but it also manifests itself as a micro-society. There is, in any organization, the impetus for organizing that springs from a number of individuals having some vision of purpose and some plan for accomplishing that purpose. When the organization is thriving, the individuals who are part of it build and rebuild a more fully developed ethos that defines not only purpose and action, but also the relationships of its members. As is true of society at the macro level, this ongoing construction is dynamic; some individuals leave the organization because it has evolved into something less personally compatible, others gravitate to it because its culture is amenable to individual belief. Especially with those who remain with the organization, the culture is likely to be accepted because they have likely contributed to its state. At the heart of recognizing the existence of such a thing as organizational culture is the reality that the organization is not (as the classical school, with its mechanistic assumptions, would have it) separate from the people who are part of it. These individuals contribute to the culture *and* are affected by its existing state. The investment that its members have in the organization led Marvin Peterson and Theodore White to define culture as "the deeply imbedded patterns of organizational behavior and the shared values, assumptions, beliefs, or ideologies that members have about their organization" (1992, 181).

Organizational culture is not merely an expression of some abstract social bond; it is a genuinely social construction. Such a statement betrays something of an analytical bias. Another approach (one that is rejected here) is that of social interactionism. The interactionist stance is one of extreme relativism; there can be no examination of the creation of meaning apart from the individual. This means that the frame of reference for beliefs and assumptions in an organization is as variable as the number of its members because interactionism is founded on the experiences, and the impact of those experiences, of each individual. The organizational culture approach does not deny that there is an individualistic element of the organization, but it suggests that there can be a social glue at work. Of course, there are obstacles to the creation of this social glue. As Nicole Stelter (2002) pointed out, gender differences (in particular, a woman as leader of the organization) and the response to the differences by members can affect the creation of cohesion. Given the nature of library organizations, libraries may be a significant and positive lesson for organizations that may experience difficulties, as Stelter observed.

The interaction of individuals is contextual; it takes place within a structure that is offered by the organization *and* by the people who affiliate themselves with it. The contextual character of culture is evident in library organizations as well as in higher education. William Sannwald recognized that culture "gives members of the organization identity. . . . It provides collective commitment to the organization. . . . It builds social system stability, which is the extent to which the work environment is perceived to be positive and reinforcing. . . . It allows people to make sense of the organization" (2000, 9). When individuals construct meaning within the organization, that meaning tends to be influenced by the aggregate. If it were not, the organization would be in jeopardy of finding itself unsustainable. The simultaneously occurring phenomena of individual meaning formation and the sharing of beliefs led Jeffrey Pfeffer to observe, "There is, then, a duality in the social constructionist view, reflecting the fact that social structures are both human creations and, at the same time, constraints on the process of meaning creation (1982, 210)."

The duality that Pfeffer noted is indeed complex. For one thing, individuals have lives apart from the organization, and the extent to which the culture of the organization is part of the rest of their lives varies from person to person. It might be said that organizational culture can be sufficiently strong to influence behavior and attitudes even when the individual is separated from the organization. If that is true, it may be that the organizational culture can become a part of an individual's identity. But there is a converse to this. It may be that people bring to the organization the beliefs and attitudes that define them as individuals and these individual contributions help to define the organizational culture. The culture is a kind of social representation, an expression of what is shared within that group. However, the creation of the representation is as complex as all of the disparate and (especially) converging beliefs brought to the organization by its members. The culture's creation is facilitated by the communication of those convergences. As such, the culture can be, in part, purposeful inasmuch as it is an articulation of a fundamental mission by the organization's leaders. On the other hand, the organizational culture can, in the absence of an articulated mission, be a result of grassroots communication of shared beliefs.

If the former is the case, if the leaders have an explicit vision and can communicate it, individuals may assimilate it into their organizational lives. Even failing immediate assimilation, it is possible that people who are sympathetic to the vision can be recruited into the organization. I should emphasize that this observation is not qualitative. Articulation of the vision and acceptance of it say nothing at all about the vision itself. It may be that the majority of people working in a given field would disagree wholeheartedly with a particular vision, but that need not impede the success of that organization. If there is agreement within the culture, the structure of the organization may be transformed. The structuralist approach asserts that there is an appropriate model for each organization. A twist on this notion is that the culture of the organization suggests that certain structures are amenable to the beliefs and their related behaviors that define the culture. The members of the organization actively create a structure that is sensitive to those things that are strongly shared. The organizational culture approach, then, is not deterministic; there is no assumption that the structure is determined by some far-reaching and powerful force that is separate and apart from the people within the organization.

The "rootedness" of organizational culture in the participants also suggests that it is not simply an emotive force born of the desire of people to share some ephemeral good feeling. There is a strong cognitive aspect to organizational culture. The shared beliefs extend to the ways of thinking about the nature of the organization's work. As we will see with higher education, this means that the fundamental conceptions of the knowledge base of the organization are part of its culture. Moreover, those conceptions do not simply accompany the organization as part of its furnishings; instead, they must be understood by the members, which necessitates that each person think about what it means to be part of that particular organization. Mary Reis Louis recognized that the individual's cognitive acceptance of the organization's culture is bound to the importance of interpretation, which is integral to the creation and sustenance of the culture. "The idea of culture rests on the premise that the full meaning of things is not given a priori in the things themselves. Instead, meaning results from interpretation. . . . The process encompasses universal, cultural and individual levels of interpretation (1987, 422)."

ORGANIZATIONAL CULTURE AND HIGHER EDUCATION

The principles discussed so far could apply to just about any complex organization. How do they fit institutions such as colleges and universities? The institutions, as is true of many organizations, are directed to specific purposes that are fairly well understood by all participants. These purposes influence the members of the organization to behave in certain ways that are aimed at the accomplishment of organizational goals. Moreover, the people who attach themselves to colleges and universities do so, in substantial part, because of an anticipated or actual affinity for the purposes of the institution. There is an assumed connection between the goals of the college or university and those of the individual. It was stated above that some conformity of behavior does not equate to uniformity of belief and action. It is important to reinforce that notion now. The idea of an organizational culture does not necessitate or reflect an absolute dissolution of self within an organization. Quite the contrary. What constitutes a culture is what can be shared freely among individuals who seek others of like mind and who are similarly directed. Even with such agreement, there may be some discord and even dysfunction. As we will see, no culture is monolithic and all-encompassing. In most instances, the culture is composed of a federation of subcultures that may disagree about other goals and differ on means of accomplishing them.

It was mentioned that an examination of organizational culture can work from the top down. Within the context of higher education, this view entails a realization that leaders, especially those in the positions of presidents or chancellors, have the greatest potential for defining the institutional mission and thus articulating a vision for the school. We need to understand that the leaders are themselves part of the organizational culture; they are not separate from, or above, it. We will not detour into the literature and thought on leadership; suffice it to say that successful leaders are able to envision an attainable goal for the organization and to communicate it. In other words, the leaders are the principal shapers of the culture, which, in turn, fosters a climate in which all organization members live. Adela McMurray's (2003) research, based in a relatively newly founded university, shows that those campus units most closely in concert with the institution's culture assessed the climate positively and those less closely aligned with the culture were less positive. Also, at this time the emphasis is on the organization as system and how all parts of the system affect all other parts.

The leader's success also is dependent on his or her living that vision, not merely stating it. William Tierney (1988) presented a case study of this top-down view. He described a public institution he called "Family State College." His focus was on the change in organizational culture spurred by the school's president. That individual seized every opportunity to state the school's mission and his vision. He made the vision real by initiating a genuine open-door policy and by being visible around campus, thus broadening the concept of the presidency beyond that of an "office." The commitment demonstrated by the president and communicated to the others in the organization influenced many people's conceptions of institutional mission and the means to accomplish it. According to Tierney, many members were able to see the beneficial effects of shared beliefs and behaviors. This case study emphasizes an organizational imperative—the vision cannot be limited to a formal statement or comment to the press; it has to be alive.

Tierney intended the example of Family State College to emphasize the observation of David Dill:

> The intensity of an academic culture is determined not only by the richness and relevance of its symbolism for the maintenance of the professional craft, but by the bonds of social organization. For this mechanism to operate, the institution needs to take specific steps to socialize the individual to the belief system of the organization. . . . The management of academic culture therefore involves both the management of meaning and the management of social integration (1982, 309).

What happens, though, when the college or university does not have a leader of the same commitment and skill as the one in the case study? The president or chancellor is not alone in influencing the formation of culture and enforcing it. If the president is successful, as is true in the case study, the success is probably contributed to by those within the institution who are sympathetic to the president's vision. Others in the college or university administration are influential in the realization of the vision. If these individuals harbor opposing beliefs, their behavior can contradict the vision of the one person at the top. In such an instance, the president or chancellor has to decide if those other individuals will remain in administrative positions. The reality is that when there is a change in the top leadership position, that person frequently makes changes in vice-president, vice-chancellor, and even dean positions. The situation is somewhat analogous to an NFL team that hires a new head coach; that person is likely to make further changes to the coaching staff to ensure consistency of thinking and strategy for the accomplishment of goals. When such administrative changes occur, there is the likelihood of a somewhat unified administrative voice and a stronger shift in organizational culture.

The prospects for change in an organization's culture are complicated by the fact that some form of culture already is in existence when a new president takes office. The existing culture may be strong and characterized by substantial sharing among participants, in which case the president is likely to face resistance if he or she seeks to change it. On the other hand, the existing culture may be factitious, with little unity or agreement, in which case the president may be able to articulate a vision that can result in greater agreement. In either instance, the faculty represent an important element within the institution. The faculty, many of whom have considerable interest vested in the college or university, also have the strength of numbers; there are many faculty relative to top administrators. In general, the faculty tend to be the most permanent members of the institution, more so than the students and, in most instances, the administrators. A president or chancellor has two principal strategies at hand to make his or her vision real—acceptance or imposition. There is no doubt that acceptance is the easier route—the change that is part of a new vision might be palatable to the faculty and may be explained in such terms that can be acceptable to them. In other words, if the faculty perceive change as advantageous, the acceptance of the president's vision will follow.

If, however, a president's vision is not seen as advantageous to the faculty, the president might resort to imposition to bring about a cultural shift. The primary mechanism that can be used in imposing change is faculty retention and, much more important, faculty hiring. In the recent past, many institutions (and not only research universities) have chosen to emphasize research for a number of reasons, including the building of graduate programs (which could lead to financial growth), the lifting of institutional prestige and respect, and the attraction of external funding (part of which can be used by the institution).

Most administrators attempt to encourage the faculty to make research a high priority, but it is not an easy matter for any individual faculty member to adopt, rather abruptly, a research initiative. Given that reality, presidents and others use attrition to replace those faculty who were not active researchers with junior faculty who are prepared to focus their attention on research. Whenever there would be a retirement or a faculty departure for any reason, administrators (who have authority to approve candidates for hire) can exert influence in the recruitment and selection process. In time, the administrators also can exert influence over tenure decisions, primarily by influencing the policies that define accomplishments appropriate for tenure at the institution. In a fairly short time, the campus's culture can be altered substantially. Also, after such a cultural shift has been made, reversal is not likely, even given that the president of a specific institution may spend a relatively brief time on that campus.

There are likely to be further changes of vision for colleges and universities. For instance, as support from government sources diminishes for public institutions, there may be more emphasis on outside sources, such as the private sector (industry and corporations). If this comes to pass, presidents and chancellors who aim to lead their schools in such a direction may find themselves imposing their vision. According to Jay Chronister, the administrators may have an opportunity to bring about change. In the coming several years, retirements will result in a massive turnover of college and university faculties. As Chronister observed,

> The implications of this turnover in the professoriate go far beyond the need to acquire qualified faculty to fulfill instructional, research, and service responsibilities. The major influx of new academics will have an enormous impact on institutional culture and faculty governance during a period of significant change and challenges to institutional management and faculty governance mechanisms—challenges that have not yet been taken into account (1991, 23).

If there will be cultural change, the question to be asked is, In what direction will the change move and who will direct it?

It becomes evident that an organizational culture approach to the examination of higher education cannot focus solely on the organization's top administration. There are multiple cultures, or subcultures, in any college or university, just as there are subcultures in any society. We have just seen that there are at least two factions on a campus—the administration and the faculty. We might ask how much agreement or conflict there may be at an institution and where disagreement may be manifest. Peterson and White (1992) conducted a study ranging over several institutions. They surveyed faculty and administrators and got responses from 1,123 faculty and 311 administrators (the overall response rate was approximately 50 percent). Their questions centered on four indices related to organizational culture that were derived from previous work done in environments other than higher education. The four indices can be placed on a matrix with flexibility, individuality, and spontaneity (one index) and stability, control, and predictability at opposite poles. At the other opposing coordinates are internal, short-term, and smooth as one index and external, long-term, and competitive as the other. Within the matrix are four types of cultures: the clan, in the flexibility/internal quadrant; the adhocracy in the flexibility/external quadrant; the hierarchy in the stability/internal quadrant; and the market in the stability/external quadrant.

Peterson and White found that faculty and administrators at comprehensive universities (those with some graduate programs) disagreed on three points. Administrators place more emphasis on teamwork and innovation (characteristics, respectively, of the clan and the adhocracy) whereas faculty tend to emphasize rational governance (hierarchy) and attention to the market. In raw scores, faculty rank teamwork and rational behavior highest, but administrators rank teamwork even higher. It is evident that faculty lean toward stability, which is not surprising because the stability index is marked by security, predictability, and productivity. Administrators lean toward flexibility, again not surprising because it involves loyalty, innovation, and consensus. It should be noted that the four types of culture are ideals; any given institution is likely to embody a mix of traits, thus placing it at some point within the matrix, but not at an extreme. The work of Peterson and White shows inevitable strains on the organizational culture of the college or university. The culture is dynamic; it is a mix of multiple subcultures, which may be at odds.

With organizations such as colleges and universities, we cannot ignore the essential aspect of mission that entails the generation and communication of knowledge. It might even be said that this aspect is higher education's reason for being. Even though knowledge is integral to the purpose of every institution, it is not separate from the institution's culture. As Tierney stated, "knowledge is a discourse constantly reconstructed over time and place. The production of knowledge cannot be separated from the contingencies and continuous reconstructions of culture that individuals experience in their work lives. As a consequence, knowledge cannot be arbitrarily divorced from organizational ideologies" (1991, 201). Tierney spoke of multiple ideologies; if there are several subcultures, there inevitably will be several ideologies. What is meant here by the word "ideology"? First, it need not be employed in a pejorative sense. If we turn to Terry Eagleton, we can see that ideology may be used in two ways:

> We can mean by it, first, the general material process of production
> of ideas, beliefs and values in social life. Such a definition is both po-
> litically and epistemologically neutral, and is close to the broader

meaning of the term "culture"; beyond this the usage regarding organizational culture has a broader meaning, which attends to the promotion and legitimation of the interests of such social groups in the face of opposing interests (1991, 28–29).

So ideology refers to both the construction of values and the justification of those values whenever there might be conflict. Because conflict is likely in an organization, the culture's (or subculture's) ideology is a powerful tool for preservation. In a study separate from the case of Family State College, Tierney (1991) conducted an ethnographic analysis of three institutions of very different mission and intellectual stance. He found that, in each instance, the faculties' beliefs and behaviors were in agreement with the institution's mission and stance. He concluded that the culture and ideology of each school guide how knowledge is produced.

Tierney's study is instructive for both its findings and the author's conclusion. He did see indications of an inextricable link between organizational culture and the means by which knowledge is created and communicated. This is important because it tells us that there is no single model of knowledge production and, moreover, that knowledge production is related to those elements of a college or university that define its culture. On the other hand, Tierney's conclusion is suspect. Although he acknowledged that disciplinary influences play a role in both culture and knowledge as discourse, he appeared to accept that the institution and its leadership have the most important part in determining culture and, by extension, knowledge production. He failed to recognize the dynamic nature of organizational culture. For instance, faculty are likely to gravitate to a particular college or university because of its stance regarding the generation and communication of knowledge, and by doing so, contribute to a strengthening of the organization's culture. In effect, Tierney separated the faculty as members of academic disciplines and centered his attention on them primarily as members of the organization. His assumptions are negated in one instance by the work of Michael Dooris and James Fairweather (1994), who found that organizational creations such as multidisciplinary research centers or institutes have less to do with the faculty's self-identification than do traditional structures such as departments. They found that artificial structures are overshadowed by the cultural linkages of discipline and rank.

THE ROLE OF FACULTY

Some attention must be paid to the faculty of colleges and universities and what part they play in the creation, maintenance, and functioning of an organizational culture. We have already seen that the culture is actually an alliance, sometimes uneasy, of subcultures. The subcultures may have very different, and simultaneously operating, foundations. For instance, the foundation for existence of a subculture may be political. The structure of colleges and departments within an institution has definite disciplinary ties, but there is also a strong political reason for their being. Resources are inevitably distributed from central sources (the administration) and there has to be a means for that distribution. It is a given that financial resources are precious, so there is naturally going to be competition among academic units for what is available. This competition may be tiered in universities, with initial disbursal to colleges and/or schools and then the deans or directors determining what departments will get. Where such tiered allocation exists, there is likely to be a subsequent tenuous subculture composed of all of the faculty of a given college (say, of engineering) because for certain purposes they share not only the principles common to all of engineering, but also the political position within the university. Where there is no college structure, such as in two-year and many four-year institutions, this subculture does not exist to the same extent or perhaps at all.

As is mentioned above, the subculture of the college is likely to be tenuous because there is another political tier—the department. Not only is there a tighter disciplinary connection within the department, there also is close geographic proximity; it is probable that all of the faculty have offices in the same building. Further, as a political entity, the department has its own meetings, which may present a further opportunity for the sharing of beliefs and activities. In the political sense of a subculture, the faculty of the department share in the strength or weakness of the unit. If the department is politically strong, all of its members share in its strength and security. If it is weak, all faculty share in the tension and unease of an insecure state. This aspect of culture is also dynamic. A strong department is not necessarily strong indefinitely. It has to reposition itself from time to time in order to maintain strength. This can involve all faculty in revising the department's stance with regard to productivity (however defined) and, perhaps, students. The department has to maintain a critical number of students declaring it as a major, as well as maintaining a critical level of enrollment in courses. This relationship emphasizes the faculty's concern with market. (See the discussion of the matrix of Peterson and White above.) Departmental weakness is not necessarily permanent either, if the faculty can attract students and heighten productivity. However, it may be difficult to arrive at agreement on *how* to accomplish those goals. Accomplishment is probably related to the level of unity of the subculture.

Another foundation for a subculture may be cognitive. Cognitive differences are usually manifest by the division of faculty into various disciplines. In a small four-year liberal arts college, the disciplinary differences—in both knowledge content and discourse—may be limited. The limitations may be such that there are no appreciable subcultures. In larger institutions there will be more, and more diverse, disciplines. There are likely to be fundamental epistemological differences among cultures so that there can be disagreement about knowledge production and communication. These differences also will lead to differences in discourses, making it more difficult for faculty in one discipline to communicate with faculty in another. A discipline, being a culturally grounded community of like-minded scholars, also exists as an ideological influence, affecting ways of thinking and also practical matters, such as the determination of appropriate research questions and methods. Even within a discipline there will be differences. A good example is library and information science, where there can be cognitive and practical differences between the two branches. In any given discipline, the question is whether the differences are apt to lead to a cultural schism.

Of course, the distinction of cognitive and political foundations is, to an extent, an artificial one. The two are constantly melded together as disciplines tend to be grouped as departments. The pressure on a subculture, then, can be at once political and cognitive. There can be misunderstandings or conflicts between disciplines regarding, for instance, pedagogical purpose. The teaching in philosophy deals with abstract concepts; the teaching in mechanical engineering deals with practical purposes. This may be an oversimplification, but it is not unusual for the dispute to be translated into one discipline/department claiming superiority over another. In part, the dispute may focus on market: one will claim more relevance to fruitful employment of its students. On the other hand, this kind of dispute may not arise; faculty may hold a cultural allegiance to disciplines first of all. Such a state could, of course, contribute to other kinds of political tension. The conflicts can spill over to the culture of the institution. The disciplinary conflict can lead to cultural conflicts. These conflicts focus on the faculty because they are at the heart of disciplinary expression. All this leads to the realization that organizational culture is problematic. This is not a failing of the organizational culture approach; rather, it is recognition of the complexity of organizations such as colleges and universities.

The cultural complexity of a university can be modeled and is represented in figure 2.1. The figure illustrates the central position of the administration in influencing organizational culture. In some ways, this figure has elements of an organizational chart; this is not accidental because of the political nature of many cultural ties. The figure reflects the strong politically based cultural ties from the administration into all formal academic units. For political purposes colleges (say, basic sciences, humanities, fine arts, etc.) have strong linkages. The strength of these linkages is founded on the continuity of aims and goals shared by the faculty in general, as reflected in Peterson and White 's study. The faculty are likely to share beliefs regarding academic freedom, teaching load relative to research responsibilities, and tenure guidelines. Especially when there may be conflict between administrators and faculty, the cultural ties among colleges may be strong. The dotted lines represent weaker cultural ties, which may at times result from a lack of political conflict or, more commonly, reflect weaker cognitive links among groups. For instance, within department X there are strong politically based cultural ties within disciplines. However, the individual disciplines may experience weaker cognitively based links. If department X is the history department, it may comprise the more autonomous disciplines of American history and English history, among others. It should be emphasized that figure 2.1 is just a model and thus a simplified look at organizational culture and faculty. In a smaller college, the intermediary level may be absent, but the cultural ties will probably resemble those illustrated in the figure.

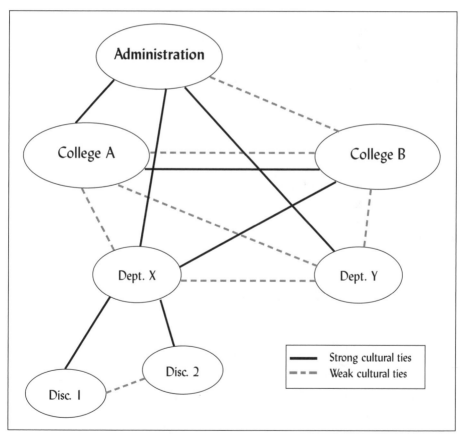

FIGURE 2.1   Cultural Ties in Higher Education

Although the faculty and academic units may well exhibit the kinds of ties described in figure 2.1, the institutional administration may be a bit removed from those ties. One reason for the distance may be that administrators constitute their own subculture, a subculture that is reinforced through frequent contact with one another and a lack of contact with the other cultures of the college or university. Schein most aptly related how the distancing might occur:

> as managers rise in the hierarchy, two factors cause them to become more "impersonal." First, they become increasingly aware that they are no longer managing operators, but other managers who think like they do, thus making it not only possible but also likely that their thought patterns and worldview will increasingly diverge from the worldview of the operators. Second, as they rise, the units they manage grow larger and larger until it becomes impossible to personally know everyone who works for the organization. At some point, they recognize that they cannot manage all the people directly and, therefore, have to develop systems, routines, and rules to manage "the organization." They increasingly see people as "human resources" to be treated as a cost rather than a capital investment (1996, 15).

Although Schein was speaking primarily about the corporate world, his remarks have clear application to higher education as well.

Schein's observations raise some important questions about culture in complex organizations. If some colleges and universities are bureaucratized, what is the resulting effect on faculty and their departments? If, as Edward Shils said, the task of the university is "the methodical discovery and the teaching of truths about serious and important things" (1997, 3), what impact does the political element of organizational culture have on that task? As we ask these kinds of questions, we quickly see how complicated the cultural structures of higher education can be.

SUCCESS AND ITS DYSFUNCTIONS

The multiple foundations for cultural bonds and the many members in various positions in the organizations suggest that there may not be a single, unified conception of success. To a considerable extent, success is a function of what is seen to be meaningful in the organization. Determination of meaning, like most aspects of organizations, is complex. As Louis said, "In a cultural view, meaning is produced through an in situ interpretive process. The process encompasses universal, cultural and individual levels of interpretation" (1987, 422). The various levels of meaning formation maintained by Louis are important to note. Success, as a function of meaning (and a function of accomplishment of objectives, which is a matter for interpretation), is tiered, as is the organizational culture itself. Some essential questions regarding success must be addressed: Who determines success? Who establishes the necessary criteria? In the event of conflict, how is agreement reached? These questions incorporate the recognition of the tiers of the culture and the existence of various subcultures.

Each of the cultures and subcultures is likely to have its own notion of success, and the behavior of members of each culture is likely to be governed or influenced by that notion. The members of each culture also are likely to share, among other things, modes of discourse that can affect meaning formation. Therefore, the criteria for success can be articulated through shared discourses. Let us look at these ideas in the context of the cultural complexity discussed so far. As has been mentioned, the college or university administration has a central role in influencing much of organizational culture. Many of the cultural determinants are established administrative expressions of the institution's mission and primary goals. The administration usually goes one step further and details the means for accomplishment of its goals. If the mission of a two-year college or a four-year liberal arts college is instruction, the administration may enforce that mission by the imposition of teaching load or office hour requirements. The faculty may have little option but to adhere to those requirements. As has also been mentioned, disagreement with the mission may be handled by replacing faculty who leave with new faculty who are amenable to the culture based on the importance of instruction and contact with students.

To take another instance, at a university there may be administrative impetus for increased research productivity and the attraction of external funding. A similar strategy to the previous example of using attrition can bring about a change in what is meaningful and in what the organizational culture is rooted in. In both instances, the administration may use rewards such as tenure, promotion, and pay increases to impose a particular meaning on the organization. In Louis's terms, meaning is not necessarily formed completely at the individual level; that is, a faculty member, if he or she wishes to remain at that institution, must accept some of the criteria for success determined by the college or university administration. Within the culture of a particular school, there are limitations to the self-determination of faculty success.

Other cultural aspects to the definition of success add to its complexity. From the political perspective, the academic units (colleges and departments) play a role in the enforcement of criteria for success. Although they are limited by the administrative initiative, the units can have a say in the determination of success. Manifestation of the unit's expression of criteria for success is affected by the strength or weakness of the unit's democracy. Where democratic decision making is both a managerial and cultural reality, the faculty within the unit may be able, within constraints, to establish criteria. Where democracy is weak, the dean or department chair is able to influence discourse and meaning, and thus influence criteria for success. The faculty in the units, then, must be aware of the political culture and its effects on the determination of success. From the cognitive perspective, those in the discipline who have reached a level of prominence and prestige through their accomplishments may be able to influence discourse and meaning. Success may follow their lead in that they can influence not only quantitative aspects of success, but also substantive aspects, such as the determination of the most important disciplinary questions and methods. As is true of all cultural issues, the political and the cognitive elements do not act independently but, instead, are parts of a dynamic mix of influences and determinants. The mix, in this case, includes the library. A library with a mission to support undergraduate and graduate education *and* research is likely to experience tugs at its limited resources.

If there is conflict regarding what constitutes success, how can agreement be reached? It should be evident by now that the cultures comprising a college or university are not equal. We have seen that agreement on the criteria of success can be achieved over time through such things as attrition. But the direction rests on the shoulders of the president or chancellor. He or she has greater say in the fundamental criteria for success than anyone in the organization. If that person proclaims that research productivity is the first principle of success, argument with him or her on that point is unlikely to be fruitful. This does not mean that the subcultures are completely disenfranchised. From both the political and cognitive points of view, it is incumbent upon the department (discipline) to define research productivity in ways that are most appropriate to the research questions and communication structures of the discipline. Dysfunction can arise if the president and administration attempt to impose a single, prescriptive set of criteria to be applied to all disciplines, whether or not that set fits the nature of work and of discourse in each discipline. In such an instance, the various subcultures may be strengthened in that they converge and coalesce around the most important and integral shared beliefs. This kind of convergence may result in a distancing of the subculture from the culture enforced by the college or university administration. It becomes evident that the institution actually is a federation of multifarious cultures held together by a fairly strong, but occasionally imposed, central culture.

ORGANIZATIONAL CULTURE AND THE ACADEMIC LIBRARY

It should go without saying that the college or university is part of the organizational culture. But how is it part of the culture? For one thing, the library contains, or offers access to, the graphic record that not only is used by students and faculty, but also has been used in the past. As such, the library represents something of a record of former states of the organizational culture. The library's collection has changed more slowly than has the institutional administration, the faculty, or even the curriculum. One reason for the slowness of change is the expense of altering the direction of the collection. It takes a number of years and a lot of money to bring about a major transformation of the physical collection. Moreover, even as change takes place, the old remains as the new is added. Let's say that at the direction of the president, a growing regional state university begins to emphasize research over teaching. The existing library collection is designed to support the curriculum, so a great deal of additional money, and no small amount of time, is needed to build a collection that can support research in several disciplinary areas. The collection that exists at the time the shift begins stands as witness to the previous articulation of the campus's culture. These statements apply to the physical collection. Electronic access, especially access based on licensing rather than purchase, can be far more impermanent. Of course, such changes in the concept of "collection" also can affect the cultures of the library and the institution as a whole.

Although the history of the library's place in the school's culture holds some interest, the library's present position is a much more pressing reality. Let's stay with the example just mentioned. The direction from the president to emphasize research is bound to result in a substantial cultural shift affecting all elements of the university. The activities of the faculty will, of necessity, be altered, as will their own conceptions of success. From a practical standpoint, the faculty will need a somewhat different set of tools to do their work. The library and its staff, sensitive to the cultural shift, will change their entire notion of collection development, taking into account the new emphasis. To bring about the change, librarians should communicate with the faculty especially so as to understand the cognitive foundations of disciplinary culture. Why is this important? In order to be supportive of faculty scholarship, the collection should include the content that is most fitting to the exploration of the research questions perceived as most important. The understanding of the disciplinary culture can be invaluable in ensuring that the most useful content becomes part of the collection. In an instance such as the one described, the librarians will have to be prepared for the possibility of some false starts in the transformation of the collection. The cultural change that is taking place, though somewhat abrupt, is not going to be immediate. The disciplines included in the university will need some time to reflect on what is important to them, and they are likely to flounder a bit before reaching some grasp of their own revised, cognitive benchmark.

The role of the library in an organization's culture does not end with its collection. The services of the library also fit into the cultural milieu. If we remember that organizational culture is a social construct and that the public services of the library are founded on social needs, it becomes easier to see the cultural basis for a library's services. For example, in a two- or four-year liberal arts college where the principal cultural imperative is founded on teaching, the library's services will be focused primarily on adding to the student's learning experience and the faculty's teaching effectiveness. In any college or university where undergraduate education is a priority, the library is likely to play a role in the shared behavior, perhaps in the form of an extensive library instruction program. At times, when the library's actions are less than effective, the reason may be a lack of awareness of the existence of a central culture and a set of subcultures that are unique to the institution. If librarians, and particularly library directors, assume that there is a sameness to institutions (for instance, all research universities are alike), they may be oblivious to a great deal of a specific school's cultural personality.

Awareness of the manifestations of a given college or university's culture is important to librarians on a personal level as well. The professional effectiveness of every librarian will be enhanced by understanding what constitutes the meaning behind the events and symbols surrounding him or her. This notion hearkens back to the tiers of culture discussed earlier. Librarians must pay attention to the articulations of vision and mission emanating from the institutional administration. This will have the greatest influence in determining what is shared. Beyond that, librarians must be aware of the political and cognitive foundations of subcultures. If a given academic department is in a tenuous political position, it may be difficult for the library to justify substantial expenditures in that area. The cognitive element is clearer; it helps to define the curricular and research directions of a discipline. Librarians also must realize that the library tends to reflect the same political and cognitive aspects of, say, a college in a university or a department in a college. In all but the very smallest academic libraries, there are some political distinctions, of which the most common center on public and technical services. These distinctions also have cognitive aspects; the culture of work in the various departments of the library can differ considerably. We'll return to these ideas when we discuss the organization of academic libraries.

There is another way that the organizational culture affects librarians on a personal level. As is true with the faculty, it may well be that the fundamentals of individual success are determined at a higher level. Although, to a considerable extent, the decisions of effectiveness are made internally and based on the particular subculture of the library, they probably will be subject to validation at some other level of the organization. If a library director decides, based on a set of criteria agreed on within the library, that a certain individual merits a promotion or a salary increase, these criteria generally must be amenable to the dictates of the dominant culture. Such can be the case in any college or university; it will almost invariably be so where the librarians have some form of faculty status. In those institutions, the librarians are attaching themselves to a culture that extends well beyond the library and there must be sufficient sharing of beliefs and, especially, behaviors if they are to be accepted in that culture. This topic, too, is the focus of discussion in a later chapter.

SUMMARY

There are many ways to examine colleges and universities as organizations. As we have seen, some of these approaches are prescriptive; that is, some of the methods of study purport to set forth the ideal means of organizing and of managing. Those methods tend to be deterministic; they tend to outline strategies that treat organizations as mechanisms or as physical organisms. One outcome of such approaches is that there is a link of attention to the social complexity that accompanies any gathering of people. The organizational culture school of thought takes into account the reality that there are many individual and group motivations and allegiances and that, for a variety of purposes, there is sharing of beliefs and behaviors. In applying an organizational culture approach to the study of higher education, Tierney advocated that students of organization:

> consider real or potential conflicts not in isolation but on the
> broad canvas of organizational life;
>
> recognize structural or operational contradictions that suggest
> tensions in the organization;
>
> implement and evaluate everyday decisions with a keen awareness
> of their role in and influence upon organizational culture;
>
> understand the symbolic dimensions of ostensibly instrumental
> decisions and actions; and
>
> consider why different groups in the organization hold varying
> perceptions about institutional performance (1988, 6).

These admonitions emphasize the social underpinnings of any human organization.

Looking into the culture of higher education, we see that there are actually multiple cultures on college or university campuses, but the cultures are not equal. As stated earlier, the titular leader of the institution—the president or the chancellor—has greater influence over the organization's culture than anyone else. Moreover, that individual, along with the rest of the campus administrators, has the ability to bring about a change in the culture by decree and by taking the time to recruit personnel sympathetic to the new culture. The administrators also are in the best position to realize what Domenec Mele (2003) called an "organizationally humanizing culture," in which individuals' dignity and rights and the common good are central. All of this is not to say that the subcultures of the faculty are ineffectual; they are integral to the workings of the college and university and are the means of articulating the goals and activities of faculty groups. The groupings of faculty have political and cognitive foundations. Sometimes these two cultural elements can work separately, as when focus is variously on the academic unit as a structural entity and the discipline, which manifests the fundamentals of pedagogy and inquiry for a cognitively linked group of faculty. According to Patrick Terenzini (1993), the complexity of the institution necessitates three tiers of intelligence to comprehend fully the organizational culture: (1) technical/analytical intelligence (familiarity with the categories, terms, and measures customarily employed in higher education institutions as well as knowledge of the methods that might be used to explore the structural elements of the university); (2) issues intelligence (understanding how the university functions, how decisions are made, what problems are faced); and (3) contextual intelligence (understanding the culture of higher education and, especially, the specific institution, including the university's philosophical stance, organization, politics, and customs).

The academic library is a part of the college or university's culture. It fits into the political structure of higher education as a unit analogous to either a college or a department within the institution. The library also is affected by the existing subcultures because its collection and services exist to attend to the needs of the academic community. Librarians also are personally affected by the existing culture because their own conceptions of success are heavily influenced by the dominant culture.

Nothing has been said in this chapter about the place of students in organizational culture. This group does constitute a set of subcultures, but its influence on the operation of the college or university tends to be less forceful than that of the faculty and administration. One reason for this relative lack of influence is the transitory, sometimes even itinerant, nature of the student population. Restrictions on time and space do not allow us to deal with this element further.

Let us consider some questions surrounding the organizational culture of higher education and use them for the purpose of discussion:

> What are the essential elements of the culture of a college or university?
>
> What constitutes some of the differences between the culture of a four-year liberal arts college and a research university?

How does a dominant culture become dominant?

What sorts of things might be shared by faculty in an academic unit?

How do disciplinary concerns affect the subcultures of the faculty?

What cultural elements have an impact on the staff of an academic library?

How do cultural influences affect conceptions of success for the library?

When a college or university puts greater emphasis on teaching or research, how might such institutional change affect perceptions within the library about individual and organizational performance?

Chapter 3

The System of Scholarly Communication

Scholarly communication has undergone some dramatic changes in recent years and will continue to evolve. Despite the changes, however, it continues to be the object of substantial criticism and suggestions for alteration have come from a number of quarters. Scholarly communication is probably undergoing closer scrutiny now than at any time in history. The concerns being expressed carry implications for scholarship, for academic librarianship, and, in all likelihood, for the organization of libraries.

It is not incidental that the word "system" appears in the title of this chapter. Scholarly communication is a complex web of connections among scholars and researchers, authors and readers, formal publications (in the broadest sense) and libraries. However, it was not always as complex as it is today. In a sense, the history of scholarly communication is a long one, dating back a few millennia. Certainly there was scholarship before there was printing; in fact, scholarship substantially predates the codex volume (c. second century C.E.). As we have seen from the brief excursion into the history of higher education in chapter 1, universities were around a couple of centuries before printing was invented. Scholars had worked, and even communicated, for many centuries, but it was the invention of printing that made possible the *system* of scholarly communication that exists today. Print made the fruits of scholarship accessible to a degree and scope that had not existed previously. As was true of all kinds of communication, scholarship could quite suddenly be mass-produced; hundreds, even thousands, of copies of works could be printed and reprinted in the relative blink of an eye. A scholar's words could spread across Europe in a matter of a few months.

One impact of printing was that it accelerated scientific inquiry. The cosmology of Copernicus and the anatomy of Vesalius, to name just a couple of works, could be shared with a relatively large number of people and subjected to critical scrutiny. By the seventeenth century, the interest in science (in the broadest sense) had fostered development of a substantial community interested in similar questions and concerned with what others were working on. The philosophy of the time also was focused to a considerable extent on science and the question of human interaction with the natural world. The work of Hobbes, Descartes, Berkeley, and others was widely distributed in print. The community of scientists grew to such a size and the activity of scientists increased to such an extent that a new medium became a necessity in the seventeenth century—the scientific journal. The watershed year was 1665, the year in which the first two journals began publication. On January 5 of that year, the *Journal des scavans* first appeared. It was soon followed by the first issue of the *Philosophical Transactions of the Royal Society* on May 6 (Houghton 1975, 12–15). These journals principally comprised brief communications, usually summaries of published efforts in some areas or presentations of short updates or inquiries. Specifically, the purpose of the *Journal des scavans* was:

> to catalogue and give useful information on books published in Europe and to summarise their works, to make known experiments in physics, chemistry and anatomy that may serve to explain natural phenomena, to describe useful or curious inventions or machines and to record meteorological data, to cite the principal decisions of civil and religious courts and censures of universities, to transmit to readers all current events worthy of the curiosity of men (Houghton 1975, 13–14).

Even those early journals were used as mechanisms to communicate the latest work in science to a cohort of colleagues and competitors.

One of the lessons learned from the work of Copernicus was the importance of open dissemination of scientific writing. By the end of the seventeenth century, scientists had come to rely on the forum of ideas that print made possible. The accessibility of print meant not only that the writings of important thinkers could be distributed widely, but also that commentary on their works could be published. This advance had two principal effects: the world was alerted to the existence of the primary work through reviews and commentaries, and the commentators added to the inquiry itself through their observations and questions. Elizabeth Eisenstein illustrated the impact that Isaac Newton had because of the availability of his work and the commentary it spurred.

> Thanks to [Edmund] Halley, who stepped in when the Royal Society's publication funds were exhausted, it had been issued in printed editions and discussed in all the major learned journals of

Europe. It had been made known throughout the Commonwealth of Learning in a Latin review which stimulated major revisions in the second edition of 1713, and which led Leibniz to turn out three articles even before he had seen Newton's work. It had been publicized for the Republic of Letters in a French translation of a long review-essay which may have been written by John Locke (1979, 638).

As formal institutions of higher education became more numerous worldwide, the scholarly profession likewise grew. This profession was certainly not limited to colleges and universities; they were too small in number and too limited in scope even in the early nineteenth century to be the primary seat of research. Larger societal movements, such as the Industrial Revolution, heightened interest in (and profitability of) technical inquiry aimed at practical ends. Such pragmatic purposes did not diminish the need for mechanisms to keep up with the most recent developments in technology. Out of this kind of need was born the *Mechanics' Magazine*. It contained "accounts of new discoveries, inventions and improvements, with illustrated drawings, explanations of mineralogy and chemistry, plans and suggestions for the abridgement of labour, reports on the state of the arts in this and other countries, memoires and occasionally portraits of eminent mechanics, etc." (Houghton 1975, 23). Although this publication was aimed less at the learned audience and more at the artisan, it can be seen as a precursor of the technical and trade journals that exist in abundance today.

In the later nineteenth century, as higher education branched beyond its traditional curricular boundaries, the need for faculty to communicate with one another was felt more strongly. Remember that the last quarter of the nineteenth century saw the rise of research as a mainstay of universities. This same period of time saw the rise of learned and professional associations. These newly formed societies tended to found journals as a means for members to keep up to date on developments in the field and to share their research with one another. Our own profession provides an example of the development of associations and their journals. In 1876, the ALA was founded; in that same year, the *American Library Journal* began publication. In short order, the ALA adopted the journal as its official publication. (After several years, *Library Journal* became an independent publication, but ALA started the *ALA Bulletin* to fill the need of an association journal.)

EVOLUTION OF THE SYSTEM

If we recall the history of higher education, particularly in the nineteenth century, we are struck by the expansion of the last quarter of the century. Not only was there growth in the number of institutions and student enrollment, but there also was diversification of colleges and universities' curricula. Academic disciplines began to realize possibilities for study that their subjects presented. Research was becoming common at universities, not simply because of political pressures to conduct research (such political impetus was minimal at the time), but also because of an awakening to the richness of potential areas of inquiry. As research became a mainstay of U.S. higher education, the need for the communication of research results likewise grew. If people were going to engage in research, they wanted to tell others of their efforts and hear about the research of others. In many disciplines, the communication need was filled by the journal. From fairly meager beginnings in 1665, journals increased in number to approximately 5,100 by 1885 (Houghton 1975, 102). The increased activities of university faculty then began to have a substantial effect on the number of journals, and by 1895, just ten years later, the total number had grown to an estimated 8,600 (Houghton 1975, 103). Many of the journals were founded in order to report the increasing volume of scientific research.

It is very difficult to separate the growth of scholarly information from higher education. By the beginning of the twentieth century, the level of research activity was increasing to match the expectations that administrators were coming to have of faculty. However, research, especially scientific research, was—and still is—costly. Even in the nineteenth century, universities were turning to private donors to help fund the materials used in the research endeavor. A fairly common practice at that time was for an individual or a family to give money to a university (more often than not a private university) for the purpose of constructing buildings that could be used for both research and teaching. A number of scientific laboratories were funded in this manner. The labs of the nineteenth century were simple facilities because the technology used by scientists had not advanced much. However, by the beginning of the twentieth century, technology and instrumentation were becoming more sophisticated and more expensive. Again, many universities turned to private endowments to help outfit their laboratories. As Roger Geiger reported,

> Probably the most ambitious and explicit plan for endowing research was formulated in 1910 by President Jacob Gould Schurman of Cornell. Complaining that "the demand for scientific investigators, for laboratories, and for the instrumentalities of research come to the president from all departments," he invited contemporary millionaires to contribute $1 million to $3 million in endowment for each of seven departments (1986, 85).

Research had become such a central part of universities' missions that any fundraising plans included seeking capital for research facilities (including, at a growing rate, research conducted in medical schools).

The place of research at universities also was having the effect of distinguishing the university from the college. As early as the turn of the century, there was such an apparent influence of research that the teaching activities of faculty at the two kinds of institutions were becoming noticeably divergent. A survey conducted by the Carnegie Foundation for the Advancement of Teaching in 1908 showed that, although there were some differences between the teaching of undergraduate and graduate students, there was a noticeable difference in time spent in the classroom. Referring to the results of the survey, Geiger wrote,

> Most striking is the pronounced disparity in teaching loads between colleges and research universities. Faculty in the latter averaged from eight to ten hours of teaching per week (nonlaboratory subjects), while their counterparts in well-established liberal arts colleges (i.e., Carnegie-accepted) were professing from fifteen to eighteen hours. To the survey's authors this represented "a difference in kind of work" that existed by this date between the two settings (1986, 69).

The practices that attract the attention, and frequently the ire, of observers today apparently have deep roots in academe.

At the same time that universities were seeking outside funding for research, they were looking for private gifts to help fund the growth of their library collections. The trend, begun with the donations to Harvard's library at the time of the college's founding, continued into the twentieth century. As Geiger wrote,

> The voluntary support received by university libraries deserves special mention. . . . For example, two-thirds of the book purchases at Columbia in 1903 were financed through eleven donated funds. In addition 319 individuals gave books or pamphlets to the library that year. The largest university library, Harvard's, was completely supported by donated funds during the first half of the 1890s, and even after that endowments and gifts managed to finance all book purchases (1986, 83).

It seems clear that the changes in institutional mission were not extended to institutional financing. By the twentieth century, research was a solid component of the university's purpose, but institutional funding had not changed much from its earlier roots.

The emphasis on research eventually created new pressures on university faculty. The mission had become bifurcated, divided between teaching and research. Thus, expectations of faculty extended to both of those realms. For instance, in his study of the beginnings of the university in the United States,

Laurence Veysey reported that by 1901, promotion of faculty at Yale University was based on a policy that stressed "productive work" (read, publication) that would result in gaining a "national reputation" for the individual (1965, 176–77). It was becoming clear that not only was the institutional mission bifurcated and research a central part of the purpose of the university, but also the faculty were pressed to communicate the results of their work. In part, the encouragement to publish was—and still is—based on the recognition that communication is essential to the growth of knowledge in any discipline. Full communication of scholarly work enables researchers to build on the total effort in an area of inquiry. It is difficult to imagine how any progress would be possible if there were no communication.

At the same time, there are additional aspects of publication beyond the goal of communication. Publication, as it has existed for some centuries, has been closely connected to authorship. The concept of authorial responsibility includes ascribing intellectual credit for ideas or research. Authorship can lend credence to the content of particular published work. For example, a scholar who has a history of reputable work in a certain field communicates her latest research in a journal article. Readers who are aware of her past work and its quality are likely to pay close attention to the new communication on the basis of a track record of reliability. Authorship also signals credit for both the idea and the publication itself. Assuming for the moment that there is selectivity in publication, having a piece of work published distinguishes one scholar from his or her colleagues. Having more publications to one's credit results in further distinction. Along with authorship is authorial affiliation. Along with the distinction of the author upon publication comes distinction of the individual's institution. Motivation to achieve this kind of distinction is not trivial, at either the personal or the institutional level.

We can see from this sketchy background that scholarly communication, even as early as the start of this century, was beginning to display the characteristics of a system. "System" is a word that gets bandied about rather loosely; what do I mean by the term? Scholarly communication is a system because its component parts do not behave absolutely independently nor do they have independent origins. The literature of any discipline is related to the inquiry of the scholars in that field. Those scholars have multiple reasons to communicate their work to colleagues: some of the reasons are founded on the desire to contribute to the growth of knowledge; some are based in the politics and structure of academic institutions. There are other connections, such as institutional reliance on external sources of funding for research and the impact of that funding on institutional operation and reputation, that we will not delve into deeply. From the standpoint of the academic librarian, the two primary elements of the system are the drive to produce research and scholarship by faculty and the communication outlets available to faculty, enabling them to share their work with others. These two elements are clearly interdependent; the goals of one are related to the goals of the other. (In the discussion of collections in chapter 8, we will see how the library is also an integral part of the scholarly communication system.)

DISCIPLINARY DIFFERENCES

Perhaps it may be more accurate to say that scholarly communication is a system of systems. I say this because there are many subparts within the structure of scholarly communication that, in some respects, are only loosely related to one another. Principally, the independence of the parts is grounded in the differences in the content of faculty research and in disciplinary literatures—in the disciplines themselves. The distinctions among the disciplines is an epistemic one; it is based on the differences in the definitions of what constitutes knowledge, in how knowledge grows, and in how the practitioners of the discipline engage in inquiry so as to add to the field's knowledge base. Granted, there are other, nonepistemic factors that serve to strengthen the systemic nature of scholarly communication, but for the time being, let's focus our attention on the differences inherent in the disciplines. Because the purpose of one discipline varies from that of another, one can expect scholars' behaviors to vary somewhat as well. To a great extent, the variance is influenced by the subject matter being studied. Different problems or questions require different methods, different theoretical foundations, and different modes of inquiry. If we accept that proposition, we can see that the disciplines also will have different communication patterns. Let's take a brief look at the three very broad disciplines so that we can understand the differences among them.

Although the parts of the scholarly communication system constitute an elaborate social network, this network has discrete elements. At a macro level, one of these elements is science. Undoubtedly, the many scientific disciplines exhibit unique aspects, but we will look here at some particular characteristics that are more or less common to scholarly communication in science. The object of study for scientists is the physical. For the most part, the working scientist believes that the physical world exists apart from our thoughts or even our conceptions of it. The aim of science, in a radically reduced version, is to understand the workings of the physical world through such means as modeling and observation. The work of the scientist is, according to some, cumulative; that is, it is a part of a continuum of development and knowledge growth wherein the past work is incorporated in some way into the present. Although this description is simplistic, it is important to note that science is continuous; its key questions do not disappear, but contemporary work tends to replace the past in some important respects. In general, scientists must rely on artificial tools to observe the physical world—telescopes, electron microscopes, other instruments. This means that scientific inquiry is expensive. On the other hand, the perceived benefits of the investigation are taken to be sufficiently worthwhile to invest large sums of money in it. This creates a competitive situation and necessitates frequent and timely communication so that individuals or teams can stake claims and reap the benefits, both material and nonmaterial, of their work. Communication in the sciences relies on media that have the capacity to transmit work quickly. Thus, it is not surprising that scientists have been open to electronic communication outlets.

Scientific inquiry leads to formal and informal structures of communication. The latter helps to establish claims and to facilitate the progress of the disciplines. As Belver Griffith said, "The formal–informal distinction is an extremely useful one. Informal exchanges atrophy under conditions of high competition; researchers speak only to 'trusted assessors,' and, in the extreme case, they may eliminate vital communicative activities" (1990, 42). The formal communication outlets serve a couple of purposes in this scheme: they provide an artifact that records the work of science for future reference and evaluation, and they offer a record that can be accessible to those on the fringe of, or outside, the narrow subdisciplinary specialization. The competition of the environment and the purposes of communication lead to an elaborate and vast publication landscape. Another factor affecting the size of the literature is the pervasiveness of scientific investigation throughout society, not just within academe. Such an impact was recognized several years ago: "The scientific and technical fields differ from the humanities in that a much higher proportion of doctoral scientists and engineers is employed outside the universities; thus, the growth of scientific and technical literature is not as closely linked to faculty members as is the case in the humanities" (*Scholarly Communication* 1979, 148).

The above observation is not the only difference between the sciences and the humanities. The object of study in the humanities is (and again this is a simplified view) the product of human creativity. The humanities embrace the intellectual, the aesthetic, and the expressive in many forms, including texts, performance, and plastic arts. The claim has been made that the humanities are noncumulative, that in many important respects the past stands side by side with the present. It is possible that an eighteenth-century commentary on one of Shakespeare's plays is as valuable and useful as one dating from last year. Further, in some ways the textual product of humanities inquiry can form the object of study as well. (For more on scholarship in the humanities, see Brockman [2001]).

In a somewhat reductionist vein, we might put the textual in opposition to the physical to demonstrate a key difference between the humanities and the sciences. Because what we usually consider secondary works (commentaries, criticisms, assessments of human ideas or creations) may take primary importance, the formal communication process is essential in the humanities. This is not to say that informal communication does not have its place, but sustained and comprehensive analysis or argument usually cannot fit into informal mechanisms. As the National Enquiry into Scholarly Communication found, humanities scholars depend on ready access (usually including browsability) to local collections of formal publications (1979, 134–35). The kinds of sustained and comprehensive scholarship engaged in by many in the humanities suggests that frequency and volume of communication is not as high a priority as it is in the sciences.

Of course, there have been some changes in humanities scholarship in recent years. Digitization projects have expanded accessibility to primary texts and images substantially. The Library of Congress's American Memory project is only one example of such efforts. A scholar examining the poetry of Walt Whitman, for instance, can view his notebooks, thus adding the potential for greater insight into Whitman's work. Some scholars may require access to original documents in order to study not only the content, but also the physical item itself (paper, binding, etc.). However, many scholars, including students, now have access to a rich trove of resources that only technological development could make possible.

The social sciences are more difficult to describe, but we might say that they are focused on the behaviors, actions, and accomplishments (outside the artistic or creative sphere) of human beings. This summary is overly restrictive but will suit our present purposes. In many ways, the social sciences are a mix of the sciences and the humanities in both thought and practice. Although the object of study in the social sciences is human behavior or endeavor, some of the observational premises of the sciences influence inquiry. On the other hand, the interpretive practices of the humanities are necessary to the analysis of human behavior. The communication patterns of the social sciences are likewise mixed. Some individual projects are based in sustained analysis; others involve experimentation or other methods of the sciences. The formal and informal communication activities tend to follow the lead of the project. Even within a given discipline, such as sociology, a variety of investigative approaches and communicative actions may exist. At times, there is some competition for research funding and for claims of specific findings. In those particular areas of competitiveness, the publication pattern tends to emulate the sciences. In those areas that rely more on the contemplation of the object of study (which might be textual), there is likely to be less activity in informal communication and formal communication tends to emulate that in the humanities.

In all of the disciplines, there is considerable activity in the form of publication as a means of formal communication. One investigation into publishing by faculty, published in *Change* ("The Payoff for Publication Leaders"), provides an indication of individual activity. The mean number of articles published by university faculty in all disciplines was 17 per capita (with a high of 33 in engineering and a low of 11 in the humanities), and a total of 45 percent of all faculty had more than eleven articles to their credit (1991, 29). More recent investigation suggests that publishing by faculty has been increasing even in the past several years. For the period 1991–1993, the mean number of publications per ARL member institution was 4,595.8. The per capita average for those years was 3.56 (Budd 1995, 549). For 1995–1997, the mean per institution had risen to 5,493.5 and the per capita rate had increased to 4.20 (Budd 1999, 310). The increases in both measures for this brief time frame were statistically significant. More is said about this publishing dynamic shortly.

TRADITIONAL MEDIA

We cannot ignore the reality that, at the present time, some portion of formal scholarly communication exists in the pages of print publications. That statement requires an addendum: many long-standing journals are available in print, but that availability is generally ancillary to electronic publication. There is likely to be even more expansion into electronic media (we have seen the continuation of such expansion), but the promise of a migration away from print will take some time. The scholarly book, for example, which has a history almost as long as the printing industry, has been an effective communication mechanism for many purposes. As long as those purposes persist, the book may well remain a viable medium. Some centuries ago, the rather new industry of printing was helped along by the demand for, and the production of, monographs on scientific topics. The impact of such titles as *De Humanis Corporis Fabrica by Vesalius* and *De Revolutionibus Orbium Coelestium* by Copernicus certainly was felt in the fields of anatomy and cosmology, but it also was apparent in the business of printing. Over time, the book as a medium evolved into the principal communication tool of the humanities. The evolution of the medium paralleled the evolution of the nature of scholarly work in the disciplines. We need to understand the present state of book publishing and its place in the scholarly communication system.

At the present time, it is common to speak of publishing as being in a state of crisis. Frequently, discussion of the crisis is couched in financial terms, with increasing publishing costs and static or diminishing sales revenue cited as contributing factors. If there is a crisis, it is not simply a financial crisis. Frederick Praeger spoke to the academic side of the crisis:

The scholar needs information and knowledge, often different kinds of knowledge—conclusions, guesses, insights, scenarios, creative interpretations, models, analogies, summaries, speculations, and the whole array of unconventional experimental thought processes and results of thought processes, the links in the chain of understanding—and, finally, more knowledge, and also wisdom. How is he going to do his job if book and publisher, the traditional depositories and transfer agents of knowledge, are eliminated from the chain (1984, 22–23)?

Here we see the complexities of the system and the effects of some elements on the entirety of the system. There is no shortage of manuscripts offered for publication, but there are severe limitations on publishers' ability to bring these manuscripts into print. A publisher concerned with profit, for example, must consider what Morris Philipson said are the costs involved in production of print copies:

the amount of money invested in typesetting for each page, the number of pages, and the size of the first printing. All three of those costs must be spread over, divided among, shared by, the number of copies that the publisher will invest in—whether considering the constraints under which he is publishing, he imagines it will take one year or three years or five years to sell out that first printing (1984, 15).

The publisher then must price the book in such a way that some profit is realized.

Such policies are to be expected on the part of for-profit publishers, but they also are a part of life for university presses. The same dynamics that elicit action from these companies in the profit sector affect the nonprofits as well. If sales decline, the presses have little alternative but to reduce costs and the reduction can take a couple of forms. One is to publish fewer titles, thus cutting production costs. If that alternative is deemed unacceptable, the press can reduce the print run for most titles. This factor is having an impact on the publication decisions of university presses and other scholarly presses. Anecdotal evidence suggests that print runs have continued to decline. Moreover, university presses, which have been subsidized for years by their parent institutions, are in danger of losing institutional support. Cathy Davidson has described the dilemma as seen by an academic administrator:

A provost trying to save money by asking her university press to bring in more revenue (making cost a major goal in book acquisition) is in an untenable position if she is also trying to maintain the same quality-based publishing standards for her faculty. At the same time, no university has enough money to fund everything, and every university wants to maintain its standards (2004, 132).

The dilemma is not faced by university presses alone; this is also a library problem and, ultimately, a problem for students and scholars. Fewer titles may be printed in fewer copies and fewer libraries may own the books. A recent examination of some university press titles demonstrates a decline in holding libraries. University press titles in the subject areas of English and American literature, philosophy, and North American history with imprint dates of 1990 and 2000 and that were included in *Choice*'s "Outstanding Academic Books" were searched for holdings. Also, titles with those imprint dates that were reviewed in *Choice* but not included in "Outstanding Academic Books" were searched. The numbers of holding libraries for both populations declined in that ten-year period. Further analysis showed that the number of reviews per title also declined for both populations (Budd and Urton 2003). It does seem as though there is cause for concern regarding access to some kinds of information in the future. Historian Robert Darnton suggested that technology could actually save the scholarly monograph.

> I think it is possible to structure [the electronic book] in layers arranged like a pyramid. The top layer could be a concise account of the subject, available perhaps as a paperback. The next layer could contain expanded versions of different aspects of the argument, not arranged sequentially as in a narrative, but rather as self-contained units that feed into the topmost story. The third layer could be composed of documentation, possibly of different kinds, each set off by interpretive essays. A fourth layer might be theoretical or historiographical, with selections from previous scholarship and discussions of them. A fifth layer could be pedagogic, consisting of suggestions for classroom discussion and a model syllabus. And a sixth layer could contain readers' reports, exchanges between the author and the editor, and letters from readers, who could provide a growing corpus of commentary as the book made its way through different groups of readers (1999, 7).

This specific idea might not be adopted, but, discipline by discipline, the strengths of electronic media might be used to produce more effective and far-reaching forms of communication.

Disciplines other than the humanities tend to employ the mechanism of the journal article as a principal communication tool. Such a mechanism is effective, again, because of the nature of the object of study. Communication in the sciences, for example, is of such focused content that the briefer communication not only suffices for the author to make known his or her work, but it also serves the reader who can more quickly assimilate that briefer communication. In many scientific fields, concentration is not on the rhetoric of presentation but, rather, on the statement of hypotheses and the analysis of data. When the communication is thus focused, the journal provides the most efficacious medium. Because the journal article serves the communication purpose so well, there are, naturally, many scientists contributing articles to journals in order to share their work with colleagues. To understand fully the communication process in disciplines such as the sciences, we have to realize that competition is a vital element of that process and of the disciplines. Intellectual credit for ideas and research depends on getting into print quickly. The need for timely communication leads to publication of the results of separate phases of a research process. A researcher, or a team of researchers, submits each part of the research as separate articles so that he or she can stake his or her intellectual claim.

Given the number of scientists (academic and nonacademic) working in the U.S. today, we can quickly see that the number of article-length manuscripts produced each year is of gargantuan proportions. Moreover, the number of scientists is growing and the competition for intellectual credit and financial support is heightening. These factors contribute to the growth of the number of papers being produced. Over the last several years, the acceptance rates of journals have remained fairly constant. For instance, if a journal in chemistry accepted for publication about 60 percent of the papers submitted to it fifteen years ago, it probably accepts about 60 percent today. However, it now receives more submissions than it did fifteen years ago, so the journal is likely to publish more pages of content. One result of the increase in the number of submitted papers has been what is referred to as "branching" and "twigging." A particular journal that is receiving more papers than it can publish may divide into two (or more) separate titles, thus effectively doubling the space it has to work with (and potentially doubling its revenue). A journal also might publish supplementary issues that may be sold and distributed separately from the subscription of the journal.

Of course, another decision that may be exercised is the establishment of new journal titles, ostensibly created to fill the need for communication outlets in dynamic disciplines. I have noted one of the results of this growth: "It has long since reached the point where it is virtually impossible for a specialist in any field to feel confident that he or she is abreast of all the latest work in that field. It has been, and continues to be, difficult for the scholar to keep up with the major journals in a narrow area of specialization" (Budd 1994, 196). Growth in the numbers of articles and journals presents a potential dilemma for everyone engaged in scholarly communication. Beyond the difficulties of acquisition and storage (which are discussed in chapter 8), there are potentially deleterious effects on the communication system. Because scholars are unable to keep up completely with the published output of their fields, there is the danger that some important work is missed by researchers who would benefit from an awareness of it. In some fields, such a lapse could be particularly harmful.

With both book and journal publication there are middle people. Because these media are physical, there have to be people involved in production. We have seen, to some extent, the role that book publishers play in the communication system. Publishers likewise have a role in the production of journals. As is true of book publishers, journal publishers exist in both the private and public sectors. University presses may be the publishers of journals, as may learned or professional societies such as the American Historical Association. These publishers get some financial breaks—university presses in the form of institutional subsidies, learned societies in the form of members' dues—that affect the prices of journals. Private-sector publishers must ensure that revenues are sufficient to realize a profit. Again, as is true of book publishers, the financial situations of individual journal publishers affect editorial decisions. Before looking at these traditional media in customary economic terms, it is important to remember that there is a major difference between a journal publisher and, say, a carmaker. The carmaker manufactures, distributes, and sells the product through approved dealers. The journal publisher does not, in a very real sense, make the product. The research community, academic and nonacademic alike, write articles that go into the journal's pages. This leads to a systemic relationship among all involved and, as we will see later, has some economic implications.

COMMUNICATION AND THE ACADEMIC REWARD STRUCTURE

As discussed earlier, scholarly communication has been tied to considerations of prestige in higher education for a number of decades. In large part, the system is based on attribution. This involves assigning credit for the production of published work through authorship and also authorial affiliation. Thus, both the author and the author's institution receive credit for the work published. Of course, the impetus behind credit for work done translates to the push for external funding of research endeavors. Funding from federal agencies and private foundations enables universities to pay not only for the research done, but also for the research infrastructure of the institution. Direct and indirect costs fund portions of researchers' salaries, graduate assistants' stipends, computer hardware and software, instrumentation, and other things. Beyond the tangible benefits of external funding, the attraction of grants further adds to the prestige of individuals and institutions. The material and immaterial benefits have a strong influence over the rewards structure of higher education. Perhaps this influence cannot be overstated. As more varied enterprises funnel money into higher education through grants, contracts, donations, and partnerships, those enterprises can help shape many aspects of higher education, including rewards. Sheila Slaughter and Larry Leslie placed this influence within the context of the political economy of resource dependence, stating that "resource dependence holds that those who provide resources to organizations such as universities have the capability of exercising great power over those organizations" (1997, 68). Their idea is too involved to delve deeply into here, but it does illustrate the complexity of the world that colleges, universities, and their libraries live in.

In recent years, there have been many more applicants for academic positions than there have been openings. As might be expected, the competition for the few openings is high. Further, there is competition among faculty for tenure and promotion. The institutions of higher education are so large that a stringent assessment of the quality of the work of applicants or faculty is difficult to perform. In the absence of a legitimate means of evaluating the teaching and research of individuals, the competition leads to the reduction of assessment mechanisms to numerical comparisons. If two assistant professors are up for tenure, the one with more publications and external research funding is likely to be the one who is successful. One of the outcomes of such an evaluation is "the fragmentation of one piece of research into as many publications as possible" (Budd 1994, 197). William Broad and Nicholas Wade referred to this tactic as reduction to the least publishable unit, or LPU (1982, 55). The resulting plethora of publications makes genuine evaluation even more difficult. Faculty members who serve on tenure and promotion committees are likely to be inundated by papers written by candidates. It's difficult, if not impossible, to read and assess all the papers. The danger is that numbers of items are counted, rather than communication taking place. Numbers have become increasingly important not just for research universities, but also for other types of institutions. In addition to research universities, my study (noted above) included measures of publishing activity by faculty at institutions tracked by the Association of College and Research Libraries (ACRL). The brief time period also saw increases in total and per capita publications by those faculty. In the 1991–1993 period, the average faculty published 874.0 journal articles; in 1995–1997, the average was 1,074.9. The per capita average rose from 1.59 to 1.78, and, again, these changes are statistically significant (Budd 1999, 312). The scholarly communication system is experiencing pressure from all educational quarters.

In an effort to arrive at some kind of distinctions among publication outlets, academic institutions recognize that journals are not all created equal. For example, some journals are more selective than others. It is not unusual for these selective journals to be the official organs of learned societies. One reason for the prestige of the journals is the wide audience they reach. Only so many articles can be published in prestigious journals, though, and their rejection rates tend to be higher than those of other journals. For example, according to one estimate, the average rejection rate of humanities journals is 87 percent whereas the rejection rate of *PMLA,* the journal of the Modern Language Association (which has about 29,000 members) is 95 percent (Budd 1991, 210, 215). Assessment of faculty and applicants takes into account the prestige of the journals in which individuals' works are published. Some simple criteria are customary at universities. For one thing, subscription by the university's library to the journal (or licensing of a source that includes the journal) in which one's work is published is essential. For another, indexing of the journal in a prominent secondary source also is necessary. Some institutions may be tempted to add citation to published works to the evaluation process as a means of gauging the impact of a scholar's work on their colleagues. However, as John Braxton and Alan Bayer (1986) noted,

> A citation count, even when carefully compiled and adjusted to compensate for artifactual weaknesses, is not a measure of scholarly performance for use without the other methods discussed here. . . . It is also a fallible tool; an occasional piece may be frequently cited for its flaws. Conversely, a high-quality piece may go unrecognized for years, uncited until long after its first appearance in the literature (1986, 37).

As can be seen from the discussion so far, the reward structure is centered on traditional media. One probable reason for the reliance on print publication is the history of prestige that many titles have. Another likely reason is the combination of relative ease of counting and familiarity with subscriptions that accompany traditional journals. The journals themselves are reasonably simple to analyze and to assess relative to such measures as acceptance or rejection rate, circulation, and so forth. The ease with which faculty publication can be counted and journal characteristics analyzed contributes to the employment of publication as a key to the academic reward structure. Perhaps this helps to explain the pervasiveness of publication in the evaluation of faculty. It should be noted, however, that the competition described above affects more than just the relatively small number of research universities. Institutions that formerly had a less prominent research focus have raised the importance of research and publication. The extent of the publication requirement may be why, at the *American Political Science Review,* "On the average, about two manuscripts come to the editor every working day" (Patterson and Smithey 1990, 247).

Because publication tends to be rewarded in American higher education, faculty must devote a substantial amount of their time and energy to research and publication. It is not hard to see, then, the kind of pressure placed on evaluation committees on campuses. Several years ago, the Harvard Medical School proposed a radical alternative to the status quo:

> Harvard [Medical School] has published guidelines that dare to suggest that someone up for promotion to full professor should be judged on no more than ten papers. Those up for associate professor could make the grade on the basis of a mere seven papers, presuming they were pretty good ones. A person could become an assistant professor with only five good papers in the literature (Culliton 1988, 525).

There is no indication that the proposal has been adopted, but raising the idea that quality, rather than quantity, should be the defining measure of success is, to say the least, intriguing.

The pressure to publish has another, extremely disconcerting, result in some instances. In order to meet the requirements of success, some individuals have turned to fraud. There are some reports that researchers have, in a few highly publicized cases, falsified data, plagiarized, and sometimes created entire projects on paper without actually conducting the research. Although some claim that such misconduct is rare and occurs only in isolated instances, others maintain that the known cases are an indication that many more transgressions do not get detected. Attention has been directed particularly to cases of misconduct in biomedical research because of the implications of false information becoming accepted on a large scale. For instance, Stephen Breuning was found guilty of misconduct; he falsified research on drug treatments for hyperactive children. Marcel LaFollette (1992) reported that "Breuning's research data had, in fact, been widely reported and accepted by practitioners; from 1980–1983, his published papers represented at least one-third of all scientific articles on the topic; a citation analysis of his publications concludes that, from 1981 to 1985, his 'impact on the literature was meaningful'" (1992, 25). In another case, John Darsee's work was repudiated when it was found that he had fabricated the data that formed the basis of a number of published articles. Despite the fact that some of his publications were formally retracted, they continued to be cited in the literature several years after the discovery and publicizing of his misconduct. As Carol Kochan and I stated, "It becomes clear that this is both a biomedical research and an information retrieval problem, and that both aspects of the problem require further investigation" (Kochan and Budd 1992, 492). Fraud, misconduct, and perhaps a more insidious result of the pressure to publish, error, are problems that are not likely to disappear as long as the academic reward structure remains unchanged.

COST OF SCHOLARLY COMMUNICATION

This section briefly addresses some of the costs incurred as part of participating in the scholarly communication system; the issue of pricing and its implications for libraries and their budgets is discussed in chapter 8. Just a few words here can serve as a bit of a preamble to that later discussion. There is a genuine awareness on the parts of academic administrators and scholars of the economic challenges that are part of the scholarly communication system. One clear indication of this awareness is the formation of the Public Library of Science, an organization of scientists who are willing to commit to a nonprofit archive of their written work. (See http://www.publiclibraryofscience.org.) Thousands of scientists have signed an open letter to publishers urging them to allow articles to be distributed freely through such an archive. Perhaps the most widely publicized initiative of recent years has been the Scholarly Publishing and Academic Resources Coalition (http://www.arl.org/sparc). SPARC has a broad agenda, but one of its programs is support for the development of journals that provide a more affordable alternative to existing publications. More is said about this later.

Of primary interest here are the costs related to faculties' efforts at producing the work that will be communicated. Education itself is a fairly expensive endeavor; research is even more expensive. Research universities spend millions of dollars to build the infrastructure in which research can thrive; they then spend additional millions of dollars each to maintain that infrastructure. (For example, in fiscal year 2002, the University of Washington spent more than $487,000,000 on research and development [*Chronicle of Higher Education Almanac Issue, 2004–05*, p. 34].) For scientific research to be possible, many tools and facilities must be in place. The university has to build and maintain laboratories that are adequate for the work of the faculty and students. The laboratories must be equipped with sufficient instrumentation and supplies. In part, an initial capital outlay is viewed as an investment by the institution. Money is spent to construct facilities and to hire faculty capable of doing research, and then the faculty are urged (or, more accurately, required) to support their research activities by attracting external funding. Financing scientific research gets much more complicated than this, but the thumbnail sketch presented here suffices to illustrate the magnitude of the financial side of research.

We tend to think that inquiry in the humanities is not expensive, but just because laboratories are usually not required does not mean that it is not expensive in its own way. The research university spends millions of dollars each year to build and maintain its library collections. A portion of that expenditure is aimed explicitly at supporting the research activities in the humanities and the social sciences. (A substantial part of the expenditures supports work in the sciences, adding to the already formidable amount needed to assist with that research.) When a university library supports special collections, those collections are frequently specifically related to inquiry in the humanities. These collections may comprise archival or manuscript collections or rare books, and their growth and development are frequently tied to needs of the faculty. Also, because scholars in the humanities depend on collections of materials, the institution may provide funds for the faculty to travel to those collections so that they can make the fullest use of the materials.

One other cost that is sometimes ignored is that of support for graduate students. One of the purposes of the support is to recruit bright students who will be researchers in their own right and who will join faculties after graduation. The students' research may be supported to some extent by the institution. The attraction of bright graduate students also serves to help recruit and retain faculty. The faculty reap the intangible benefit of being able to work with these students. A more tangible benefit is the assistance these students offer to the faculty in exchange for a stipend and learning experience. The faculty then can use these graduate assistants to help with the work of research. Moreover, the graduate assistants may teach, thus freeing the faculty from those responsibilities and providing time that can be allocated to research.

What all of this means is that when a manuscript is written and is ready to submit to a journal, a substantial amount of financial support (from one source or another) has made the manuscript possible. All the equipment, supplies, computer time, personnel time, and so on has gone into the production of that unit of communication. In the case of a book on, say, twentieth-century French literature, the faculty author has likely been supported substantially. One form of support may have been a sabbatical or research leave that enabled the individual to devote time to the manuscript's completion. These are part of the institutional costs of the scholarly communication system. The producers incur the costs associated with production; these costs vary according to the requirements of the subject matter. Because they affect the ultimate price of materials, discussion of them is delayed until it can be conjoined with the library collection.

QUALITY AND CONTROL

Regardless of the medium, the question of control is an important one. Because of the potential for openness with electronic information, some individuals advocate a policy of freedom. The argument is usually that unfettered access by authors to the communication structure ensures that no biases can prevent creative and risk-taking work. That point of view is usually countered with the assertion that such freedom of submission would exacerbate the already calamitous state of information overload. Although there are merits to both sides of this issue, the present state (influenced very heavily by a reward structure that places great stock in selectivity and prestige) is weighted in favor of control. One of the jobs of the journal editor is to ensure that control is based as much as possible on quality. "There is scarcely a pretense that the process is flawless, but diligent editors do what they can to assure that the literature reflects that segment of the field that is most serious about its work and most thorough in its execution" (Budd 1992, 45).

The editor as gatekeeper still has to come to grips with the conception of quality. Felix Berardo offered what is perhaps the most enlightened view of quality; it

> refers not just to the proper execution of the technical and mechanical aspects of analysis and manuscript preparation. . . . It involves judgments with respect to originality of ideas, the elaboration of new techniques and conceptualizations, and the significance of the work for the field. Sometimes an editor will decide to accept a manuscript on the basis of these factors, even if the type of data utilized, sample size, etc., fall short of the exacted standards (1981, 773).

Such an idea of quality transcends the criteria that may be applied narrowly as a template to see if a manuscript fits a particular model of the published paper. Berardo's notion incorporates some ideals of inquiry: it is intellectually challenging; it is competently executed; it transforms the disciplinary context; it is not limited by restrictive standards. Not everyone is of the opinion that Berardo's ideal is currently realized, though. Benjamin Singer wrote, "The academic world faces a crisis of standards. The crisis is symbolized by increasing incidents of academic fraud, confusion over quality, intense criticism of the slipshod way in which faculty members are hired, tenured and promoted to the highest ranks, and by outlandish proposals that threaten further decline" (1989, 127).

We have to remember that the editor is in a sticky situation. Editors sometimes bear the criticism some dispense when they see a lack of quality work in the pages of journals. The editors do not write the articles, though; they exercise judgment over the papers that authors choose to submit. The editor also is not isolated from the discipline in which he or she works. The editor is usually someone who has, in some way, reached a level of distinction, usually by virtue of a record of scholarship and an understanding of the communication system. Thus, he or she is in a good position to appreciate the universalistic standards for scholarship in the discipline. This means that the editor usually has a clear understanding of discipline's goals regarding inquiry and contributions to knowledge. Janice Beyer recognized this:

The degree to which norms and/or counternorms govern the behavior of journal editors and the publication practices of journals is bound to affect communication channels and reward structures within scientific fields. It is evident journal editors must make judgments, and like other scientific actors, must rely on the criteria available within their scientific field or subfield to make these judgments. In the absence of universalistic criteria, they are likely to rely on more particularistic ones (1978, 69).

The particularistic criteria are focused on the specific purpose of the journal and the standards that govern the execution of research and communication. When particularistic, rather than universalistic, criteria are adhered to, there is the chance that too much attention may be paid to the technical and the mechanical and that the contributions a manuscript may make to inquiry in a field could be obscured.

As we have seen with electronic information, the communication system has both formal and informal elements. Even with a formal process such as publication in a journal there can be ancillary, informal parts to the process. The scholar who submits a manuscript to a journal may not simply wait silently throughout the evaluation process. If that scholar believes his or her work is important, he or she may share it with colleagues before actual publication of the paper. He or she may wait to learn of the disposition of the manuscript and then, if it is accepted for publication, may send preprints to selected researchers. Figure 3.1 presents an illustration of the possible dissemination of an idea, including formal publications.

The process of formal communication is not perfect. Perhaps the imperfections cannot be corrected; perhaps they are connected with human nature. Singer offered that "One of the earliest cures [for the glut of publications] in 1939 by J. D. Bernal, was to do away with journals entirely in favor of a central organization for editing and distributing scientific papers. Although a quixotic scheme, it would at least compel the reading of papers by evaluators instead of their depending on the frequently false filters of refereed journals" (1989, 140). However, there are no guarantees that a central organization would necessarily be any more selective than the current spate of journals. The pressures to allow a free flow of information probably would not abate (especially if we recall that the participants in the system are authors as well as readers). Furthermore, as Michael Hill pointed out, the smaller journals that presently exist are, in many instances, sympathetic to work that may be out of the mainstream (1990, 298–300). A centralized organization may, by its very nature, embody the mainstream and leave no room for alternative or dissenting work. The bottom line seems to be that the scholarly communication system depends on an evaluative

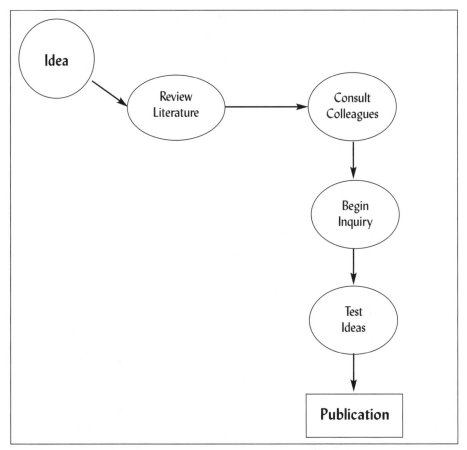

FIGURE 3.1   Idea to Publication

structure that may not please everyone. To date, no one has been able to suggest any other reasonable choice.

The editors do not exercise complete dominion over the communication process. Concern for quality is the reason for reliance on referees, knowledgeable people who are asked to assess submissions according to the journal's standards for quality. One purpose for the employment of referees is the notion that there is strength in numbers. When several qualified people evaluate a manuscript, there is a greater chance that if it passes muster, readers will view it as a genuine contribution. However, the referee's position is about as sticky as the editor's. A considerable amount of responsibility is entrusted to referees, and if they should make an error, it could be of drastically different types. Insufficient critical assessment could lead to the encouragement of poor research. Being too critical can result in wasting the time of researchers and authors and delaying the communication of valuable work. Communication from an editor to a referee regarding specific evaluative criteria eliminates the ambiguity that sometimes accompanies the referee's task. Not all journals provide detailed instruction to their referees, although the majority require referees to complete some kind of evaluation form.

ALTERNATIVE COMMUNICATION

This is a daunting subject to approach because it covers potentially immense territory. However, many aspects of electronic information will not be dealt with at this time. Libraries are concerned with matters such as accessibility of databases and aggregators, document delivery (such as is available through commercial outlets), and other forms of information. These are certainly pressing matters for libraries, but they are somewhat tangential to scholarly communication (in the sense of the formal distribution of the work of scholars). This section delves into the aspects of electronic information that are related to the scholarly communication system. Toward this end, this section will not spend a great deal of time on the structure of networked information. For one thing, this is not the best place to deal with such matters; for another, the readers' time would be better spent consulting the writings of experts in this area, such as the late Paul Evan Peters and Clifford Lynch.

To offer just a few words about electronic information, we need to remember that networks, in this country, began as a government-sponsored effort at facilitating the sharing of research. The origin of the Internet is based in such government research initiatives. Today, large sets of data are relatively easily accessible to researchers (when those data sets are not proprietary). For instance, in our own field the ARL makes its library statistics available in a number of ways, including via the World Wide Web. In the case of commercially available data, online access is used as a medium to make available large bodies of data, images, and other information.

The upshot is that technology offers a means of greatly accelerating access to information that is related to scholarship and not just scientific scholarship. Some institutions and groups (including many universities), led by the Library of Congress (LC), are digitizing early texts, manuscripts, photographs, images, and other things that are important to scholarship in the humanities. As was mentioned earlier, the American Memory Project, for instance, LC is digitizing collections of American history and literature so that scholars can study materials with far less cost and effort. From this, we can see that one impact of electronic information is on the opening of a great amount of information that is vital raw material for scholarship. Faculty at almost all institutions have much easier access to those things that form the foundation of their study.

Many would claim that some of the current activities of electronic journals do not make the most of the medium's potential. For instance, there is no technical reason why an article cannot be transmitted to readers as soon as it is in an acceptable form. Readers, though, may want (at present) a more convenient packaging of the information so that they are not constantly on the lookout for new contributions to the literature. It is almost inevitable that the attitudes and needs of authors and readers will vary (perhaps greatly) from one discipline to another, and perhaps even within a discipline. If that is true, no one solution will meet the disparate scholarly communities. In the course of deliberating on policy matters, it is important that the diversity of need and usage be considered as the electronic element of the system evolves.

Electronic access to scholarship also applies to monographs. This kind of access takes a particular form at this time–digitized versions of works already published in print. Commercial providers such as netLibrary and Ebrary market numerous titles to libraries. These commercial providers generally enter into agreements with publishers so that revenue protections for the publishers and authors and copyright protections can be assured. This alternative is limited to medium; that is, the same work, in essentially the same form, is available in print or electronically. There are some advantages to this alternative for libraries and readers alike. Libraries might choose such electronic access instead of acquiring a physical item so that stack space (which is at a premium in many libraries) is not used and concerns such as loss of an item are no longer an issue. Readers may be able to take advantage of retrieval structures in order to locate specific relevant passages of a book. It is likely that we will see continued evolution (perhaps along the lines Darnton (1999) suggests), particularly in storage and reading devices.

The possibilities of electronic media are only beginning to be explored. One of the possibilities centers on institutional information repositories. Clifford Lynch described this: "[A] university-based institutional repository is a set of services that a university offers to members of its community for the management and dissemination of digital materials created by the institution and its community members" (2003, 328). As David Prosser (2003) pointed out, a repository can be the virtual location for many types of information, including data sets, images, teaching materials, working papers, and student products. In a rapidly growing and changing area, the maturest repository is MIT's project, D-Space (http://www.dspace.org), although its success to date has been limited. As can be expected, many questions accompany a new idea such as the repository, including regarding matters of expansion beyond a single institution and standards for compatibility should the eventual decision be to develop some overarching access mechanism. Some of the questions, such as in which direction will participants (particularly faculty) take a new development, are asked by Ann Wolpert (2002).

Part of the evolutionary process will necessarily involve considerations of matters such as ownership, copyright, pricing, and accessibility. These are the most intractable matters. Present copyright law is inadequate to handle questions of rights and ownership in a networked environment. Perhaps the heart of the matter is control, that is, who can legally and effectively control the access and use of information in the electronic world. The slow growth of electronic journals is undoubtedly tied to answers to questions regarding control. Eldred Smith addressed the matter of control from the library's point of view, saying that

> this emphasis on control is an inevitable consequence of the need to preserve the scholarly record. It provides the discipline that enables research librarians to manage the organization, maintenance, and use of research library collections with minimum threat to their preservation. Scholarly information is a chaos, out of which the research librarian is charged to bring order. Control is essential (1990, 10).

I would not argue with his implied point that intellectual access is founded on the control that is effected by organization. However, he missed the boat in his statement about scholarly communication. The principals (authors, editors, publishers) involved in the scholarly communication system are certainly concerned with legal and economic control, as well as with intellectual control. (See, for example, Peggy Hoon 2003.) Realizing workable control has, to this time, remained elusive.

One effort at seizing control, in one sense at least, is what is being called the open-access movement. In short, open access means free (to readers) access to the products of scholarship. For example, an open-access journal would have a funding base other than library and individual subscribers and would make its contents available to anyone. The most ambitious journal at the time of this writing is *PloS Biology,* produced by the Public Library of Science (described briefly above) and first published in October 2003. In the case of *PloS Biology,* published authors pay a fee to be published. At present the fee is $1,500. This pricing model definitely does not suit all disciplines and all authors, but it may be a workable solution in some subject areas. (This topic is discussed in greater detail in a later chapter.) Although this has been a brief and sketchy presentation, these observations on electronic information present some of the important developments, potential, and challenges facing the scholarly communication system now and into the future.

SUMMARY

The system of scholarly communication has a fairly long history. Recent development has been marked by changes of scale and changes in kind. The systemic character of scholarly communication becomes evident when we try to stake out a vantage point from which to survey the landscape. It seems that there is always some territory that is out of view. For instance, we cannot examine authorship without taking readership into account. When we give our attention to readership, though, we run the risk of ignoring the structure that emphasizes the importance of authorship. We also have to remember that research that is communicated is valued in several contexts. Of course, it has value within the community of scholars, which depends on the exchange of ideas for growth and advancement. It also has value on a personal level for the researcher because it leads to promotion, tenure, and some tangible monetary rewards. Further, it has value on an institutional level because prestige and reputation depend to a considerable extent on the product of the research endeavor.

The system is perhaps on the brink of unprecedented change. There is displeasure with some elements of the communication system. The cost of communicating is affecting the efficacy of the system. The amount published threatens the ability of individuals to make full use of the system's output. I say "perhaps" because this is a system, and change in one area depends on, stems from, or necessitates change in other areas. The system has several potential new faces. It is likely that some time will pass and some turmoil will be endured before there is any semblance of stability. The library is a part of the system, and chapter 8 investigates the effects of the other elements on the library and its possible role in the transformed system. There is much more to be said about specific developments, including open access and the bundling of serials, which are addressed in detail in a later chapter.

Here are a few questions to spur discussion on the scholarly communication system:

> Is there any way to define a beginning or starting point of the scholarly communication system?
>
> What has the growth of higher education since 1960 meant for scholarly communication?
>
> Is there the possibility of one vision of scholarly communication that covers all disciplines?
>
> Can a different reward system be envisioned?
>
> If you were an editor, what changes would you impose on the customary operations of a journal?
>
> What are the implications of electronic media for the glut of publications?
>
> What is the future of the book?

Chapter 4

Perceptions
of the Academy

In chapter 2, we saw how colleges and universities as organizations embody purposes, practices, and cultures that are essentially different from other human organizations. The behavior of faculty, for instance, is influenced by a variety of forces, including the political (which is common to almost all organizations) and the cognitive or intellectual. The political side of higher education is likely to be readily understandable to anyone who works in a corporation or business. The elements of the political that are common to most environments are the urge to survive, the desire for autonomy, the resistance to external control, the strategic positioning of the unit within the organization, and the attraction of resources. These elements would be seen by many as integral to the nature of work in such companies as AT&T, IBM, or Wal-Mart. The political aspect of the organization incorporates these means of sustaining existence in dynamic environments characterized by finite resources, changing goals, and fluid participation. When the organization can afford to keep only so many employees on the payroll, there will be competition among units for available positions. Downsizing (which is a term usually reserved for the scaling back of the number of members of the organization) exacerbates already existing competitive behaviors. As goals or products change in an organization, the various units try to adjust their own behavior patterns and beliefs in order to maintain—or to ascend to—a place of importance. The changes that take place in most organizations mean that, at any given time, some units and/or individuals will have roles that are more central to the primary purpose than others. However, further change almost inevitably upsets patterns of participation.

Although the political aspect of organizations may be common to most environments, the cognitive aspect is unique to education. This is not to say that there is no thought in businesses or corporations, but the thinking in those types of organizations is, for the most part, pragmatic. What counts as "knowledge management" in the corporate world usually consists of managing information and data flows so that all elements of the organization have access to strategic or design knowledge. The result is greater efficiency (in terms of responsiveness to market change, speed of product design and production, and coordination of departments) for the business. The company has a product or service that can be defined quite discretely, and its efforts are aimed at selling that product or service. The product of higher education is less easily defined. Are students the product? If so, what constitutes the market for the product? Are students customers? What are they buying? Do they simply want the academic degree, or is the product something as nebulous as knowledge? If students are customers, why do they not pay the full cost of the product? Is higher education distinguished from corporations and businesses by being a public good? How does the public benefit from higher education? I do not intend these to be imponderable questions. As is seen in this chapter, a great many people are questioning the purpose of education, so these questions should spur some initial discussion before we proceed. Throughout the reading and discussion, it should be kept in mind that the academic library is part of the educational endeavor and thus may also be subject to many of these questions.

If we focus briefly on one of the above questions, relating to students paying the full cost of education, we can examine some data that illustrate the discrepancy between tuition paid and cost. The University of Missouri recently studied educational costs for programs at all four of its campuses. At the University of Missouri-Columbia, the cost of providing instruction to undergraduate students was $288 per credit hour when the study was conducted. Tuition and fees at the campus at that time amounted to $141.50 per credit hour. The discrepancy increased for graduate education. The cost per credit hour for Ph.D. student instruction at the University of Missouri-Columbia was $1,981, and tuition was $179.10 per credit hour. The gap between cost and tuition was even greater at the University of Missouri-Rolla campus, which specializes in engineering ("State Legislatures Examine Funding for Public Higher Ed," p. 3). Tuition has increased recently, but not enough to come close to covering the costs. The cost of libraries is part of the cost of instruction on any campus. Although library expenditures are a relatively small portion of the total institutional budget, they are certainly not insubstantial. Add to libraries the cost of the technological infrastructure of a campus (which also can enable students and faculty to gain access to electronic information sources) and the reasons for the cost of instruction become readily evident.

What we have to keep in mind as we inquire into the perceptions of higher education is that colleges and universities are fundamentally different from businesses. It is true that there are business aspects of educational institutions (purchasing of products, employment of personnel, operation of a physical plant), but these are not the essential elements of either the mission or the culture of higher education. The work of teaching, learning, and inquiry engaged in by faculty and students is not the same as the manufacture of durable goods, the production of entertainment products, or the sale of such services as telecommunications or even legal advice. The work of higher education is essentially intellectual. Even in practical and professional disciplines, such as engineering, computer science, allied health fields, and library and information science, the educational purpose is not limited to questions of how but also includes questions of why. The impetus behind higher education is not merely to ensure that students will be technically proficient, but that they will be critical, inquisitive, and grounded in the theory that underlies the practice. Such a goal is not always easy to communicate, and this may be at the heart of some of the disputes between those in and out of higher education. This chapter examines the criticisms of, and visions for, higher education. As will be seen, some of the criticisms are legitimate and must be taken seriously. Academic librarians need to be aware of the disputes and the directions they take because these disputes can have an impact on the structure of the academic environment, including institutional mission and financial support.

TRADITIONAL CRITICISMS OF HIGHER EDUCATION

Criticisms of higher education in the U.S. are not new. In the past, many of the perceived shortcomings of colleges and universities led to changes within the institutions. For instance, the social, political, and economic forces of the Industrial Revolution contributed to reforms in teaching and curriculum in the nineteenth century. The alterations in the nature of higher education—the new focus on research, the institution of graduate programs, revised requirements for faculty–spurred considerable discussion on what education *should* be and how it should be accomplished. Some perceived a diminished value placed on learning among the professoriate in favor of the validation that comes with the doctoral degree. In 1903, William James (who was a member of Harvard's faculty) wrote that the doctorate was essentially a sham, a reward for meaningless work and a marketing tool for the administrators of Harvard and other universities. Despite such an indictment, however, possession of the Ph.D. became an essential criterion for hire to a university faculty.

As professional education was added to their repertoire of offerings, colleges and universities came under the scrutiny (and probably rightly so) of some critical observers. Just after the turn of the century, the state of medical education was chaotic, with few standards guiding educational purpose or practice and with a number of academic programs of questionable quality. Abraham Flexner studied the condition of medical education and published a groundbreaking report in 1910. In the aftermath of the report's publication, some medical schools closed and many more changed their operation substantially. Flexner's report was a reminder of educational purpose and both a jab at programs that had lost sight of that purpose and a blueprint for incorporating professional education into the academic sphere. In a subsequent study, Flexner (1930) looked at American universities and found them lacking. Again, he paid attention to professional education and accused many institutions of establishing courses, and sometimes entire programs, that were empty of intellectual content. For instance, Flexner wrote, "Does library training belong to a university? And if it does not necessarily belong there, it has no business there at all—such is the importance of preserving university ideals pure and undefiled" (1930, 2). Too often, according to Flexner, institutions rewarded meaningless work with educational degrees. He saw little distinction between the rudimentary education of entering students and the work that claimed to be at the graduate level.

Other criticisms have been leveled at higher education for some time. Throughout this century, as more people have been able to attend colleges and universities, the differences between the academic world and that of commerce, industry, and so on have come to be realized by a larger population. There has been a tendency for some to conceive of that world of business and labor as the "real" world. It is the venue in which people earn their livelihoods, practice their trades and professions, and interact with people who have similar aims and behaviors. Some see this world as removed from the ivory tower of the academy. In part, this perception comes with removal from the college or university in space and time. As a person becomes accustomed to work in the office (or elsewhere), he or she may recall the days as a student as a place and time when the pressures and demands of a working life did not exist. This is a very real perception; for the vast majority of people, life changes dramatically and irrevocably upon graduation. Even if a person worked and studied long hours to earn the degree, that kind of work is very different from his or her eventual occupation. Although the perception is real, it is limited. For the most part, students do not see the kind or amount of work that the typical faculty member does. For this reason, the perception is one-sided, but it can be—and frequently is—extended to the entirety of academic life.

It is true of most criticisms, as it is of most stereotypes, that there is at least some basis in fact. One manifestation of the charge that faculty are out of touch with the rest of life is the curriculum. There are instances where courses are created and offered because someone wants to teach them, not necessarily because someone to take them. It is not unusual for a university's catalog to have several thousand courses listed, primarily because faculty, who have specialized interests, want to extend their specializations to their teaching. Some graduate-level courses on the books at various universities include: "Occupational History and Folklore," "Interdisciplinary Water Resources II: Modelling and Communications Lab," and "The Politics of International Humanitarianism." Over the course of the twentieth century, education at the graduate level has become so specialized that a student's principal work of scholarship, the dissertation, is so narrow that no one else has approached the subject in precisely that way (or so go the instructions given to the dissertation writer). The specialization of graduate school can lead to specialization of the faculty. It can be argued that the experience of the dissertation need not lead to a faculty of overly narrow pedants. There are sufficient examples of absurdly specialized courses in institutions' catalogs, though, to prompt some to ask if such "pickyness" is the norm. It probably would be more instructive to look not just at courses listed in catalogs, but also at courses actually taught. It may be that the narrowest courses are seldom, if ever, taught. Also, even at the institutions where the above-named courses are on the books, there is a substantial number of broader and more general courses.

Another long-standing criticism is that higher education structures foster an elite. For some time, this criticism of elitism was tied to the rest of society. Well into this century, only certain people were able to take advantage of higher education. A family had to have the financial wherewithal to send sons, and eventually daughters, to a college or university and be able to spare them from work at home. This economic stratification has been, and may always be, a part of society at large. In addition, gender and race (among other things) have contributed to stratification. At the most fundamental level, the existence of higher education leads to a bifurcation of society: those who can attend a college or university, and those who cannot (for whatever reason). In more recent years, attending college has become more egalitarian because there are opportunities for student aid and a somewhat heightened institutional sensitivity to the need for many to attend on a part-time basis. Whether such egalitarian opportunities will continue and what forms they may take are matters for speculation. Further, even among students attending an institution there are elitist and egalitarian conflicts. At colleges and universities with diverse student populations, there is the potential for stratification within that population. It becomes, one might assume, inevitable that some sort of elitism be a part of higher education. Julius Getman observed that education "separates those who have experienced it from those who have not, in terms of learning, language, aspirations, and self-perception. It certifies ideas, books, art, and intellectual achievements. By setting standards, it generally announces that certain works, ideas, and people are not entitled to serious attention in the world of ideas" (1992, 2).

RECENT CRITICISMS OF THE ACADEMY

As we have seen, critiques of higher education are not new. In the early days of the twentieth century, there were those who accused colleges of selling themselves for the glory of sports, particularly football, victories. There were occasional scandals when a school hired a "ringer," someone enrolled in name only who could spark the team to a win. Although the formal charges of "pay for play" have dissipated, it is certainly not unusual to hear voices raised in anger over athletes who fill their course schedules with less-than-challenging offerings in order to maintain their eligibility for sport. More serious critics decry the seeming injustice perpetrated against the students. Frequently, the argument is that the institution is using the athlete for the financial gain of major sports resulting from the sale of tickets and the negotiation of television deals. That athlete is not educated while at the college or university and, in too many instances, never earns a degree. Although this is a serious matter, and one deserving close scrutiny, it is a bit off the track for the present discussion. What we will focus on is the charge that there is something wrong with the very essence of American higher education today. There are several elements to that charge; we will explore them in some detail in order to gain the most complete understanding of the environment of higher education. I must emphasize this point in anticipation of the question, Why is it important to know about these criticisms? It is important because they strike at the most fundamental elements of the college or university: mission, teaching, research, funding, expectations of students, and eventually the collections and services offered by the library to fill those diverse needs.

For an examination of recent critiques of higher education in the U.S., a reasonable starting place is the late Allan Bloom's best-selling polemic, *The Closing of the American Mind* (1987). The subtitle of Bloom's book, *How Higher Education Has Failed Democracy and Impoverished the Souls of Today's Students*, provides a synopsis of his principal thesis. One important observation of Bloom's should be heeded especially, in part because it is reflected in the world of the academic library as well. He said that the act of teaching and the role of the teacher are not neutral; rather, they incorporate a stated or perceived authority. From the beginning of formal education this notion of authority has gone along with "professing." The teacher creates the context for learning: he or she selects the required readings, plans the progress of the course, and chooses what to impart to students. This assertion gave Bloom the platform to accuse higher education of abandoning the moral responsibility to seek truth. He asserted that the responsibility is abdicated by the claims that truth and knowledge are relative. He stated, "the relativity of truth is not a theoretical insight but a moral postulate, the condition of a free society, or so (students) see it" (Bloom

1987, 25). He claimed that the presumed democracy of the college or university "is really anarchy, because there are no recognized rules for citizenship and legitimate titles to rule. In short there is no vision, nor is there a set of competing visions, of what an educated human being is" (Bloom 1987, 337). His point was that higher education exists to foster democracy, which is not served by any negation that there are no underlying truths. Bloom sought philosophical foundations for both the malaise (which he found in Nietzsche, Heidegger, and others) and the solution (which he found in Plato). It is not necessary to delve into his philosophical excursions here; the key at this time is his accusation of the misuse of the authority of education.

As an aside, a similar authority could be imparted to the college or university library. Although the claim is not as strong because both students and faculty frequently use the library without any mediation, some aspects of the notion of authority are worth attention. The library's collection does not simply appear miraculously; it is selected in some way. In the past, the means of selection varied between librarians choosing which published items to acquire and faculty recommending that specific materials be purchased (or usually some combination of the two). In any event, some authority was claimed for the selection of particular works. Libraries' policies and collection development texts make mention of the "authority" of the author or the publisher, or of the reviews that have assessed the worth of the book. In such cases, whether an active judgment or deference to some other source, authority is exercised. We should seriously question the nature of such authority and what it suggests for the library's collection. In more recent time, selection has been removed from the library to varying degrees through the use of mechanisms such as approval plans. This does not negate authority, but it may serve to relocate it to the vendor with whom the library has an approval plan. Perhaps even more important in recent years, the bundling by some producers of journals in their electronic access packages may effectively mean that the publishers assume authority. Again, the question is what the location of authority means for the collection. I am not an advocate for Bloom's opinions; he tended to speak ex cathedra with, at best, some anecdotal evidence to support his claims. On the other hand, the notion of authority and the responsibility that goes with it is one worth giving some attention to in higher education and in libraries.

The idea of authority is carried a step further in another best-seller published at about the same time as Bloom's book. Although higher education is not the topic of his book, E. D. Hirsch (1988) does suggest that there is an authoritative base of information in *Cultural Literacy: What Every American Needs to Know.* Neither Hirsch's philosophical foundation nor his philosophical critique was as strong or well developed as Bloom's. In fact, it would be tempting to dismiss the book if it had not received so much attention, even praise, and had it not given birth to other, equally presumptuous works. Bloom's vision of authority means not submitting to nihilism but, rather, seeking fundamental truths that guide thought and life. Hirsch's authority embodies a faith in the efficacy of mere exposure to a list of names, places, and things, selected by one person who is not in the position to comprehend the essential elements of *all* academic disciplines. He wrote, "To be culturally literate is to possess the basic information needed to thrive in the modern world. . . . It is by no means confined to 'culture' narrowly understood as an acquaintance with the arts. Nor is it confined to one social class" (Hirsch 1988, xiii). Although he made such a claim, his list (what he referred to as a "national vocabulary") is narrow and omitted most references to any but the white, Western European, middle class. I offer Hirsch as an example of the concept of authoritarianism, rather than authority, so that we can appreciate the distinction in critiques of education.

Other recent critiques of higher education have focused on the operations of colleges and universities. Some of these have come from writers who are outside educational structures. Perhaps the best known of the attacks from without is *ProfScam*, by Charles Sykes. Sykes wasted no time in ascribing blame for the death of higher education: "Almost single-handedly, the professors—working steadily and systematically—have destroyed the university as a center of learning and have desolated higher education, which no longer is higher or much of an education" (1988, 34). (One might wonder if he was being facetious when he claimed that professors act systematically.) He provided a laundry list of what he called the crimes of the professoriate. Among these indictments were that faculty are underworked and overpaid, that they do not teach, that meaningless research constitutes the only activity, and that publishing has degenerated into a self-serving scheme to advance careers. The ferocity of Sykes's invective may tempt one to pay little heed to his book, but the popularity of *ProfScam* suggests that some believe his accusation to be true in fact and indicative of a crisis in higher education. His evidence was entirely anecdotal, but the perceived malfeasance he cited begs for some reply (though not necessarily an apology). Sykes noted that on many campuses freshmen are subjected to class sizes of 500 or more. There is no doubt that this is not a desirable situation, but what would be required to change it? Let us assume that these class sizes are common in required courses at large public universities. If this is undesirable, what would the most effective class size be? If that number is 100, the class of 500 would have to be divided into five sections. If the number is 50, ten sections would be needed. If, at present, there are three of these 500-student classes and 50 is the optimal level, this means that the three sections of the one course would have to be transformed into 30 sections. Let us further assume that professors teach three sections each; ten faculty would be occupied with this one course. Would the university have enough faculty in this department to offer courses beyond the freshman level? The absurdity of Sykes's claims becomes quickly obvious.

Let us take another common complaint on university campuses. Freshman English classes are taught by teaching assistants, graduate students who are just a bit older than their students. On a large university campus, a hundred or more of these sections of freshman English will likely be taught. If there was a revolution and graduate students no longer taught, full-time faculty would have to teach these sections. If the English department at this hypothetical university had twenty-five full-time faculty, each one would have to teach four sections of freshman English each semester. Would the department be able to offer any other courses? The real insidiousness of Sykes's accusations is that there is no acknowledgment of the possible reasons for the current state of affairs. His jabs have a ring of truth about them, especially when he offered evidence that some faculty scarcely teach at all. Sykes was a bit short on suggestions for remedies for the ills he chronicled nor did he examine the potential costs of an altered state.

The principal difficulty in Sykes's book is not its negative slant nor is it his exclusive reliance on anecdotal evidence. Rather, the main problem is his almost willful misunderstanding of the structure of higher education. His examples of large class size, good teachers not receiving tenure, and inflated publications came from the largest and most prestigious public and private universities. Based on those instances he condemned all of higher education; he painted all institutions with the same brush. As is stated above, there undoubtedly is some reason for concern. But it is a disservice to the institutions, the students and faculty, and all readers of the book to equate surreptitiously, say, Oberlin College and Harvard University. The institutions are not comparable by any of the measures he mentioned. Sykes quoted data stating that 60 percent of all faculty do not publish. This figure should not be surprising considering that, according to the classification of institutions by the Carnegie Association for the Advancement of Teaching, just over 100 of the more than 1,800 four-year schools are considered research universities. Sykes tended to look on all of higher education as a single organizational type. This would be analogous to judging all computer software producers by the behavior of Microsoft. The damage he did by being so uncritical of institutional differences is to damn all four-year colleges by not acknowledging their very different teaching and learning patterns and to dilute some serious concerns we all should have regarding the remaining colleges and universities. I will return to these concerns momentarily.

Sykes is not alone in his attacks from outside the academy, although his books do set the tone for others. Another celebrated polemic is *Illiberal Education: The Politics of Race and Sex on Campus*, by Dinesh D'Souza (1991). The critiques of Bloom, Sykes, and D'Souza are conservative, but in different ways. Bloom's analysis of the state of higher education might be termed intellectually conservative. He accused the academy of forsaking Platonic ideals in favor of intellectual and moral relativism. Sykes and D'Souza, on the other hand, are politically conservative. They see higher education as being dominated by a fairly radically leftist faculty who are creating an intolerant atmosphere for any dissenters by prescribing the curriculum and the discourse of colleges and universities. D'Souza claimed that, because of the changes wrought by the faculty,

> an academic and cultural revolution is under way at American universities. It is revising the rules by which students are admitted to college, and by which they pay for college. It is changing what students learn in the classroom, and how they are taught. It is altering the structure of life on the campus, including the habits and attitudes of the students in residence (1991, 13).

According to D'Souza, the agenda of the faculty is, essentially, an ideological one, and he used the word "ideology" in a pejorative sense. We will return to the concept that there is one (or more than one) ideology influencing the current state of higher education. The claims of a leftist orthodoxy and the denigration of conservative viewpoints are echoed in recent books by Ben Shapiro (2004) and Mike S. Adams (2004).

On every college and university campus, there are pulls and tugs between and within disciplines and departments centering on the production of meaning. Sykes, D'Souza, and others were right to decry any efforts to silence anyone in such discourse. Their critiques are precariously positioned in that they sometimes advocate a refutation of the openness of discourse when they argue against feminist, deconstructionist, or multiculturalist statements of aesthetics, argument, or curriculum. Higher education is founded on the principles of dialectic; that is, the open attempts at resolving conflicts within or between reasoned positions. If the critics cited here are engaging in dialectical debate, they are doing a service to American higher education. To the extent, though, that they are closing off debate, they are doing equal disservice. The same can be said of the individuals and stances they write about. The library, its collection, and its access mechanisms exist in large part to foster the dialectical debate. One manifestation of the debate, mentioned by all of the critics, is the place of an intellectual canon in the curricula and teaching of colleges and universities.

The canon, too, is a thorny matter. The invocation of a canon assumes that there is complete agreement as to its contents. The complexities of a canon are appreciated by Harold Bloom, who wrote,

> The Canon, once we view it as the relation of an individual reader and writer to what has been preserved out of what has been written,

and forget the canon as a list of books for required study, will be seen as identical with the literary Art of Memory, not with the religious sense of canon. . . . Pragmatically, aesthetic value can be recognized or experienced, but it cannot be conveyed to those who are incapable of grasping its sensations and perceptions. To quarrel on its behalf is always a blunder (1994, 17).

Hirsch, Sykes, D'Souza, and others are clear, however, in their call for a unified canon that expresses the essential cultural elements of the United States. What might be questionable is whether the canon, expressed as the best writing of those who have stood the test of time in the forums of education and informal discussion, embodies all cultural elements of the U.S.

The discussion of ideology and canon has particular relevance to academic libraries. An often-stated goal of library collections and services is egalitarianism, representation from as broad a spectrum as possible. But are there influences over what is produced and made available? Is the system of information production as egalitarian as the library's goals? If the two are at odds, it is incumbent upon librarians, first, to be aware of the differences and, second, to examine the implications of the unity or differences for the decisions they make. This is a difficult matter now; as academics have become heavier participants in electronic information production, the dilemma has grown even more problematic. The landscape of publication has changed substantially of late. Some publishers have disappeared; others have changed their focus. Some kinds of works are no longer published. Also, if there is a canon, librarians should understand who has influenced its formation and maintenance. If there is opposition to the canon, librarians should comprehend the grounds on which the opposition is based. Each side has a say in what gets published, how published works are received (for instance, through reviews), what is adopted for courses, and what is recommended for acquisition by the library. Like it or not, libraries are part of the dialectic and librarians should be able to appreciate the ramifications of the debate.

INTERNAL CRITIQUES

Outsiders are not the only ones to offer assessments of the state of higher education; some faculty also have written books chronicling perceived ills of colleges and universities. One of these books is *Up the University: Re-Creating Higher Education in America,* by Robert and Jon Solomon (1993), faculty members at the University of Texas and the University of Arizona, respectively. As did the journalists mentioned previously, these writers observed some serious deficiencies in the operation of higher education. The Solomons did not examine the philosophical ideals and justification of education, as did Bloom. Their approach was more akin to those of Sykes, D'Souza, and others. For one thing, they accused "research" of being an ill-defined term used to rationalize time- and space-consuming activities aimed at personal self- interest. They wrote,

> A university cannot be a "great" university without a dynamic research program and an industrious, productive professoriat (sic). But much of the research on campus today is only secondarily the pursuit of knowledge. It is the search for status, for notoriety. Much of it is sheer junk, although we know that everyone thinks of their own interests as utterly important and essential to the future of the world (Solomon and Solomon 1993, 67).

Again, as is the case with their journalistic predecessors, the Solomons offered only anecdotal evidence of the shoddiness and self-serving aspect of research. The lack of emphasis on, or attention to, teaching also received their wrath: "The university has trained and hired too many so-called teachers who have little interest in, and perhaps even contempt for, teaching. They are taught to dislike, disdain, or at least be annoyed by students, and they confront no institutional incentives to feel otherwise" (1993, 6).

The Solomons did go beyond the likes of Sykes et al. in both their understanding of the context of higher education and their responses to some of the problems they perceived. For instance, they observed that, all too often, the "free marketplace of ideas" that the university is supposed to represent is not all that free. There sometimes is a resistance to new or different ideas. Moreover, they wrote that students are far too infrequently traders in this marketplace. The Solomons also recognized that the metaphor of the marketplace can be taken only so far, that the college or university is not, at its foundation, a business. They blamed corporate thinking for the valuing of research over teaching. (In actuality, the ability to attract funding from outside sources does weigh heavily in evaluation of faculty, including promotion and tenure.) The tone of *Up the University* is not uniformly negative, however; the Solomons took pains to offer suggestions as to how higher education might reclaim its mission. For one thing, they advocated that teachers need to be learners as well and that faculty can learn from other faculty. An openness on the campus would allow faculty to seize the opportunities that the institution represents. Whether one agrees or disagrees with their assessments, it is clear that the Solomons took a serious look at higher education and found it lacking.

There is no denying that the Solomons (and others) have written about some serious concerns regarding the state of higher education. But just as did Sykes and the other journalists, the Solomons tended to wrap all of higher education in the cloak of the university. Their observations do not necessarily apply to liberal arts colleges, which adopt missions that are substantially different from those of universities. Further, the problems they enumerated have little relevance to community colleges, which tend to have clearly focused purposes. That said, some of the points raised by the authors discussed here do have some relevance to all types of institutions. Emphasis on research is certainly not evil, but an overemphasis on research and publication can, of, course, correspond to an inadequate attention to teaching. A rewards structure that provides financial incentive for research productivity is likely to influence the faculty. As Christopher Lucas said, "part of the answer (to a perceived incentive dilemma) probably inheres in the reluctance of individual academics to question a system in which they have acquired—or are earnestly seeking to acquire—a vested interest" (1996, 195). Even though some critiques have merit, what is generally lacking from the critiques of higher education is a close examination of the purpose of the college or university. To understand higher education, and the place of the library within it, we need to delve more deeply into this matter.

IDEAS OF PURPOSE

For many years, those who would examine or suggest the purpose of higher education have invoked the name of John Henry Cardinal Newman. His *Idea of a University*, written in the middle of the last century, set forth his conception of the ideal university for the day. In many ways, Newman used the Oxford University of his younger days as a foundation for his examination of that ideal. We will not spend much time on Newman's thought here, but the discourses that comprise his book have long provided successors with either a model (on which to base their own conceptions of higher education) or a foil (to disagree with and propound alternative visions).

The Debate Rages

We have seen, represented here, some diatribes against higher education. We also have seen some recurrent themes loom through these critiques: inadequate attention to teaching; too much attention on research and, especially, publication; the creation of an orthodox way of thinking that pervades today's pedagogy and curriculum; politicization of the academy; and an abandonment of moral traditions that extend back in time as far as Plato. There is some foundation for each of the points raised by the critics; otherwise these factors would never be mentioned. We have to accept that higher education in the U.S. today is not perfect, that it does have warts. Further, the specific aspects that are mentioned repeatedly should be examined carefully so that we can understand as completely as possible the challenges facing colleges and universities. However, we as students of this particular organizational type (or environment, or ecology, or culture) must take care not to allow some particular incidents to be necessarily indicative of the whole of higher education. For one thing, we must keep in mind that the college or university is essentially a place of questioning, of dialogue, and, unavoidably, of conflict. In every discipline on every campus, there will be adherents to multiple intellectual and practical positions. The environment of the academy, when it is working at its best, not only allows those divergent views, but also encourages exploration through civil argument. To adopt a particular stance, an individual must question the tenets of that stance and of its competitors. The closing off of debate and conflict would serve only to create a genuinely dismal and sterile place.

The ideal of the college or university, as suggested by Bloom, Hirsch, Sykes, D'Souza, and others is one in which there is an orthodoxy determined by one group of people. To make the case for the determined orthodoxy, these writers claim that an opposing group is now dominant and is propounding a way of thinking that is damaging to the heritage of Western thought. The writers listed are able to find examples of the domination in the form of efforts at containing speech on campuses, courses that seem to have no substantive content, and publications that appear to exist only to allow credit for the authors. There is no doubt that some of this does occur; the question is—and it is an open question—is how prevalent are these examples. At a more fundamental level, the controversy turns on the degree to which knowledge is objective and absolute. Hirsch argued for a determinacy to knowledge, saying that we can know enough to arrive at a singular, invariable interpretation. Bérubé (1993) posited that the acts of reading, interpreting, and knowing are at least somewhat indeterminate and complex. These two positions necessitate very different conceptions of the college or university.

Something of a variation in the discussion of purpose (and, incidentally, on objective knowledge) is also evident. Some observers suggest that higher education has transformed itself over the past years from an environment where learning is the goal to one where training replaces learning. They see a corporate ethos underlying the transformation. A collection of essays, entitled *Campus, Inc.,* is grounded in the idea that "The university is not a corporate personnel training agency, a research subcontractor, a business, a state agency, a graft machine, or an instrument for oppressing unwelcome facts and opinions" (Dugger 2000, 26). The attention to a corporate model, according these critics, leads to an abandonment of the ideal of learning that should be at the heart of the academy's purpose. Stanley Aronowitz articulated the gist of the criticism:

The current academic system has fudged the distinctions between training, education, and learning. Administrations of most colleges and universities have responded to the economic and cultural uncertainties provoked by budget constraints and a volatile job market by constructing their institutions on the model of the modern corporation. Consequently, many have thrust training to the fore and called it education. . . . Under these imperatives colleges and universities are unable to implement an educational program that prepares students for a world of great complexity (2000, 158).

Even more sweeping is Derek Bok's (2003) examination of the commercialization of higher education. He saw corporate interests influencing both the kinds of research undertaken and the reporting of the results (citing some delays in publication when the results could benefit a corporate funder of the research). He also observed commercial or profit motives affecting teaching. He did conclude on a positive note: "Although universities show signs of excessive commercialization in every aspect of their work, the trend is not irreversible in any area (barring a few high-profile competitive sports). In the all-important domains of education and research, academic leaders still have the power to develop appropriate policies" (Bok 2003, 205–6). David Kirp sounded a more dire note in the conclusion of his book: the university "might conceivably evolve into just another business, the metaphor of the higher education 'industry' brought to life in a holding company that could call itself Universitas, Inc. If there is a less dystopian future, one that revives the soul of this old institution, who is to advance it—and if not now, then when" (2003, 163)?

The conceptions just mentioned imply different perspectives on the academic library as well. The view embodied in the perspectives carry with them the suggestion that the library is—or should be—the repository of the correct interpretation of literary works, human behavior, or scientific progress. This also means that the services of the library can be directed to the proper teaching of students, proper learning, and proper inquiry. It also implies that the library has a role in the perpetuation of a canon, an accepted and ordained body of knowledge in each discipline. This role is accomplished through building collections, providing access, and offering intermediary services. The stance of Bérubé (1993) questions the correctness of interpretation and thus the existence of an approved body of canonical knowledge. A point of view sympathetic to Bérubé suggests that there are competing interpretations, texts, modes of learning, and pedagogical methods. It also suggests that the library be open to the existence of disagreement and variety. It is probable that most librarians hold to the latter view and advocate a willingness to develop diverse collections and offer services that recognize the absence of an absolute. The critique of corporatization, if at all correct, could further include a critique of collections and services aimed at material success in training programs, rather than at creating a deep understanding of the complexity Aronowitz spoke of. Librarians, however, may not realize fully the debate that exists on their campuses and what forces may be employed to influence the library.

A Careful Assessment

The foregoing creates the awareness that many people have certain conceptions of higher education. It would be useful now to look closely at a couple of explicit notions to see what types of institutions they advocate and what atmosphere campuses should have. We begin with Bruce Wilshire and his assessment, published in *The Moral Collapse of the University: Professionals, Purity, and Alienation* (1990). It is obvious from the book's title that Wilshire believes something is seriously wrong with higher education. He restated some of the criticisms already stated, but his analysis went a little deeper than the rest and he did not look for easy answers to the complex questions. For one thing, Wilshire tended to agree somewhat with Hirsch that students do not arrive at college with a common foundation of knowledge on which to build. Wilshire looked for some source of students' preparation and attitudes toward education and saw a problem that has been some time in growing.

> I thought more about the ideology of consumerism as a reason for their numbness and detachment. After spending their lives barraged by images equating buying with goodness, they seemed deeply to believe (if they believed anything deeply) that anything good can be bought, and without ever looking closely at the images on the money. A college education meant a degree, and this is a commodity which can be bought by paying fees and serving time. The possibility that knowledge could only be earned through diligent and at times drudging effort to come up to standards native to the enterprise of knowing itself, had apparently never entered most of their minds (1990, 13).

Throughout Wilshire's critique—and not just in his recommendations for change—he sketched a picture of the college and university as an ideal, that is, as it ought to be to meet the challenges of teaching and contribution to knowledge. Wilshire, although not explicitly acknowledging the existence of various cultures on campus, observed that there are factors that influence both the political and cognitive structures. With regard to the first, he cited the bureaucratic organization of the college or university as a stifling factor. By the word "bureaucracy," he was referring to "a system for organizing human activity so that persons become almost totally absorbed in the welfare of their particular module, and are only dimly aware of the role this plays in the whole, or the way in which the welfare of the whole affects the part. It is organic and desiccated connectedness" (1990, 50). As was hinted at in the last chapter, the political culture is typified by competition and positioning. The goals of the department are largely material: a larger student base, more faculty, a bigger budget. When the resources on a campus are finite, the gains of one department are offset by the losses of another. According to Wilshire, the latter structure, the cognitive culture, has led to a narrowing of the intellectual territory of the scholarly group, again to achieve material ends. Implicit in Wilshire's critique is its opposite. Actually, he made that opposite explicit, but not until he had offered his analysis of the ills of the system. There is the need for advances in both political and cognitive (especially cognitive) cultures in cooperation. In the simplest terms, his solution would be a reassessment of the goals that the department or the discipline sets for itself. As stated above, the goals can become essentially material or instrumental; they tend to be focused on the departments and disciplines themselves. The revised state of higher education would embody a shift in attention to students and learning and to the growth of knowledge. Wilshire recognized substantial obstacles to the shift in goal orientation, not the least of which is professionalism which, he claimed, can distort purpose and insulate faculty from the broader goal by emphasizing the narrower, material, ones. He wrote,

> (Magali) Larson (who has written on the sociology of the professions) puts her finger on one of the most hidden and troublesome influences of technology and the money economy. The university is the gatekeeper on the road to money and power, and the society supplies most professors with a guaranteed monopoly of clients and a serviceable salary. So the professor is free to define his or her status through relationships, not to the clients, the students, but to fellow professionals. The dependency on student-clients is masked, but I think that unacknowledged dependency upon them generates guilty and destructive feelings toward them (1990, 137).

Change requires fighting against the distortions that the artifice of professionalism promotes and urges awareness of the essence of education—the teaching and learning processes and inquiry that looks to the connections among the fields of study.

Everything that Wilshire said culminates in what is taught to students and how it is taught. The material goals that can arise in the political and cognitive cultures do not serve teaching and learning. It comes down to a matter of commitment. When faculty are committed to the instrumental values that lead to strong political positioning for the department or to individual gain through the mechanisms of tenure and promotion, something important gets lost.

As Wilshire said, "Without that tissue of commitment in meaning-making and knowing in which we confront our own freedom and responsibility in the world, the curriculum becomes an arbitrary sequence of courses; there is no connective tissue" (1990, 206). Although these critiques and responses share some ground with other writers mentioned in this chapter, it should be noted that Wilshire is not exclusionary in his goals for learning. The connectedness he speaks of so much is a pervasive concept in his ideal institution. Toward the end of achieving connectedness, he disagreed fundamentally with Allan Bloom:

> how can a thinker such as Bloom fail to discuss how self-pro-claimedly universalist views of human nature nevertheless manage to exclude the vast majority of the human race? Bloom does not face this issue, and I think I know why. He must sense that it would be disastrous, for his prejudice and aversion would be so obvious that it would be impossible to conceal it. . . . Bloom refuses to see the hatred and belittlement by oppressors through the years is incorporated in the souls of the oppressed as their own inner attitude toward themselves (1990, 154–56).

Wilshire's ideal is overtly democratic, even though he sees many practices and structures that confound his ideal.

A Different Kind of Ideal

Another ideal vision was propounded by Jaroslav Pelikan in *The Idea of the University: A Reexamination* (1992). Pelikan explicitly drew on the previous idea of the university articulated by Newman in the middle of the last century. Pelikan likened the university to a table supported by four legs. The legs that provide the foundation are teaching, research, preservation of knowledge in libraries, and communication through publication. This idea is a somewhat limited one; its focus is explicitly the university. This means that his idea does not necessarily apply in full to the college. Pelikan warned that an unclear vision can lead to confusion of purpose. He observed that "the transformation of 'college into university' has often accomplished the change of designation and sometimes of little else, at great cost to the essential business of the college and not always with a clear sense of the business of a university" (1992, 17). There are points raised by Pelikan that have relevance to all of higher education, though. For instance, he advocated that the institution itself foster compassion and caring because education is based on a moral imperative and involves attention to the individual. Pelikan's ideal in this regard would inevitably be met with favorably by the most vocal critics of higher education. He wrote,

Any definition of the university that does not explicitly incorporate this dimension of personal caring betrays the deepest traditions and highest ideals of the university and is woefully inadequate, and any citizen of the university who feels squeamish about a definition of the university that includes this dimension should reexamine both the intellectual and the moral imperatives that underlie the university as community (1992, 54).

From the outset Pelikan asserted that the university has obligations that should be fulfilled through the four key elements.

When Pelikan speaks of the essence of the university, he states that a first principle is the realization that knowledge is, in and of itself, valuable. He asserts that knowledge alone is a worthwhile goal and does not have purely utilitarian purposes. Moreover, he recognizes that an intent on utilitarianism may fail to foster the kind of utility that may be its goal.

Yet today it is necessary to sharpen, more than Newman did, the polemical point that utilitarianism is a threat to utility, and that therefore a rigid application of the utilitarian criterion could deprive the next generation of the very means it will need for the tasks that it will face, which will not be the tasks that this generation faces and which therefore cannot be dealt with by those particular instrumentalities that this generation has identified as "useful" (1992, 34).

The goal that is inherent in this first principle transfers to the key element of preserving knowledge in libraries. Having access to what has gone before contributes to the dynamic creation of knowledge; it is not static or ossifying. "In the modern university . . . the new knowledge has repeatedly come through confronting the old, in the process of which both old and new have been transformed. . . . For the university . . . these two conceptions, memory and expectation, are finally inseparable" (Pelikan 1992, 120).

In some ways, Pelikan provided responses, though not explicitly, to the critics of higher education. Teaching, one of the key elements of the university, is essential to the purpose and to the moral obligation of the university. He recognizes that good teaching is a challenge to the faculty; it requires attention and effort, just as does research. He also recognizes the need for teaching to be more than the passive transfer of information; it must engage the minds of students and teachers in order to create an atmosphere that fosters understanding of how to learn so that learning does not end with a classroom bell. Pelikan further notes that successful teaching manages to communicate facts, method, and also the excitement and exhilaration that can be part of each discipline. As another response to the critics, Pelikan acknowledges that the academic community is a diverse one, that it naturally and invariably includes a pluralistic environment. Of course, there will be methodological, ideological, and political differences within the university and attempting to impose one approved or official ideology will not make competitors disappear. The freedom and responsibility of the university necessitates resistance to the establishment of any single stance or position.

The most consistent aspect of Pelikan's idea of the university is the moral imperative that governs all of the university's work and effort. The critics already mentioned write of the moral failure of higher education by injuring teaching, overemphasizing research and publication, and politicizing institutions. Pelikan focused on the positive elements of the moral imperative and arrived at a conclusion that is somewhat at odds with the critics. He spoke of the "moral obligation to convey the results of research to other," and said, "There is an imperative of communicating that corresponds to the indicative of knowing. . . . Research, teaching, and publication are ultimately inseparable for the university, because they are all functions of this single obligation" (1992, 51). Wilshire agrees that teaching and research are not absolutely distinct and that the university has the obligation to do both. The obligations of the university extend to professional education, which, according to Pelikan, has a definite place within higher education. He quotes Edward Levi (1969), who wrote, "The professional school which sets its course by the current practice of the profession is, in an important sense, a failure" because "the professional school must be concerned in a basic way with the world of learning and the interaction between this world and the world of problems to be solved" (1969, 38–39).

The ideas of purpose discussed here have important implications for the academic library. For instance, Wilshire, although he communicates an ideal for higher education, focuses on some specific ways in which the ideal is not realized. He speaks of material goals of bureaucracy that define organizational structure. If we accept that the bureaucracy embodies such material goals, they will be transferred to the library. If the organizational culture is so affected by materialism, what the faculty and even the departments will want from the library will be those services and information that support the political positioning of the department. If professionalism leads to a narrowed scope of self-reflexivity among faculty, the faculty will transfer that narrowness to their expectations and demands of the library. On the other hand, Pelikan's idea could have significance for the library. First of all, the library features prominently as one of the key elements of the university. A realization of Pelikan's ideal would ensure centrality for the library on campus. With such a prominent place would come the obligations and responsibilities that are part of the university's moral imperative. The obligations would be focused on freedom of inquiry, the communication of research, and the pluralism that is part of the academic community. It should be noted that Pelikan's ideal is just that—

an ideal. As is in the next chapter, the internal workings of the institution are usually not subject to tight administrative control and the status quo can be powerful. That said, academic librarians need to be sensitive to the goals, ideas, and ideals of their campuses in order to be able to respond to the needs of their environment.

SUMMARY

A number of assaults against higher education have been launched in the past several years. Cary Nelson and Michael Bérubé (1995) have provided a litany of the most common complaints:

> Academy-bashing is now among the fastest-growing of major U.S. industries, and the charges are as numerous as the bashers themselves: teachers don't teach; scholars fritter away their time and your tax dollars on studies of music videos; campus regulations thwart free speech; the Western cultural heritage is besieged by tenured radicals; heterosexual white men are under attack from feminist, multiculturalist, and gay and lesbian groups; universities are buying luxury yachts with federal research dollars; academic standards of all kinds are in tatters; undergraduates lack both reading skills and moral foundations; and, in the midst of all this, to add financial insult to intellectual injury, college tuitions are skyrocketing (1995. 1).

Other critiques focus on the institution itself. Bill Readings (1996) addressed the purpose of higher education, as expressed in a great amount of discourse. Colleges and universities today, according to Readings, are becoming fixated on the idea of "excellence." Excellence, he observed, is not contestable; how could anyone refute the assertion that education should be excellent? However, excellence is almost meaningless, though, because it doesn't really *refer* to anything (internally or externally) and it isn't a fixed standard of judgment. The attachment to excellence, as Readings sees it, includes the danger of reducing the institution and what it does to a commodity that can be bought and sold in a market that has no clear demarcations.

The criticisms of colleges and, especially, of universities should not be dismissed. Many of the critics are serious about pointing out perceived problems and solving them. It may be easy to disregard some accusations based on scant anecdotal evidence, but recurrent mention of some particular areas of concern should prompt some attention to the subjects of the critiques. Through any assessment of criticisms, the mission of the individual institution should be kept in mind. It may be that the mission itself should be evaluated in light of the needs of the larger community served as well as the institution's ability to fulfill it. The next step in assessment should be to determine if actual practice is departing from the mission. If such is the case, answers should be sought as to why this departure is occurring. It may be that the practice is justified on some grounds, but assumptions should not replace investigation. The thoughtful ideas of Wilshire and Pelikan, for instance, can be used to examine the direction of the college or university and the actions of the academic units and the faculty. As Wilshire noted, self-reflection is essential to education; it should govern assessment.

The future will depend on an effective higher education system, and colleges and universities will have to be sensitive to the societal needs (not that they have not been in the past). As James Duderstadt, former president of the University of Michigan, said, "The needs of our society for the services provided by our colleges and universities will continue to grow. Significant expansion will be necessary just to respond to the needs of a growing population that will create a 30 percent growth in the number of college-age students over the next two decades" (2000, 321). Serious critical assessment of higher education is needed, and responses to all critics will have to be a part of the assessment.

The topics covered in this chapter suggest some questions for further discussion:

> What is the purpose of the college, and what is the purpose of the university?
>
> Is there a connection between research and teaching?
>
> Does higher education have a moral obligation? If so, what is it?
>
> Should tenure be abolished?
>
> Should the four key elements of Pelikan's idea of the university be coequal?
>
> Is the library a participant, a pawn, or an outsider in the problems that critics complain of?
>
> Can the library have an influence in the formation of an idea of the institution?

Chapter 5

Governance

The organizational culture of higher education was discussed in chapter 2. As we saw, the cultural foundation of colleges and universities is structural, at least in part. It is evident that not all cultures are equal, that the administration is more influential than any other group in influencing the culture of the organization. This chapter explores a part of the formal structure—governance. In the simplest terms, governance refers to the official chain of authority, but that chain of authority is not so simple. We must understand the governance structure in order to grasp the path of decision making and financial support. This statement implies that colleges and universities are not completely independent, and this is, in fact, the case. Every college and university is answerable to some outside body; major policy decisions almost invariably must be approved by that body. The governance issues illustrate most clearly the differences between public and private institutions.

Matters of governance also point out the odd place higher education has in the United States. As George Keller wrote,

> American colleges and universities occupy a special, hazardous zone in society, between the competitive profit-making business sector and the government owned and run state agencies. They are dependent yet free; market-oriented yet outside cultural and intellectual fashions.... The institutions pay no taxes but are crucial to economic development.... They constitute one of the largest industries in the nation but are among the least businesslike and well-managed of all organizations (1983, 5).

Although colleges and universities can enjoy a degree of independence, that independence is by no means absolute. The nature of the work done in today's institutions is particularly difficult to classify, to find an analogy for in the rest of society. Higher education forms a puzzle for those who would exercise some management control over it. The enigma of higher education seems to create a contradiction. Robert Birnbaum said,

> The apparent paradox that American colleges and universities are poorly run but highly effective is easily resolved if either or both of these judgments are wrong. But what if they are both right? . . . Or, strangest of all, it might be that to at least some extent our colleges and universities are successful *because* they are poorly managed, at least as *management* is often defined in other complex organizations. If this is true, then attempts to "improve" traditional management processes might actually diminish rather than enhance organizational effectiveness in institutions of higher education (italics in original) (1998, 3–4).

Birnbaum's suggestions indicate that the conventional wisdom of management that takes its cue from the business world may not apply, or may not apply fully, to higher education. Much of management thought and activity focuses on control—financial control, control of personnel, control of the product and its production. These aspects of control have quite different meanings in colleges and universities. One reason for the lack of agreement about meaning is the ambiguity regarding the product of higher education. It is very difficult to translate what happens in the typical educational institution into the terms that the typical business might employ. These dilemmas will recur throughout this chapter, but first we should take a look at the formal structures that are common to public and private higher education.

TRUSTEESHIP

Practically all institutions of higher education are answerable to a governing board. From the founding of Harvard College in the seventeenth century there has been some form of trusteeship, some body of individuals who have exercised authority over the schools. This is the way Robert Rosenzweig described the situation of higher education: "The university is held in trust by a lay board of trustees. They are absentee landlords, remote from the actual work of the institution, and, if they insist on being an active force in the governance of the institution, that is usually seen as a sign of a deep political dysfunction" (1994, 301).

This description is not a portrait of a particularly rational structure. Rosenzweig's assessment may have been colored by his tenure as president of the Association of American Universities. Involvement by governing boards varies considerably. Let us begin the investigation of trusteeship with a description of governing boards of private institutions.

Private Colleges and Universities

The private college or university is, by and large, an institution with either ties of dependency or connection to a private, nongovernmental agency. Many private colleges are affiliated with religious denominations or with particular churches. Although this religious affiliation seems to suggest uniformity of governance, we must remember that the scale of governing authority can be very specific and localized or quite dispersed. For instance, an institution such as Oral Roberts University has strong ties to a particular source and to specific individuals. The governing board of such an institution may be drawn from a relatively small pool of people with similarly close ties to the same source. One potentially favorable result of such control is that members of the governing board may be more likely to share primary goals for the institution and may even share ideas on how to accomplish those goals. In other words, there may be fairly high levels of agreement among board members. On the other hand, such high levels of agreement may not be particularly advantageous to the college or university if the board has a conception of the institution that is substantially at odds with the school's administration and/or faculty.

Affiliation with a religion does not necessarily ensure levels of agreement that are high. When the college or university is affiliated with a religious denomination, rather than with a particular church, membership on the board can be as diverse as the denomination itself and disagreements within the denomination may spill over to the college or university. The Catholic University of America (as a hypothetical example) has such a broad base of governance and, although there is sure to be greater agreement on orthodoxy than is true with a public governing board, there can be disagreement regarding the means by which the institution achieves its educational aims. For instance, the board may agree about religious matters but disagree about managerial matters. It sometimes is assumed that such institutions serve a national audience, a goal that can create pressures on the college or university to spread itself rather thin. It should be remembered that with institutions with church or religious ties, the tenets of the particular church or religion usually form the foundation upon which the school is based, a reality that is understood by the administration, faculty, and students.

It is certainly not unusual with these kinds of institutions for the church or religious denomination to determine who serves on the governing board. A formal process of nomination and/or appointment may be in place. Again, an advantage of such a system may be that those on the campus (administrators, faculty, and students) can assume that serious rifts among board members will be rare and that there probably will be continuity of board decisions because the principal beliefs that influence decisions are unlikely to change and the incoming board members are likely to be in substantial agreement with outgoing and present members on the essential areas of decision making. It is possible that, at times, even a governing board will make a policy decision that has a considerable impact on the institution. These decisions can be far-reaching, such as the recent action taken by Brigham Young University. As Denise Magner reported, "Professors at Brigham Young University now must have their spiritual worthiness certified annually by local Mormon Church leaders in order to keep their jobs. . . . Starting this year (1996), local ecclesiastical leaders will receive annual letters asking if B.Y.U employees in their congregations have met standards for temple membership" (1996, A17). Details of the requirements of faculty are in the BYU handbook, which is password protected.

Other private colleges and universities that have no (or very weak) religious ties are likely to have independent governing boards. In most instances, the institution's charter dictates how their governing board is formed and what its authority is. Almost invariably, a primary concern of the private college or university's governing board is the institution's finances. For example, the board may have authority to establish the amount of tuition to be charged. The board also may have authority over the expenditure of funds generated from the income of endowments (or of those endowments that are not otherwise restricted). For instance, the board may have the power to make decisions regarding capital expenditures such as new buildings, renovation, or large-scale projects (such as wiring the campus as part of improving telecommunications access). Because the boards of these private institutions are unlikely to be as homogeneous as the boards of church-related schools, some conflicts may exist among board members. Conflicts are almost inevitable when it comes to issues such as the institution's debt or alternatives to the missions. The conflicts that can occur can be intensified if the board's position is in opposition to that of the administration or faculty, or both. At Bennington College, the president, with the full approval of the board, eliminated tenure in some departments and dismissed twenty-six faculty. As could be expected, the atmosphere on that campus was tense in the aftermath (Wilson 1994, A19).

Public Colleges and Universities

With public higher education, two characteristics of governing boards are most striking: the board customarily has authority over more than one institution, and appointment to the board is part of a political process that extends well beyond the college or university. These aspects set public institutions' governing boards apart from those of private ones. For our purposes, we can focus on state control of higher education, although there may be municipal or county control, especially with regard to two-year institutions. Most states have multiple systems of higher education institutions. For instance, California has the University of California system and a separate system for the state universities. Sometimes a mandated set of regulations limits the decision-making purview of a governing board. To use the state of California as an example again, the state universities are prohibited from establishing doctoral programs. Whether the board wants to start a doctoral program in chemistry at, say, San Jose State University is irrelevant; it cannot consider such an offering.

In many states, the structure of governance is complicated by the existence not only of multiple systems, but also of hierarchical governing boards. Louisiana has the Louisiana State University system with its board of supervisors, the Southern University system with its separate board of supervisors, a board of the University of Louisiana system to oversee most of the rest of the public institutions, *and* the board of regents, which is largely responsible for coordinating the efforts of all of higher education. Other states have similar structures. In most cases, the coordinating board is charged with ensuring that there will be no unnecessary duplication of effort. If one university has a doctoral program in romance languages, another university may be unable to begin a similar degree program. Almost invariably, membership on public higher education governing boards is a matter of gubernatorial appointment (usually with legislative approval). This means that the political mix on governing boards can lead to internal and regional tensions. Because board members serve fixed terms that overlap, it is very possible that half (roughly) of the board members were appointed by a Republican governor and the other half by a Democratic one. Add to the mix the desire or requirement that all regions of the state be represented (and perhaps equal representation from both major political parties), and the stage is set for potential battles.

How might conflict arise? Internal conflict can result from a couple of sources. One (and the one that may seem most obvious) is the possibility of board members belonging to different political parties. The parties may influence the members' thinking on matters such as budgeting, degree program offerings, administrator hiring, enrollment, capital projects, research, and even the institution's overall direction. Internal conflict also can result from the regional dispersion of representation on the board. Because the board is probably governing several campuses, there could be competition for resources. A board member from one part of the state may see her or his job as that of advocate for the nearest college or university. When resources are finite (as they always are), and especially when resources are scarce, there will inevitably be competition among the colleges or universities. The board members will be graduates of specific school and thus may also feel the association that comes with being an alumnus/alumna of that institution.

All of the above paints the picture of a political snake pit where there may be little agreement on any but the most trivial issues. I do not want to give the impression that progress is impossible because of permanent political gridlock. Most board members are dedicated individuals committed to ensuring the best educational institutions for the state's citizenry. Moreover, these individuals, in both private and public higher education, take on the demands of serving on a board while working in full-time careers. Because of the underlying selflessness of their motivations, most of the tension is caused by honest disagreement over important issues. Let's say that a state university system is facing the likelihood of drastically increased numbers of people wanting to enroll at its campus in the coming years. The current physical plants of the universities are inadequate to meet the potential increases in student body size. One faction of the board may believe that the answer to the problem is increased capital expenditures so that the campus can be expanded to take on more students. Another may believe that admission standards should be raised so that the student population does not increase. Still another may be of the opinion that the physical plant should not be expanded but, rather, that distance education opportunities should be increased so that the state's citizens can be served. These are three very different solutions, each requiring a certain vision for the expenditure of resources. There is no purely objective guide that leads to one solution over another, so the conflict will have to be resolved politically. It is the board's job to make such difficult decisions.

Frank Rhodes eloquently described the primary responsibility of all governing boards:

> The role of the board is governance, and there is a world of difference between governance and management. Governance involves the responsibility for approving the mission and goals of the institution; for approving its policies and procedures; for the appointment, review, and support of its president; and for informed oversight of its programs, activities, and resources. Management, in contrast, involves the responsibility for the effective operation in the institution and the achievement of its goals (2001, 220).

DECISION MAKING

Speaking of making decisions, how do decisions get made in the varying governance structures? First, all of the policy decisions that affect the direction of the institution or system will ultimately be the responsibility of the board. However, the issue to be decided does not begin with the board. Generally speaking, the campus and/or system administrators will be much closer to the matter to be decided than will the board members. The administrators will see the need for a decision before the board is aware that a problem or opportunity exists. The administrators will examine that matter and, frequently with advice from a number of parties and groups, will arrive at what they believe to be the optimal decision. If it is a matter of sufficient importance that the governing board needs to be involved, the administrators will provide information to the board members and usually recommend a decision. If the problem is systemwide, the administrators of each campus probably will have separate assessments of the problem and separate visions for a solution. The system administration weighs these potentially different views and arrives at a compromise to present to the board. Compromise may be the most important element in effective decision making,. Not all players may get exactly what is wanted, and the interests of the whole need to be weighed.

Even within a particular college or university, institution-wide decisions may be a product of compromise. A number of constituencies may want a voice in the decision-making process and may well have legitimate claims on the attention of administrators. Various departments or colleges are likely to have different emphases and foundations for reasoning. Again, effective decision making takes into account the diversity of purpose and functioning. It is not necessary to delve deeply into that nature of effective decision making here. Robert Stueart and Barbara Moran cover the topic in *Library and Information Center Management.* Many of the aspects of decision making in libraries are universal and apply to any organization at any level. For instance, they wrote, "Decision making is a conscious choosing, and it is a much slower process than one would like to imagine. . . . The decision-making process involves a blend of thinking, deciding, and acting; information is key to the process. Deliberation, evaluation, and thought must be brought into play" (1993, 60).

To some, the decision-making activities of the college or university can be summed up in terms of the difference between administration and management. Keller asserted that management is the embodiment of leadership, and that means taking an active role in the overall purpose and direction of the institution. He described what he sees are some differences between administrators and managers:

> The behavior of education leaders dedicated to good management is different from the behavior of those who are traditional administrators. Administrators prefer people, individual projects, specific routines; managers prefer ideas, linked initiatives, new ventures.

Administrators tend to be cool, amiably neutral, businesslike; managers tend to be spirited, committed, entrepreneurial. Administrators are usually cautious, passive, and conservative; managers are often risk-takers, active, and adventurous. Administrators love details and efficiency; managers love large objectives and effectiveness (1983, 68).

However, there are some problems with Keller's notion. The characteristics of managers, according to him, center on control at high levels. (His view of administrators includes control as well.) The kind of control Keller spoke of is difficult in an educational institution. The principal personnel in a college or university are more self-determined than in just about any other type of organization. Faculty are not nor do they assume the roles of employees of the president or chancellor (or of deans or department chairs). Again, there is the difficulty of defining the product of higher education, which contributes to the difficulty of defining administration.

The three branches of purpose in higher education illustrate the problems with management in the business sense. Teaching, research, and service each has a problematic locus, for instance. Teaching, although integral to the mission of every college and university, tends to be largely a department concern. It is the department that establishes its curriculum (including what is to be required of all majors) and schedules courses. Research is generally an individual activity for each faculty member, and although collaboration may cross disciplinary lines, it certainly cannot be managed from above. Service resides in many places—the campus, the community, the profession. As Birnbaum noted, "It is important in some situations for administrators to intervene, make decisions, initiate programs, and take other actions that are generally considered the hallmarks of a good leader" (1988, 224). On the other hand, he realized, efforts at too much control can disrupt functioning relationships and have effects opposite to what is intended. Faculty will tend, on various grounds (including rational and nonrational), to resist the control of management.

All of this has implications for the locus of decision making at any college or university. To hearken back to the concepts central to organizational culture, there are things that can be imposed by dominant cultures on others, but even that has limits. The decisions that can be imposed are usually large-scale ones that will have an impact on the entire campus. The effective college or university administrator will recognize the autonomy that faculty have (in part a reflection of cultural manifestations) and the interest they have vested in particular spheres of activity. That administrator will include faculty (at least by representation) in the advising process prior to major policy decisions, out of a realization of the knowledge and expertise that faculty can bring to bear on the matter and out of an awareness of the necessity for cultural integration to smooth operation. There are occasions where faculty know more about an issue than administrators can, so the administrator should admit to and incorporate that knowledge. As we will see, though, there are reasons why things can go wrong and this ideal is not achieved. To a considerable extent, the problems center on a set of difficult questions asked by Jonathan Cole. He wrote,

> The fundamental problem of choice at research universities has more to do with basic ambiguity over governance than with the ability to articulate alternatives. Who has the authority, beyond the formal authority registered in the statutes or the table of organization, to make such choices? Who has the power to "veto" the choices made? What are the processes by which the choices of the decision makers are legitimated within the university community? What is the role of faculty, students, administrative leaders, trustees, and alumni in making such choices? (1993, 6)

SOURCES OF FINANCING

As noted above, the governance structure of any institution or system is charged with devising a means of attracting financial resources. Whether private or public, no single source of support is sufficient to enable the college or university to accomplish all of its goals. All institutions have to turn to multiple sources in order to continue operation. Let us look first at the predicament of private colleges and universities. Because of scant (if any) state funding, private institutions have to consider tuition a principal source of income. However, there is a limit to what schools can charge students. Administrators of private institutions have to find a tuition level that both provides a substantial amount of money and allows for at least a stable, if not an increasing, student population. If tuition is increased to the point where enrollment begins to drop, there may be no financial gain (and, in fact, may be a financial loss) as a result of the increase. As might be expected, this puts private institutions in competition with one another for students and tuition dollars. Small liberal arts colleges probably feel the competition even more keenly than do larger schools. These colleges are fairly numerous and may be in close geographic proximity to other, similar, institutions. Indeed, relatively small towns may be home to more than one college. For instance, William Woods University and Westminster College both reside in Fulton, Missouri.

Private institutions find themselves having to work hard to attract gifts from individuals and businesses. Much of the money given is invested in endowment accounts, properties, or other sources that generate income. Endowments are extremely important to private colleges and universities because the funds represent capital that can be invested and can grow. The institutions generally invest the endowment monies in any of a number of places, such as stocks, bonds, real estate, and so on. The college or university takes a portion of the income generated from the endowment and uses it for operation or capital projects. The rest of the income rolls over and is added to the endowment fund so that it can grow. The endowment is usually not a single, monolithic fund but may comprise a number of funds, many dedicated or restricted to specific purposes. Some funds may provide for scholarship for students; some may fund faculty positions; some may be limited to the purchase of library materials. There also is competition for gifts that can be used to improve the institution. Naturally, college and universities turn to their graduates and launch campaigns aimed at asking alums for monetary donations. The more graduates a school has, the larger the potential donor pool. When the institutions move beyond their graduates to businesses, corporations, or philanthropists, competition for funds begins in earnest.

These funding opportunities for private colleges and universities are limited. Only so much money is given to higher education and only so many students can, or are willing to, pay many thousands of dollars a year in tuition. As the costs of operation increase, the predicament for some institutions can grow dire. Many issues of the *Chronicle of Higher Education* report the financial troubles of colleges. The financial problems of some schools place their futures in jeopardy. Although there is some federal support for private higher education (for student financial aid, some programs, and research conducted at universities), this source does not provide a large percentage of school's incomes. As Keller stated, "Not every existing institution of higher learning will, or should, survive the 1980s, or the twentieth century. . . . Nine out of ten institutions in the United States, therefore, are precariously financed, and many live at the brink of jeopardy and instant retrenchment" (1983, 152). In times of financial trouble, those governing the institution have responsibility for devising plans to continue operation, which may include revision of the school's mission (which, in turn, may affect the student population, the faculty, and potential donors).

Public higher education receives its financial support from somewhat different sources than do private schools. Funding from states comprises the largest source of income. Of course, by definition, public college and universities receive support from public funding. For most public institutions, the path of this financial support follows a complicated route. On a given campus, the administration is responsible for arriving at a funding request that is to support the plans formulated for, and by, that campus. That request may then go to the system administration, who must weigh it against the requests of other campuses in the same system. The system administration then has to devise a funding proposal for all of the campuses (plus the system office) and then, perhaps, submit it to the administration of a coordinating board. That board may have to reconcile the requests of all of the systems and campuses and come up with a single funding request for higher education in the state. The board usually submits the request to the governor or the state legislature or assembly. Add to all this, the realization that the state's governor may submit a separate budget request for higher education. Further, a legislative committee also may come up with a funding plan. When the state's legislature approves an appropriations bill, the funding may travel back down the same path. Although procedures vary somewhat from state to state, the process is almost always a complicated one. The people on that initial campus must be aware that a lot can happen to its funding request as these various bodies review it and, possibly, alter it.

Of course, tuition also is an important source of revenue for public institutions. Some colleges and universities have stopped referring to themselves as "state-supported" institutions and have begun to call themselves "state-assisted" institutions. This change in rhetoric reflects the reality that public higher education must look to several sources for financial support. It is not unusual at large public universities for state appropriations to account for 25 percent or less of the university's annual expenditures. The stance regarding tuition is much the same for public and private institutions. Each institution must determine the optimal tuition rate, the rate that students are able and willing to pay and that will not result in a loss of students. The tuition rate, however, is considerably lower for public than for private colleges and universities. Because public support is provided by some form of taxation, people are willing to pay only so much in tuition. That said, the tuition rates charged in the various states differ substantially. Local matters must be taken into consideration when deciding tuition rates. If the population's per capita income is low, a lower rate will have to be charged so that the state's citizens can have access to public higher education.

As is true of private colleges and universities, public schools likewise look to the federal government to provide student aid support, as well as assistance with program and research initiatives. The questions that may be asked at this point include: What proportions of support do public and private institutions receive from various sources? What has been happening to the sources of support over the past several years? Table 5.1 provides a glimpse at answers. As is evident, public schools now receive a smaller proportion of state funds than they used to. Because the difference has to be made up somewhere, we look for areas of increase. The percentage of support coming from tuition has risen, which means that students are bearing more of the costs of education. In addition, there has been an increase in the category labeled "Sales and Services." This category includes many and varied operations, with no one (except hospitals,

TABLE 5.1 Sources of Financial Support over Time, by Type of Institution

	PUBLIC		PRIVATE	
SOURCE	*1996–97*	*2000–2001*	*1996–97*	*2000–2001*
Tuition	19.0%	18.1%	27.8%	38.1%
Federal Govt.	11.0%	11.2%	11.7%	16.3%
State Govt.	35.6%	35.6%	1.0%	1.4%
Private Gifts & Grants	4.3%	5.1%	12.3%	19.3%

Source of Data: National Center for Education Statistics, 2003.

where they exist) forming a large percentage of the total. Private institutions also have seen increases in tuition relative to other sources. The most substantial decrease has been in federal support. If the trends continue, all of higher education will soon be hard-pressed to find resources sufficient to continue the kinds of programs, services, and operations that have existed in the past. The challenges that likewise face academic libraries cannot be overstated. It is incumbent upon library directors to be entrepreneurial when it comes to seeking financing and to build close ties with the institution's development office.

BUSINESS MODELS

Because most members of governing boards are from the outside (that is, not from the inner academic circles), there may be some discordance between the board and the campus when it comes to a model for organizing and operating. Board members who come to their positions from the business world may be tempted to see the college or the university as a nascent business. This view may be especially tempting when the board member sees the amount of money that goes into the running of academic institutions. The business approach of boards is not new; Thorsten Veblen saw it at work in 1918. The board, he said, tends to adopt a particular point of view: "the university is conceived as a business house dealing in merchantable knowledge, placed under the governing hand of a captain of erudition, whose office it is to turn the means at hand to account in the largest feasible output" (Veblen 1957, 62). The business approach is not limited to the governing board; system and campus administrators may adopt a corporate stance and attempt to frame their decisions accordingly. If such is the case (at the board level or lower), some elements of higher education may stand out in the administrator's mind. For instance, given that financial resources are not plentiful, the business model may lead to a deliberative process that focuses on the attraction of money from heretofore untapped sources, including product development (such as technologies that might be marketed broadly). The process also may fix on those segments of the college or university that have the potential for attracting funds. Benjamin Johnson, Patrick Kavanaugh, and Kevin Mattson make the rather extreme statement that "Universities have changed with this world. They no longer collude with big business; they have become increasingly identical to business. The wall between the two has grown thin" (2003, 12).

Let's take a look at a hypothetical scenario. At a public university there is an acknowledged need for expanded resources. However, the state is not going to be appropriating larger sums to higher education. Further, the tuition rate is almost as high as students are willing to pay. Thus, the university administration must look elsewhere. As a matter of course, the university upgrades its development effort so that it can seek higher levels of giving from individuals and businesses. Development is a long-term commitment, though, and the administration wants to see more immediate growth. At present, the strongest academic units are in the humanities and the social sciences. There is not much hope that these departments will be able to attract external funding. The decision is made to enhance the science and technology units on campus. Available funds are used to improve some facilities and to attract faculty who will be able to compete for outside money. Within three years, the faculty increase federal research funding received from $12 million a year to $30 million. Some of the direct costs of these research projects are used to improve laboratory facilities and to purchase scientific instrumentation. The negotiated indirect cost rate at this university is 49 percent. Even given that some budget items are not subject to accompanying indirect costs, the university receives about $6.5 million (of the $30 million) as indirect costs, part of which may be used for the further enhancement of those departments attracting the funding. What happens to the humanities and the social sciences?

Speaking of the university as a holding company (as opposed to a single, unified entity), Steven Muller offered his view of the effects of a business model for higher education. He said,

> the arts and sciences, or liberal arts, no longer constitute the acknowledged and determining core of the university institution. This erosion of the centrality of the liberal arts, the descendant of the faculty of philosophy of the historic Western university, is one of the most significant and disturbing features of the current state of the research university in the United States. All of the implications and consequences of this erosion are as yet neither manifest nor understood, nor is the occasion to examine them in much greater detail (1994, 120).

The concept of holding company implies that the university comprises a number of semiautonomous units, each with its own notion of success (unit as subculture) and its own attachment to, or detachment from, the governance structure. Muller suggested that there is another effect of the holding company thinking that is related to governance issues: the people in each unit look first to the leader of their unit. As he stated,

> those individuals in any one of the components relate far more directly and continuously to the chief executive officer (CEO) of the component than to the CEO of the company as a whole. In short, the members of each school, college, or division within the holding company model of the university look to their dean rather than to the university president for leadership. If a component unit lacks adequate leadership, the appropriate response is to select and appoint a new dean but definitely not for the component to be governed by the leadership of the holding company itself (1994, 121).

Those at the top of the structure must work through the intermediate administrative ranks in order to govern.

There is difference between the academic and the corporate. Because the key elements of academic life—teaching, research, and service—are only peripherally controlled at the highest levels, the faculty can choose how they are going to meet the requirements of the administration. Again, we come back to an elusive product, conceptions of which can vary greatly even within an institution. At the above hypothetical university, the administration conceives of the product as becoming self-sustaining. To produce that product, decisions are made regarding potential for attraction of outside funding, costs of operation, student tuition dollars, and, only then, academic issues. The administration may be looking at the institution in terms of its ability to sell its offerings in a competitive market. Michael Cohen and James March observed that in such a marketplace,

> Students, faculty, donors, and communities select from a list of alternative universities (willing to accept them) the one (or more) that comes closest to satisfying their perceived needs. Quality, price, and quantity are determined as in the usual competitive market. The distribution of wealth is the key to the distribution of power. Internal organization is entirely arbitrary. Effective "governance" takes place through the operation of markets (e.g., labor market, student market, employer market, donor market, legislative market) (1986, 30).

The problem, as Cohen and March noted, is that higher education does not fit the assumptions that usually fit a free market: there are frictions in the academic world that can limit students and faculty from exercising unlimited alternatives; there is a general lack of awareness about the alternatives that exist, and the market is not amenable to new institutions entering it.

The above paints a fairly bleak picture and is not intended to portray all, or even a majority of, academic institutions. For one thing, not all institutions attempt to incorporate a business model of governance. The examples given tend to be of universities, and there is a reason for this. Four-year colleges have substantially definite, and fairly fixed, missions. Colleges generally do not possess the infrastructure to support a move to research; major changes to the physical plant, curriculum, student–faculty ratios, teaching loads, and emphases of the faculty would have to come about for a liberal arts college to make a move toward enhanced research with potential for external funding. At universities, where there already are some research and some graduate programs, the increased emphasis on research seems, to some, natural. What may not be fully appreciated is that some of the same major changes listed above will accompany that emphasis, even on a university campus. In particular, governing boards may not have such an appreciation of the current state of the institution and the impact that change will have.

FACULTY AND GOVERNANCE

A purely business approach to governance has some severe limitations, and institutions have some structural features to counter the event of the scenario presented in the previous section. One such element is faculty involvement in governance. On most campuses, this involvement takes the form of a faculty senate, a group of faculty elected by their colleagues to advise the administration on matters affecting the institution. The idea of collegial governance has been the product of a fair amount of rhetoric over the years, but it is still not entirely clear to what extent the collegial community is able to govern itself. This is essentially an open question. Cole said that this and other questions are difficult to answer. There is no consensus on the ability of faculty, who have diverse and often competing interests, to agree on issues of governance, on the possibility of administrators consulting with faculty on matters of change, or on the faculty's consultative strengths (1993, 7). Cole asserted that the dichotomy between faculty and administration is a false one, that administrators are faculty who have altered their roles. Collaboration, he believes, should exist in the development of academic priorities, but articulation of vision and translation of goals into accomplishments are administrative tasks. It should be noted that, as he expressed these opinions, Cole was serving as provost of Columbia University.

There are supporters of faculty sharing in governance. John Dempsey wrote, "Shared, collegial governance is one of the real treasures of life at four-year colleges." He added that such collegial governance is not common in community colleges, but that "Community college faculty should more properly be treated as professionals—people with unique insights into what is possible and proper for their institutions. Community colleges need to move forcefully in the direction of greater faculty participation in governance" (1992, 45–46). Emily Stipes Watts reported on the success of the faculty senate at the University of Illinois in opening formal communication between faculty and administrators. She concluded that "the current stirrings of unified and assertive faculty leadership hold promise for a continuation and revitalization of shared governance through a strengthening of the role of the academic senate" (1991, 33). John Dimond reported that faculty on campuses where they have substantial roles in institutional budgeting tend to be satisfied with their voice on governance matters, whereas those on campuses where they have lesser roles report far less satisfaction (1991, 67).

More writers, however, express skepticism regarding the effectiveness of faculty sharing in governance. The disunity that Muller mentioned is sometimes spoken of as an inhibition to collegial governance. For instance, Birnbaum wrote, "The loss of faculty control is related to increased institutional size and complexity and the division of faculty into different departments, committees, and other units. This fractionation prevents the development of a holistic faculty perspective" (1988, 15). The environment that creates such inhibitions operates against not only faculty, but administrators as well. Birnbaum added that "neither faculty nor administration feels able to take command, since neither group fully understands the enterprise or has control of enough of its resources" (1988, 15). The complexity of higher education does not seem to work in anyone's favor; all participants are stymied by the scope of factors influencing the educational enterprise and by the intellectual and functional diversity on the campuses themselves. Rozensweig observed that whenever there is stress in the organization, factions can be created and the absence of strong and legitimate decision making can inhibit the effective resolution of conflict (2001, 113).

Faculty participation in governance also is hindered by faculty's organizational position. It is generally quite clear in the corporate environment who is management and who is not; the same cannot be said of the educational environment. It is stated above that the determination of what is taught, of what research to engage in, and of what kind of service is important is largely a matter for the faculty to decide, individually or in departments. Are these managerial tasks? If they are not, it appears to be clear that faculty might be considered labor and could, through collective bargaining, exercise some control over their setting and conditions. If, however, these tasks *are* managerial, collective bargaining is not an option. The question has never been fully resolved, despite the U.S. Supreme Court's decision in the case of *NLRB v. Yeshiva University.* In 1980, the majority opinion held that the faculty of Yeshiva University are management and, as such, are ineligible for collective bargaining. If faculty are managers, the means that may be most fruitful to explore is to voice their managerial concerns as members of the formal governance structure. If faculty are managers, their official positions are inherently the same as administrators. Perhaps the obstacles are too great to overcome, but the question remains as to what might be the most effective means of governing colleges and universities.

The above constitutes a dilemma for the official determination of managerial roles and thus lines of governance. It is likely that most faculty do not see themselves as managers. Although faculty do exercise control over their own teaching, research, and service, they do not impose on other faculty to teach or conduct inquiry on certain subjects in certain ways. The view that faculty are managers is a tenuous one. Even the official faculty bodies and groups, such as faculty senates and promotion and tenure committees, generally serve in an advisory capacity but do not have the authority to make and enforce decisions. If we also consider the aspects of organizational culture, discussed in chapter 2, we see further indications that there is a distinction between the roles of faculty and of administrators. Although faculty do live their lives in politically based cultures, these cultures are focused primarily on survival and advancement of the department. Simultaneously, the faculty also live within cognitively based cultures, and these cultures exert the stronger influence on a faculty member's teaching and inquiry. The issue of collegial governance will not go away, but the existence of "professional" administration and faculty reaction to that administrative structure ensure tension into the future. Academic librarians need to be aware of such issues because they may find themselves organizationally allied with either faculty or administrators (or may have some different place in the organization). Librarians, then, will have their own perspective on governance.

OTHER VIEWS OF GOVERNANCE

What has been presented so far has assumed that governance is a matter of rational thinking and practice. However, some are skeptical of that assumption of rationality. Cohen and March have devised the most elaborate conception of this mix of the rational and the nonrational. Their conception is based on the metaphor of "organized anarchy" as a description of higher education. Organized anarchy presents some particular challenges for governance because it is a realization that there are aspects of the environment that are independently influential and not easily controllable. According to Cohen and March, there are three particular properties of the organized anarchy: problematic goals, unclear technology, and fluid participation (1986, 3). They hastened to mention that these properties do not necessarily lead to disorganization, but they do result in a puzzling condition for a college or university. The organization itself is difficult to analyze, or even describe, if we accept that these properties exist.

What, exactly, do the three properties indicate for higher education? Each carries a set of features that, the authors say, are present in many organizations and are common in higher education. "Problematic goals" generally means that there is a fairly loose collection of changing ideas (that have a number of sources); the organization tends to operate according to a variety of inconsistent and ill-defined preferences (for instance, the decision to stress "teaching" as opposed to "research" without a clear definition of the two terms or a clear conception of the similarities or differences of the two); the educational institution discovers preferences through action more than it acts on the basis of preferences (that is, the pragmatics of everyday activity tends to suggest short-term direction or policy); and it is difficult for the institution to establish clear goals when what it wants to do is subject to change (although the overall direction or mission may be fairly stable, the means by which goals are achieved are at least somewhat malleable). "Unclear technology" employs the word "technology" in the broadest sense and implies that colleges and universities do not have a clear understanding of their own processes (or it may be interpreted that understanding is not consistent and does not extend to everyone in the institution); things do tend to get done, but this may occur by trial and error or through imitation of other, like organizations; and there is residual learning from what went wrong in the past or, at times, action is dictated by immediate necessity. "Fluid participation" means that participants, both faculty and administrators, vary in the time and effort expended on the institution (for instance, committees or task forces whose membership changes fairly frequently); and the boundaries that define participation can shift.

To the extent that these factors exist in colleges and universities, there will be uncertainty. The uncertainty is especially evident at the higher administrative levels of the organization because those individuals are charged with instilling or maintaining order. As Cohen and March observed, the anarchistic elements of higher education lead to ambiguity for the president. Specifically, they see four types of ambiguity complicating the president's life: ambiguity of purpose, ambiguity of power, ambiguity of experience, and ambiguity of success (1986, 195–203). These manifestations of ambiguity put the institutional leaders in anomalous positions; the customary conception of management and effectiveness is questioned by the very nature of the educational institution. We have already seen that colleges and universities face particular governance challenges because of the dispersion of decision making and the independence of the principal workers. These factors make higher education quite different from the typical corporation and put the individuals who occupy presidencies in uneasy situations.

Let's take a closer look at the ambiguities faced by the president. Cohen and March said that "Almost any educated person can deliver a lecture entitled 'The Goals of the University'. . . . For the most part, such lectures and their companion essays are well-intentioned exercises in social rhetoric, with little operational content" (1986, 195). The question that suggests itself is whether the stated goals are clear, specific, attainable, acceptable, or problematic. Further, does the observed behavior of those in the organization make it possible to infer goals and objectives? A number of tricky issues surround purpose: behavior of those throughout the institution may or may not be consistent; there is no easy way to determine what motivates behavior; and past behavior is, at best, an imperfect predictor of future behavior. The ambiguity of power that a president faces is the realization that although the person in that office has greater ability to set direction or initiate change than anyone else, he or she has less power than most may think. The power the individual has is dependent, to a considerable extent, on what he or she wants to accomplish. Acceptance of authority is neither automatic nor universal; faculty, for instance, may be skeptical of the person who moves into the office of president because they may believe that person has more affinity with, say, the board than with them. The president can decide little by fiat; negotiation and validation are more often the rule.

Cohen and March said that a simple learning paradigm usually describes how a president adapts on the basis of experience:

1. At a certain point in time a president is presented with a set of well-defined, discrete action alternatives.
2. At any point in time he has a certain probability of choosing any particular alternative (and a certainty of choosing one of them).
3. The president observes the outcome that apparently follows his choice and assesses the outcome in terms of his goals.
4. If the outcome is consistent with his goals, the president increases his probability of choosing that alternative in the future; if not, he decreases the probability (1986, 199).

This model is a rational one. In an anarchy, however, reality can take some non-rational turns. If the president tries to apply a model like the one above, the result may be false learning because experience is bound to be partial and unable to capture the complexity of the phenomena that form the thoughts and activities of a college or university. The president is further subject to the ambiguity of success. One common measure of success is promotion, but this measure becomes increasingly limited when one reaches the level of president. Another measure common to other organizations is the accomplishment of widely accepted operations outputs, such as profits. The measures in higher education, though, are largely imprecise and unstable. For instance, the amount of money appropriated to a state college may have little to do with the president's policies or accomplishments but, instead, may be based on the state's general economic well-being.

Throughout the governance of higher education there is an insistence, usually tacit, on rationality. There is the possibility of rational choice and there should be tools to help ensure rationality. As Birnbaum offered,

> The concepts of the organized anarchy are counterintuitive. They defy the common expectations that are part of the more familiar ideas of organizations as communities, as bureaucracies, or as political systems. To understand them requires suspension of some commonsense ideas about organizations that we "know" are correct— ideas that we have internalized and that are potent enough to filter and distort our perceptions (1988, 153–54).

The insistence on rationality negates the utility of other tools, such as intuition. Given the nonrational aspects of organized anarchy, decisions in colleges and universities follow a "garbage can" model (Cohen and March 1986, 81–82). Inside a metaphorical garbage can swim an array of problems, solutions, participants, and choice opportunities. For one thing, a decision is a product not just of the relevant information, anticipated impact, and so on, but also on the politics of its timing, its affiliation with other issues, and its initial sources of support. (For example, the impact of a particular technological development on a library may present problems related to personnel, finances, and services; solutions may be varied and elusive, and its impact is likely to involve staff from all parts of the library.) Given the obstacles, mentioned by Cohen and March, it seems as though there is nothing a president can do to govern. However, Cohen and March do offer some strategies to overcome the anarchistic tendencies of higher education. These strategies depend on an awareness of the problems and ambiguities that are likely to exist. They include persistence (spending time and energy on those things that are deemed most important and returning to them even after initial resistance), focus on substance (and not letting attention to self-esteem rule behavior), and managing unobtrusively.

Karl Weick offered another conception of higher education that has decided implications for governance issues. His image of the educational organization is as a "loosely coupled system."

> By loose coupling, the author intends to convey the image that cou-
> pled events are responsive, but that each event also preserves its own
> identity and some evidence of its physical or logical separateness.
> Thus, in the case of an educational organization, it may be the case
> that the counselor's office is loosely coupled with the principal's of-
> fice. . . . Loose coupling also carries connotations of impermanence,
> dissolvability, and tacitness all of which are potentially crucial prop-
> erties of the "glue" that holds organizations together (1976, 3).

Although his example is taken from an environment other than higher education, his idea applies equally well to all educational organizations. Also, the notion of loose coupling fits well with organizational culture. Most especially, the
realization that there are multiple cultures and subcultures on a campus leads
to the awareness that there will be multiple, and fluid, opportunities for the
coupling of any of the existing entities.

One example suggests itself immediately. Let's suppose that a university is
going to establish a center for American studies. The first thing that must be
agreed to is a definition of American studies. If we assume that it is an inclusive
concept that embraces, say, history, literature, sociology, and anthropology, we
understand that the various units are going to be coupled in some ways. When
it comes to some very specific purposes, such as budgeting for a central office
or political positioning for the purposes of creating a degree program, there
may be some strong coupling. However, most of the individuals and units involved with the project will be loosely coupled. A faculty number in the history
department may be involved in the center only insofar as particular courses are
listed as highly relevant or some advising of students in the American Studies
program is necessary. The departments themselves may be loosely coupled because no one department may have administrative responsibility for the center
and involvement may be limited to the identification of courses and faculty that
might contribute to the center's effort. The university administration, however,
may take advantage of such loosely coupled systems because they can allow for
flexibility in operation and can be responsive to some specific needs within the
environment.

Weick outlined a set of seven potential advantages that loose coupling may
have for an educational organization:

> Loose coupling lowers the probability that the organization will have
> to—or be able to—respond to each little change in the environment
> that occurs. . . . A second advantage of loose coupling is that it may
> provide a sensitive sensing mechanism. . . . A third function is that a
> loosely coupled system may be a good system for localized adapta-
> tion. . . . Fourth, in loosely coupled systems where the identity,

uniqueness, and separateness of elements is preserved, the system potentially can retain a greater number of mutations and novel solutions than would be the case with a tightly coupled system. . . . Fifth, if there is a breakdown in one portion of a loosely coupled system then this breakdown is sealed off and does not affect other portions of the organization. . . . Sixth, since some of the most important elements in educational organizations are teachers, classrooms, principals, and so forth, it may be consequential that in a loosely coupled system there is more room available for self-determination by the actors. . . . Seventh, a loosely coupled system should be relatively inexpensive to run because it takes time and money to coordinate people (1976, 6–8).

Some of the advantages accrue to the participants, such as the faculty, but some work in favor of the administration. Some advantages, such as the ability to isolate breakdowns to specific areas of the college or university, may indeed be useful to a president or a chancellor.

At the heart of the concept of loosely coupled systems is the admission that organizations such as colleges and universities are inescapably complex. Moreover, absolute control is impossible; there will be attachments that form for particular, and frequently short-lived, purposes and then will dissolve. Sometimes the formation of the attachments will be prompted by administrative will; sometimes that will occur for purposes perceived by the participants themselves; sometimes they will form in opposition to the policy or action of the administration. To an extent, loose coupling occurs because colleges or universities cannot easily be managed at the level of individual activity; there is a lack of detailed coordination and a considerable degree of independence. Both Birnbaum (1988) and Keller (1983) observed that loose coupling may be indicative of a pathological state, that is, of things occurring that were unanticipated or even unwanted. Weick himself is aware of the pathological potential and states that administrators may misunderstand the connection between intention and action. Action may, in fact, precede intentions, which may actually be justifications for action, rather than guiding principles. For this reason, planning may be an overrated activity because the action may proceed independently and loose coupling may be the mechanism used for responding to immediate or short-term needs. In any event, awareness of loose coupling may be, according to Birnbaum and Weick, a means not of correcting pathologies, but of adapting to the unpredictability of an open system: "Effective administration may depend not on overcoming it but on accepting and understanding it" (Birnbaum 1988, 41). "They sensitize the observer to notice and question things that had previously been taken for granted" (Weick 1976, 2).

THE LIBRARY IN THE GOVERNANCE STRUCTURE

There is an easy answer to the question, Where does the library fit into the governance structure of the college or university? The library occupies a formal position analogous to other units on campus. In the two- or four-year colleges, this usually means that the library is essentially the equivalent of a department. In the university, the library is more often the equivalent of the college. The library director not infrequently holds a position equivalent to that of a dean and may even hold the title of dean. The position of the library on a campus is not a trivial matter. At a college, the department chairs may well form, collectively, a governing body. The deans at a university usually comprise a similar body. Within these bodies, some decisions are made regarding academic programs and recommendations that may carry substantial weight are forwarded to the institutional administration. The library director who has a seat on this body will have a voice in the determinations emanating from the group. He or she can advise the other department chairs or deans on matters of library and information resources to support existing and proposed academic programs. The group may decide to speak with one voice when it comes to recommending enhanced resources for the library because their own interests may be dependent on those resources. It should be noted that in instances of potential self-interest, there usually is the need for negotiation and compromise and conflict may arise when individual interests collide.

On most campuses, the library director reports to the chief academic officer (a dean at colleges or a provost or academic vice-president at universities). The more common view is that the library exists to support teaching, learning, and research through its collections and services. Steven Atkins observed,

> Library directors at the large academic libraries are often one of these deans, and at the smaller libraries the director reports to a dean. Either way, the relationship between the library and the university is determined by the relationship of these deans to the library. A "pecking order" is established among these deans through force of personality or by the strength of the dean's department. It is in this pecking order that the library finds itself at risk, because so much depends on the personality of the library director (1991, 108).

In some instances, the library director reports to the chief financial officer. The rationale for this structure may be that the library is unlike academic departments or colleges in that it usually has no students of its own and may not be included in funding formulas. The differences between the library and other academic units are real and must be recognized if a relationship between the library and those units and between library and administration are to be fruitful.

The library has the broadest constituency (the entire campus), but that constituency is secondary. The English department, for instance, has its majors and students enrolled in the courses it offers and, so, has a primary constituency. The library is at least once removed from such a relationship. Kaye Gapen recognized the disparity: "the library director or library dean does not have the responsibility for academic programs and, therefore, is not comparable to the academic dean" (1988, 54). This, she maintained, is so even though there are some important congruencies between the positions of director and dean.

When it comes to governance, there is another distinction between the library and other academic units that tends to be tacitly accepted and potentially schizophrenic. The library is generally the only unit on campus for which there is an extraordinary committee. On most campuses, there is a separately constituted library committee, frequently existing as a faculty senate standing committee, with a membership of faculty that is representative of the campus. Sometimes the library director or his or her designate is a member of the committee; sometimes that individual serves ex officio. When the library is in good standing with the faculty, this committee can be helpful in articulating the needs of the library on the grounds that a strong library contributes to a strong institution. On the other hand, when the library is out of favor, the committee may seek to become involved in internal management issues. In either case, such a committee is unique on college and university campuses; there is no such thing as the chemistry department committee. Nonetheless, it is a reality and, as Atkins observed "Special effort should be given to this committee because it can be a good friend in crisis situations, or a liability if the members have been alienated. Another important function of this committee is that in many institutions it plays an important role in the hiring and firing of library directors" (1991, 111).

SUMMARY

As is evident in table 5.2, support for the library has declined at all types of institutions. Although it is not a comforting realization, support for instruction has seen a similar decline. These data may be taken as signal of the general tenor of governance at the present time. Resource allocation is perhaps the most crucial exercise of governing authority, and the breakdown of allocations is indicative of the fiscal and policy pressures faced by administrators. There is no simple devise that can be used to divine administrative purpose or individual motivation. Volumes could be (and have been) written on the transformation of the presidency over time and of the changes wrought on and embraced in colleges and universities. The constant at the present time is the complexity that

TABLE 5.2   Percentage of Educational and General Expenditures over Time on Academic Libraries, by Type of Institution

	E&G EXPENDITURES	
INSTITUTION TYPE	*1990–91*	*2000–2001*
Public Universities	3.0	3.0
Public 4-Year Colleges	3.1	2.8
Private Institutions	2.4	2.3

Source of Data: National Center for Education Statistics, 2003.

both accompanies and defines the governance of higher education. This complexity can be reflected in the anarchistic or loosely coupled nature of colleges and universities.

Discussion about governance matters can be lively. Here are some questions that might facilitate conversations:

What would be the ideal makeup of the membership of a college or university governing board?

Is there a need for a genuinely professional academic administration, as opposed to the academic training ground most administrators go through?

Would you be willing to serve on a faculty senate? If yes, what would you hope to accomplish?

To what extent do you see Cohen and March's three properties of the organized anarchy at work in higher education?

Does the library director face the same ambiguities that the president does?

If you could set the agenda for your campus's library committee, what would it include?

Chapter 6

The Organization
and Management
of Academic Libraries

For many academic libraries, questions of organization and structure are not particularly pressing. Why? A substantial number of libraries are small. Most two-year college libraries have staffs of just a few people, as do many small four-year college libraries. The small numbers of staff do not mean that the libraries do not provide adequate, or even excellent, services; it is much more often simply a reflection of the size of the institution. For the college library with, say, four professionals and a total staff of nine, there are some limitations regarding choice of organizational structure. There are some choices to be made, however; and one option may well be better than another for a specific library. This chapter looks at the past and then moves on to some variations on traditional modes of organizing. There are some conscious efforts at devising an organizational structure that can enable the library to meet challenges more effectively. The chapter also examines some possibilities that do not necessarily constitute completely different structures but do reflect different ways of thinking about the library's place in the college or university. Management in those various kinds of organizations is not explored in great depth, but some essential managerial features are discussed.

BACKGROUND

Libraries are human organizations and, as such, are subject to the same sorts of influences that many other organizations must deal with. This means that the various schools of management thought that have enjoyed supremacy in the past—scientific management, human relations, systems—have been adopted to some extent by library organizations. There is no need to cover such things as scientific management here; it was introduced in chapter 2.

Some of the thinking that underlies such approaches to organization such as scientific management still pervades libraries. Beverly Lynch observed, "The management literature of librarianship, like the field itself, looks for ways to organize the work in efficient and rational designs. Articles on library economics, cost analysis, personnel planning, job analysis, all reflect that interest in efficiency and cost effectiveness" (1988, 69). If we accept that efficiency and rationality have been—and are—goals of libraries (albeit not the only goals), it seems eminently reasonable that the most common form of organizational structure in libraries has been the hierarchical bureaucracy. This bureaucratic organization became more common a number of decades ago as the size of academic institutions, and their libraries, began to reach magnitudes that seemed to necessitate formal structure. The dictates of scientific management and the influence of Max Weber suggested that bureaucracy would be an organizational form that would allow the kind of control that managers wanted.

As academic libraries grew in size throughout this century, increasing attention was paid to the functions that seemed to define libraries. Libraries were generally organized according to a bifurcated structure. The two functional branches of this structure were public services and technical services. The assumption that accompanied the bifurcation was that the efficient management of an academic library depends on a clear definition of every aspect of the library's work. The relationship between this assumption and scientific management is obvious. Primary attention goes to the elements that comprise each task and then the individual tasks are linked so as to fulfill the goals of each function. One characteristic of the bureaucracy is the containment of a discrete set of tasks within the purview of an office. For some time, academic libraries fit that model well. For instance, the tasks related to cataloging were within the control of the cataloging department. In some libraries, it was not unusual for the tasks and the knowledge and skill that go along with them to be guarded jealously. Sometimes the members of the organizations themselves could perpetuate the sharp lines between departments. Individuals in some libraries tended to view themselves as members of a priesthood that was privy to knowledge that would not, could not, be shared with others. A question may arise at this time: Is such proprietary and exclusionary behavior peculiar to libraries?

The answer to this question has to be a rather emphatic no. Although the example may seem a bit extreme, the structure itself tended to foster the territorial boundaries. (The boundaries would be more than metaphorical; they may have determined use of the library's physical space.) The attributes of library organizations, mentioned above, are common to all, or virtually all, bureaucracies. A bureaucracy tends to be more than merely a system of organizing; it is a shaper of the modes of thought and behavior of those in the organization. Ralph Hummel (1994) argued that bureaucracy creates a way of living for those within it, and this way of living is different socially, culturally, psychologically, linguistically and cognitively, and politically from the rest of life. Hummel's critique of bureaucracy is one of the most complete and most cogent; I will draw substantially from his attack against bureaucracy. Fundamentally, the bureaucracy structures the life and thought of those within it. One purpose of a bureaucracy is to create uniformity. A primary goal is to ensure that the same decision resulting from the same, or largely the same, circumstances is reached regardless of who makes it. Such uniformity is accomplished by the establishment of a set of rules and regulations that are to be followed closely. Individual discretion is limited so that control can be maximized and outcomes can be predicted with considerable accuracy. The duties of the office and the requirements of, and constraints on, the officeholders are as detailed as possible; the objective is to minimize the individuality of behavior by the officeholder.

The rules of the bureaucracy shape not only the way people in the organization think about and react to the work, but also the ways people think about and react to people and things from outside the organization. The ideal is the application of the rules and regulations to all situations. Hummel maintained that this attitude has far-reaching implications for the people who must function in such organizations and that the structure can act to transform people. He wrote,

> Psychologically, bureaucracy rips control over conscience and mastery out of the psyche of the individual bureaucrat and deposits these functions in organizational structures: hierarchy and division of labor. What sense of self is left to the individual comes in terms of organizational identity—what the organization says he or she is—not personality—who a person becomes when left to grow and utilize all of individual psychic potential (1994, 21).

The transformation is related to effects of bureaucracy itself. Hummel provided some specific statements to illustrate how bureaucracy differs from the rest of life in the ways mentioned above. For one thing, bureaucracies tend to be impersonal, so they tend to transfer this impersonal aspect into social interaction with the result that they deal with cases rather than people. The cultural outcome is a focus on control and efficiency, not the myriad emotions and events that typify the richness of culture at large. Bureaucracy alters its members psychologically, insulating them against the people they deal with and making them, in the extreme, heartless and soulless. Bureaucrats structure language and thought according to the impersonal nature of the organization, rendering complete dyadic communication very difficult. Although the ostensible goals of the organization are aimed at service, the actual goals tend to be focused on control and efficiency. The complexity of the psychological element of bureaucracy is very important; we should take care not to reduce the impetus or impact of bureaucracy to simplistic excuses. As David Beetham (1996) pointed out, "to see administrative behaviour (sic) as subject to a constant calculation of self-interest is to overlook what is distinctive about norms of conduct: whether by a process of conscious acceptance or unconscious internalization, they become recognized as valid or binding on the individual, and hence an autonomous determinant of action" (1996, 34).

Given this picture of the bureaucracy, it is not at all surprising that so many writers have inveighed against it. Speaking a bit more practically, it is not surprising that many libraries have sought alternatives to bureaucracy—in rhetoric if not in action. The words of Faleh Alghamdi are typical: "Bureaucracy with its mechanistic approach is no longer accepted. . . . The problems associated with bureaucracy and its classical principles as a dominant form of governance indicate to us that another organizational model ought to be sought" (1994, 15–16). It would be a mistake to think that because more attention is being paid now to organizational alternatives, bureaucracy is dead. We should now turn to the present to see what the state of organization is.

THE RECENT PAST AND THE PRESENT

Although bureaucracy and hierarchy do not always co-occur, it should be noted, as indicated above, that bureaucracies have not disappeared. Many libraries are still organized along traditional hierarchical lines. In some instances, the hierarchy has expanded a bit from the customary bifurcation that has typified libraries for a number of decades. In addition to the division by public and technical services, some libraries have added such functions as collection management, automation (or some designation based on the use of technology), personnel, finance, and others. The organization's structure, even with these additions, is still frequently bureaucratic. The typical organizational chart illustrates specific lines of authority and decision making and, implicitly, communication. Most human communication centers on the construction of meaning, with two or more individuals engaged in the use of language to establish a shared context in which meaning can be constructed. Hummel maintains that bureaucratic communication is not genuine communication in the above sense; rather, it is more often the structuring of meaning by one source (usually at the top end of the bureaucracy) and the imposition of that meaning on others in the organization. For this reason, Hummel says that bureaucracies involve exchanges of information, rather than communication.

Hummel offered an illustration of his point by borrowing Herbert Simon's observation that bureaucracies consist of frozen decisions.

> In other words, the office of the sales manager in a vacuum cleaner
> company is set up to perpetuate the decision that whenever a cus-
> tomer comes in to buy a vacuum cleaner there will be adequate sales
> staff to effect the sale. Setting up this structure once—the structure of
> the sales manager's office—for all time hence, or until another deci-
> sion is made, obviates the need to have unqualified and ill-informed
> personnel run around, when a customer comes, searching desper-
> ately for vacuum cleaners, price lists, and the proper procedures for
> recording the sale so that inventory can be brought up to date, new
> machines ordered, and so on. In this sense, the office structure is not
> simply one frozen decision—the decision to sell—but many frozen
> decisions: on how to sell, what price to ask, how and when to reorder
> (1994, 171).

It does not require a large leap to see that similar kinds of "frozen decisions" are integral to academic libraries. The acquisition of materials depends on preordained sets of procedures so that orders can be placed, materials can be received, and, eventually, things can be made available to users. These kinds of frozen decisions are essential. However, we should question whether all library functions or events should be subjected to such information without communication. It is the absence of communication that is at the heart of many criticisms of bureaucracy.

Much of the information in formal organizations (such as libraries) that have fundamentally bureaucratic structures is written rather than spoken. Memos, frequently in the form of directives, are issued from one of the upper tiers of the hierarchy and disseminated to lower tiers. Many memoranda are written so that no response is necessary; that is, the memo is intended as one-way communication. At times, the questions that might be raised by memos go unasked, because the unidirectional nature of the information suggests that questioning should not be necessary and probably will not be welcomed. Even when these assumptions are incorrect from the viewpoint of the writer of the memo, the nature of the form of communication, combined with the structure of the bureaucracy, sends messages to the recipient of the memo. Those messages may indicate that the memo is not the imitation of a dialogue. Much of management literature, emanating from LIS or from other disciplines, speaks against the limitations to communication within bureaucracies. This literature includes observations on the dissatisfaction with the communication mechanism, the lack of clarity that can result from unidirectional communication, and the time that is sometimes required to interpret information and to correct misinterpretations. All of this notwithstanding, many academic libraries embrace bureaucratic structure.

Fundamentally, some academic library directors may focus on the efficiency of the organization. Bureaucracy is a representation of the effort to enhance efficiency through the simplification offered by established rules and regulations and "frozen decisions." The promise that bureaucracy appears to offer is attractive. If bureaucratic organization precluded all possible individual autonomy and flexibility, it would not have survived this long. What we have been talking about here is an extreme and dysfunctional type of bureaucracy that is, unfortunately, possible in part because of the structure of bureaucracy. The focus on efficiency may not ensure the longevity of bureaucratic structure in academic libraries, but it does suggest that some elements of bureaucracy, such as establishment of regulations and simplification of the flow of information, may well endure. They are likely to endure because the organization provides a structural means for decisions to be made (not an unimportant matter). Although there is no necessary link between technology and bureaucracy, the connection of the two is not infrequent. Lynch articulated the connection: "As to the impact of technology on library organization, libraries as organizations will continue to seek ways to become more efficient. How the technology will influence that drive or quest for efficiency will be important" (1988, 76). The problems with bureaucratic organization, some of which are discussed here, are substantial enough that some people have sought alternative structures.

Charles Townley observed that "even though many librarians have come to accept reasons for change and to espouse different organization structures, few library organizations have been redesigned. Most academic libraries continue to use bureaucratic structures to carry out their mission" (1995, 149). He further stated that one possible reason for the adherence to familiar structural models is the inexperience of most librarians in devising some organizational design that may increase library effectiveness. This is a somewhat different view from the one focused on efficiency. The most efficient structure, from an internal perspective, may not result in the most effective service to the library's community. Reorganization based on effectiveness may well lead the library away from the bureaucratic model, especially if it can be accepted that the bureaucracy is not conducive to open communication and may not be sufficiently responsive to user needs. If such reorganization is attempted, it is important to keep foremost in mind the core mission of the library and its reason for being.

One alternative to bureaucracy, or possible complement or addition to bureaucracy, is a collegial structure. In the past, this form of structure has been related to academic status for librarians. In fact, in the 2001 ACRL "Standards for

Faculty Status for College and University Librarians," it is stated that "College and University libraries should adopt an academic form of governance similar in manner and structure to other faculties on the campus" (ACRL 2001). Beyond the issue of status, there are few organizational reasons offered in the standards for a move to a collegial structure. This is not to say that there may not be reasons for a library to adopt such a structure. Alghamdi detailed the characteristics of the collegial structure; they include mutual respect and equality of power, group decision making, and peer evaluation (1994, 17). He went on to point out both the strengths and weaknesses of collegiality.

A couple of the weaknesses are worth mentioning. Decisions made by groups present the problem of determining responsibility. This should not be confused with ascribing blame; rather, the group process can make it difficult to chronicle the rationales or justifications for decisions and it can be difficult to make corrections or emendations to decisions or actions taken. Another potential weakness is that a collegial model can require a considerable amount of time. This can be particularly true if consensus is required for decisions. The most important lesson to take from the discussion of collegial structure is the same lesson we can learn from the focus on organizational culture. There is no prescription for the ideal organizational model. The most appropriate structure for a library depends on the mission of the institution, the culture of the institution, the purpose of the library, and the library personnel. Another factor to be considered is the size of the library. There are some constraints on a staff's ability to discuss issues and to make decisions in a timely manner.

Even without adopting a collegial structure, some libraries have sought ways to flatten their organizations. This is not a new trend, but it is surely an ongoing and dynamic transformation. The change is spurred by an altered vision of the purpose of the library. This vision emphasizes that, as emerging information technologies have been incorporated, the library is less an archive and more an organism. This means that there is a heightened awareness that the library does not consist of autonomous parts but, rather, of interdependent and living parts. Those libraries that exhibit commitment to change and to a different vision, in eschewing bureaucracy, accept an alternative to the aim of control that comes with clear differentiation of tasks. Such libraries tend to be characterized by a genuine focus on their purpose rather than on their inner workings. The purpose is usually expressed in terms of use and users. Hummel anticipated the difference between the bureaucracy and the changed library in terms of the relationships that form an integral part of organizational structure. In the bureaucracy, relationships may be one-sided; the manager defines the work and the means by which it is accomplished, while the worker is supposed to orient him- or herself to the manager and to following the rules and guidelines set down by management. The changed organization is oriented on the basis of social interaction, interaction that recognizes the "reciprocity of relationship based on authenticity of both members of the dyad and of mutual orientation" (Hummel 1994, 58). This social interaction imbues the organization and characterizes the relationships of its members. It also characterizes the relationship between those inside and those outside the organization.

One example of a library's effort at emphasizing social interaction and eschewing potentially negative effects of bureaucracy is the organizational change at the Harvard College Library. Part of the change has been to flatten the organization, to impel a move from isolated work to an integrated approach, to emphasize the work of the whole organization and the contribution of collaborative effort, and to encourage individual autonomy, rather than excessive central control (Lee 1993, 227–28). It is possible that larger academic libraries can tend to rely on inertia and to continue existing organizational structure because of the momentum that such a structure has built up over time. The inertia can be tacitly encouraged by the traditions and, frequently, the resistance to change of the parent organization. The kind of change articulated at Harvard does not come about by accident. It has to be a conscious decision founded on a planning initiative that begins by looking closely at the essential purpose of the organization. Harvard began its change effort by revising its mission statement. One passage from that statement captures most effectively the altered perspective that the Harvard College Library vision embraces: "The College Library will pursue a deliberate strategy of identifying and satisfying user needs. Information services will be tailored to meet differing instructional and research needs" (Lee 1993, 227). It is certainly true that for effective change to be realized, the vision must inform not only all further organizational statements, but also the actions of the organization's members. In other words, for change to come about, the library must practice what it preaches. As Townley stated, change necessitates action and is not itself a static, or even a linear, phenomenon: "Some aspects of a new organizational structure will not be quite right. New reasons for change will emerge. New structural options will arise. And at some point in the future, incremental adjustments will not suffice to make the library responsive to reasons for change that it must address. At that time, organizational design becomes appropriate once again" (1995, 162).

CHANGE: THE TEAM-BASED MODEL

James Neal and Patricia Steele observed that the organizational structure in place in many academic libraries at the present time have been unchanged for the better part of the last three decades (1993, 81). Their observation may be dated; most of the world around those libraries (for instance, their own campuses, the system of scholarly communication, the economics of information) have undergone change, including changes wrought by technology. The changes in those other areas necessitate revisiting the libraries' organizational structures. As illustrated in the preceding section, the efforts of the recent past have been aimed at eliminating some of the more negative elements of bureaucracy. The strategies employed have been principally the flattening of the organization. At this time, some libraries are looking at more sweeping changes to their structures. Neal and Steele enumerated some important principles that inform libraries', especially larger libraries', thinking with regard to structural change. One of the principles they included is the need for organizational flexibility so that the library can respond more quickly and effectively to the environment in which they exist. A couple of the other principles they mentioned are portentous for reorganization: "Work is increasingly accomplished through project teams, and research library organizations must reflect this clear matrix-oriented style," and "Small-group collaboration is essential to real and effective empowerment. The organization must promote and support unit-level and inter-unit discussion of improvements to increase the effectiveness and efficiency of services and operations" (1993, 83–84). Again, technology, such as Web-based information, both influences the responses to change and enables libraries to enact change.

The library that has probably been the first to take the team concept to a pervasive extent is that of the University of Arizona. Members of the library staff report that the effort at reorganization was prompted in part by the arrival of Carla Stoffle as dean of libraries, but also that "An assessment of changing factors in the environment (rising serial prices, a pattern of yearly budget cuts, the implementation of an integrated library system, etc.) was leading us to rethink how our services and work processes were organized" (Giesecke 1994, 196). They further report that all staff were urged to participate in the examination and deliberations and that Susan Jurow, from the ARL, facilitated a workshop aimed at self study. The result is the abandonment of traditional hierarchy and traditional departments. Throughout the process, which was not quick or cursory, the librarians worked at clarifying the library's purpose and vision and aimed at keeping the redefined purpose before them as restructuring proceeded. The staff described the results of the process:

> The chart is now very flat. All teams report directly to the dean. Each team is organized with a specified customer orientation, e.g., a discipline focus or a general customer. The assistant deans are staff positions in support of a specific function or activity, e.g., Human Resources and Finance Systems or Team Facilitation. The actual chart shows the dean at the bottom in a support role for the organization.

The Library Faculty Assembly and the Staff Governance Association have representation on the leadership group, the dean's cabinet, which also consists of team leaders (eight), assistant deans, and the Assistant to the Dean for Staff Development, Diversity and Recruitment (Giesecke 1994, 198).

More recently, representatives of the University of Arizona reported that the early stages of reorganization into teams led to some confusion and duplication of effort. These difficulties were addressed as soon as they were recognized, and the flexible response to, and efforts directed at, change remain the benefits observed with the structure (Diaz and Pintozzi 1999). Although not numerous, there are a few dissenters when it comes to team-based organization. The most articulate is Phillip Jones (2000), who questions where accountability may reside in a team structure and the role of the director in assessing the work of teams (wondering, in particular, if a director who holds ultimate decision-making ability actually vests the team with any real authority).

The team structure, where implemented, is most likely to be implemented in larger libraries, where the existence of teams make sense within the complexities of the large organization and the context of the larger staff that can be focused around team-based criteria. However, the imperative of staff participation, which is central to the success of a team structure, can become an integral part of smaller organizations. In recent years, the emphasis on an orientation aimed at library users has prompted the search for means outside librarianship that might be borrowed from in an effort to explore the structural implications of such an emphasis. The literature on academic libraries in recent years was rife with articles on total quality management (TQM). Attention to TQM is not limited to libraries; colleges and universities in general have turned to TQM in the hope that it will provide the tactics needed to accomplish the institution's strategic plan. The team approach, as embodied at the University of Arizona, is not necessarily an application of TQM, but the principles that guide a team structure tend to be common to most definitions of TQM.

As is mentioned above, TQM incorporates evaluation into the entirety of the workings of the library. TQM is seldom mentioned any longer in our, or in other, literatures, but some of the basic tenets just expressed endure in some form. For example, many who have written on TQM have asserted that the evaluation of an organization should be quantitative in nature, so as to facilitate comparison of a library with other libraries and with itself over time. Some of the quantitative measures of a library are statistics related to inputs, such as volume count, volumes added, expenditures, staff size, and so on. These are not useless measures; they can be used to analyze the effects of decisions that have been made in the library. For instance, if, over time, analysis shows that a library has had a constant number of serial subscriptions, but payment for those subscriptions have become a larger portion of the library's materials budget, there is an indication of the decided, or assumed, importance of maintaining subscriptions to those serials. In itself, such a measure is not very telling, but viewed in conjunction with an examination of budget decisions and deliberations regarding user needs, these data can help in reaching an understanding of the library's practice as it relates to stated purpose or user opinion. On the other hand, some quantitative measures deal with outputs, such as items circulated, reference questions answered, and so on. Although some count can be attached to those things, the counts may be artificial. For instance, keeping track of turnstile count, the daily number of people entering the library, contributes little to an understanding of the reasons people have for coming into the library, much less the effectiveness of the library's services and collection.

There is no doubt that evaluation is challenging, especially because many of the activities that take place in the library are of an intellectual nature and thus not readily amenable to quantitative measure. Some have tried to face this challenge and suggest ways that the library and its services and collections can be evaluated. *Measuring Academic Library Performance* is such an attempt. However, the primary focus of this manual is on outputs such as those described above. For instance, most of the measures the authors advocate using are relatively easily quantifiable: materials availability and use, including circulation, in-library materials use, total uses, facilities use rate, service point use, and building use; and information services, including reference transactions (Van House, Weil, and McClure 1990, 5). The three measures that depend on user assessment are reference satisfaction, online search evaluation, and general satisfaction. However, there are some problems with the approach to assessment advocated by this manual. For one thing, satisfaction is based in part on user reports of success. Success, however, is not defined and, in fact, is a complex phenomenon that may not yield a binary assessment (e.g., satisfied–unsatisfied). For another thing, the measures tend to be instrumental; that is, the measures are assumed to be instruments of user behavior and correspond to the thoughts and deliberations that underlie action. This is a questionable assumption at best. In operational terms, this drawback can be seen as a library being managed so as to maximize these quantitative outputs. It is an open question whether such a management practice leads to an increase in effectiveness. A more recent means of assessment centers on use of the balanced scorecard. This method focuses on four areas: users, finances, internal processes, and the future. Although it attempts to assess outcomes to some extent, some instrumental measures are still used (Self 2003).

Effectiveness could, conceivably, be a measure of efficiency, according to goals some libraries might set for themselves. In fact, efficiency is the primary goal for academic libraries, or so said Malcolm Getz. He said, "The 'better' library yields services that are more valuable than they cost, indeed, as much more valuable as possible" (1990, 194). He then urged libraries to measure what he calls outcomes, but which are, in reality, the kinds of outputs listed in the manual. Getz's approach is little removed from scientific management, as it was defined in a previous chapter. He assumed that all of the pertinent variables could be assigned quantitative values and that those values represented qualitative outcomes. As is true of *Measuring Academic Library Performance,* important concepts such as "success" in information retrieval go undefined. He further assumed, and portrayed graphically, that those complex variables are linear functions—as one ill-defined variable "increases," another may "decrease" proportionally. Underlying all of Getz's work is his particular notion of analysis, which "means the careful examination of cause and effect relationships" (1990, 192). Human behavior does not frequently have a single ascribable cause, though, and the quest for that elusive cause may be ill-advised.

The equation of quality in the private sector with quality in libraries can become a pervasive rhetorical device. In the corporate context, defining the customer base is essential to survival, especially because that customer base is likely to be a specifically targeted subset of the population. Not all drivers want to own a minivan; the automaker must understand the characteristics of consumers who want features that comprise the minivan. Who are the customers of the academic library? The answer is inevitably the academic community, or in other words, the entire population of the college or university. Why is the "customer" base so large? For one thing, the library's "product" is not so narrow as a minivan, or even a particular subject area or a single kind of service. The library world at large has a long commitment to egalitarian and universal service. The rhetorical device, however, suggests that customers can be identified in some ways, according to the same criteria, regardless of the organization or its purpose. Such rhetoric can lead many to think that academic libraries are no different from businesses. It can lead to the kinds of statements that Christopher Millson-Martula and Vanaja Menon made: "With the development of the online catalog, customers experienced a faster, easier, and more efficient method of searching" (1995, 33). Although faster, easier searching is no doubt evident but not necessarily universal. Moreover, the population that uses the academic library exhibits different, sometimes contradictory, needs. For instance, undergraduate students would prefer multiple copies of those items that are most frequently assigned, whereas faculty may want specialized, esoteric materials that only a single individual may use. Who is the customer then?

Irene Hoadley recognized the rhetorical dissonance created by the word "customer." She wrote, "Without question libraries provide some services that are purchased by patrons. But, to the best of my knowledge, the large majority of library services are provided without a direct cost to the user" (1995, 175). Perhaps the thing to be most wary of is the influence that language and its use has on thought. When a certain vocabulary is adopted, thinking may well follow. To focus on the negative for just a moment, usurping the language of another source can have at least two effects: there can be the tendency to see things in terms of the vocabulary adopted (in this case, to see all library users as customers who are to be sold some product); and the language used can become empty and devoid of meaning (Budd 1997). In the latter instance, the only concession is to the terminology itself, without any necessary improvement to service. Especially with the rhetoric of customer service, it may be forgotten that the academic library does not serve the same need as a retail outlet, in terms of either the users' needs or the library's services and collections. All this is certainly not to imply that libraries and the business world are absolutely distinct. Allen Veaner expressed the problem and the potential very well: "I am very critical of business management derivatives—they tend to be deterministic, highly reductive, and transient. But I do not suggest we cannot learn from business and industry or should not apply appropriate business techniques to managing academic libraries. The key is in the words appropriate and proper" (1994, 398). Problems with the idea of "customer" are not limited to librarianship. Within the public administration sphere, Lisa Zanetti and Guy Adams observed that the "movement toward commodification means that phenomena that were formerly outside the market acquire economic-use values. . . . Viewing citizens as consumers/customers/clients of government exacerbates a rights mentality, and continues an assumption that citizens can only be motivated by self-interest" (2000, 544–45).

The emphasis on users is not brand new to academic libraries. In 1983, Charles Martell published *The Client-Centered Academic Library*. In that work, he pinpointed the heart of the problem: "In theory, the academic library is sensitive and responsive to changing client needs for information. In practice, the library is relatively insensitive and unresponsive to these needs" (1983, 22). The book also illustrates one of the potential pitfalls of an orientation ostensibly aimed at users and their needs. Martell's focus was predominantly on the organizational structure of the academic library and the work of the academic librarian. As stated earlier, there are many occasions when the user's need is elusive and meeting that need is problematic. Martell did not address such a dilemma, which does not mean that his book has no value. At some point, librarians must address the structural means of responding to their users. Prior to that, though, any notion of quality has to center on all elements of the user as he or she approaches the complex world of information from some content-based and contextual structure. The content focus of a user's need is not always fully understood by the user. It is not unusual for students, and even faculty, to turn to the library, and sometimes to librarians, out of a rather dim awareness of absence, that is, out of a sense that there is something they don't know and they are not at all certain what it is. Quality service and quality system design includes a recognition that their need is elusive and some means—partly cognitive, partly affective, partly structural—must be employed to meet the need. Success is not simply a measure of items circulated or reference transactions completed. Because success is not easy to define, evaluation is not easy to measure. I am not advocating the dismissal of output measures, but I am suggesting that *outcomes* are not the same as outputs.

The most recent effort (on a large scale) to assess quality of services and other elements of libraries is LibQUAL+™. Building on earlier and broader tools, LibQUAL+™ is intended to be a mechanism for listening to the library's communities. It encompasses measure of total quality as well as for subdivisions of users' perceptions: service affect (such as willingness to help); the library as place; personal control (including the library's Web site constructed to enable unassisted location of information); and information access (convenient hours, among other things) (Cook, Heath, and Thompson 2003, 114). As part of their inquiry into the results of applications of LibQUAL+™, Cook, Heath, and Thompson found that the subdivisions "service affect" and "personal control" are rated as most important by users of all types and across institutional categories (2003, 117). The intention of the tool is ultimately the provision of a large database of assessments so that a library can measure and track its own performance and compare it with the performance of other libraries.

OTHER MODELS

These are not so much variant organizational structures as they are models for organizational purpose or initiative. In some cases, these models have implications for structure but do not necessarily preclude, say, a team approach. An internal team orientation can still function, even though there are differences in the library's stance relative to the rest of the institution and to the college or university community. These suggestions represent some possible ways (and the models presented here do not constitute an exhaustive list of possibilities) of envisioning the ways the library might serve the institution. Further, these models are not mutually exclusive; it is conceivable that they could be employed in combination on some campuses. It is essential that the library staff of any college or university devise the structure that has the potential to work best given that institution's culture, mission, student body, and personnel. The structure selected for a particular organization will inevitably and necessarily incorporate current, and try to anticipate future, technologies in its development.

The Institutional Information Model

The library in this model is one component in the entire institutional information environment. In this conception there are some fairly obvious potential partners. I should hasten to add that, though partnership may be possible or even desirable, there may be obstacles to a full partnership among institutional units. Political concerns, as well as cultural incompatibilities, may prevent successful partnering. At least initially, the potential problems should not prevent the exploration of cooperation between the library and some other campus units. Such units include institutional records and archives, instructional media of various types, and campus computing. Robert Hayes presented some of the arguments in favor of strong cooperation among information enterprises:

> There are some good arguments for any of these alternative (sic) and perhaps others. On the one hand, establishing an information czar would be consistent with the view that information resources are essentially substitutable for each other. Placing computing and libraries under one manager makes good sense if the perception is that electronic means for information distribution will become the dominant form in the future. Merging various kinds of libraries and archives makes sense if one looks only at the similarities among media. Indeed, several universities have accepted this view and established positions for vice president for libraries and information resources, chief information officer, or similar titles (1993, 62–63).

Hayes was speaking specifically about a formal merger of units, with a recreated organizational structure and one person with ultimate responsibility for decision making. He observed that a merger of this sort would more likely be characteristic of institutions with an established hierarchical structure. He also saw some points against a merger:

> First, the different kinds of information resources require different kinds of management and technical expertise; there is no reason, in principle, to expect that one person will be sufficiently expert in each of them. Second, most information facilities, the library and the central computing facility among them, are already major bureaucracies; there is no reason to expect that there would be returns to scale in combining them. Third, most of the information resources are closely tied to specific academic programs, and the political and operational problems that would be created by combining them in some overall agency far outweigh the advantages to be gained from doing so. Fourth, the acquisition budget of the library must be carefully protected from

a wide range of forces that would dissipate it; if the library were to be combined with data archives, film archives, media centers, and the wide range of other resource-acquiring agencies, the result would be a dramatic increase in those pressures (1993, 63).

Hayes is certainly correct that such a mega-unit would be extremely difficult to manage and direct given the diversity of purposes of the subunits. It could create an organizational black hole, with resources sinking into the information unit, but few effective services coming out.

On the other hand, cooperation among a campus's information enterprises need not result in a formal structural merger. On some campuses, the library and the computing center and the institutional records office do not communicate with one another in any regular, purposeful way. The lack of communication is unlikely to result in a linking or sharing of technical, organizational, or mediation expertise. It is unproductive for the computing center and the library to think that one does not have anything to learn from the other. Sheila Creth (1993) explored some of the possible benefits of library–computing center cooperation, cooperation that does not necessarily involve the surrender of organizational autonomy for either. These two units could collaborate on a campus information policy, addressing issues such as technical compatibility of information systems, widespread access to electronic information from a variety of sources, and equitable availability of connections and services. They could join together to support curriculum development, including incorporating information into the physical classroom. They could jointly devise tools to teach students and faculty about information technology (for instance, classes to instruct in the accessibility of networked information). They could work on large-scale initiatives such as institutional electronic publishing, converging with institutional administration and the university's press (if it has one) to transform the scholarly communication network. Richard Dougherty and Lisa McClure (1997) reminded us that unifying information services on any campus is a formidable task; libraries and campus computing are complex organizations that are likely to have unique cultures and their own ideas of service.

As we can see, the possibilities can be attractive and need not entail subordination of one unit to the other. As information technology becomes more pervasive in instruction and research, the absence of a collaborative model could have deleterious effects on effective teaching, learning, and inquiry. We should remember that collaboration is not a quick fix to complex information challenges. No matter what technology is used to produce, store, or retrieve information, some deeper access and organizational issues can be persistent. This means that the campus cannot look to more widespread technology or technical access as a replacement for careful planning. The planning necessary involves curricular development, the content of what is taught, students' learning of substantive matters, and the purposes of scholarly communication. Discussion of these matters can be informed by technological possibilities but is still dependent on pedagogical purpose and creativity of inquiry.

The Unbounded Model

This model has metaphorical significance, but it also has practical significance. The metaphor that may spring to mind is that of the "library without walls." There is the stubborn notion of the library as a warehouse or a repository. This notion is more common outside the library, but some librarians adhere to it as well. I would suggest that the idea of a library without walls is not completely appropriate to the needs of faculty and students on a college or university campus. Perhaps a more appropriate conception would be a "library transcending walls." Although it is not as catchy a phrase (perhaps "gateway" would be more palatable), this expression incorporates the traditional collection, which suits many needs very well, along with other ways of providing information to users. Also, this metaphor necessitates the realization that information defies the limitation of any one medium and that we should not be constrained by any one means of delivery. Current thinking frequently interprets this realization as an assertion that print is inadequate and digitization is the solution to all information needs. Such an interpretation ignores content and the match of content and use with medium. Full realization of the unbounded model means that librarians and libraries are not limited to a single means of service provision but are responsible to the academic community to devise a convergent service structure that brings together the information (in the most effective format) and the user.

This model does not necessarily imply a distinct organizational structure, but it does mean that the library must be a flexible organization able to respond to members of the academic community on the basis of the nature of individual need. It is definitely a user-based model, with all of the concerns that accompany rhetorical expressions of quality. The unbounded model recognizes that users and content are elements of a complex fluid in motion. This, of course, is another metaphor, employed here to convey the fact that the user population, the students and faculty, are unpredictably diverse within certain constrained limits. The limits are defined best by the curriculum, the institution's mission, the body of available information, and the faculty's research activities. Within these limits, a finite, but extremely large, number of possible requests may be made of the library. Users and content attach to one another, then detach, then reattach in different configurations. In sum, the use of information is effectively unbounded.

Given that use is unbounded, the media should be unbounded as well. This means that electronic, as well as print, media can be effective for use. Electronic information has qualities that can, in many instances, emphasize unbounded use. Michael Buckland enumerated some of the qualities of electronic information (and although his observations were made some years ago, we should still keep them in mind):

1. Electronic documents are not localized. . . .
2. In practice several people can use the same database or electronic records at the same time.
3. Electronic documents are easily copied.
4. Documents stored electronically are very flexible. They are easy to revise, rearrange, reformat, and combine with other documents. . . .
5. Collections of documents stored in electronic form are now less bulky than paper version (1992, 43).

It is tempting to use this list to compare electronic with print media. Such a comparison should only be reflective of the nature of particular need and should be an evaluative tool only be the standards of that tool. The unbounded model needs to extend, perhaps even transcend, Buckland's list. As electronic information has begun to mature, its differences with print-based information are starker. An additional list might accompany Buckland's:

1. Electronic information is not stable; it can change over time and the changes can be wrought by many individuals or entities, not just by the author.
2. Electronic information incorporates all possible media (text, audio, video, etc.).
3. Access to electronic information is not as readily controllable by a single source, such as a library, or even a publisher.
4. Electronic information necessitates a different access structure.

One organizational alternative necessitated by the unbounded model is that the conception of collection must be fluid (according to the usage of fluidity exemplified by the above discussion). This does not mean that traditional notions of the library's collection disappear but, rather, that they form part of the set of possibilities that can best meet users' needs. In some cases, users want and need a personal interaction with a physical collection; at other times, they need specific bits of information and, essentially, means of delivery is one expression of an unbounded service. A traditional version of document delivery is interlibrary loan (ILL), but the service is broader than only ILL. In fact, to be consistent with the unbounded model, the service probably should be renamed information delivery. The most important organizational aspect of this service is the fact that it is frequently a mediated service; that is, the librarians work with the user to fulfill a need. Information delivery implies ILL, or use of commercial document delivery systems, or electronic communication between librarians and users, or any structure whereby people have fairly explicit needs and have them met.

I just mentioned that in this model the librarian works with the user. If the library is to break down physical bounds, the library staff has to be aware of constraints and opportunities presented by information sources other than traditional collections. For one thing, librarians have to realize the importance of the communication process (which, of course, is integral to all user-based services) to the success of any services that depend on bibliographic or other access. In the unbounded model, the librarian's role of selector may be lessened, but there is likely to be added pressure on librarians to understand and communicate about the structure of information and access mechanisms. Such a model forces us to examine information environments and user needs that may be separate from what is most familiar to us.

The Education/Research Consultant Model

The preceding two conceptions suggested ways of looking at academic library service center on the structure of information, particularly as it may exist in an academic institution. This conception focuses more on what the librarian can add to the instruction and research of the campus. It also is less dependent on technology or collection for identity. In it, the librarian is in partnership with faculty with the principal purpose being the enhancement of learning and the furthering of inquiry. Partnership of this kind is quite natural, but only if certain barriers can be broken down. It cannot succeed without full recognition of the potential contributions of librarians to teaching and research. By the same token, it cannot succeed if librarians do not accept responsibility for those features of the educational enterprise.

Conceivably, the librarian and the faculty member can be partners in the instructional process. Perhaps the most reasonable way to accomplish the partnership is to focus attention on freshmen. Those entering the college or university are the ones who most need exposure to the complexity of the academic experience. Not only are entering freshmen unlikely to be aware of the depth and breadth of the information base, but they also are usually unaccustomed to taking a critical approach to their own educations. They have to be acculturated into the cognitive aspects of academe before they can adopt a stance of questioning and discovery. The faculty, along with the librarians, can open students up to inquisitiveness and exploration of the accompanying record of accumulated knowledge. When freshmen are used to inquiring, rather than constantly being told, they may be in a better position to investigate the subject matters of their major fields of study. Of course, that point in their educational careers presents another opportunity for the faculty–librarian collaboration to add depth to the students' experiences. At that stage of their academic careers, they have the necessity, and perhaps the desire, to move beyond the surface and to engage in more complicated inquiry. The partnership may aim at integrating the existing body of knowledge into the presentation in the classroom and the work of the students.

Openness on the parts of all individuals also is key to the faculty–librarians partnership in research. It may be that the partnership does not necessarily express itself in actual collaboration on formal research projects (although that is certainly possible wherever individual interests and abilities mesh). Instead, the librarian may indeed assist through some sort of consulting role. The faculty member may well be very familiar with a body of knowledge relevant to specific questions. The information base is widely dispersed, even though a few journals may have some highly relevant materials. A librarian, especially one familiar with the subject area the faculty member is working in, may have sufficient knowledge of the language of the subject to explore more fully the literature that touches on it. Also, much of the inquiry engaged in by faculty is of a multidisciplinary nature. The faculty member may be expert in one aspect of the project but may be a student regarding other aspects. In such instances, he or she may seek out a librarian with different, but complementary, expertise in order to learn more about the body of knowledge in related fields. Their partnership can enrich not only their own work, but also the product of inquiry.

The consultant model means that librarians are, at minimum, liaisons between the information base and the faculty. This model has at least two implications for librarians and the library. The librarians are going to be challenged by the liaison work. They have to be willing to increase their knowledge in certain academic disciplines in order to understand the kinds and purposes of inquiry engaged in by faculty. They also will have to struggle to persuade some faculty of the benefits of partnership. Some individuals will be open to the possibilities for teaching and research; others will be resistant, perhaps thinking that they have a proprietary claim on the knowledge base of the discipline by virtue of their academic appointment. Some faculty will never accept librarians as partners; the librarians may have to concentrate their efforts on those faculty who can see benefits to their own work by teaming in some way with librarians. The challenge for the library that would like to incorporate this model into its operation is to recruit librarians with knowledge that can be pertinent to partnerships with faculty and with an understanding of the value of a partnership.

Moreover, the library may have to make a commitment to provide staff members with the wherewithal to enhance their knowledge bases. It is a major commitment, but the success of the consultant model would be in jeopardy without it. The minimal level of passive liaison, however, is unlikely to enhance learning and inquiry on a college or university campus. The limitation of passivity is recognized by Donald Frank and colleagues: "Librarians must aggressively customize, filter, synthesize, and market information for students, scholars, and administrators. . . . Consultants customize and personalize information services, adding value in the process, and facilitating collaborative efforts to transform information into knowledge" (2001, 95).

A particular strategy for realizing the consultant model has emerged in recent years. On several campuses of all sizes and types, a specific environment has been created that frequently goes by the name "information commons." The idea of information commons can be described quite explicitly, as is the case with the University of Toronto:

> We propose that the Information Commons have a front help desk serving as a single point of contact for information technology support, supported by specialized support desks and electronic printed resource guides. . . . The front help desk should be accessible by telephone, e-mail, and the World Wide Web. . . . We envision the Information Commons as a highly visible and easily accessed place staffed by librarians, research assistants, and technology experts, where students, faculty, researchers, and staff can come to find out about information technology, to learn how to make use of it, and to actually use and develop appropriate tools to retrieve and manipulate information (Biderman, n.p., quoted in Beagle 1999, 85).

Not all conceptions of an information commons focus so strongly on information technology, but ease of access and community space are consistent elements. Sometimes the undergraduate library is seen to evolve into a commons space where all technologies are available in an open environment that invites collaboration by information seekers and unifies services designed to meet educational and research needs. (See "The Fate of the Undergraduate Library" 2000). Donald Beagle (1999) used the word "consultant" to illustrate the potential of an information commons to meet the multitiered needs of all information seekers. A recent review of several implementations of information commons, as well as a substantive assessment of the strengths and weaknesses of the model, should be consulted for a clearer picture of this popular idea (MacWhinnie 2003). The instructional role of the library is central to this model; more is said about instruction in a later chapter.

MANAGEMENT ISSUES

The organizational and operational models discussed so far depend on management support for their success. First, there has to be a vision behind any move away from the traditional bureaucracy; the director has to see the efficacy of some other organizational approach if any transformation is to occur. Many things occur in libraries without the director's personal involvement, or even approval, but organizational change has to be implemented from the top. As is evident from the alternative organizational types presented, the academic library must be concerned not only with its internal workings, but also with how it fits into its institutional environment. These concerns imply that any organizational restructuring or reorientation is a part of strategic management, which Hayes defined as "that part of the general management of organizations that emphasizes the relationships to external environments, evaluates the current status and the effects of future changes in them, and determines the most appropriate organizational response" (1993, 3). The strategic element further implies that the library has to be very sensitive to that external environment. Specifically, the librarians have to be very careful with the assumptions they make regarding the college or university. They must realize that it is not a business and is not going to behave as the typical business does. The notions that best fit the business world may inappropriate in the educational world. At the least, they will have to be altered; at the most, they will lead to false learning.

A fundamental difference between the business organization and the educational one is what Henry Mintzberg called its "ideology." We can see that his conception of ideology is closely related to what we've identified as culture. He takes ideology to mean

> a rich system of values and beliefs about an organization, shared by
> its members, that distinguishes it from other organizations. For our
> purposes, the key feature of such an ideology is its unifying power: It
> ties the individual to the organization, generating an "esprit de
> corps," a "sense of mission," in effect, an integration of individual and
> organizational goals that can produce synergy (1989, 224).

This is a rather generic notion of ideology; any organization that is successful may have such a system of beliefs and values. The organization, and more particularly the differences among organizations, is defined by the composition and purpose of those beliefs and values. Mintzberg's usage is neutral, but an ideology adopted or accepted by an organization certainly need not be.

Sherman Hayes and Don Brown wrote, "If one were to map the financial relationships and examine the energy that goes into those relationships, it would be clear that the library is a business and will continue as a business for the foreseeable future" (1994, 404–5). The thrust of their paper is that the academic library engages in financial relationships with a number of internal and external sources. This observation is certainly true, but it does not necessarily mean that a library is, at its heart, a business. It seems evident that Hayes and Brown are urging a particular ideology for academic libraries. Before adopting that ideology, we should ask how it fits with the purpose of college and university libraries and how its adoption might transform the library's mission.

Purpose, mission, and vision are, of course, mentioned with some frequency in the literature on leadership. There is no need to delve deeply into this literature here, but some mention of leadership as it relates to the management of libraries is necessary. There are always challenges to managing a complex organization, but the challenges that face library administrators are compounded by developments in information technology, financial uncertainty, and the possibilities presented by alternative organizational models. Because of the demands on management, the matter of leadership becomes increasingly important. First, we need to focus on one particular element of leadership. It must be substantive; that is, the leader must know the organization and its purposes and believe in its efficacy. In short, the academic library leader has to have a clear understanding of the purpose and the means of accomplishing it. Sue Faerman put this leadership definition into a library perspective and summed up the requirements for success in leading a library: "Library administrators leading their organizations through a transition must first take responsibility for establishing the vision for the organization's future, setting the direction for the organization based on an understanding of the trends in the social, political, economic and technological environment and projecting an image of what the organization might look like in 10 or 20 years" (1993, 67).

The aforementioned aspects of leadership have pertinence for both the individuals in management positions in libraries and the organizations themselves. It would be a grave mistake to see the leader *as* the organization. Perhaps this statement is especially true for a professional organization, where autonomy of decision making and independence of thought should be valued. The complexity faced by libraries as organizations accentuates the need for attention to purpose and, further, the need for organizational, rather than simply individual, initiative. Within the context of complexity, there is a term that has gained currency in the last few years: "the learning organization." This term is relatively new and has been made popular by Peter Senge, who uses it to reflect the organization that is able to overcome limitations, understand the force of pressures against it, and seize opportunities. Senge offered what he saw as the key to the learning organization: "Systems thinking is a discipline for seeing wholes. It is a framework for seeing interrelationships rather than things, for seeing patterns of change rather than static 'snapshots'" (1990, 68). The ability to see the big picture enables leadership to emerge and to foster alignment (that is, the coordination of individuals' efforts and the focus of their attention on goals and on working together to achieve the goals).

To become a learning organization, a library must overcome some obstacles and embrace some different states of mind. The obstacles are formidable and have been recognized in the past; they include falling prey to linear thinking (looking at successions of events instead of systemic shifts in order to understand phenomena), seeing positions as isolated (separate from others in the organization), and seeing problems as existing "out there" without recognizing the bridges that link the inside with the outside. The changes in thinking that Senge mentioned are based on realizing the power that mental models have in shaping our actions (and reconstructing more effective mental models); sharing vision, and thus establishing "a common identity and sense of destiny" (1990, 68); and fostering team learning, which involves being open to thinking together without the barriers of preconceptions or of trying to "win," as in a debate. This is a capsule version of Senge's idea; he developed it much more fully in his book. His idea was seen to have such a potential for impact on libraries as organizations that it prompted Shelley Phipps to write, "I am convinced that (Senge's) definitions of leaders as designers of organizations, as stewards of the vision not possessors of the vision, as teachers committed to creative tension involved in pursuing the vision and incorporating the truth of reality are key to the successful transformation of libraries in their role as transmitters of knowledge from generation to generation" (1993, 21). The success of Senge's model relies on the administration of a college or university taking a long-term commitment to the betterment of the institution; otherwise, planning, development, and growth efforts will be controlled by only a few people (Avdjieva and Wilson 2002, 373).

Senge is not the only advocate for the learning organization stance. Robert Stein and Gifford Pinchot also have spoken of the importance of the discretion that members of the organization have. According to them,

> The structural architecture of an intelligent organization is flexible and responsive, shifting to meet new challenges and current situations. What makes it flexible is not the brilliance of organizational designers sitting at the top, but the free choices of people in the middle and bottom of the organization choosing the connections needed to make their particular enterprises thrive while developing synergistic integration with what is going on elsewhere (1995, 33).

The literature on learning organizations, which is now less frequently cited in librarianship than it was in the past, has a tendency to be utopian. Moreover, it can have unintended consequences. Cliff Oswick and colleagues pointed out that "the convergent pursuit of an uncontested outcome (i.e., the 'right answer' or the 'solution') is at a price; some voices are silenced and, as a consequence, certain perspectives are marginalized while others are privileged" (2000, 900). The learning organization can, at times, suggest that adoption of this way of thinking can solve many of the organization's problems. But solving problems is not that easy. There are impediments to achieving the ideal of the learning organization.

Edgar Schein noted that shortcomings may have cultural foundations. For instance, he wrote that the culture of which the manager is part can lead to a distancing from many of the other members of the organization:

> as managers rise in the hierarchy, two factors cause them to become more "impersonal." First, they become increasingly aware that they are no longer managing operators, but other managers who think like they do, thus making it not only possible but also likely that their thought patterns and worldview will increasingly diverge from the worldview of the operators. Second, as they rise, the units they manage grow larger and larger until it becomes impossible to personally know everyone who works for them. At some point, they recognize that they cannot manage all the people directly and, therefore, have to develop systems, routines, and rules to manage "the organization." They increasingly see people as "human resources" to be treated as a cost rather than a capital investment (1996, 15).

The lesson we can learn from Schein is that the substance of a complex organization resists any simplistic solution; if the learning organization mode of thought is to be fruitful, we must understand the organization's political, intellectual, and cultural elements. Beyond the learning organization model, there are some leadership dynamics that apply universally. In chapter 2, we saw the profound contribution that Bolman and Deal (1997) have made to our understanding of organizations and leadership. Another important point they have made is that, regardless of the frame that is deemed applicable in any given situation, there can be effective and ineffective leadership strategies. For example, given the human resource frame, an effective leader might be a catalyst or a servant and may adopt processes of support and/or empowerment. An ineffective leader in this frame might be a weakling or a pushover and may abdicate leadership responsibility (Bolman and Deal 1997, 303). Further, Bolman and Deal recognized that there are barriers to change that may be manifest in each organizational frame, as well as essential strategies related to change. In the symbolic frame, there can occur a loss of meaning and purpose and a clinging to the past. The leader needs to create some transition rituals within this frame and celebrate the future while mourning the past (1997, 321). Again, their contributions are substantial and meaningful and should be heeded.

SUMMARY

Libraries have been reluctant to alter the traditional modes of organizing that have characterized the twentieth century. Because most colleges and universities are traditional in their organization, it is not terribly surprising that libraries have followed suit. The tradition has been to emphasize bureaucratic organization, but as we have seen, bureaucracies have some severe limitations. Perhaps the most important effect of bureaucracies is to shape the society and social outlook of the organization. The traditional structure also tends to be at least somewhat mechanistic, using a machine model as the guide to effective organizing. This machine model has led to a tendency in libraries to focus on events or parts of the library's purpose and to manage them.

There are some alternatives to traditional organization, and some libraries have tried to transform their structures by using different models. The possibilities for physical organization are certainly limited. For instance, we haven't spoken about the question of centralization or decentralization of the physical facility. For many libraries, this simply is not a question; the organization is too small to decentralize. For other, larger libraries, the question was probably addressed some years ago and the answer now dictates some of their organizational decisions. Within those limitations, though, there are many ways of conceiving the purpose of the library and its relation to the external environment. The possibilities are magnified when we realize that conceptions can be merged or that many hybrids may exist. There is no single appropriate or most effective way of organizing. The best choice depends on a clear understanding of the institution of which the library is a part, what it values, and how best to contribute to its aims. This does not mean that the library should be reactive only; on the contrary, the library should seek out what is meaningful on the campus, recognize why that is meaningful, and use that knowledge to reconceive its purpose. Attention to Senge's idea of the learning organization may well assist such an active stance.

Because we all have been involved with various organizations, we are likely to have thoughts regarding what seems to work and what doesn't. Here are some questions to get discussion going:

> How have you felt when you've been part of a bureaucratic
> organization?

Is it possible to have an effective organization of professionals with a bureaucratic structure?

If bureaucracy has inherent shortcomings, how do we in libraries avoid it?

What do you see as strengths and weaknesses of a team approach to organization?

What influences outside the library might affect the adoption of one or a combination of the conceptual models discussed?

What does it mean to be part of a learning organization?

Chapter 7

Libraries
and Money

L ibraries are resource-intensive organizations. They require the influx of resources, especially financial resources, to fulfill their missions. Given the demands on institutional resources (including the need to fund emerging technologies), funding for libraries from their parent organizations is likely to be
insufficient for everything the libraries need. Seeking funding, especially endowments that can provide ongoing support, is very common. Many of the library's resources *are* appropriated to the library by the institution. In some instances, the materials budget is a matter of legislative appropriation, but that
still constitutes an external (to the library) control of funding. As can be expected, the management of finances in a college or university is complicated
and has its political side. There are other tugs and pulls at the institution's purse
strings and many difficult decisions must be made. This chapter explores the
primary elements of a library's budget and the factors that affect institutional
resource allocation. Through this exploration, we will come to a fuller understanding of the constraints within which the entire institution must operate.
One factor to stress at the outset is that, regardless of the sources of funding, the
library's responsibility is to make the most effective use of available resources
(which may mean departing from the status quo).

WHAT DO STANDARDS RECOMMEND?

As we look at academic library budgets, we can turn to standards from various
bodies regarding what should be the appropriate level of support for libraries.
For instance, all colleges and universities are concerned with institutional

accreditation. Without it, the college or university cannot remain viable. Institutional accreditation is not, as it is in many European countries, controlled by the government (state or federal). It is a largely voluntary, but generally acceded to, system of review and evaluation based on a wide-ranging set of standards. To complicate matters further, there are several regional accrediting associations, each charged with the review and accreditation of educational institutions at all levels within a specified geographic area. Even though each regional association composes its own set of standards, there is a substantial amount of conformity among them. Each set of standards includes a section dealing with the library. In some respects, the content of these sections is problematic. Although many standards include some variations, the individual set of standards has to be applicable to both the four-year liberal arts college and the research university. Because of their broad applicability, the standards cannot have a high level of specificity. It should be noted that in the past some standards did include specificity with regard to one element of the library—the amount of financial support it receives. In the past, some standards have recommended that the library receive five percent of the institution's educational and general (E&G) expenditures. As we will see, for some time this standard has presented an insurmountable obstacle for many libraries.

In the absence of specificity, what is the significance and what constitutes the application of such standards? The significance is obvious; colleges and universities depend on accreditation, so they pay attention to the standards and demonstrate the ways in which they meet them (or legitimatize their decisions and operations in light of the standards). The application of the standards is not so straightforward. Because they are stated generally, they must be interpreted. The interpretation process is necessarily repeated in each case with each institution being assessed. This means that the accrediting team assigned to review a particular college or university is exercising its own interpretive discretion. It is possible that a different team, composed of other individuals, might interpret the standards and the institution's adherence to them somewhat differently. However, there are mechanisms, including the training of team members, to keep variance to a minimum. The standards related to the library may require the college or university to launch into some fairly lengthy explanatory statements. If a standard calls for an "adequate" library collection, the library may have to suggest a justification for the equation of access to information through a number of remote electronic sources with ownership of materials in a traditional collection. Many times, it is necessary to anticipate concerns the accrediting team might have and include them in the self-study.

Institutional accreditation also presents an opportunity for the library that can be used but should not be overused. The college or university administration is likely to rely on the library for much of the analysis that will form an integral part of the self-study document. By default, then, the institution is relying on the library for the stance that will be adopted and presented to the accrediting team in order for the team to ascertain whether the standard is met. The library has the chance to focus on specific aspects of support for either inclusion in the self-study or institutional use. If financial support has been diminishing, accreditation may be used as a tool to persuade the administrators of the college or university that the accrediting body would look more favorably on the institution if support for the library were enhanced. The accreditation standard and its interpretation can have tactical importance. It would be a questionable tactic, however, to threaten the administration or to use the standard as a bludgeon to get what the library wants. The library is not in a position to threaten and could be placed in a tenuous political position if administrators were to call its bluff. On the positive side, the accreditation self-study presents the library with the opportunity to compare itself with libraries at a cohort of institutions as identified by the administration. Such comparisons frequently are noticed by institutional administrations. It also provides an opportunity for genuine self-study; that is, while the institution is in an evaluative mind-set, the library can seize the opportunity to undertake a relatively large-scale examination of its impact on, and benefit to, the academic community.

The challenge for us in libraries and for our academic administrators is that interpretation lies in the wording of the standards themselves. For instance, a library standard of the Southern Association of Colleges and Schools (SACS) states, "The institution provides a sufficient number of qualified staff—with appropriate education or experiences in library and/or other learning/information resources—to accomplish the mission of the institution" (SACS YEAR, 26). This version of the "Principles of Accreditation" (not standards, but principles) is softer and more vague than previous versions, which called for graduate degrees to be held by personnel. A statement such as the foregoing should be cause for concern to us and to our profession. An institution that does not happen to be firmly committed to genuine service might construct a self-study that appears to meet the standard. The task of a visiting team responsible for evaluating the institution is formidable; it would have to demonstrate inadequacy somehow if its assessment were negative. On the positive side, standards such as those of SACS now include distance learning activities and the resources and access that are essential for their success. Many regional associations are turning their attention to outcomes assessment, rather than measures of inputs (as are many organizations). Bonnie Gratch-Lindauer (2002) has reviewed this trend and provides a valuable compilation of statements from the agencies. Librarians should pay close attention to such outcomes assessment; it is likely to be required of libraries by several bodies.

For some years, the ACRL has offered a set of standards for college libraries.

The most recent revision of the standards is dated 2000. These latest standards ask sets of questions that individual libraries should answer within the context of their home institutions and their own goals and objectives. Because this represents a new approach to standards, it will take a bit of time to see how libraries respond to and use an outcomes-based approach.

When it comes to inputs, though, we can create a hypothetical situation that displays the impact of a declining percentage of an institution's E&G budget on the library. (See table 7.1.) This hypothetical example is based a few premises: (1) the university's budget increases at an annual rate of four percent (admittedly this would be wishful thinking, but it serves this example); (2) the library's share of the institutional budget begins at 3.50 percent and declines at an annual rate of 0.05 percent; and (3) the library's budget at a constant E&G percentage is based on the starting point of 3.50 percent. As is evident from table 7.1, at times when the institution's available resources increase, the library budget may increase, even though the library's piece of the pie is getting smaller. That increase may cloud the decline suffered by the library. When we

TABLE 7.1 Hypothetical Budget Growth for a University Library, 1994–2006

Year	University's E&G Budget (Assuming a 4% Annual Growth Rate)	Library Budget as a Percentage of E&G Budget (at a 0.05% Rate of Decline)	Library Budget at the Declining E&G Percentage	Library Budget at a Constant E&G Percentage
1994	$57,142,857	3.50%	$2,000,000	$2,000,000
1995	$59,428,571	3.45%	$2,050,285	$2,079,999
1996	$61,805,714	3.40%	$2,101,394	$2,163,199
1997	$64,277,942	3.35%	$2,153,311	$2,249,727
1998	$66,849,060	3.30%	$2,206,018	$2,339,717
1999	$69,523,022	3.25%	$2,259,498	$2,433,305
2000	$72,303,943	3.20%	$2,313,726	$2,530,638
2001	$75,196,101	3.15%	$2,368,677	$2,631,863
2002	$78,203,945	3.10%	$2,424,322	$2,737,138
2003	$81,332,103	3.05%	$2,480,629	$2,846,623
2004	$84,585,387	3.00%	$2,537,561	$2,960,488
2005	$87,968,802	2.95%	$2,595,079	$3,078,908
2006	$91,487,554	2.90%	$2,653,139	$3,202,064

get to 2006, however, we can see that, had the funding remained constant at 3.50 percent, the library would have in excess of $500,000 more than it does in a state of constantly declining support. We also have to remember that the effects of the difference are cumulative. Suppose the materials part of the library's budget remains steady at 30 percent. That would mean that in 1995, the materials budget (at the 3.45% rate) would be $615,085. The materials budget at the constant 3.5 percent rate in 1995 would be $623,999, a difference of $8,914. Moving ahead in time to 2006, the materials budget at the 2.90 percent rate would be $795,941. At the 3.5 percent rate, it would be $960,619, a difference of $164,678. The problem is even worse than it looks; the library loses in each year the E&G percentage declines, so the decrease in total materials expenditures for the entire time period is considerable. This hypothetical example is offered solely to illustrate the potential impact of a declining level of institutional support.

Perhaps the most striking aspect of the ACRL standards is that they do not carry so much as the threat of enforceability. Because they do not carry the imprimatur of any accrediting agency, college and university administrations can ignore them with impunity. Furthermore, because they depart so radically from the reality of funding, they may not be taken by those administrators as reasonable guidelines. It should be noted that subject accreditation (such as business, teacher education, etc.) frequently includes a library standard. Some of these standards may be looked at closely by both the accrediting body and the institution. At times, these standards can be used as justifications for a reexamination of the library's financial resources. On the other hand, administrators are becoming frustrated with the many areas of subject accreditation and the costs associated with the accreditation process, so the future of such subject accreditation is not altogether certain. At any rate, as is true of institutional accreditation, standards demand a rhetorical response, which may entail justification of current practice rather than a substantive change in allocation of resources.

Carla Stoffle and Kathleen Weibel offered an assessment of the present utility (or lack thereof) of standards:

> Nationally developed standards for library funds are inadequate since these standards currently focus solely on the library and rely on input measures—the presence or absence of specific services and formulas for staffing, collection purchases per student or faculty member, and type of educational program. These standards are also based on print collection definitions that reflect storehouse functions but do not address the effect that access or even the local collection has on meeting campus needs (1995, 137).

Stoffle and Weibel expressed, albeit by implication, a particular vision for the academic library that transcends the notion of the library as a repository of materials. Such a vision can have an effect on budgetary requests and expenditures. The incorporation of technology, as well as print materials, in libraries is discussed later.

COMPETITION FOR RESOURCES

The library is not alone in its quest for enhanced funding. Every unit on every campus argues for more money, and most can put forth persuasive rationales for additional funding. The competition for funding that occurs within any college or university is not simply a matter of unit heads articulating reasonable plans for expending the money in keeping with the institution's mission as it fits into a state or national vision. Nor is it simply a matter of administrators weighing requests according to a rational plan for the entire campus. I do not mean to imply that funding requests and decisions are unreasonable and irrational but, rather, that political pressures come to bear on all involved that complicate the picture considerably.

As mentioned in chapter 5, almost every institution is governed by an external board. The members of such boards may be elected or appointed; in either case, they are sensitive to the political world of which they are a part. In private institutions, this world can be at once local and global. Members of boards at private institutions are not so much influenced by the party politics of the state as they are by the political necessity of survival. This is frequently translates into a concern for the tenuous mixture of tradition and attraction of students. It may be that neither is the best guiding force for the future of a particular institution, but the board may move those factors to the fore and insist that administrators address them. In public institutions the structure of the state system(s) of higher education exerts a great amount of influence over the resources available to any given institution. In reality, institutions may be in competition with one another for funding. The decisions that are made are affected by party politics, personality, and the wishes of each section of the state. If boards decide to assert their wills, funding is inevitably affected. In some instances, the board may find itself at odds with the state legislature and funding may suffer. In other instances, the board may differ with the administrators of one institution, and that institution may have to surrender some stability, at least for the short term. We cannot afford to forget that the decisions that affect the library are frequently made in a complex and far-reaching environment.

In the more local environment there is also complexity. There also are tough choices. Perhaps the most frequently voiced external demand is that students be educated as effectively as possible. The problem for the college or university is in determining how that may best be done. The customary category "instruction" may seem inclusive, but it is impossible to separate entirely what the library provides from instruction. Likewise, it is impossible to separate entirely scholarships (financial aid) from instruction. The category "instruction," however, has progressively declined over the years. Data collected by the National Center for Education Statistics (2003) indicate that the funding for instruction declined at public degree-granting institutions from 35.1 percent in 1980–1981 to 30.4 percent in 2000–2001. The decline was even steeper for four-year colleges (excluding universities), from 44.8 percent in 1980–1981 to 37.4 percent in 2000–2001. Support for libraries also suffered a decline. Degree-granting institutions saw a drop from 2.8 percent in 1980–1981 to 2.2 percent in 2000–2001. Again, when universities are excluded, the loss in support is even more precipitate, from 3.9 percent in 1980–1981 to 2.8 percent in 2000–2001. When the two academic functions—instruction and libraries—are pitted against one another in the quest for funding growth, the aims of the institution can be endangered. Looking at the predicament another way, when funding for instruction is declining, it may be difficult to construct the argument that the library needs increased resources to be able to contribute to instructional goals. The institutional administration may not be sympathetic to such an argument, even as it oversees continuous degradation of the proportion of E&G expenditures on instruction. To anticipate a question that the data on instruction and libraries might raise, two areas of expenditure have seen a substantial increase in funding. One area is research, which increased at degree-granting institutions from 19.7 percent in 1980–1981 to 22.5 percent in 2000–2001, and when universities are excluded, from 7.9 percent in 1980–1981 to 11.4 percent in 2000–2001. The other area of expenditure is administration, from 12.9 percent in 1980–1981 to 17.0 percent in 2000–2001 at universities.

The question that may spring to mind is, Why are colleges and universities putting more of their resources into research? It is tempting to reject a simplistic answer, but the seemingly simple answer must be stated. There is the hope, perhaps even the expectation, that money spent on research may reap a return. If an institution's research enterprise is enhanced, it is usually hoped that the effort put into that construction will enable the institution to attract funding from many potential external sources. In many ways, it is an operation of the old maxim, "You have to spend money to make money." The attractiveness of the possibility of external funding is a powerful driving force; we will leave to one side the question of whether it is a promise or a siren beckoning institutions toward dangerous waters. That said, emphasis on research is not just an instrumental action. Administrators are generally communicating a priority in stating such an emphasis. It is incumbent on librarians to listen and heed these statements and to seize opportunities to establish or call attention to the library's contributions to the research enterprise.

Anecdotes abound regarding the growth of administrative structures at institutions; usually they stress the negative side of the growth. In part, the increase in expenditures on administration has accompanied the expanded missions of some institutions. As some colleges have initiated a few limited graduate programs, expanded extension and/or distance education offerings, or increased the emphasis on research, some administrative costs have been realized. To an extent, some of the increases are inevitable; as a college strives to do more, it may have to create or enlarge the structure to allow for the expansion. It is practically impossible to make the general statement that increased cost in administration is an indication of waste. No doubt, there is some waste in higher education, but the dynamics of a particular college or university would have to be examined very closely before an accusation of waste could be leveled.

Something that does not show up clearly in most reports on expenditures is technology. The costs of technological enhancements or upgrades on most campuses are spread through just about all of the spending categories. For instance, creation of a computer lab for use by students may be declared an expense related to instruction. Other technological expenditures may be assigned to research or administration. Subsumed in each of the categories is equipment, which is where the money for computer hardware (and sometimes software) comes from. Undoubtedly, there has been a growing demand for expenditures on technology in higher education. This is true of libraries as well. In light of the technological necessities for libraries to serve the students and faculty on their campuses, the declining proportion of E&G expenditures allocated to libraries presents an even more dire predicament. It is, in part, a predicament shared by the rest of the campus, but the problem is exacerbated for libraries by a diminishing funding level. The library, then, probably faces the expectation by the academic community that all existing services will continue and that new technologically based services will be added. The library's dilemma is the quest to do more with less.

SELF-GENERATED INCOME

At most institutions, the possibility exists for the library to engage in activities that may bring in money. One of the initiatives open to libraries is the attraction of gifts or the establishment of dedicated endowment funds. A dedicated endowment fund is an income-generating source of finances that usually is built from donations by individuals, groups, corporations, and so on. A dedicated fund is one where the income is restricted for use by the library. The structure and management of such funds can vary from institution to institution. On some campuses, alumni/alumnae can designate donations for the library as part of an institution-wide effort at seeking gifts. Sometimes specific donors are targeted and their support is solicited for the library. One important thing to remember is that before representatives of the library go abroad contacting potential donors, they should consult with the institution's development office. The campus may already have an integrated development plan in place, and university representatives may have made an initial contact with potential donors. This does not mean that the library cannot be the beneficiary of donations, but it may mean that fund seeking is controlled centrally. Librarians may certainly be a part of the effort, but the development office may direct it. It is certainly not unusual for the library to have a full-time or part-time development officer who can facilitate donations, bequests, and other ways of giving to the library.

Another way to coordinate or organize financial giving to the library is through a Friends of the Library group. Such groups are commonly associated with public libraries but also exist to assist academic libraries. They are usually independently constituted so that they have no legal ties to the college or university. The Friends of the Library group may charge membership dues, make initial contact with donors of money or materials, oversee book sales or auctions, or undertake the fund-raising projects. Being independently chartered, the group may collect the money and then donate it to the library so as to remain independent. (The Friends group also might serve the less tangible purpose of providing positive public relations that could influence the college or university to look favorably on the library.) Whether supplemental funding comes from an endowment or from the efforts of a Friends group, its use may be restricted. For example, it is not unusual for there to be a requirement that the money be spent on nonrecurring items. That is, the money cannot be spent on salaries and perhaps not even on subscriptions but, instead, must be spent on materials, equipment, or other one-time expenditures. This requirement only makes sense. Income from an endowment fund can vary according to prevailing interest rates, the ups and downs of the stock market, or the less-than-predictable nature of other investments. The fund is usually invested as part of the entire institution's portfolio; the library probably will have no say in how the money is invested.

According to a survey sponsored by the Association of Research Libraries,

> ARL respondents earned anywhere from 0.4% to 40% of their revenues from supplementary (non-university) sources. Among the different supplemental revenue categories, gift and endowment income and grants showed the largest range. While a handful of U.S. public and private institutions reported over 10% of their total funding from either of the two sources, others at the opposite end of the scale

reported almost zero. . . . Responding libraries . . . obtained, on average, about 8% of their revenue from supplementary sources (Melville 1994, 11–14).

In addition to endowments and grants, respondents reported that they earned income from fees for photocopying or document preparation. With regard to the other sources, "income" may be a misnomer; the money collected for those services usually affect some or all of the costs of providing the services. For instance, a library may charge patrons for interlibrary loans only when there is a charge levied by the lending library. "Several respondents (to the ARL survey) commented that such services (especially interlibrary loan) ran at a deficit or on a 'no loss' basis. One administrator added that fees for these services were regarded more as an 'offset' for expenditures than 'income'" (Melville 1994, 10).

The results of the survey make sense when we consider certain factors affecting libraries' ability to attract outside sources of revenue. The larger institutions also are more likely to have larger and more active development programs, so they are in a better position than most smaller institutions to seek donations and gifts and to build endowment funds. Smaller colleges frequently do not have the resources available to engage in large-scale development programs.

Another consideration when it comes to the aforementioned sources of income is whether the library can keep the money that is generated. The assumption may be that because the library is responsible for the money coming in, it can keep it. However, it may be that the library has to turn over some or all of that income to the institution. The ARL survey provides an indication of what the disposition of self-generated income might be. Of the eighty-five libraries reporting that they receive gifts, fifteen stated that they keep part of that revenue. It may be that the institution, or its development office, keeps a percentage of any gift as a charge for processing, accounting, and/or investing the donation. With some sources of revenue the library may retain even less. A total of eighty-three libraries reported income from overdue fines, but in thirty-two of those cases none of the money is kept by the library. Some institutions may have policies that require funds generated from sources such as fines to go into the institution's general fund or some other fund. Librarians must become familiar with the rules and regulations of the college or university before taking any generated income from some sources for granted.

RESEARCH AND INCOME

As mentioned above, there is little doubt that universities look on research as a potential income generator. The potential is twofold. First, faculty who have ideas for research projects can propose the ideas to funding agencies, public and private, and request money to pay for the project. Also, the funding agencies may pay for indirect costs. Indirect costs are unrelated to the project itself but, instead, refer to the costs associated with the research enterprise—administration, facilities, and so on. Agencies such as departments of the federal government may pay an added percentage of the actual costs of a project to cover some indirect costs. For institutions with active initiatives, the amount of money attracted under the rubric "indirect costs" can be substantial. In fiscal year 1999, for example, the University of Missouri-Columbia received about $15.3 million in indirect cost reimbursement (MU Research 1999, 4). It is customary for a portion of the indirect costs to be allocated to the college and department of the investigator(s). With some constraints, the institution then can use the remainder of the funds for some of its operating expenses. A portion of the indirect costs on some campuses may go to the library.

Why would a college or university give up some of that funding to the library? All of the research done in the academic world depends, at least to some extent, on information. Drafting a grant proposal necessitates a review of pertinent literature. Conduct of the research itself is preceded by an examination of information that may influence method, sampling, research question, or even the general direction of the project. The research endeavor relies on information derived from the library's collections and services. The information that assists research is not cheap. Some institutions may view the library and its contributions to research as a necessary indirect cost. The materials and services that are useful to research tend to be specialized; they do not necessarily support instruction on campus. Assistance in the form of a piece of the indirect cost pie can be valuable to the library's effort to support a research mission. The role of information accessibility and information services, both of which are indispensable to research and expensive, is frequently taken for granted by faculty and administrators. Academic librarians may be able to learn from librarians in businesses and corporations and demonstrate the tangible benefits of what they have and what they do for the research enterprise.

A small minority of higher education institutions attract substantial research funding. Agencies frequently demand evidence that the researcher and the institution have the intellectual and material wherewithal to accomplish the proposed project. Two-year colleges and four-year liberal arts colleges (along with many institutions that have missions that go beyond instruction) generally do not have sufficient laboratory facilities, instrumentation, or computing power to engage in ambitious research. Moreover, their faculties have heavy teaching loads and research records that are not competitive with counterparts at research universities. In other words, to succeed at research there has to be a substantial institutional investment in an infrastructure that will enable faculty to build research programs. Smaller institutions cannot afford such an investment. There is a very real cost that comes with an institution's positioning itself to attract funding for research. As Derek Bok wrote,

> In competing for federal grants, scientists frequently spend 10 or 20 percent of their time preparing grant applications, receiving site visits, or sitting on expert panels to review the proposals of other investigators. . . . These burdens may be well worth enduring, given the benefits of independence and competition, but it would be pointless not to acknowledge that the burdens do exist (1986, 27–28).

The institution must be able to afford to build an infrastructure, which includes an adequate library, and must be able to afford the costs of the necessary shift in faculty time from teaching, which is usually primary at smaller colleges, to research and scholarship.

Even if the institution were successful at attracting research funding, there is no guarantee that the library would reap any financial benefits. In fact, it is a very hard sell persuading administrators to take some of the indirect cost money and allocate it to the library. As mentioned above, the institution must invest capital in the research enterprise, building a structure that enables faculty to conduct research, which provides a stepping-stone to writing successful proposals. The administration may well be tempted to reinvest the indirect cost reimbursements in the structure it created, while overlooking the library as an integral part of that structure. The argument by the library director probably would have to be based on the point that information and information services are tools that are integral to research success. It will be especially useful if some costs could be quoted. If, for instance, librarians consult with faculty on their specific information needs, or if faculty must use interlibrary loan or document delivery services, the costs of these activities might be cited by the director as being related to the research process. It would be even more helpful to the argument for funds if the faculty can estimate the benefits of the information and services to their proposal writing and research. This doesn't mean that administrators will acquiesce and give the library some of the funds, but evidence of cost and benefit is more likely to succeed than appeals to altruism or generosity.

WHERE DOES THE MONEY GO?

After the money has been allocated to the library, what happens to it? In simplistic terms, we could say that the bulk of the budget goes to personnel and materials. In a sense, this statement is true, but there are complexities to the personnel and materials expenditures that have to be recognized. In the simple version, we can look at past data to see if the proportion of libraries' budgets expended on personnel has changed. In my 1990 study, cited previously, expenditures were analyzed and the proportion spent on personnel examined. Although there were some short-term variations, in the longer term the percentage expended on personnel changed little. In 1976, 46.549 percent of the library's budget was devoted to personnel costs; in 1985, the percentage was 47.168 (Budd 1990, 157). When types of institutions are analyzed more specifically, we see that the proportion spent on personnel rose a bit at comprehensive and general baccalaureate institutions, but fell from 45.952 percent to 44.836 percent at doctoral-granting universities (1990, 157). These data show little change in budgeting patterns over time but do demonstrate that personnel represents a major expenditure for academic libraries. Spending on personnel may be variable at this time. Expenditures by ARL members in 1994 on total salaries and wages averaged 49.8 percent of total expenditures; in 2003, the percentage was 46.7. Given the service imperative of libraries, it isn't surprising that so much of the financial resource base is concentrated in personnel; however, if is a decline, at least in some institutions, there may be cause for concern regarding library services.

There has been very little analysis of more complicated aspects of personnel expenditures. One question that comes to mind is, Has there been a shift in expenditures on professional personnel, as compared to expenditures on support personnel? It is a matter of conjecture whether libraries have retained some proportion of professional and support staff in recent years and whether the salary differential between the two personnel classifications has remained constant. Over the past few years, there have been some discussions of different ways to accomplish library goals and deploy personnel. For instance, consideration has been given to other means of cataloging materials. One option that has gained currency is outsourcing of cataloging, that is, using external services for cataloging copy rather than doing copy cataloging in house. Libraries that have exercised this option have altered utilization of personnel. In one instance, at the Jackson Library of Stanford University, Karen Wilson reported that

> One indisputable fact is that the number of Jackson Library staff performing cataloging and physical processing work at the beginning of the pilot project (4.75 FTE) was reduced by 2.25 FTE by the end of the one-year study. Another .25 FTE reduction was made shortly thereafter. All outsourcing costs incurred by the library, by way of fees paid to BNA and BHB and additional internal costs, were more than offset by the staff salary savings resulting from the removal of 2.5 FTE from the technical services division (two full-time library specialists and two quarter-time student assistants). The remaining staff in the cataloging department at the end of the project consisted of one full-

time cataloging librarian (by then, the department head), one full-time copy cataloger, and one quarter-time student responsible for physical processing work. The sole cataloging librarian also works part-time on the reference desk, so that particular full-time position is not devoted entirely to technical services work (1995, 378–79).

A problem arises from the above case. We can wonder to what extent budget cuts are borne by library personnel and what the impact on the goals and objectives of the institution might be.

The Stanford experience shows that with redeployment may come a shift in personnel expenditure patterns. In some libraries, the changes in personnel utilization may have been a necessary reaction to imposed constraints. Many academic institutions have had to deal recently with less-than-optimal funding levels and have had to initiate hiring freezes or at least allow some vacant positions to go unfilled. Sometimes the libraries have had to change staffing patterns because of institution-wide practices. Even when there have been no college- or university-mandated hiring constraints, some libraries have made changes in response to perceived needs. Barbara Dewey (1994) pointed out that the incorporation of information technologies, pressures to innovate, incremental demands for services, enhanced library focus on use and users, and the development of new programs have added to the complexity of budgeting for personnel. Most of what Dewey discussed translates into additional demands on the library. There is certainly nothing wrong with high expectations for library services, but with insufficient resources, frustrations result both within and outside the library. The situation has changed little in the intervening years. Recently, there was an economic downturn in most states and one result was a decrease in state funding for higher education. The libraries at public institutions had to take their share of the cuts. Meanwhile, the information universe expands, bundled packages of information cost more, and the academic communities continue to demand a great deal from libraries.

Just as the proportion of the library's budget expended on personnel has been variable in recent years, the proportion of expenditures on materials has seen changes. In 1985, libraries spent about 30.0 percent of their budgets on books and periodicals. The percentage altered some by type of intuition at that time (Budd 1990). In 1994, the average ARL member library spent 34.7 percent of its total budget on materials (including "other" materials). By 2003, the average expenditure on materials was 39.7 percent. There also has been a substantial shift within the materials budget. Doctoral-granting universities, comprehensive colleges, and general baccalaureate institutions spent a smaller percentage of their budgets on books in 1985 than in 1976. The rise in the prices of serials (along with the changing dynamics of serial literature) is largely responsible for the shift. (This phenomenon is investigated in greater depth in chapter 8.) In recent years, there probably has been some more complicated shifting of the materials budget. In 1994, the average ARL member library spent 32.4 percent of its materials budget on books and 59.0 percent on serials. By 2003, the figures were 26.2 percent on books and 63.3 percent on serials. The purchase of, or subscription to, electronic resources is likely to come from the materials budget. In some libraries such expenditures can be considerable. An ARL report indicated that member libraries spent about 3.6 percent of their materials budgets on electronic resources in 1992–1993 and 10.56 percent in 1998–1999 (Kyrillidou 2000). It could reasonably be expected for the percentage to have continued to rise. Charges for other electronic formats or media also may be made to the materials budget. Whether the library's focus is on ownership of physical packages of information or access to information regardless of where it resides, there are—and will continue to be—costs associated with the essential services provided by the library.

Beyond the two traditionally large categories of expenditures, libraries spend money on a variety of products and services. Libraries will customarily have a separate line in the budget for equipment, but the amount of money in that line is seldom sufficient to meet all of the library's equipment needs (if it ever has been). As Dewey pointed out, there are pressures to innovate and increasing demands for services. Many of the innovations and service demands have technological components, but libraries frequently are constrained by the amount of financial resources available to fulfill the innovative ideas librarians may have. Some of the grants that libraries are able to attract are targeted specifically at technology-based solutions to some of the perceived needs of libraries' communities. For example, The University of Alabama Libraries, in cooperation with the University of Wisconsin-Madison's General Library System, recently received a grant of about $226,000 to digitize some materials related to the book trade (Galloway 2004). External sources of funding are limited, however, and federal programs in particular cannot be counted on as possible sources of fiscal enhancement. In addition to equipment, the library's budget is likely to include lines for supplies, postage, telecommunications charges, and travel. Most of these budget lines are similar to the equipment line in that they are not really adequate for most of the goals and aspirations that librarians have. Postage costs have risen dramatically in recent years, especially in the library rate, which has an impact on services such as interlibrary loan.

Libraries are making more varied and more extensive use of telecommunications for a number of purposes. Access to information frequently depends on telecommunications connections. The connections can be used for access to databases or for internal and patron uses of networked information, such as Web-based information. At present, on most campuses the network charges for

Internet usage, electronic mail, and so on are paid centrally by the institution. The charges are growing sufficiently rapidly and are reaching such amounts that institutions may begin charging units for usage of network connections. The charging of units on some campuses may be difficult at this time because there may be a multitude of systems and servers and users may have multiple passwords. Colleges and universities might well attempt to exercise greater control over access so that they can charge departments and other units more efficiently. Admittedly, this is speculation, but institutions have shown a proclivity to charge units for other services, such as maintenance, repair, local computer usage, and other things. The cost of networked sources is a genuine concern in libraries, and the concern will grow as more private enterprises market their wares over the Internet and the World Wide Web for a fee.

The incorporation of technological development, and the several possibilities that accompany any technology, presents opportunities for libraries but also creates pressure on their budgets. Not only is the expense associated with access, but also the attendant costs of hardware and related items, such as furniture intended for use of computer hardware. As we have seen, personnel and materials account for the major part of the average academic library's budget. At most institutions, large-scale upgrades or purchases of computer hardware and sometimes software have been funded by one-time appropriations. For instance, if the library has to, or wants to, migrate to a new integrated online library system, it usually has submit a request to the institution's administration. The administration (assuming it concurs that the move is needed) sends the request upward perhaps to the governing board and, in public colleges and universities, to the state. This path of requests takes time, and success is by no means guaranteed. Because the process takes so long, the library may have to live for a time with inadequate technology. Stoffle and Weibel recognized the problem and offered an imminently reasonable suggestion:

> Library capital budgets will need to be created in most libraries and reconfigured in those institutions that now have them. Capital budgets are required for equipment, major software purchases, online services, and research and development funds. The current tendency to deal with most of the library capital needs as one-time requests is no longer in the institution's best interests. This method of funding tends to pit the library's needs against other academic needs and often has meant that library equipment is kept long past its useful life. It has also meant that libraries could not take advantage of newer equipment to improve services and/or productivity on a timely basis, thus leading to a decline in library service. And it has meant that academic administrators are continually having to handle

capital requests that are really ongoing operating expenses. The solution is to establish a regular replacement cycle for library equipment (including furniture) and to budget the replacement of a specific portion of the equipment yearly while at the same time establishing a specific portion of the library's capital budget for new equipment (1995, 139)

Ideally, this solution should apply to the entire campus and not just to the library.

SUMMARY

There is some dispute as to the purpose of the library; the dispute focuses on what the library should be doing to best serve the community. In part, the dispute includes the conception of community. Some, such as Michael Gorman and Walt Crawford, envision community writ large (that is, a community of users that transcends the geographic boundaries of any single institution and temporal boundaries as well). Gorman and Crawford stated, with confidence, the purpose of the library: "libraries are *not wholly or even primarily about information.* They are about the preservation, dissemination, and use of recorded knowledge in whatever form it may come so that humankind may become more knowledgeable; through knowledge reach understanding; and, as an ultimate goal, achieve wisdom [emphasis in original]" (1995, 5). Their vision is based on a skepticism regarding information technology. All academic librarians should read their book, *Future Libraries.* I do not intend this statement as a blatant endorsement of all of the book's contents, but the book does present arguments that require critical evaluation and response, either favorable or unfavorable. None of us should automatically accept the traditional operation of the library *or* the complete transformation to an electronic resource. Stoffle and Weibel saw the challenges faced by libraries and presented a different take on the issue of purpose:

> Funding the academic library to effectively serve the campus mission assigned to it was not easy in the best of times when institutional budgets were growing and library technologies and activities were stable. The current unsettled environment of higher education, the debilitating state of information economics, and the rapidly changing information technologies have made the task even more difficult. There are no guidelines or formulas for library funding that are applicable in this environment. The politics of the campus favor support for the collection in their attempts to increase their budgets. Yet in today's environment support for the collection no longer equals support for the library (1995, 146).

This dispute is examined further in chapter 8. For now, though, the point is that the perceived purpose of the library will have a tangible effect on its budgeting strategy, the argument for resources, and the expenditure of funds.

That said, there are some almost universal factors that affect the financial position of libraries on campuses. One is the reality that the library belongs to everyone and to no one. What does this mean? Well, much of the funding of units or departments in colleges and universities is based on some measure of size, usually taken in terms of students or student credit hours generated. In other words, the teaching activity of the department frequently influences the funding it receives. Apart from library instruction programs, the library doesn't engage directly in teaching. Even when library instruction exists, the library may not benefit from the student credit hours generated by the program. Some other department may claim the credit hours, or they may not be part of the accounting when library funding is determined. The library is viewed as a universal resource; it exists to serve the needs of all academic programs. As a result, the library has no group of students that it can call its own. Other academic departments are generally reluctant to relinquish any of their own funding in order to support the library, but, occasionally (especially in times of dire financial straits for the library), some departments will lend support. That support is usually focused on the acquisition of materials. The fact that the library exists to serve everyone is the primary rationale for using the E&G expenditures of the institution as the pot from which the library's budget is taken. The E&G monies are the universal source of funding, so they should be the source for the universal service that is the library.

As we can see, the competition for financial resources is quite strong. Just as there are increased expectations for the library, so, too, are there increased expectations for all academic departments. Many departments are expected to incorporate the latest technology into their teaching and research, for instance. Also, the departments are expected to retain current levels of enrollment in their courses or to increase enrollment. Those other departments are encouraged to generate new income, principally by attracting external funding for research and instruction. The department can reap the benefits of both the direct costs of the project and some portion of the indirect costs. However, the opportunities for external funding are limited for the library. As we have seen, the possibilities for self-generated income for the library are not numerous. Certainly, libraries should be encouraged to build their donor bases and to establish or add to endowments. However, this is unlikely to occur without the active support of the institution. Development is a complex activity requiring a strategic plan and a team of people who can contact potential donors and oversee the investment and management of funds. The library should be part of the institution's development efforts.

Concern regarding funding for libraries is not new. It probably has been heightened in recent years by the increasing prices for materials and by the costs of technological tools that can be incorporated for internal purposes and for service to the academic community. Goudy wrote,

> There are no easy answers to the current fiscal crunch. Librarians must first seek to maximize the efficiency and effectiveness of current resource usage. It is unlikely that vast new sums of money will be forthcoming, and each unit of the university will be increasingly held accountable for the cost effectiveness of its operation. Nevertheless, librarians must become more assertive and more savvy in presenting the library's case—in demonstrating how a proper funding level for the library will, in the long run, promote the quality of the institution (1993, 215).

Goudy's point is a particularly important one. Funding processes are a local matter; each institution addresses the processes on the basis of its mission, the pressure that it feels from internal and external forces, and its culture. Librarians do not have a packaged strategy they can use to increase funding. There is no substitute for the effort it takes to understand the workings of the college or university. Money problems will be with libraries for the foreseeable future, as will high expectations for them. It will not be easy for libraries to explore creative ways of attracting or expanding money unless the institutions themselves welcome challenges to the status quo.

Although this chapter has emphasized the attraction of resources and some of the demands of the library budget, the managerial imperative of librarians with regard to funding is twofold. As stated at the beginning of the chapter, the budget is, to an extent, flexible and it is the librarians' responsibility to look beyond the past to make effective, even creative, use of resources. The other side of the imperative deals with the responsibility, mainly (but certainly not solely) of the director, to address the institution's mission—the needs of the academic community. Success in this endeavor requires full and truthful communication with the institution's administration (for example, about the costs and benefits of what the library offers to the community) and with library personnel so that all understand the institutional mission and the internal fiscal decisions.

Money tends to strike responsive chords in people. The financial aspects of academic libraries can generate some lively discussion; the following questions can be used to get the discussion going:

What impact could the revision of ACRL standards have on libraries' planning and evaluation?

What arguments could be used with administrators to increase the proportion of E&G expenditures going to libraries?

What key political issues are related to public funding for higher education?

Can libraries build internal research programs that will attract external financial support?

Do libraries employ too many or too few people?

To what extent does the increased use of information technology lead to increased personnel needs?

Chapter 8

The Collection(s)

For almost as long as academic libraries have been in the United States, they have been associated with the collections they have selected, acquired, organized, and housed. This historical association is one reason for some of the care that must taken in a discussion of the topic of the library's collection. As was noted at the end of chapter 7, there is some dispute regarding the purpose of the library. On the one hand, there are those who advocate breaking through the constraints a physical collection imposes on library services. On the other hand are those who make the case for the preservation of recorded knowledge. Of course, both points are correct; what is constricting is a narrowness of vision that puts libraries in an either/or stance. This chapter and chapter 9 examine the communication media of the past, present, and future. They will show that the key to effective integration into the educational enterprises of higher education is an intellectual commitment to understanding the content needs of students and faculty and the content of the communication media. That intellectual commitment entails an acceptance of media for what they are–conduits through which content can be transmitted from a voice to an ear, from a sender to a receiver, and also shapers of the content. The media are to be viewed in light of their effectiveness and success at accomplishing the aim of communication.

As seen in earlier chapters, much of what the library exists to do is driven by the processes and products of scholarly communication. Some of the motivation behind scholars to produce evidence of communication is material. That is, there is an effort to produce things, artifacts, measurable units of communication that can be used for evaluation and comparison. In other words, there is a motivation to create material products in the form of articles in journals, books, or other, similar physical items. Another motivation stems more directly from communication. Scholars are interested in sharing the fruits of their work and thought, not just to establish claims or to receive credit, but also to subject their ideas to the critical assessment of their colleagues. This motivation is non-material; rather, it is emotional or intellectual in nature. The library, then, is a part of the communication system whose aim is to evaluate the work of partic-ipants and to add to knowledge. The scholarly communication embodies the paradox of the material and the nonmaterial. Note that this is a paradox, not a contradiction. The material and the nonmaterial aspects exist simultaneously and the one does not negate the other. For instance, if an assistant professor writes several papers on a particular subject and the papers are published in journals, the material presence of the papers may well contribute to his or her tenure and promotion. The material aspect, however, does not preclude the pa-pers' potential intellectual impact on the discipline. The library also is affected by the paradox of the material and the nonmaterial. The traditional collection is physical, but it is not merely physical. It embodies the nonmaterial element that enables faculty and students to be informed and to learn. We cannot lose sight of this nonmaterial aspect of the collection, even as we examine the material.

TRADITIONAL MEDIA AND TRADITIONAL COLLECTIONS

Books

As was just stated, the library is affected, if not imposed on, by the scholarly communication system. The system was treated in chapter 3, so there is no need to describe it here. It has been formed by the purposes and media of commu-nication in the past and the present. As a result, the library's collection (as a record of formal communication) has been shaped by the media that have ex-isted. Print on paper has been the principal communication medium in the form of books, journals, reports, and so on. For centuries, the medium was a part of the only effective means of communicating over space and time. In par-ticular, the book has a substantial history as a mechanism for transmitting and sharing ideas. Its place of importance was especially marked in the time before increased academic and intellectual specialization and pressure to publish. Regardless of the discipline, the book was seen as the medium of choice to com-municate a fully developed idea or program of research. For many years, then, books were published and libraries acquired them. Of course, there had to be authors of those books. Many scholars of the past sought to unify their work in book-length presentations. Time was not as much of a limiting factor as it has become, so publication of work as a book did not present problems for the scholarly community, from either the author's or the reader's point of view.

Time is still not a major factor in communication in some disciplines. Especially in many humanities disciplines, the subject matter studied is not dependent on new developments or discoveries in the same way that, say, the sciences are. If a scholar is working on the interpretation or reception of the works of a particular writer, the key to inquiry is the writing itself. Further, many studies in the humanities acquire extensive narrative or discursive treatment because the study depends on language for its development. It may require hundreds of pages of exposition, argument, and interpretation in order to treat the subject matter fully. The nature of inquiry in the humanities means that the structure of communication is unlikely to change drastically in the foreseeable future. If the nature of inquiry doesn't change, it is likely that the medium of the book will be with us for some time. Of course, the "book" does not necessarily refer to print on paper. Robert Darnton (1999) has offered an alternative vision for book publishing. He advocates employing electronic books in a creative and innovative way, presenting the content in multiple layers that can be used for different purposes. The structure would include teaching aids and full documentation, as well as the text itself.

In addition to the intellectual and communicative efficiency of the book in the humanities, an organizational imperative works in the book's favor. As discussed in chapter 3, college and university administrators are accustomed to evaluating faculty on the basis of their productivity in producing things such as books. To some extent, faculty are conditioned by this fairly long-standing reward structure. Partly because of the rewards that await productive faculty, and partly (or mostly) because of the motivation to communicate ideas to colleagues, scholars in a number of disciplines in the humanities and social sciences tend to conceive of projects as book-length communications. Some, such as Robin Wilson, have observed that the bar is constantly rising when it comes to the evaluation of scholars' publication, resulting in greater numbers of publications being required. The scholar may think in terms of a large-scale question that necessarily involves an extended treatment. It is an open question whether this is the only way to conceive of questions in the humanities and the social sciences. Undoubtedly, some extended treatments are necessary; there is no other way to handle, for instance, the history of a large geographic area over a substantial period of time. However, it may be that some things that are published as books may be as effectively, or more effectively, presented as a journal article or an essay.

The relationship that scholars as authors and as readers have with books affects the library's operations, collections, and services. Because the book is an important medium for the communication of content, it is important that the library pay attention to it because it is important that libraries link content with users. When there were fewer choices of media, the library's job was simpler and so was its collection. Even today, though, the content that is enveloped in the medium of the book is essential to many disciplines. However, the book is not the only medium; therefore, librarians have choices when it comes to providing access to content. This level of choice translates into pressures on the library's financial resources, which also means that finite resources can be used to acquire or provide access to information. The fiscal pressures do not stop with the library; they extend to book publishers. If libraries are spending a smaller portion of their resources on books, the publishers of those books are sure to be affected. The market for scholarly publications consists of scholars and libraries. Individuals, as might be expected, have limited money to spend on books, so libraries tend to be a more important market for scholarly works.

More than three decades ago, William Harvey and others wrote, "The craft of university publishing is a fragile and skittish vessel at best" (1972, 195). In the 1970s, the sales revenue of university presses failed to keep up with the Consumer Price Index. Perhaps more important, unit sales declined. This means that prices had to rise for revenues to increase. It is extremely difficult to ascribe causation to these phenomena, but we have to wonder if rising prices have influenced unit sales. Of course, we can find ourselves wondering if the chicken or the egg came first because declining unit sales are likely to influence the unit price of a university press book. In the 1980s, the trend continued. It is estimated that libraries spent about $17.4 million on university press books in 1983. The unit sales to libraries that year were 1.19 million. This trend has led to some strong measures by university presses. University press titles, by and large, have shorter print runs than in the past.

Concern about the publication of scholarly books is not limited to university presses. Commercial publishers face some obstacles from the financial state of academic libraries, which, it is popularly believed, are buying fewer books as their budgets undergo shifts in the face of pressures to pay for serials, electronic media, and online access. According to ARL data, the median amount of money expended on monographs rose only slightly from 1994 to 2003. The median in 1993 was $1,309,807; the median in 2003 was $1,827,006. The increase is relatively small, but the median number of monographs purchased increased from 27,293 in 1994 to 35,577 in 2003 (http://www.arl.org). The figures for other academic libraries, however, indicate a trend that more closely resembles the popularly held view. For example, a recent study indicates that the mean numbers of holding libraries of items published by university presses in three subject areas and that were reviewed in *Choice* (English and American literature, philosophy, and North American history) declined from 1990 to 2000 (Budd and Urton 2003). Projections related to publishing activity indicate that book publishing and sales may reverse the recent downward trend. For example, total university press sales may increase from 17.6 million units in 2003 to 18.6 million in 2008.

Also, professional book sales may increase from 170.9 million to 173.8 million units over the same time period (Book Industry Study Group 2004, 9).

In addition to matters of content and supply, libraries are interested in the prices of books. The authors of *University Libraries and Scholarly Communication* reported that from 1963 through 1990, book prices rose at an annual rate of 7.22 percent (Cummings et al. 1992, 85). This rate of increase was greater than the average annual inflation rate for the period. Moreover, the authors wrote, "It appears, then, that price increases have been more significant since the mid-1980s and that the most expensive books are also those that have been increasing most rapidly in price. This evidence suggests that book prices are now showing some of the tendencies characteristic of serials—not an encouraging sign for those who must be concerned about library budgets" (Cummings et al. 1992, 86). However, more recent data provide some better news for libraries. Overall, hardcover book prices have been rather stable in the past few years. In 2000, the average price of a hardcover book was $60.84; in 2001 (preliminary data), the cost was $59.80 (*Bowker Annual* 2003, 495). If we look more specifically at academic book production (excluding reference books), we again see that there is some price stability. In 1999, the average academic book cost $56.30; in 2001 (preliminary data), the cost was $57.65 (*Bowker Annual* 2003, 497). This time period is too short to conclude that the upward trend has ended, but it certainly provides some reason for optimism.

Serials

Yes, it's true that books and serials are both print materials, but they are treated differently and present their own challenges to libraries. Although the production of scholarly books has been declining in recent years, at least from some sources, there has been no similar decline in the production of serials. Again, we have to turn to the complete view of higher education to see potential reasons for the state of serials in libraries. Our attention first will be on elements of production; pricing and economics will be discussed separately. We have already explored the driving force of authorship in academia and how widespread the publishing imperative has become for faculty at many institutions (and not just the largest research universities). Through our examination, we have seen that there is a substantial push for both quantity and immediacy of published work by faculty. Gary Brown noted that when it comes to publishing, success really can breed success: "In a sense, there is a circular process that instigates research and publication: one publishes to further a field of knowledge, which brings recognition and promotion; this in turn makes one highly eligible for research grants, which also in turn bring monies to the parent institution and foster both the progress of research and the researcher's career" (1990, 35). The more who become involved with publication, the more who are likely to succeed and to continue writing and publishing.

Regardless of the motivation, faculty in all disciplines contribute papers to journals. Faculty in some academic areas are more active publishers in journals, principally because of the natures of those subjects and the accepted areas of communication in the disciplines. It's fairly safe to say that where the subject matter can be treated discretely (that is, when the subject can be divided into tightly focused, independent objects of inquiry), the article is the most commonly produced and read unit of communication. Scientific, technological, and medical (STM) fields certainly fit that model. Other disciplines, including some social sciences, also rely on the journal articles for communicative purposes.

The faculty, however, do not act alone in the production process. Although Karen Hunter of Elsevier Science Publishers maintained that the research community, not the journals, produces articles (McDonald 1990, A6), the publishers of journals are not bystanders in the production process. When a new journal begins publication, it may be, to an extent, a response to a perceived need for a communicative mechanism, but it also serves to create a market. The new journal represents yet another option for faculty who, for whatever reasons, want to share their work with colleagues. If the journal exists, those faculty who want to publish in it probably will want their college or university library to subscribe to it. The faculty who want the library of their institution to subscribe to journals in which they might want to publish exert some not-so-subtle pressure on the library to meet their needs. I mention this to illustrate that demand emanates from authors as well as readers. However, authors and readers are largely a secondary market for journals. They read and write for publication in journals, but the journals are paid for predominately by libraries. This complication in the serials market renders conventional economic analysis a bit problematic. It also complicates libraries' roles in the communication process.

It would be less than responsible to blame publishers for what has been called "the serials crisis." Publishers—commercial publishers, that is—are in business, which means that they aim to make a profit from their enterprises. Imagine you're in business. Your costs go up by, say, five percent in a year and you decide to increase the price of your product by 10 percent. The margin creates additional profit and gives your business more capital that could be used to expand the business. Suppose you find that you lose no customers, even though you've increased the price by 10 percent. The next year, you do the same and, again, you lose no customers. One conclusion you may be tempted to reach is that your product has been underpriced, that the market will pay more for what you have to sell. A scenario similar to this (although this is a gross oversimplification) may describe journal pricing for several years. Libraries paid for journals for some years even though subscription prices were rising sharply.

It should be noted briefly here that the journal–library relationship is different from most economic relationships; for one thing, the purchaser of the product is not the ultimate consumer. In a little while, we will look at some economic analyses of library expenditures. The above scenario is not intended as a defense of journal publishers. They have been much more than simply an outlet for the work of scholars and researchers; they have contributed to the growth and direction of the market.

One of the ways in which publishers affect the market is by expanding their products. They may make decisions to increase the number of pages in a volume. Another strategy may be to branch a particular title. A given title may be split into two or more parts; if a library wants to provide the information in that area to its community, it may find itself subscribing to two (or more) titles instead of one. Some years ago, *Physical Review* was a single title; now it exists as *Physical Review A: General Physics, Physical Review B: Condensed Matter and Materials Physics, Physical Review C: Nuclear Physics, Physical Review D: Particles and Fields, Physical Review E: Statistical, Nonlinear, and Soft Matter Physics,* and *Physical Review Letters.* This expansion hasn't gone unnoticed by the readers of journals; some scientists were talking about the problem a few decades ago. David Mermin related a joke told him by Rudolph Peierls in 1961: "An extrapolation of its present rate of growth reveals that in the not too distant future *Physical Review* will fill book shelves at a speed exceeding that of light. This is not forbidden by relativity, since no information is being conveyed" (1990, 57). Branching of the sort described exacerbates the difficulty that libraries are facing. Publishers also affect the market by their packaging of products. With a substantial shift from print to electronic accessibility in recent years has come the bundling of journals by publishers and aggregators. Whereas, in the past, a library made a decision about each title, the decision now can be whether to license the entire bundle. This kind of packing has several effects: (1) libraries' budgets are less controlled by librarians than they once were; (2) an institution's faculty has access to the bundle regardless of whether it is the most appropriate set of titles; and (3) publishers have been able to ensure the profitability of these products.

The pricing of journals is at the heart of the notion of crisis. Pricing is a focal point of *University Libraries and Scholarly Communication.* The report shows that the average annual rate of increase in subscription process for the period 1963–1990 was 11.30 percent (Cummings et al. 1992, 85). Most of the increase seemed to come from the late seventies through the eighties, but the increases continued. The average price of a journal in 1984 was $78.35; in 2002, it was $543.96 (Dingley 2003, 493). Causes for the crisis are not simple. Specialization of content is linked with price increases, although it is impossible to say that there is a causal relation. Some external factors contribute to higher prices:

currency exchange rates have been less stable than in the past and the dollar has had periods of weakness relative to other currencies; the cost of paper has increased; the cost of the reproduction of graphics has increased; postage rates have risen. Although all of these factors have had an impact, the price increases outpace the cost increases.

In recent years, the trend toward higher prices has continued unabated. Brenda Dingley (2003) has provided an analysis of overall pricing in a number of subject areas. The percentage change in all categories (excluding Russian translation) in 2003 was 7.7. The average annual increase for the period 1994–2003 was 9.4 percent. Unlike previous years, where science and technology areas saw the highest increases, the social sciences represented four of the five subject categories (political science, psychology, library and information sciences, and labor and industrial relations). The category of medicine has seen the largest average annual increase from 1994 through 2003—11.4 percent. Serials price indexes have risen far more rapidly than either the Consumer Price Index or the Higher Education Price Index. The ARL data illustrate the dilemma that libraries face. In 1994, the median amount spent on serials was $2,892,898; in 2003, the median was $5,340,158. During the same period, the median number of serial titles purchased increased from 14,956 to 21,192 (http://www.arl.org).

As might be expected, some libraries have reacted to the continuous price increases. That response has generally been in the form of cancellation of subscriptions. It has not been unusual for academic libraries of all sizes to engage in some program of evaluation leading to cancellations. In fact, these programs have been frequent at institutions; over a period of years, a library may have had to engage in multiple cancellation projects. In many cases, the emphasis is on *programs;* that is, there has been effort to gather information on pricing as well as on local need for specific titles. Decisions are usually not made without consultation with the faculty. It is essential to understand how individual periodicals fit into the instruction and research of the faculty before titles are cancelled. It should be emphasized that this is a consultative process. Anecdotes abound of faculty who zealously defend subscriptions to particular titles and it turns out that the faculty member either doesn't know what the journal's contents are or assumes on the basis of the title that it must be important. For the most part, however, faculty understand the problem and are sympathetic to the library's dilemma. Beyond the information that the faculty may offer, involving faculty in the deliberations offers a political benefit. In a political environment, support for difficult decisions is very important. Regardless of the decisions made, the library should inform everyone on campus of the nature of the problem, including the history of price increases, the reasons for the cancellation program, and the process by which decisions will be made. We should never assume that everyone is as attuned to the problem as we are. Furthermore, the collection exists for users; that maxim should be the guiding principle in the cancellation program. How, though, do we make decisions about what to cancel? Some libraries turn to global data sets, such as citation frequency and impact factor. These means of examination are not without problems, as would be any local application of universal data. What is likely to be more effective is longer-range planning engaged in with the faculty. This planning would focus on the kinds of information individual titles provide and how essential that information is for local need. Ideally, the institution's administrators should be part of the conversation so that they comprehend fully the nature and scope of the problem. The entire landscape of serials management is getting progressively more complicated because of, among other things, open access. The open access movement is discussed in chapter 9.

ECONOMIC ANALYSES OF SERIALS PRICING

In recent years, a number of studies have been conducted on the economics of serials production and pricing. Some of these studies have been undertaken by economists, applying methods, models, and sometimes assumptions of economics to the serials predicament. It is not only useful, it also is important that we look at these analyses critically because some of them include not only examinations of serials as a commodity and libraries as a market, but also recommendations for actions by libraries. One such analysis was performed a few years ago by David Lewis (1989). Lewis focused a substantial amount of attention on demand. He maintained that there are two markets for journal producers—individuals and libraries. The library market, he said, is inelastic; pricing has limited impact on subscriptions. Individual demand is based, to a much greater extent, on pricing. Lewis further examined some potential pricing models available to journals, such as marginal cost pricing and dual pricing (different pricing for individuals and institutions). His analysis, as is common to economic analysis, assumed some deterministic aspects of markets; for instance, all consumers behave the same way for the same reasons. It is difficult to avoid assumptions of this kind, but it likewise is difficult to conceive of a law-like structure for commodities. Further, some statements are made ex cathedra; they are actually propositions but are not necessarily supported or defended. Lewis wrote, "To the established scholars who manage much of the journal system, it is the journal's role as bestower of academic recognition that is paramount, not its role as distributor of scholarly information" (1989, 684). This is a sweeping statement that, no doubt, is an accurate assessment of some specific instances, but a rather gross oversimplification. Lewis concluded with speculations on the impact of electronic information. He recognized that the online environment both enables and creates structures of use and distribution that differ from those of print.

Roger Noll and W. Edward Steinmueller (1992) offered a rather simple take on the journal pricing issue in a preliminary piece of work on the subject. Their conclusion was that variations in journal prices are due primarily to variations in circulation, or subscription rates. Circulation rates are affected, at least to some extent, by the increasing number of journal titles in a market that has finite financial resources to spend on the products. As more journals are started, the existing journals are likely to lose some subscribers. Noll and Steinmueller spoke to demand and suggested a particular source of demand for journals: "The fundamental factor determining faculty demand for academic journals is the desire by faculty to have their work published" (1992, 33). The urge by faculty to be published leads to the establishment of more journals, which in turn leads to economic problems based on subscription rates. The authors wrote, "as more faculty seek publication outlets, the demand to be published in a fixed number of 'best' journals grows, and a smaller proportion of scholars succeed in publishing at the top of the hierarchy. Recognizing this, both publishers and scholars seek to create new publishing outlets that create a new hierarchy, rather than enter at the bottom of an established one" (1992, 37). This statement begs the question of why the lowest tier of journals doesn't fail due to subscription rates that render costs higher than revenues. The assumption does not address why the number of journals continues to climb in the face of some debilitating economic challenges. Haworth, for instance, proliferates titles in our own field, and institutional prices are high. The price, as of this writing, of *Cataloging & Classification Quarterly* is $325 per year. Volume 37 (2003–2004) appeared in only two issues, numbers 1/2 and 3/4, even though the journal is putatively a quarterly. Further, the relationship between pricing and subscription rates is a complex one and is not unidirectional; subscriptions have an impact on price and price has an impact on subscriptions.

Let's take one more example of economic analysis. Michael Stoller, Robert Christopherson, and Michael Miranda (1996) proposed a different view of journal publishing as a monopoly, although they maintained that a monopoly does exist. These authors differ from others in that they admit that, at a certain price level, demand is indeed elastic and libraries will cancel subscriptions if prices rise too high. Also, they stated that as some libraries cancel subscriptions, publishers are forced to raise prices even further. Some of their recommendations have raised some questions, though; they stated, "Despite publishers' printed statements that individual subscribers may not pass their journals on to libraries for other readers, that proscription is of dubious legal validity and publishers have never tested it in court. . . . Selling or letting others use a product that you purchased is certainly another matter, and this practice has never been illegal in the United States" (1996, 18). The authors may wish to take a look at the predicament of textbook pricing, where college and university bookstores routinely resell books. Albert Henderson (1996) took issue with the study. In particular, Henderson said the dynamics of institutional support for libraries has been decreasing at the same time that the institutions have been increasing support for research.

It may seem that I've been hard on these analyses. It is no doubt important to increase our understanding of the economics of publishing and information production, but the issue is neither simple nor linear. The library is a somewhat odd market because in many instances the purchaser is not the consumer. Also, the library does not generate the funds it has to spend on journals. These and other factors may render the employment of conventional economic models less useful. As we have seen, some assumptions tend to underlie the studies we've looked at. The assumptions could be problematic and should be questioned. Many of them could be the basis of inquiry that would help guide future economic analysis. A more effective economic analysis would investigate all elements of the system—the branching and twigging of titles (as both response to and creation of a market), the rising prices of journals, the cancellation of titles, the bundling of titles, the institutions' roles in fostering production, and so on. Finally, as discussed in chapter 10 and reiterated in this one, there are multiple motivations behind the production of information and a complex of players in the mix of production and consumption. Although these difficulties complicate examination, ignoring them is likely to result in work that is less useful to us in making decisions.

Hypothetical suppositions and conventional economic analyses of serials prices can be helpful, but the complexity of the business necessitates more complete analysis, including of the marketplace. Mark McCabe (2001), for example, illustrated that mergers among journal publishers have contributed to increases in serials prices. Also of note is the realization that serials price increases are not limited to the STM fields. Elsewhere, I have investigated the prices of a selected group of journals in the social sciences (Budd 2002). The prices of these journals increased substantially in the 1990s, and the steepest increases were those journals published by commercial producers. When all factors are examined, the fact remains that journal prices have increased at a rate faster than libraries' budgets. Some libraries have responded rather forcefully to the pricing predicament. Bensman and Wilder (1998) reported on a project conducted at Louisiana State University (LSU) based on a complete analysis of all facets of scientific and technical journal publication. They found that LSU libraries, taking advantage of a variety of available mechanisms, including technology, could cancel a number of titles with no discernible impact on access to information.

The challenge to libraries may be shifting (as we will see in chapter 9), but it is not diminishing.

SPACE CONSIDERATIONS

One of the library's considerations related to the publication of books is the growth of library collections. Physical collections require space, and space is limited and costly. Throughout this century, academic library collections have grown continuously, which has created space problems for many libraries. The problem is not limited to the large libraries, even though, in raw numbers, their collections have grown more than those of other institutions. For instance, the library of a two-year college is limited in space and many libraries are at maximum capacity. This problem is not just a management concern, a matter of deciding where to put materials (although this is an important concern). The space problem has serious implications for access and services. If the library's stacks are full, it can become more difficult to find physical items on the shelves. One reason for the difficulty is the chance that more things may be misshelved. Also, as more shelving space is used, the likelihood increases that items may be crowded on the shelves and placed so that book spines are difficult to read. It stands to reason that crowding makes browsing more difficult. Browsing is inhibited by the density of shelving, which requires the user to concentrate attention on a fairly small area of space in order to examine all items. In a sense, the crowding constitutes noise that inhibits communication. Finding potentially relevant material becomes more difficult. Services also may be affected because space is taken up with shelving. Many libraries have been forced to reduce the space allocated to readers and users so that more shelving can be installed. Less space may be available for instruction, group work, and the use of reference materials. The limitations imposed by space problems can force libraries to re-examine their ability to fulfill some of their goals and objectives.

The space problem seems to cry for efforts to expand existing facilities and construct new ones. Some of the difficulties caused by space constraints could certainly be alleviated by the addition of space. However, the problem has political aspects that are related to the expenditure of money necessary to expand or construct facilities. If a library needs additional or new space, the director must try to make the case to the institution's administration that money would be well spent on the library. The director's recommendations would have to be specific, with regard to the impact of the new space and cost estimates. He or she is in the position to construct an argument for the expenditure of funds based, in all probability, on the benefits that would accrue to the entirety of the campus. Of course, the library proposal will be in competition with other proposals.

The campus administration then must decide on the priorities of the proposals before them and prepare an institutional proposal for presentation to the governing board. In public higher education, the board then would develop a proposal for presentation to the state legislature because the money would come from the state's capital budget. In private colleges and universities, the decision might rest with the board, which might have to consider embarking on a capital campaign to seek money from donors to pay at least some of the construction costs. At each decision level the priorities can be reordered. It is not unusual for a library's proposal, even if it is eventually successful, to be presented for several consecutive years before there is agreement on its priority status. It is becoming more difficult, though, to persuade local administrators of the need for library space. Some administrators are convinced that electronic information will soon supplant print materials, thus eliminating collection growth in the future. Such an attitude may reflect a lack of understanding of the dynamics of scholarly communication or a willful rationalization for a decision not to spend money on library space.

In the event that space problems grow too severe to ignore, some institutions look for alternatives to the construction of traditional library space. Traditional space is quite expensive because it includes space for readers (space not used for the storage of materials), shelving space that is designed for browsing and user access (which means compliance with the Americans with Disabilities Act), and areas for user and staff traffic. One alternative that has captured the attention of administrators is the separate storage facility. A storage facility may be constructed locally, in the heart of the campus, or remotely. As might be expected, remote storage facilities tend to cost less because the cost of land is very high on all college and university campuses. The storage facility is usually not intended to be browsable space, so some economies can be realized, including denser storage such as deeper shelves, storage based on size rather than classification, and taller shelves to make more complete use of space. On the plus side, because the facilities are not intended for heavy foot traffic, climate control is factored in at the beginning and is likely to have preservation benefits. Such economies mean that more materials can be stored (than in traditional library space) for a particular sum of money. Let's look at a hypothetical breakdown of costs for some different construction models—traditional space, compact shelving attached to an existing facility, and remote storage. Table 8.1 presents some comparative costs. (The models are based on an assumed cost of $175 per square foot for construction and estimates for ancillary costs that are intended for illustrative purposes only. Actual construction costs will vary by geographic region and actual ancillary costs will vary greatly as well.)

The intention is usually to place infrequently used materials in such facilities so that the more heavily used items can be stored in the library itself.

TABLE 8.1   Models for Construction Costs (at $175/square foot) for a Library of 500,000 Volumes at an Institution of 10,000 Students

Type of Construction	Amount of Space Needed	Additional Costs	Total Costs
Traditional	117,500 square feet*	N/A	$20,562,500
Movable, Compact Shelving	20,000 square feet**	$3/volume for the system	$ 5,000,000
Storage Facility (Automated Retrieval)	6,000 square feet***	$1,500,000 for retrieval $600,000 for climate control	$ 3,150,000
Storage Facility (Mechanical Retrieval)	6,000 square feet***	$750,000 for retrieval $600,000 climate control	$ 2,400,000

   * Adhering to Formula C: Facilities of "Standards for College Libraries" (1995, 254).
  ** Assuming 50 volumes per square foot plus space for browsing and use of materials.
*** Assuming 150 volumes per square foot plus staff space.

Arguments against the use of storage facilities include the claim that removal from ready access influences requests for materials, with users deciding not to spend time waiting for the retrieval of materials. One concern is that the reluctance of users to request materials may affect the content of scholarship in the future and contribute to an ahistorical approach to some areas of inquiry. The matter of storage also is politically charged, and librarians must be aware of the political importance of decisions regarding the expenditure of money. Moreover, librarians must realize that capital expenditures are subject to procedures that may differ from those related to operating expenditures. It is extremely rare that the decision to spend funds on a capital project is a local one, so external bodies and individuals will be involved in the deliberations.

COLLECTION DEVELOPMENT

All of the considerations mentioned so far constitute issues relevant to collection development or collection management. (These two terms are used most frequently in the literature; I use "collection management" here to mean not only selection of materials, but also fiscal management, analysis, and evaluation.) There are more extensive works that tackle collection management matters (Johnson 2004); this discussion focuses on some particular aspects of managing collection that are relevant to, and perhaps sometimes unique to, academic libraries. So far in this chapter, little effort has been made to differentiate among types of libraries because the prices of books, the serials crisis, and space problems tend to affect all types of academic libraries. When it comes to collection management, the missions of the institutions play a major role in management considerations. For instance, there are differences between four-year college libraries and research university libraries. The needs of the institutions, their faculties, and their students will vary; what is most essential is attention to the curriculum and research of the individual institution. Realization of the diversity of needs makes generalization difficult, if not impossible. As C. Roger Davis (1991) pointed out, the maxims used in the past—the college librarian will know the institution better than will the university librarian; college libraries have to manage serials collections more carefully than do university libraries; students are more important clientele than faculty for college libraries; and so on—are lacking in substance and could do some harm when misapplied.

On the other hand, Davis wrote, "There are major differences between college and research libraries in working conditions that affect the context in which collection development decisions are made, but the overall approaches and principles are the same. The chief difference is dollars. All other differences flow from it" (1991, 31). Without a doubt, there is a difference in dollars, but the money does not create, or even symbolize, all the differences between colleges and universities. The most fundamental difference between the college and the university is mission. This difference affects just about every aspect of the library, including collection development. It is not just that the college library tends to have a smaller collection than the university library, but also that the collection is different in kind. Mary Casserly recognized the differences between college and university libraries and further observed that these are not pure types, that there may be varying levels of research and emphasis on the curriculum.

> Very few academic librarians involved in collection development do so in the quintessential college or research library. Rather, most librarians function in a setting that occupies a place on a continuum anchored by these archetypes. Further, this place may shift across the continuum, closer to one anchor or the other, as different aspects of philosophy and practice are considered. It is therefore important that librarians understand and appreciate collection development not

only from the research library perspective but also from the perspective of the college library setting (1991, 12–13).

It is true that wherever on the continuum the library falls, the publishing of books, the prices of serials, the challenges of space, and (as we'll see in chapter 9) the complexities of electronic information present difficulties for collection management. Add to this mix the necessity of understanding the institution's mission and priorities and fitting into its culture, and collection development becomes a tall order. The responsibility of collection development is, first, to create a decision process wherein selection is based on a set of goals that are, admittedly, collection based, but librarywide. This means that the collection is seen as the primary resource that enables access and services to succeed. The collection, then, does not *belong* to collection management. In a very real sense, it does not *belong* to the library; rather, it is a resource that is used by community members who are external to the library. It is up to everyone in the library to determine on what basis the collection will be developed and then it is up to collection development, as both a unit in the library and a process, to bring about that vision. As we can see from the discussion on the different organizational cultures that exist on campus, the different institutional missions, and the varying motivations and activities of faculty as authors. The inadequacy of funding for libraries and the tumultuous nature of publishing—the realization of the vision is problematic.

A concern of academic librarians (in all types of libraries, but particularly in college libraries) has been the role of faculty in collection management. For at least the first half of this century, faculty largely controlled selection in college libraries. To a lesser extent, faculty control still exists in some libraries. This means that faculty have (or take) responsibility for the selection of specific items and thus have a substantial say in the shape of the library's collection. A common criticism of faculty activities in collection development is that faculty lack the broad vision necessary to build a collection of sufficient breadth to meet the needs of the whole academic community. Faculty selection has tended to be based on individual need, and instructional purposes have not always been considered. Since the turn of the century, some libraries have formalized faculty involvement through the allocation of financial resources to academic departments. Over time, there has been something of a lessening of such allocation, with the library retaining more control over the expenditure of funds. Mary Scudder and John Scudder (1991) pointed out some of the difficulties of faculty control of collection development but also insisted that faculty involvement is essential for effective collection management. The consultative relationship they advocated is indeed a necessary one. As discussed in earlier chapters, the faculty tend to be the most permanent members of the academic community and the people who are most familiar with the disciplinary literatures. Liaison work usually succeeds because librarians both work with the disciplinary community through public services and contribute to managing those disciplines' collections. The Collection Development and Evaluation Section (CODES) of the Reference and User Services Association (RUSA) has established "Guidelines for Liaison Work in Managing Collections and Services" that are intended to help libraries establish liaison programs to assist effective work with the libraries' communities (http://www.ala.org/ala/rusa/rusaprotocols/referenceguide/guidelinesliaison.htm). With staff reductions and more for librarians to do, effective liaison work may be placed in jeopardy. Although faculty involvement is important, it must be remembered that the faculty may well have something of a skewed notion of what the library exists for. In particular, faculty may equate collection with library.

The aforementioned challenges suggest that perhaps more attention should be paid to the management aspects of collection-related activities. Robert Hayes (1993) emphasized the importance of collection management, principally because of the number and magnitude of external influences on the library. These external influences include the institutional administration, academic program needs, publishing activities, financial resources, and technology. These factors led Hayes to assert the need for strategic management, "That part of general management of organizations that emphasizes the relationships to external environments, evaluates the current status of them and the effects of future changes in them, and determines the most appropriate organizational response to them" (1993, 22). Awareness of the external influences is vital because so many players can have some effect, sometimes indirect and subtle, on the collection of academic libraries and their management. The challenge for librarians is to analyze the potential influences of those outside players without becoming opportunistic. By that I mean that libraries should take care not to focus on potential short-term and narrow advantages to the detriment of a thoroughly considered and encompassing vision. Such vision is, of course, at the heart of strategic management. Collection management necessitates not only analysis, but also action targeted at the solution of problems. For instance, many libraries in recent years have responded to the serials crisis by devising programs of across-the-board cuts of serial subscriptions. Although this action meets a short-term need, it really doesn't address the reality that price increases are not universal or uniform but, instead, are linked to some subject areas and some producers of information. Charles Hamaker wrote, "I have remarked . . . that across the board cuts generally protect the publishers whose price increases have been the major villains in our libraries" (1992, 95–96). What Hamaker speaks of is managing the collection by taking a more careful look at the library's most important goals.

As might be expected, the management considerations have implications for collection development policies. There is no need to go into great detail on policy here, but a few particular aspects are worth noting. In particular, policy outlines who will be responsible for selection and what criteria will be used. It is in academic libraries that the concept of levels of collecting are most relevant. On just about every campus, there are differences in the depth of instruction in the various subject areas and in the depth of inquiry of the faculty. In a given department, the specializations are not given equal attention or emphasis; some will be featured more prominently in the curriculum. An understanding of the varying emphases is required to be able to assign collecting levels to the many subject areas. To arrive at the most accurate picture of emphases, it is important to consult with the faculty to become informed about current curricular structure and the direction of the academic department. Likewise, not all subject areas are equal when it comes to research. In many ways, research is more challenging than the curriculum in the determination of collecting levels. Although the curriculum is likely to change less drastically and less frequently, research can be variable as the faculty on campus at any given time and also is affected by the agendas of funding agencies and the perceptions of what constitutes the "cutting edge." Research, in other words, is more dependent on changeable external factors than is the curriculum. The problem for collection development is how to develop collections in a dynamic environment and how to adjust collecting levels.

The matter of collection development itself has been challenged lately. The most frequently stated criticism is that given the dynamic environment just described, a policy statement is bound to be insufficiently flexible to reflect changes within and among disciplines. Dan Hazen wrote, "Collection development policies reify scholarly distinctions that no longer carry meaning. They are exercises in obsolescence that cater to nostalgic longings for order, precision, and prescription" (1995, 30). Hazen aims his criticism at collection development policies, but his comments are more descriptive of the uses of policy. It is easy to see how a policy, when formulated, can be allowed to stagnate. A policy (which is more than simply a *statement* of policy, that is, more than just a rhetorical device) can be flexible enough to be responsive to the needs of the community, the evolution of publishing, and the adoption of technologies. What is required is constant inquiry into these external matter and evaluation of the ability of the collection to fulfill all that is asked of it. The main obstacle to flexibility, as Atkinson (1992) said, is financial resources. The library has no choice but to compose and conduct its strategy in the face of an inadequate budget and a system of financial allocation at the institutional level that is mired in a tradition of operation.

The success of realizing the goals of the policy and, in fact, the success of collection development is dependent on people. The librarians are charged with building and managing a collection that enables the college or university to fulfill its mission. As is the case with much academic librarianship, no one single model best fits all institutions. In the past, university libraries tended to rely on a few subject specialist bibliographers to manage their collections. College libraries, by and large, didn't have the luxury of a large staff, some of whom could be assigned only collection management duties. In libraries with smaller staffs, assignment of multiple responsibilities has been more common than not. More recently, university libraries have come to emulate the approach of some of the college libraries. Some university libraries have reorganized to disperse collection management responsibilities. There are two fundamental reasons for the shift. The first reason is the recognition that it is impossible for a humanities or social sciences bibliographer to know the entirety of the collection in the humanities or the social sciences in any detail. A finer breakdown enables librarians to become more familiar with a smaller segment of the collection. The second reason is the recognition that, in the former model, the bibliographer is unable to get to know the faculty in these broad areas and be in close contact with academic departments. Dispersion of duties allows an individual to have, perhaps, only one department, or very few departments, to work with. Liaison can be more successful if the librarian can get to know faculty and speak with them frequently about both library and academic matters. Each college or university library should determine its own goals for collection management and then devise an organizational strategy to meet them. The models of the past, if deemed inadequate, should not be retained in the interests of tradition or comfort.

Given the demands on the library and librarians, the demands on the collection, the dynamic nature of the institution, and the limitations on library staff growth, some mechanisms are used to help meet collection management objectives. One of the most frequently used mechanisms is the approval plan. Vendors and jobbers are generally willing and able to work with just about any library with a sufficiently stable budget to construct an approval plan to ensure the acquisition of materials in at least some subject areas. From a management perspective, the plan's profile is the most essential element. Details of the profile can't be rushed; the point of the plan is to receive items that would have been selected and not to receive items that would not have been selected. The profile is based on a clear understanding and articulation of the curricular and research needs of the community. It makes sense that faculty, as the segment of the community most responsible for assigning readings and engaging in scholarship, be consulted as part of the profile stage. When the profile is created, the approval plan constitutes, according to some, a preselection device. For instance, Hunter Kevil wrote,

> The job the vendor wants to do is preselection, not the actual selection, which is done at the library. This preselection is accomplished

by the library's profile which, of course, is a record of its collection development policy. To the extent that this record is accurate, preselection will simply exclude those titles library policy would have excluded, . . . and will send for consideration those titles the library has determined its selectors should see. Selection can then be done at the library in the best way, with book-in-hand (1985, 16).

When in place, the plan should be evaluated. Joan Grant (1990) provided a very useful list of considerations related to evaluation that all academic librarians should be aware of.

One concern that is expressed occasionally regarding approval plans is that they represent the library's abdication of responsibility. In other words, the fear exists that library collections are being built by vendors, who are in business to make sales and may not be as inclusive as librarians would like. In libraries where the profile has been constructed carefully and reviewed frequently, where the quality of the plan is monitored, and where there is not sole reliance on an approval plan, the fears can be allayed. A movement in some libraries, however, may heighten concern. In some instances, libraries are foregoing approval; that is, they are agreeing to accept all materials sent by the vendors and are not sending materials back. The constraints on the library, already mentioned, may be the cause of the movement, but the library must be aware of some of the effects of such a decision and should use the plan as only one of a number of means of carrying out collection management responsibilities.

The constraints on libraries present other challenges and responsibilities. Everyone knows that no library can possibly meet all user needs. The breadth and depth of those needs are too great, as are the library's limitations. The inability to be fully self-sufficient naturally implies the need for cooperation. Cooperation has been talked about and written about for many years, but it is still not as widespread or as encompassing as some would like to see. One inhibitor is the potentiality of a library giving up more than it gets; another is the fear of loss of autonomy and identity. The first concern tends to be a more realistic concern, especially because there are costs to cooperation. One way to cooperate is simply through resource sharing (that may be typified by traditional interlibrary loan). A more concerted effort is cooperative collection development. As Ann Thompson (1993) pointed out, cooperative collection development is much more than just resource sharing, it hinges on libraries building and maintaining collections that are founded on strengths, describing those collections, and being willing to share them. These factors are important, but they are joined by the necessity for planning and envisioning both the benefits and the costs of cooperation. The desire to cooperate is not enough, which is why Patricia Buck Dominguez and Luke Swindler said that successful cooperation is dependent on circumstances being conducive to the effort (1993, 487). This means that there has to be mutual willingness among participants to engage in cooperation and share costs, a realistic mechanism to share materials, and institutional support for the program. The last item may be the most vital; without institutional support, libraries may come up against insurmountable governance obstacles. That support has to be sought early in the planning stage. Moreover, no single library should take advantage of the others; all should make an equivalent commitment (equivalent rather than equal because libraries of unequal collections and resources may enter into a cooperative agreement). As always, the guiding force should be providing needed contact to the user community.

EVALUATION OF THE COLLECTION

This section is not intended as a treatise on the measurement of use in libraries. Rather, it is a brief look at the considerations related to use that are important in academic libraries. The primary reason libraries build collections is use. It must be stated that use is conceived of very broadly in college and university libraries. This conception includes the most familiar measures of use, such as circulation of materials and tabulation of in-house use. Although these categories sound simple, they are more complex phenomena than they first appear. Because of time and the demands on library staff, it is very difficult to gain a full understanding of the motivations for use, the kinds of uses that may exist, and reasons for nonuse of library collections. The default, then, is frequently a set of mechanistic evaluation measures. Kristine Brancolini (1992) provided a thorough discussion (with examples) of kinds of use studies conducted in academic libraries. A user survey constructed at Indiana University, and included by Brancolini, reflects the typical sorts of questions asked of faculty and students but also exemplifies some of the problems of many user surveys. Some of the questions ask what materials are used, but no definition of "use" is offered. Different individuals may interpret the word quite differently; what constitutes use for one person may not for another.

As an example of the use of locally available circulation data, we can turn to Hamaker. He has used this information to engage in some probing examinations of collection use at Louisiana State University (LSU). I will mention only one of these examinations and urge all academic librarians to read his work. For some years, librarians have put considerable stock in what has been termed the 80–20 rule. This "rule" asserts that 20 percent of a library's collection will satisfy 80 percent of users' needs, usually defined as circulation. Hamaker's analysis indicated that, in a 45-month period, 856,000 unique items circulated in LSU's main library collection of less than two million volumes. This means that 43 percent of the collection circulated in that time period (1992, 72). Hamaker's work (and the work of some other prolific writers on academic libraries) tends to challenge common assumptions on which some decisions have been based in the past. If it is to be informative, evaluation should examine such assumptions to see whether they are based on evidence and are indications of actual behavior in libraries.

Thomas Nisonger (1998) provided a thorough set of possible mechanisms for libraries to use in evaluating serials collections. He included several in-house measures that enable libraries to make local decisions, such as reshelving, photocopying activity, checklists, surveys, and other measures of use. He also reported on larger-scale measures that also may be used in decision making. Means such as citation analysis and journal rankings also can offer libraries valuable data that can be added to local measures. Nisonger's contribution may be especially valuable, given the inevitable difficult decisions libraries continue to face with regard to serials.

SUMMARY

Recently, there was a listserv posting regarding collection development. The author of the posting claimed that collection development should be abandoned in academic libraries. The reason, according to the author, is that it is foolish for libraries to select and acquire materials in advance of a demonstrated need. Therefore, collection development should be replaced with document delivery and other access mechanisms. This assertion betrays a dangerous ignorance of the dynamics of collection use and the purpose of scholarly communication. For one thing, students and faculty are not willing to wait, and certainly aren't willing to pay, for information that is needed immediately for specific purposes. Beyond this, though, the existence and structure of a library collection constitute information retrieval devices themselves. As a faculty member or a student consults the library's catalog or browses the stacks, he or she is informed of the existence of potentially relevant materials. These discoveries can affect individuals' thought and the ways they approach questions and problems. Abolition of the collection and reliance on demand can only be based on the assumption that all information users (1) completely understand their information need, (2) can articulate it explicitly, and (3) can translate it into packages of information that can be acquired or accessed when needed. These are decidedly questionable assumptions. Moreover, these assumptions are antithetical to almost all of the working of colleges and universities; higher education aims to foster learning through discovery, which implies that knowledge grows as students (and faculty) find connections previously unknown to them. In addition, the author's statement includes the tacit assumption that the information exists somewhere and is deliverable to the library or the individual at an affordable price.

All of the above points to a particular purpose of the library collection. It is a means to understanding. It is a record of the thought that has gone before. It is a dynamic entity marked by an abundance of potential energy. And it is vital to the mission of higher education. The packages of information that make up the library's collection are certainly commodities. Their values as things, however, may be dwarfed by the value their contents add to learning and inquiry. Some may be tempted to center attention on the exchange value of the collection (what its components are worth in monetary terms). However, it is far more productive to think of the use value of the collection (the contributions it makes to students' progress, faculty scholarship, etc.). Inevitably, librarians will be concerned with some of the material aspects of the collection. The budget is a material thing, so the price of serials constitutes a serious problem. The items themselves are material, so librarians must deal with space constraints. The most important considerations of the collection, though, focus on content. Whatever the material aspects, the collection represents intellectual content and contributes to intellectual growth. This focus compels us to think first about content. This chapter has explored the physical, tangible manifestations of content; chapter 9 explores access and electronic sources of information,

The physical collection is obviously the subject of some debate in academic librarianship. Following are some questions that may help to frame further discussion:

> Is the book dead?
>
> How effective are books and journals as communication
> mechanisms?
>
> What would you, as a librarian, tell faculty they could do
> to help resolve the serials crisis?
>
> Should collection development be the province of one person
> or unit in the library?
>
> What options exist for the library that is almost out of available
> space?
>
> What does the collection contribute to education?

Chapter 9

Electronic Information
and Academic Libraries

In the past several years, no area related to academic libraries has changed more dramatically than that of electronic information. The technology involved has undergone considerable change, but the information markets have been even more greatly transformed. This chapter examines some actual and potential uses of electronic information in college and university libraries. In some ways, this discussion builds on chapter 8 on collections. Electronic information is envisioned by some as a replacement for print collections. According to this vision, we should abandon consideration of print as a communication medium and look to supplant our existing collections with access to electronic information. As is obvious from chapter 8, I do not share this vision completely. Assertions that electronic information will replace print completely are misplaced for many reasons. Some of the reasons are related to libraries, their communities, and the needs of diverse users. Some are external to the library and are related to the production of information (including those things that authors write as well as the activities of information producers), the cost of information, legal considerations, and technological realities. These external reasons include the growth and seeming inclusiveness of the Web (e.g., Googling retrieves everything needed). I hasten to add that a fully Luddite stance is likewise misplaced. There are obvious benefits that libraries can realize if they take advantage of some of what electronic information has to offer. It is clear that this is a mixed bag of benefit and mirage, and there are complexities we must be willing to examine if decisions are to be well informed.

As we look at electronic information, we see that this is not a single issue or a single product. "Electronic information" is an umbrella term and sometimes refers to physical artifacts that house digitized information, locally created databases, and, most frequently, access to information stored remotely. The variety of objects and access form some of the complexities we must be aware of. The different kinds of electronic media present different concerns regarding cost, ownership, and control, among other things. These are not trivial concerns, and electronic media, including the Web, do not comprise a panacea that will cure all information-related ills. That warning notwithstanding, there is certainly no reason for libraries to assume that the print medium is inherently superior to all alternatives for all purposes. We must examine the various possibilities and the context in which they arise. Before we begin in earnest, I should state that this discussion does not rely heavily on specific technologies because information technologies are at least somewhat transient, as we have seen recently. The emphasis here is on the more sweeping questions, and some technologies will be considered as examples of possibilities.

GENERAL CONSIDERATIONS

Certain specific aspects of electronic information require attention, but some more broad-based matters need to be addressed first. In the recent past, some of the concerns that have occupied librarians have become less pressing. For instance, the 1970s and 1980s saw a push to automate basic library functions. It is almost impossible to think about an unautomated library; concern now is focused on maintenance and, at times, replacement and upgrade of systems. In some cases, the automation projects have been spurred by large-scale cooperative efforts. This means that multicampus automation initiatives have been undertaken to assume a high level of interconnectivity, resource sharing, and communication. Sometimes these efforts have included most, or even all, state institutions, and, on occasion, the cooperative endeavors have included both public and private colleges and universities. Automation now is sufficiently widespread that attention can turn to matters that go beyond a single library. The automated systems frequently are able to support at least limited networking among libraries. The potential that networking presents is still being explored; the beginnings have centered on the sharing of holdings information, coordination of collection management decisions, the sharing of access to databases, and other initiatives having to do with the handling of certain bibliographic control issues. (For examples of the consortium approach, see the OhioLINK [http://www.ohiolink.edu] and MOBIUS efforts in Missouri [http//www.mobius.org].) MOBIUS includes public and private colleges and universities, and is expanding to bring in some public libraries. Of the many changes that consortia influence (not the least of which is enhanced bargaining power when negotiating prices with information providers), one of the most important is the need to make decisions in a cooperative environment. The good of the whole, as well as the good of each member, must be considered.

As we know, most of the history of academic libraries has entailed the organization and control of print on paper. The beginnings of automation also have entailed the management of information in print. Over time, although print has remained an important and pervasive medium, electronic information has emerged and grown, frequently as the preferred medium of communication. The diversity of media has led to increased responsibilities for libraries. The library has to provide its community with books and journals because some information is only available in print on paper. In addition, the library has to be open to other possibilities. No longer are services limited to bibliographic access to journal literature; many provide access to full text and/or full image of the contents of many periodicals. The difference between full text and full image is that full text involves the transmission and availability of an article's content (usually in HTML format) whereas full image is the availability of the article's content exactly as it was published, including the original typesetting, pagination, and graphics (usually as a .pdf file). I'll return to these services shortly.

There is no doubt that the academic library is evolving at a fairly rapid rate. The reasons for its evolution are many and have internal and external impetuses. Librarians have become attuned to the possibilities offered by automation and electronic media and have begun articulating demands for products and services. Some of the demands are based on the opportunity to get more for the existing financial resources. (Note that I didn't say that libraries can save money. Saving is difficult, if not impossible, but it is possible to get better service and more access for the same expenditure.) Automation, in part, enables libraries to enhance access to materials held locally and materials available from other libraries (e.g., the consortial environment). Librarians have voiced their concerns to information providers, which has led the providers to enhance their products. The internal impetus for development also has come from the academic community. Students, and especially faculty, have been able to see potential developments in the storage and retrieval of information and have communicated their concerns to the library and, at times, directly to information providers. There have been external developments as well. Technological developments, particularly in the area of networked information, have proceeded at a rapid rate and have inspired products and services that libraries find attractive.

The evolution has proceeded in the direction of electronic information, but there remains diversity of communication media. Michael Buckland has observed the course of the evolution:

> Hitherto, the dominant interpretation has been the judicious assembling of local collections as the only effective means of providing

convenient physical access to items, augmented by retrieval tools and advice. Contemporary changes in the technology underlying access to information indicate a need to reconsider how information services are provided as well as changes in relationships between systems and between local and remote collections (1991, 205).

He has extended his view of the future more recently and speaks of the difference between the automated library and the electronic library. The automated library, which is the stage at which most academic libraries exist now, has developed computerized mechanisms for many of its technical operations but still relies on print or paper as the primary medium. The electronic library incorporates digital and digitized media into the totality of its information base and its services. This view is echoed on a larger societal scale by Nicholas Negroponte (1995), who described the evolutionary tracks as proceeding from atoms to bits. It is obvious that there is no absolute consensus on what the future of libraries will be. Now let's turn to some specific media and content to see what exists and what is possible.

ELECTRONIC JOURNALS

It is impossible to consider electronic information in academic libraries without dealing with electronic journals (e-journals). We've already seen the place that print journals have in the communication patterns of some disciplines, the weight they carry in the evaluation and rewards of faculty, and the effect of their prices on library budgets. According to various statements and visions, the e-journal has the potential to transform each of the aforementioned problem areas. Before addressing any claims regarding e-journals, however, we must examine what they are. It is not easy to define and describe *the* e-journal; it is a varied resource. It seems almost quaint to talk about the history of e-journals; there has been a considerable degree of development in a very short time. Many of the earliest e-journals were more akin to newsletters. Their content tended to be limited in length and scope, and the topics included were frequently of the nature of reporting news. I do not mean this as a negative criticism; newsletters can be valuable sources of information. Many of the early electronic newsletters were established by small groups, or even by individuals. The workload of the editor, which was customarily in addition to the duties of a professional position, was considerable. These factors, along with the absence of formal support such as the release time, subsidy, or financial resources that might accompany the editing of a print journal, may well have affected the content and scope of e-journals. The resources put into them also may have affected the reception of early e-journals.

Early e-journals were not all newsletters. There were some electronic counterparts to print journals, which served the purpose of extending and expanding the audience for the journal's content. Also, in cases where the journal also was published in print, the release time, subsidies, and financial assistance may have been available. Print journals also tended to carry some kind of institutional attachment (a university or a learned society), which may have affected the popular and official institutional perception of them. In the earliest days, there may have been at least a tacit assumption that an e-journal is ephemeral and transitory. Of course, such a notion has disappeared utterly. Others of the earlier e-journals were efforts to use the technological possibilities of networked information to create and distribute content only in an electronic format. These journals tended to be similar to print journals in manuscript review processes and arrangements of content. That is, the tendency was to develop a journal that would include full-length articles reviewed by peers and grouped in issues distributed at regular intervals. The content and use of these e-journals did not differ appreciably from print ones.

One technical point needs to be made here. The early e-journals predated the World Wide Web and the widespread incorporation of graphical user interfaces in networked information. Because of these factors, the contents of the early journals were exclusively, or almost exclusively, text. Textual or ASCII data were easiest to work with and distribute. The limitations contribute to a phenomenon that is not surprising: many of the early e-journals were in the humanities and the social sciences. In other words, they tended to have content that was amenable to textual discourse. Not too long ago, e-journals were relatively (especially to the number of print journals) scarce and journals in the sciences were even scarcer. Many of the sciences depend on figures, tables, and other graphics as part of the communication process. The inclusion of graphics was no simple matter, and it may have been avoided in an experimental medium whose reception was uncertain.

The number of e-journals, defined generously, has been growing remarkably recently. Some individuals, such as Michael J. O'Donnell, were willing to make predictions about e-journals' success: "extrapolating from the success of journals that are currently published electronically, it is clear that electronic media will capture a large share of scholarly publication in the next five years, and that printed media will not be competitive in journal publication beyond a few more decades" (1995, 183). His prediction may have been just a bit optimistic; academic libraries still subscribe to many print journals. However, a number of persistent and plaguing nontechnical issues may be much more difficult to resolve. Among others, these include copyright, archiving, access and indexing, academic rewards, and profitability for producers.

With the development of the Web, a wealth of possibilities has opened up for e-journals. The inclusion of elaborate and sophisticated graphics, sound, and moving images presents some potential to enable e-journals to be something very different from their print counterparts. It may be possible to imagine a sociological study that can incorporate ethnographic research methods to include sound features (e.g., the voices of interviewees responding to questions) and perhaps photographic images of places and people. In this example, what might be communicated is not (or not just) a textual compendium of research findings but, rather, aspects of the subject of investigation. Such communication may be able to provide audiences with a fuller and richer appreciation for the question researched, the method employed, and the conduct of the study, as well as the findings. This kind of communication is demanding on both producer and receiver. The time that might be required to create the presentation may well be an inhibiting factor, especially considering the requirements of, and need for, rapid demonstration of productivity. Nonetheless, Web-based communication presents opportunities that are being seized in a number of disciplines.

E-journals of the kind just described may have additional features that set them apart from print journals. In addition to incorporating various media, the electronic journal may be accompanied by an integrated access mechanism. That is to say, the potential exists for a sophisticated access mechanism to be created simultaneously with, or just after, the creation of the presentation itself. A set of protocols, including thesauri to describe textual, graphical, and other content, could be established and imbedded in the presentation in order to provide full-content access of semantic richness to the journal. This potential, I must add, has not yet been fully realized. The potential of the medium in this regard demands that organization and access mechanisms be developed in conjunction *with* the content. This may well be an unrealizable ideal in its most complete incarnation. Other possibilities loom larger, however. For instance, the e-journal need not be constructed in the same temporal fashion as the print journal. It need not necessarily exist as a set of periodically appearing issues. Contents could be transmitted as soon as they have been reviewed, accepted, and formatted. Again, this can create demands on the receiver (subscriber). The flow of content is unlikely to be regular, so the receiver would have to be attuned to the possibility of new content appearing at any time. An example of a growing body of information resources is Paul Ginsparg's e-print archive (a large searchable database of scientific papers, submitted prior to publication in formal mechanisms such as journals; see http://xxx.arxiv.cornell.edu).

Another potential presented by the e-journal is interaction. Many print journals include letters to the editor that comment on published articles. However, the letters appear some time after the article's publication and are separated from it by being in a different issue of the journal. If a reader wants to comment on the comment, the time lag would render such communication at least a little absurd. The electronic medium can allow for commentary that may appear quickly after the appearance of the original presentation. Further, the commentators can be linked to the original paper for easy reference. The creator of the presentation can respond quickly to the commentary. The interaction could facilitate debate and discussion of the ideas or research that is included as the journal's content. It should be noted that discussion and disputation occur in all disciplines. In fact, narrative comment may be most amenable to the humanities and the social sciences. Once again, however, the demands on the receiver of the communication can be formidable. The magnitude of the content could, at times, become greater than an individual can, or is willing to, absorb. Overload is a distinct possibility with the interactive capabilities. Also, without some editorial control of the comments, there may be repetition of statements or observations by a number of commentators. Moreover, the comments could diverge from civil discourse and become personal and inflammatory. A completely open forum may not be desirable. (A number of academics have created their own Web logs, or blogs, in order to comment on disciplinary, as well as social and political, issues. A discussion of blogs is beyond the scope of this book.)

Academic librarians face the challenge of understanding not only the potential that e-journals represent, but also the uses to which the academic community puts them. The latter demands that librarians comprehend the reasons why individuals submit manuscripts to journals, why they read them, and how they incorporate their content into their own work. One uniting realization is that communication is essential to scholarship, research, and teaching. Another factor of substantial importance is that publication, including or perhaps especially, in journals is a universally accepted measure of scholarly productivity. The challenge, then, is to appreciate the epistemic and the practical purposes journals serve. In arguing in favor of the centrality of e-journals in the academic world, Teresa Harrison and Timothy Stephen addressed what they saw as the most important aspects of scholarly communication:

> Most discussions of discourse communities are based upon the assumption that members orient themselves around its media—that is, the specific channels and genres that members use to communicate, which, it is worth pointing out, have been regarded implicitly as print-based, principally because, until recently, there has been no apparent alternative. Most scholarly communities are oriented particularly around refereed journals as channels for communication and the research article as a genre of communication. While scholars share information and debate issues at conferences and other face-to-face meetings, for most disciplines, the refereed journal is the primary "site" for communication (1995, 595).

Although, on the whole, their comments of are reasonable, Harrison and Stephen made some generalizations that are problematic and, I think, misrepresent to some degree the communication process as it works in various disciplines. They mentioned that conferences serve a communicative purpose but asserted that journals are the principal means of communication "for most disciplines." In many scientific disciplines the journal article is more of an archival artifact, a record of communication that, in many important respects, already has played out in a forum of interested participants. The conference is an important site of informing, discussion, debate, and, as Karl Popper has said, conjecture and refutation. At conferences many presentations are of work in progress. Such communications serve to establish intellectual claims of some researchers regarding questions or problems. These initial claims are subjected to the scrutiny of the research community, and the ensuing interaction may involve disputation of some or all of the research, affirmation of the work's efficacy, or questioning of method, data, or other elements of the research. The journal article reporting the full results of the research frequently is not new to the community, but it does serve as a tangible summary that can be acknowledged, built upon, or refuted in future work. However, the actual incorporation or refutation probably has already begun based on earlier, interactive communication.

In the humanities, the primary "site" for communication tends to be the book. The journal article usually is reserved for two purposes: addressing questions that are too limited in scope to be dealt with in a book, or communicating specific aspects of a larger question. In many instances, the latter purpose is supplementary or preliminary to the fuller treatment of the book. Scholarship in the humanities relies heavily on extended discursive narratives to develop premises, construct arguments or propositions, and (most important) address problems that are themselves based in textual communication. Reliance on the book means that journals, although not unimportant communication mechanisms, are not of overwhelming interest to humanities scholars. The state described by Harrison and Stephen is most descriptive of some, but not all, social science disciplines. It seems evident that academic librarians need a better understanding of the wide-ranging purposes and practices of communication in the various disciplines. Some future inquiry focused on such questions could be very beneficial to the discipline of library and information science in general and the work of each academic library in particular.

"E-journal" has, at this time, been integrated into the mainstream of information retrieval on campus and university campuses. The mergers and consolidations of information providers in recent years has accelerated the profusion of products that offer full text and full image of the contents of thousands of journals. Products such as ProQuest, Ebsco's Academic Search Elite, and many others are mainstays in the lives of students and faculty. There are still a number of paper-only serials, but it may be safe to speculate, especially where undergraduate students are concerned, that electronic access, including Google and other tools, is the primary educational and scholarly source of information. The challenge remains for librarians to help all information seekers make the most effective use of information resources, including educating people that the Web is not a reasonable substitute for scholarly resources that have been vetted by editorial and review processes.

THE ROAD AHEAD

There may still be some administrators and faculty do not invest much credibility in e-journals. At least part of the source of faculty skepticism rests with the acceptance of contributions to independently produced e-journals in the academic reward structure. In time, and with the demonstration of a rigorous review process for the journals, the prejudice could wane. Given the mainstream publication of so many journals by long-lived publishers (such as Elsevier, Wiley, Academic Press, etc.), the prejudice may soon become meaningless. Libraries are concerned about some particular aspects of e-journal publishing, especially as they might affect the services and information that libraries can provide their communities. As might be expected, one concern is the amount of information available. This translates to a concern regarding the number of e-journals published, the number of articles or other contents published, and the growth in e-journal publishing. In addition, librarians and faculty share interest in the credibility of these journals: who edits them, who contributes to them, who sponsors them, and so on. Naturally, librarians are concerned about the potential costs of electronic access in the future and their concern is certainly legitimate. There is one feature of e-journals that publishers are going to relish and libraries are going to fear—control.

The answers to the thorny questions challenge us, in large part, because the questions constitute a shifting ground. In all likelihood, whatever I state at this time will be outdated by the time the first reader browses this book. With a bit of trepidation, though, I would like to raise a few issues as they may be defined now. Many college and university libraries are migrating from print to e-journals. Until now, the migration was a bit difficult because of the requirement of some publishers, or by publishers with regard to some products or packages, that libraries maintain subscriptions to print journals in order to license electronic versions. A few years ago, Elsevier began offering electronic-only subscriptions to many of its products. Its strategy has been emulated by other major publishers. On the face of it, this may be good news to some subscribers. However, things are more complicated than may first appear. Elsevier manages some bundles of journals: its ScienceDirect package at present comprises about 1,800 journals. (See http://www.sciencedirect.com.) The costs of bundles such as this can vary, and a number of factors determine the price of an individual library. Kenneth Frazier (2001) has exhorted librarians to be skeptical of bundling, which he calls "The Big Deal," because of usurpation of choice by the publishers. These bundled deals resemble the present state of cable television. There may be some limited options, but the options are predetermined by the provider.

The bundling of journal subscriptions in licensing agreements can benefit some libraries, especially those that would want to provide access to all or almost all of the titles included in the agreement. For libraries that would like to be more selective, cost and benefit are more difficult to calculate. In consortia, it may be that smaller libraries realize considerable savings as a result of the buying and negotiating power of the collective. Other benefits provided by the consortium—a union catalog, reciprocal borrowing agreements, and so on—may offset some costs of licenses. Consortia and licenses do change the meaning and practice of selection, at least as far as some information products are concerned. As Curt Holleman pointed out, "To the degree that selection takes place, it is believed that it will be on a grand macro scale and not in the selection of individual materials" (2000, 694). In this environment of the licensing of electronic information, it is absolutely essential that academic libraries remember that their collections, access, and services exist to support the institutional community. With the growth of distance learning initiatives, and even with different attitudes toward information use among resident groups, academic libraries increasingly serve what Bryce Allen (2001) referred to as "electronic communities," typified not by geographic place, but by common interests, activities, and goals. Such physically dispersed communities already rely on dispersed information accessibility to help them achieve their academic objectives. The importance of licensing cannot be overstated; fortunately, there are resources to help libraries wade through the licensing quagmire. One vital source is Lib-License (http://www.library.yale.edu/~llicense/index.shtml), which offers advice and sample licenses to help guide decision making.

In the realm of the traditional print collection, the library has substantial control over the accessibility and use of materials. The library buys books and subscribes to journals, and then chooses how to make them available to the academic community. On the whole, this means free and ready access to the contents of the collection by faculty and students. If the library subscribes to a journal, a large number of people can read, and even photocopy, articles. The library doesn't pay extra for heavy use. The charging options for electronic access are expanded because the producer maintains substantial control over dissemination. In the future, the publisher could opt for pricing on a per-use basis, for instance. Such a structure may not be frowned on by all libraries. A particular library, instead of subscribing to an expensive journal, might pay for limited access to the journal's contents as needed by members of the community. On the other hand, we could envision how such a pricing structure could increase the costs to a library when there is considerable demand for access. It may well be that publishers eventually will establish multiple pricing structures in order to optimize their markets. There could be quite a bit of instability before workable practices can be instituted.

It may sound clichéd, but there are more questions than answers at this point. Sara von Ungern-Sternberg and Mats Lindquist (1995) lumped some of the questions into three major categories, and the categories are still important:

(1) the authority of information: who will take the role that the traditional publisher has today with regard to stability and authenticity of material?

(2) the cost of information: who will pay for maintaining the collection? This includes archiving, long-term storage and access. While electronic publishing can save costs in some aspects of publishing, the consequential costs are still significant.

(3) the access to information: who will grant equal access to information? A higher technological level in publishing will require more sophisticated equipment to use the information, but whose responsibility is it to make sure that this equipment is available (1995, 400)?

It would be a mistake for librarians to wait and see how the answers to these questions unfold. It is incumbent upon all academic librarians, and academic librarianship as a whole, to envision answers that will best serve the needs of the users of information while conceiving a mutually workable relationship for libraries and publishers.

Although the providers of electronic information are altering their business models almost constantly, dissatisfaction remains with the pricing and availability of electronic products. There are additional concerns about the archiving of electronically available journals, the stability of access to the database of information, and the rules that will determine future access to today's information. One response, led by the ARL in partnership with many other organizations, to these plaguing concerns is the Scholarly Publishing and Academic Resources Coalition (SPARC). (See http://www.arl.org/sparc.) A major goal of SPARC is to increase competition in the information marketplace by facilitating the creation of alternative sources of scholarly and research work. Working with several professional and learned societies, SPARC has fostered the development of several new journals that are based are more user- and library-friendly pricing models. The newly created journals have realized some success luring away editors, editorial board members, and contributors from higher-priced commercial journals. What remains to be seen is whether SPARC can spur the development of enough such competing journals to make a real difference in the information landscape. At this time, the number of SPARC-initiated titles is small. Future success probably will depend on the actions of the learned societies and others, such as the Public Library of Science (http://www.publiclibraryof science.org) toward developing new journals.

NETWORKED INFORMATION

Electronic access to journal literature constitutes only one element in the world of networked information. There are vast numbers of information sites of almost indescribable diversity of content available form educational, government, commercial, and individual sources. However, most of this content can be dismissed readily by the academic library because it has little or nothing to do with the academic enterprise. Still, that leaves a massive amount of information that has potential utility for faculty and students. Before exploring some of that content, I'd like to look at the human side. For the array of information to be useful, people must be connected. Essentially, this is a trivial concern for physical campuses, but such trends as greatly expanded online distance education may make it important. Students in more remote areas may only have the option of dial-up access. Their potential use of the possibilities of networked information may be severely limited.

Much of the information, including text, produced today is in machine-readable form. People use word-processing and database management packages, spreadsheets, and other tools to give tangible form to their ideas; and Web-authoring skills are widespread. Because of this behavior, no huge technological leap is required to make information available to a potentially large audience using means that are becoming more and more accessible. If, say, a sociologist wanted to share a draft of a paper with an undetermined community of readers, he or she could include the text of the paper in a Web site and perhaps inform potential readers via a listserv. He or she could benefit from the constructive comments and suggestions that readers might make and then submit a revised paper to a journal for formal publication. One caution: if such a paper were readily accessible, the author might fear that some less-than-scrupulous person might appropriate the idea and submit a paper based on it to a journal. As is the case with much of life, there are benefits and pitfalls to networked information. (A critique of access mechanisms, such as Web search engines, would certainly be possible, but it is not my intention to engage in such a critique here. Suffice it to say that the commercial nature of many search engines, including the practice of displaying sites on the basis of money paid by the owners of the sites, renders genuine academic use of the Web somewhat problematic.)

Because much existing data are in a digital form, organizations, associations, and even governments can distribute information quickly and with less cost than is involved in printing and mailing physical items. The amount of information is so vast that no one person can be aware of everything, but this situation has existed for a long time. At present, no subject specialist in a library can know the contents of every book and journal article in a subject area. However, the parallel between services in print and networked environments is clear. Librarians have to keep up as much as possible with the growth of information in order to meet the needs of the community. For example, a political science subject specialist should be able to guide an undergraduate student seeking information on the present state of the legislative branch of the federal government to the URL http://www.senate.gov so that the student can explore some specific aspects of the U.S. Senate. If a faculty member wants data on college and university enrollments, the education specialist might direct him or her to http://www.ed.gov/NCES/ and show the information that is available form the National Center for Education Statistics.

The diversity of subject matter available, the wide distribution of the locations of information, and the seeming fluidity of movement form one site allows us (perhaps forces us) to conceive the relationship between information user and what is used. In the traditional library, space is obvious and has a specific meaning for the user. Part of the notion of space in the traditional library is related to content. A library's classification joins and separates materials on the basis of content. Physics is not only intellectually apart from religion; it is physically apart. Networked information signifies a different kind of space. When the student or the scholar is at a workstation, the information is "there." The advantages of such an information space are quite evident; foremost among them is the ease with which the user can move through space. The travel through space is far less a physical one than a mental one. In the traditional library, movement through information space also is largely mental, but the physical movement is sufficiently pronounced that it may affect the mental operations. The space of a library is closely related to what Ross Atkinson identified as goal values. The primary goal values are functionality and maintenance, and are based on the ability to move information objects, to break them down into smaller parts, to ensure the stability of content, and to make sure the content survives over time (1998, 12–13).

One factor has a tremendous impact on movement through networked space. It is a factor that librarians have been struggling to come to grips with for centuries—organization of information. To an extent (at least to those of us who work in and/or study libraries), "library" is defined by organization. An unorganized mass of information is not, in some important sense, a library. For example, it is common to find only collection-level descriptions for archives and for special collections such as large numbers of photographs, where the costs of producing detailed cataloging for very large numbers of individual, unique objects is prohibitive (p. 9). Networked information (or at least some of it) is more transient than much of print information, which increases the importance of the economics of organization. Moreover, networked information is not subject (in the same way that most print information is) to gatekeeping. In all probability, the creator of the message can find a channel by which to communicate it. Control, and this includes control over what is removed as well as what is available, is so dispersed that the possibility of imposition of a uniform means of "thick" description of content is remote. Organization, or at least ex post facto subject-based access, is afforded through the use of any of a number of search engines designed to retrieve information available via the Web. It would be fruitless to describe these search engines in detail here because evolve quickly and new ones appear fairly frequently. Some outside of librarianship have been critical of the kind of access available to Web-based information today. Notable among the critics has been Clifford Stoll, who wrote, "Keyword-in-context lists are weak substitutes for a genuine index. Such searches profane the whole idea of research. In their facile expediency, they deliver information too effortlessly to be trustworthy. I know neither the depth nor breadth of the search: what databases did I miss? Would I get different results if I'd capitalized the name" (1995, 197)? Regarding his last question, the mechanisms of the Web are such that case sensitivity could alter what is retrieved in a search. Again, it is the librarian's responsibility to understand the workings of search engines so that the user can benefit form the librarian's knowledge of principles and practices of organization and the application of that knowledge to particular retrieval problems. Despite some claims by search engines, and despite assumptions by many Web searchers, the information world is much more complex than a Google search implies.

Whatever the shortcomings of networked information, faculty are taking advantage of the availability of this source and it seems apparent that networking is affecting the scholarly work of this segment of the academic community. A number of faculty are using networks to gain access to such things as texts or statistical data that may be useful to their research. Many also are using electronic networks as sources of information about grant and funding sources. A popular use of the Internet seems to be the searching of library catalogs other than those of faculty's local institution. The availability of electronic networks seems to be facilitating changes in disciplinary communities. For instance, some faculty say they are coauthoring more works because of the networks and some report that they are collaborating with people they haven't met in person. On the other hand, a recently published citation study in the social sciences revealed that less than half of the journal citations were potentially accessible to authors through commonly subscribed to services. Further, only about 10 percent of books cited had electronic versions (Budd and Christensen 2003, 648). When surveyed, a sample of authors included in the study indicated that a minority (9 out of 30 respondents) was likely to use full-text articles from library-held databases (Budd and Christensen 2003, 649). These factors are central to the enduring debate regarding the building of local collections and the availability of information by other means.

OPEN-ACCESS MOVEMENT

Anyone writing at this time (late 2004) about open access should do so with trepidation. Some open-access titles are available and a number of them appear to be flourishing. We have to be careful at this point to look on these successes within the scope of their limitations and not to predict a sea change just yet. The first matter to consider is the question, What is open access? To some extent, the term is self-explanatory, but there is a quite complex design behind it. Several organizations and individuals have been instrumental in developing open-access publication and attempting to make it both intellectually and financially viable. The Public Library of Science (http//:www.plos.org) is just one of the organizations that have pushed for more open-access journals, going so far as to create a couple of them itself. An explicit purpose behind open access is the provision of an alternative to commercial journals. Another goal is the provision of a rich environment for publishing, using emerging technologies to enhance communication products. Open access as an idea has been a driving force behind electronic access to information for some time and the goal of many of the earliest e-journals. The online journal *Postmodern Culture*, to give just one example, began in 1990 and still offers free access to its contents. In that same year, Stephan Harnad began publishing *Psycoloquy* online. Harnad has been a strong supporter of open access for many years.

Through the National Library of Medicine, PubMed Central offers scientists access to a digital archive of journal literature, demonstrating the federal government's role in open access. It must be said that open access does not necessarily mean "free." In fact, many models of open access, including that of the Public Library of Science (PLoS), do involve a cost, but the cost may be shifted from traditional payers. PLoS journals require authors to pay a publication fee of $1,500 to publish in them. Lila Guterman points out that,

> In 2003, scientists and social scientists at Duke published about 4,500
> papers, according to a search of the Science Citation Index and Social

Science Citation Index. If those reports had been published in author-fee journals, and if those authors had paid PLoS's $1,500-per-paper fee, the total cost for Duke (if the university picked up the author fees, in place of subscription costs) would have been $6.75 million (2004, A11).

There are a number of "ifs" in that statement, but the germ of a point is made. Supposing that at a given university four faculty members publish papers in *PLoS Biology;* the cost would be $6,000. Is this situation more practicable than subscribing to commercially produced journals? On the other hand, there are indications of success for open-access journals. "The number of visitors to the *PLoS Biology* Web site is robust—the number of full-text downloads of individual articles . . . was over 60,000 in January 2004" (Doyle 2004, 135).

Of course, the author-fee model is not the only possibility for open-access journals. John Willinsky has pointed out that several types of open-access archives and journals are actually operating right now—from e-print archives to institutional support for journals (2003, 264). Further, as David Prosser (2003), director of SPARC Europe, observed, the erosion of library collections over the years has led to U.S. and U.K. institutions having far less access to the journals published in other nations. Open access has the potential to eliminate national bias that may be an outcome of the marketplace and to provide scholars and scientists a much wider range of research. It also is important to note that, according to recent inquiry by Kristin Antelman, open-access journals may have greater research impact than those published traditionally. She writes, "Shedding light on this category of open access reveals that scholars in diverse disciplines are adopting open-access practices at a surprisingly high rate and are being rewarded for it, as reflected in a traditional measure of research impact" (2004, 380). Ann Wolpert said that the surest thing about scholarly communication is that it will change, with ever-increasing use of network technologies coming in a close second (2002, 18). A sourer note is offered by Joseph Esposito (2004), who counters that open access will actually increase the overall cost of scholarly communication. He argues that just as the price of a long-distance telephone call has fallen dramatically, households spend much more on telecommunications today than did the previous generation precisely *because* unit costs and potential use have expanded. We'll see, probably sooner than later, what impact open access will have.

ACCESS AND OWNERSHIP

Framing the debate as access versus ownership is an unproductive start because it assumes that a binary choice always exists and that one correct answer always emerges. There is no doubt that the potentialities of access have expanded greatly in recent years through the availability of commercial online databases and information networks. Likewise, there is no doubt that, in many instances, the information provided by electronic resources has supplanted the print versions of that same information. The *reductio ad absurdum* of the argument is that because electronic resources have successfully supplanted some print resources, it is a matter of time before electronic information fully supplants print information. There is no reason to think that such a reduction will be fully realized in the next few decades. That said, it would be foolish not to acknowledge that electronic resources will continue to expand and that some of these resources will have advantages that print cannot match. Walt Crawford and Michael Gorman are skeptical of the ability of electronic information to drive print away, as noted at the end of chapter 8. Their skepticism, though, is tempered by the ready admission that electronic information is better than print for some purposes. They wrote, "Print-on-paper has never been the best medium for many kinds of data and information. The legitimate promise of electronic publishing is to provide better (that is, cheaper, more ecologically sound, more up-to-date, easier) access to certain kinds of text—replacing books and journals where books and journals have never worked very well" (1995, 71).

We have to acknowledge that the entire conception of access and ownership as some sort of dialectic carries potential problems with it. One of the first, and most important, problems is the confusion of being informed with information-as-thing (or "physical objects such as data and documents that are referred to attributively as information because they are regarded as being informative" [Buckland 1991, 43]). Michael Keller expressed an important concern regarding the emphasis on access rather than ownership; his "concern is that the 'new paradigm' (of access rather than ownership) leads ultimately to an environment where 'all is meta-information,' with no or few ideas on the shelves" (1992, 8). At the heart of Keller's concern is that libraries will be transformed from a site of knowledge growth due to the collection of pieces of the graphic record to a virtual site of retrieval of data about information. This distinction may seem a bit subtle, so let's take a closer look at it. The library as we've known it for a long time has been a place where information (not merely as thing but information-as-knowledge, or the "knowledge important in the process of being informed" [Buckland 1991, 41]) has been readily available to those who want it. This goal has been accomplished in the past primarily through the building of physical collections. The attitude of academic librarianship has been transformed, at least in part, into one focused on the provision of information about information. That is, the access model is accompanied by attention to the mechanisms of access, including bibliographic mechanisms. The library, then, is no longer a site for knowledge growth; according to some conceptions it need not be a real site at all.

Bart Harloe and I have suggested that academic librarianship has become trapped by the discourse it employs. That discourse affects how we think about access/ownership and other key issues. As we noted,

> The new vocabulary needs to be less 'stuff' and more use-based. Decisions (whether to own or to provide access to) should be based first on the needs of the community and then attention should focus on the content required to meet the need. Only after that should the package (or actual container) be considered. . . . It should not be assumed that a particular package is most effective because it is familiar or because it is new (1994, 85).

The kind of discourse used can be influenced by the past operations of libraries. For instance, Katina Strauch wrote, "We have a mission to collect materials that appeal to our user base over time, and to make them locally, readily available" (1992, 12–13). We could easily imagine a countering statement to the effect that the library's mission is to respond to user need by providing access to information at the time it is needed. Both views demonstrate a single shortcoming—the assumption that the information/library user is after some kind of access, physical or otherwise. As Harloe and I said,

> This ensnaring discourse makes it very difficult to think in terms of content as distinct from package. It forces libraries into a mode that does not move easily beyond the physical artifacts or the electronic counterparts to artifacts that currently determine the product of libraries. Product is defined as what the library has or what it has access to (what Strauch refers to as collecting materials), rather than as the content that might be needed at a particular place and time. The latter is what libraries should be attending to (1994, 85–86).

The reality for academic libraries, and for libraries in general, is that there will be a shift away from ownership of physical collections, to some extent anyway, to access to content. Someday, perhaps, that transformation may be complete. However, we are a long way from a complete shift because of economic and other obstacles. Nonetheless, the transformation is in process. Ross Atkinson (2000) stated that the transformation necessitates a more serious look at the mediation and delivery services that have existed in libraries and will continue, albeit in a different form in the future. Moreover, he said, the need for intermediation in an online environment will *increase*. The delivery function's purpose is the movement of information from one place to another. This movement can entail traditional activities, such as acquisition or circulation of physical items. It also could entail the provision of electronic resources. Presently, a great deal of attention is devoted to the storage and retrieval aspects of delivery, and this attention is essential. In the midst of storage and retrieval work, however, the mediation function must not be ignored. Mediation, as an activity, involves the critical distinguishing of content and the marriage of user need to the appropriate content. The mediation function is more difficult in the electronic environment, but no less important than it is in the traditional library. The challenge to libraries is to reconcile the needs of users with the fact that the content is not locally housed. As Atkinson pointed out, "Librarians have a very special service ideology, and as librarians now begin their journey into the new online environment with all of its complexities and uncertainties, they must take care to bring with them above all else that defining ideological perspective" (2000, 62). Although this challenge of meeting local need with remote resources has always existed, it will become increasingly common and increasingly severe. The severity and commonness of the split makes mediation all the more important. Buckland wrote, "as electronic resources multiply, the need for a convenient ordering of differentiated accessibility increases. . . . Value judgments are still needed concerning which resources are most suitable for any given user group. The privileging of the better and, by default, the nonprivileging of the rest remains an important needed service" (1995, 157). The demanding challenge will be how to formulate and communicate the value judgments inherent in mediation.

In the midst of the troubling dilemma of mediation are some additional, and equally troubling, concerns. One of the most troubling of these is control. In the world of print, control also is a potentially troubling matter because the publication decisions that lead to the content of books and journals are made by people outside the library and at the front end of the formal communication process. For example, we saw in chapter 7 that university presses are experiencing fiscal constraints that are necessitating the publication of fewer titles by some presses. In the electronic world, this constraint is absent in that an author can ostensibly take the initiative in making his or her work available. The control issue does not reside at the front end of the communication process but, rather, in the channel itself. An academic institution could exert control over the use of its servers. A college or university could, for reasons as seemingly nonideological as storage space and cost, remove some individual Web sites. The result is that the communication process is aborted. A commercial provider might determine that a particular product is not profitable and so terminate access to particular content. Clifford Stoll offered an example of such a decision:

> You probably think that digital archives are permanent. Then consider Coffee Line. For the latest scoop on coffee beans, we'd call the Dialog system to sip information on growing, marketing, and packaging. Here's where we'd get the number of tons of Kona coffee

shipped. All updated weekly. Well, it's gone. Log into Dialog and we see this greeting: "Coffee Line is unavailable as of October 1." Why? It was uneconomical to carry (1995, 186).

The library does not just lose access to current information in such a case; it may lose access to the archive as well.

As we can see, the access/ownership debate may miss the essential point that is at the heart of the services a library offers. We can turn to Sheila Dowd, who articulately pointed out the essential aspect of information service that we should not forget:

> Information is the raw stuff from which knowledge is derived; but information must be organized to foster connections and relevant interpretations before it will lead to knowledge. Life is not a trivia game. Bits and bytes of information are important only if the mind can link them with other pieces of information to build the orderly patterns that are fabric of knowledge. Hence the mission of libraries is more properly identified as the provision of access to organized information, for the fostering of knowledge (1990, 63).

SUMMARY

It is evident from the preceding discussion that there are many, sometimes different, views of the place of technology in society and in academic libraries. As each of us seeks to learn more about the technological world of today and tomorrow, we should be cautioned that some points of view paint very rosy pictures and others are bleak. The review by Rob Kling and Roberta Lamb (1996) can help us sift through utopian and antiutopian visions of technology. They examined the varying ways technology can be envisioned and offered a cogent assessment of these perspectives as they both reflect and influence social thought with respect to technology.

Electronic information is undoubtedly evolving. The products and services that are common in libraries as this book is written probably will be replaced by other, more sophisticated information resources. As the medium changes, the content also may change, though at a somewhat slower pace. The medium, whether print or electronic, will always be something different from the thought that it tries to capture. This is an important realization because knowledge, which is higher education's true reason for being, is not merely an amalgamation of sustained exposure to information. Buckland's (1991) reminder is one we should keep before us at all times:

> The physical representation of ideas, knowledge, beliefs, and opinions can be viewed as a translation or representation from something

intangible to something tangible, from knowledge to recorded knowledge. . . . Recorded knowledge, like all other representations, can be expected to be more or less imperfect. Even if it were not, people might well misunderstand it and so be able to derive knowledge from it only imperfectly or not at all, as in the case of texts in lost languages (1991, 40–41).

The importance of recorded knowledge should not be minimized; it plays an essential role in knowledge growth. Recorded knowledge, though, also is a statement of the product of ideas, inquiry, and research. I mention this to emphasize the fact that medium is not more important than content, even if medium affects content.

The movement from print to electronic media is continuing and must do so if librarians are to provide the most complete access to content for users. Will the move be a complete and absolute one? Some futurists say yes, but there is no reason to think that print will disappear in the short term. There is no reason for print to disappear; formats such as the book are still very effective means of recording, transmitting, and preserving ideas. They also are relatively inexpensive, widely available, and constant "stand-alone systems" (that is, they require no hardware or operating systems for use). In the future, the success of electronic media in academic libraries will depend on the media's ability to fulfill the information needs of users both immediately and in the future. This means that librarians, students, faculty, and academic administrators must understand the continuing existence and use of electronic media. As Peter Graham (1995) observed, the aforementioned populations already share such a widespread understanding of the traditional media that have been used for the communication and preservation of research and scholarship. He further observed that a similar future for electronic media will require an organizational commitment (libraries committed to providing services that best fit electronic information and its use), a fiscal commitment (long-term, continuous funding that can enable the library to keep pace with a dynamic information environment), and an institutional commitment (acceptance by the college or university of the evolving role of the library as a communicator and preserver of recorded knowledge).

The evolution in recent years is reflected in some of the changes in the second edition of this book from the first. The earlier edition contained a section on CD-ROMs. It now seems superfluous to speak at any length about that medium. To be sure, libraries still do have some data and information stored on CD-ROMs and DVDs, but much of the information that was stored that way, such as bibliographic databases, have migrated to online access. Libraries may have to make decisions about retention and future use (including the technological side of future use and compatibility between the media and the hardware) of these physical media. The earlier edition also included a section on information delivery, focusing on document delivery. Again, libraries continue to avail themselves of document delivery services, but more information sources and services, such as EBSCO (mentioned earlier), are more readily available and more inclusive than they were not long ago. Concerns such as the variability of licenses for electronic information and the aggregation of electronic versions of journals are more prominently on the minds of academic librarians today.

Another aspect of electronic information, e-books, is currently problematic. Some companies in the past few years have developed readers designed to be portable and to store a number of books. Only a few of those companies are still viable. Standards for e-book readers have yet to be agreed upon, so the marketplace is relatively small at this time. Some libraries, more often public libraries, have purchased stand-alone e-book readers and provide them on loan to their communities. Academic libraries have cause to worry about future access and archives for such e-books. Other products, recently developed, are intended to provide longer-term and more stable electronic information. The companies behind these efforts also have been less than stable. As an example, netLibrary, which could count a number of academic libraries as customers, has been purchased by OCLC, and there have been some changes to its business plan. Another effort aimed more at the end-user market, especially college students, is Questia. It is in business at this writing, but the company cut back dramatically on its personnel in 2001. Doubtless there will be more efforts to make book-length works accessible electronically; the success of the efforts will depend on sound business plans, but also on an understanding of the uses to which books are put and the media that can best support those uses.

The changes brought about by electronic media necessitate transformation in the way librarians think about their jobs, the users of information, and the communication process of which they are part. Or so it seems. Some commentators from outside librarianship say that changes will have to come about because of the nature of electronic information. Richard Lanham, for example, wrote, "Librarians of electronic information find their job now a radically rhetorical one—they must consciously construct human attention-structures rather than assemble a collection of books according to commonly accepted rules. They have, perhaps unwillingly, found themselves transported from the ancillary margin of the human sciences to their center" (1993, 134). It is true that the librarian's job is a rhetorical one in the electronic environment; the job is not limited to pointing, directing, or locating. But then it never was or never should have been so limited. Perhaps the difference strikes Lanham so strongly because his professional life has been steeped in a familiar object—the book. He either has not needed or hasn't realized that he needed someone to assist him with the conception and relation of ideas and their representations. When the medium is less familiar, there may be a diminution of confidence in both the medium and oneself. To the extent that such a predicament befalls library users, the job of the librarian is increasingly rhetorical. For many library users, however, the confidence and familiarity have never been strong, so the rhetorical function has always been a part of modern librarianship.

So much is yet to be discussed and decided about the nature of electronic information and its place in the library that there is much room for speculation. The following questions may be used to spur some of that speculation:

> Will e-journals and their capacity to transmit more information more cheaply facilitate or inhibit knowledge growth?
>
> What are some of the potential costs, financial and other, of the bundling of journal subscriptions into packages that must be licensed as a whole?
>
> Can librarians carve out a place for themselves as organizers of networked information?
>
> Could access completely replace ownership?
>
> Does browsing for information have a future?

Chapter 10

The Communities of the Academic Library

Previous chapters have discussed some aspects of the behavior, organizational patterns, cultures, and needs of the people on whom the academic library has an impact. One point recurs in any examination of the communities served by the library: the mission of the institution shapes the emphases of students and faculty and thus their information needs. This statement sounds absolute. I don't mean that the college or university's mission governs every aspect of behavior; many complicated influences will have an impact. But the mission is a pervasive and defining factor. It informs everyone about the institution's commitment to research and/or instruction, with its focus on (or avoidance of) some subject areas, existence or extensiveness of graduate programs, and size of the student body and faculty. The mission is not externally imposed, or at least not entirely. It is affirmed daily through the retention and recruitment of students and (especially) faculty, the practical application of the curriculum, and other activities that are engaged in by those who people the college or university. The affirmation, the attractiveness of the school's mission to faculty and students, helps to create and maintain community. The library does not develop its collections and services in ignorance of the community; rather, the community is the reason for the collections and services. This chapter explores the impact of the community on the services offered by the library.

FACULTY

The pressures on faculty have already been mentioned. At institutions where publication is valued and publishing productivity is a measure of success, much of a faculty member's time is occupied with the process of scholarship. One study shows that over a three-year period, the median number of publications per capita by faculty at ARL universities more than four. This may sound like a low number, but the numbers were derived only from the three citation indexes (in science, social sciences, and the humanities). The number, then, doesn't reflect books and doesn't include articles in journals not covered by the three indexes (Budd 1999). Even with such caveats related to the study, it is apparent that faculty at research universities spend much of their time engaged in formal inquiry. Faculty at other types of institutions may spend less time on research and publishing but are likely to have heavier teaching loads, so the time commitment to the requirements of the position are still considerable.

Teaching

Why do I mention the time spent by faculty on research and teaching? One thing that must be clearly understood by librarians is that faculty are inevitably going to be concerned with efficiency regarding their information needs. Also, I mention time to convey the probable nature of those information needs. Faculty will look to support their scholarly and instructional endeavors. Their priorities will likely depend on the kind of institution at which they work. Faculty at two-year colleges and liberal arts colleges probably will look for support of their teaching. This may take the form of looking to the library to provide print materials on reserve, to collect materials that will supplement instruction, to provide access to information, and/or to provide access to nonbook media that can be used to augment and enhance instruction. The libraries at junior and community colleges are frequently named learning resource centers; that name is reflective of the role played by the library. As might be expected from discussions in previous chapters, electronic information is playing an increasing role in the service of two-year college libraries. The financial resources of those institutions are limited, and libraries are exploring ways to provide more information to more faculty and students. To support the instructional mission of two-year colleges, David Dowell and Jack Scott advocated adopting three strategies: "(1) reaching every faculty member, (2) building library infrastructure, and (3) placing the library within the academic decision-making process and the information resource decision-making process of the college" (1995, 27). The last of these strategies could apply to all academic libraries and is becoming more important as both the institutions and the world of information become more complicated.

Implicit in the first strategy offered by Dowell and Scott is the importance of interpersonal connection between librarians and faculty. It is difficult to conceive of reaching faculty without taking the time and effort to get to know them and help them get to know the library and librarians so that more of a partnership can be formed. Again, this notion applies to all libraries. One way to forge a partnership is through well-developed library instruction programs (more is said about library instruction later). It is only reasonable that the more librarians know about the faculty's interests and work, the better placed they are to work with them. Donald Dilmore explored the interaction between librarians and faculty at nine liberal arts colleges and found that "those where library service appeared to be most valued by the faculty were those on which librarians reported the most frequent interaction with faculty members" (1996, 283).

The nature of the community (and the kinds of services offered by the library) changes somewhat as the mission of the institution changes. This is evident with instruction, particularly the different instructional imperatives that arise with increased graduate programs. Instruction of graduate students can be substantially different from instruction of undergraduates. Not only are classes likely to be smaller and the course content more specialized and deeper, but an increased responsibility is likely to be placed on the students for learning. In many disciplines, there is greater reliance at the graduate level on more diverse and more specialized materials because the subject matter is delved into more deeply. Also, in many disciplines the requirements of the students include individual exploration of relatively narrow topics. The job of the library is different with graduate instruction; the needs of faculty and students are less uniform. The difference does not mean that librarians should not work with faculty. Perhaps close relationships between faculty and librarians become even more important because the students are likely to have a greater need for the library's materials and services and may need mediation to assist them with use of the information system. The faculty may not automatically think of working with librarians; the contact may have to originate with librarians. The librarians may find a productive tack in proposing a fairly specific suggestion for working together, rather than simply extending an offer of assistance. For instance, a librarian might contact the faculty member in charge of a graduate research course and offer to present the secondary information tools (indexes, abstracting sources, networked resources, etc.) to the students during one class meeting. The specificity of a proposal communicates to faculty that substantial thought has gone into thinking about collaboration.

Of course, teaching and learning are not static. One pressure on teaching is the impetus from a variety of sources to increase offerings made available at a distance. Regardless of its relative merits and demerits, distance education is a kind of communication that is different from face-to-face classroom instruction. Because the contact students may have with faculty could be lessened with some distance education, the faculty may have to consider more seriously the students' access to information that is integral to and supplementary to instruction. The teacher cannot assume that students will leave the classroom and go to a library that he or she has confidence in regarding the availability of materials and services. Distance education requires thinking about the relationship between instruction and information in some new or revised ways. It is an environment that is relatively new to both faculty and librarians. In the future, close collaboration between librarian and faculty member will be even more essential than it is with traditional education. The level of support for instruction on campus will have to be replicated at a distance, although in a different form with different delivery mechanisms and mediation.

Even when faculty use commercial courseware, such as WebCT or Blackboard, they and their students still have a need for access to information resources. Librarians should not assume that faculty can and will create information access mechanisms to integrate into online courses. Librarians are already reasonably well positioned to assist faculty with course development and should aim to be an even more essential resource. The databases and electronic journals that libraries have licenses for provide a starting place for remote information access. Given that the licensed sources include some, and possibly an extensive number of, full-text and full-image content, students can be offered at least some information to support distance courses. There may be some important considerations in providing access. For example, from a technical standpoint, the library may have to install a proxy server so that off-campus users can gain access to information sources; from a planning and fiscal standpoint, licenses may have to be negotiated so that remote users are part of the agreement (which may add cost). More and more libraries are instituting electronic reserves services that also enhance the information available to distant students. Those libraries that have purchased e-books from sources such as netLibrary and E-brary may be able to enhance the students' information environment still further. More is said about the challenge of distance education in the section on students.

Research

At some institutions research is a major activity of faculty. The faculty must conduct formal, structured inquiry in order to earn tenure and promotion. Where does the library fit into the research activities of faculty? There is no single, simple answer to this question. For one thing, there are substantial variances among disciplines. The determining factors (if we can reduce variability to one, overwhelmingly important factor) are the object of the researcher's study. If that object is physical, as it tends to be in the sciences and engineering, the library (and information generally) serves a fundamentally supporting role. Information is necessary, to be sure, so that the researcher is alerted to prior intellectual and research claims. Furthermore, the scientist or engineer will need to be aware of current and recent developments that might have an impact on his or her own work. To the extent that awareness is important, the faculty member must employ some strategy for acquiring or accessing information. The library is taken for granted as a source for both information and bibliographic and intellectual access to information. Traditionally, the library has provided access through general and specialized indexing and abstracting sources. This role has neither disappeared nor diminished. If anything, it is a more important role for libraries.

The bulk of information is too large and its growth too massive for individuals to be able to browse, much less read. David Mermin wrote about the problem of the size of the information universe: "I went systematically through the current periodicals section at the Cornell Physical Sciences Library to count how many journals I felt I ought to look at but didn't. . . . I . . . found 32" (1990, 57). In attempting to help faculty manage both the bulk of information and their time, the library integrates technology into its operations and services. The technology (discussed in chapter 9) enhances access to surrogates (bibliographic data) and to the information itself (full text and full image). The library genuinely becomes a gateway to information for scientists, engineers, and others whose object of study is physical.

For those whose object of study is textual, the library takes on a somewhat different character. Much of what is mentioned above applies here as well. The humanist and the social scientist also are burdened by the amount and growth of information. They, too, need the enhancements to information access that other researchers need. A major difference may be that the very object of study resides in the library. A literary scholar may depend on a library for access to manuscripts, letters, and other primary sources that are the foundation of his or her study. The historian may rely on collections to examine the documentary record or certain events. To some extent, technology can alter the dependence of these scholars on the library. The Library of Congress, for instance, through its American Memory project (mentioned in chapter 3) is engaged in digitizing some of its collections and making the images available via the World Wide Web. Although more and more of these kinds of materials are becoming available, the number of manuscripts and other special collections nationwide is huge, though, and the cost of digitizing all of those collections is enormous. Many scholars will rely on libraries for some time to come to meet their research needs. Even if we are not limiting our consideration to special collections, in some ways the library is the laboratory of the humanities scholar. What is frequently referred to as secondary literature may be the primary object of study. For instance, a Faulkner scholar may be examining the critical acceptance of Faulkner as evidenced in the publications of other scholars and critics.

Likewise, scholars in the social sciences, particularly those using discourse analysis as a research method, may use secondary literatures as the object of study.

The nature of study in the humanities and many of the social sciences is different from the sciences in some important ways, most especially in the conception of what knowledge is and how it is created. There may be some dissonance between the ways that, say, humanities scholars conceive of knowledge and how the profession of librarianship conceives of it. Gary Radford suggested that this profession "holds that knowledge, as contained in texts, constitutes an independent object that can be stored, classified, and arranged in an objective manner" and that descriptions of librarianship tend to focus on the store of information containers that can be searched to find specific items and the protection and preservation of the store of information containers (1992, 410). A different view of knowledge matter captures the work and thought of the humanities. That view is embodied in a metaphor based on the library that is offered by Michel Foucault. In this alternative conception, knowledge is a creative product of the imagination that thrives in the environment the library offers. This environment includes some things we take for granted—the collection, the catalog, the classification. It can thus be an embodiment of Foucault's metaphor in which

> the visionary experience arises from the black and white surface of printed signs, from the closed and dusty volume that opens with a flight of forgotten words; fantasies are carefully deployed in the hushed library, with its columns of books, with its titles aligned on shelves to form a tight enclosure, but within confines that also liberate impossible worlds. The imaginary now resides between the book and the lamp (1977 90).

As Radford said, "The library makes the creation of new knowledge possible at its most fundamental level. . . . From the Foulcaudian viewpoint, the fantasia of the library is the experience of the labyrinth, of seeking connections among texts as well as their contents" (1992, 419–20). This seems to be an excellent depiction of the way knowledge is created in disciplines that rely on the study of texts.

Especially given the idea of the library articulated by Radford, we have to take very seriously the part the librarian plays in the conduct of formal inquiry. Stephen Lehmann and Patricia Renfro wrote, "The most fundamental distinction between researchers and librarians is perhaps the emphasis on content by the one and on access by the other (1991, 410). Herein lies a potential pitfall that can hinder the success of the library and the librarian as a facilitator of research. It is true that the profession of librarianship has concerned itself with matters of access and that access is essential to the services the library offers. However, access is not a discrete and separate concept that can be applied without consideration of some other vital factors. When a library provides access, it is providing access to what? Access is an intellectual entity and activity and, as such, is inextricably linked to content. It is impossible to provide access to *something* without knowing what that *something* is about. By the same token, selection is linked to content because it is material *about* something that is selected. In short, the librarian must consider *content, users,* and *media* in order to fulfill the ideal of access. Omission or ignorance of any one of these elements is likely to render attempts at access ineffectual.

FACULTY AND LIBRARY GOVERNANCE

At times, faculty can take a rather proprietary attitude toward the library. This may be especially true of the collection; faculty may look on part of the collection as *theirs.* I don't mean to imply that their attitude is either inappropriate or undesirable. After all, faculty are the main producers *and* consumers of the collection's content. That proprietary view may be most pronounced when the library allocates funds to academic departments. When that happens, the faculty may be doing the selection of materials themselves, so their ownership tendency may be enforced by selection. Where allocation does exist, the faculty may feel that they are de facto policy setters with regard to the library. Some faculty may develop particular and strong opinions about how the library should operate. Because responsibility for what has been historically a major function of the library—building the collection—has been given, at times, over to faculty, their ownership tendencies are understandable. As might be expected, this tendency can pose potential difficulties for the library. If the library would like to change policy or activities, there may be resistance from some faculty, who might cite their vested interest (through selection of materials) as lending legitimacy to their resistance. It is at just such loci that the need for partnerships is clearest. Open communication is the best way to ensure that faculty have the resources they need, provided in the most effective and efficient way. This brief example is offered to illustrate the point that a decision or an action that seems to be placed in a particular sphere can have repercussions beyond any assumed boundaries. There is usually a systemic impact when an operation or a function is altered in some way. The political aspect of organizations can quickly present themselves, whether they have been anticipated or not.

Another formal structure can give faculty a say in the operation of the library—the faculty library committee. Such a committee is common to many campuses. Sometimes it serves no more than an advisory function, giving some credence to decisions made by librarians. In many cases, though, the committee sees itself as a policy-making body and tries to suggest (or sometimes impose) policy on the library. It should be said that good working relations between the library and the committee are the norm, but those good working relations don't simply spring from the innate good will between the two. Some points are requisite to a positive relationship. First, the committee's responsibility and authority need to be stated very clearly and agreed to by all concerned. There should be as few questions as possible regarding the committee's role and purpose. Its reporting must be clear; there should be no uncertainty about whom the committee reports to and what the nature of its reporting should be. The library's place within the committee also has to be understood. It is usually more helpful if the library has formal representation on the committee; sometimes the library director is an ex officio member. The committee should serve as a vehicle of communication in both directions. Advice from the faculty should flow through the committee to the library; decisions made by the library (especially policy decisions) should be communicated to the committee without delay. If the ground rules are explicit and are followed, the relationship has an opportunity to be productive.

One additional brief item regarding governance affects the library less directly. In general, the nature and structure of the institution's curriculum is a matter of faculty determination. In the event that major changes are suggested, such as a new degree program, approval of the administration and usually the governing board also is required. When faculty are contemplating changes to the curriculum, it should be recognized that the changes could have an impact on the library and/or the library could have an effect on the changes. In the example just noted, the proposal of a new degree program, it should be realized that the program will require some resources and access to succeed. This factor should be considered early in deliberations so that appropriate actions can be taken. The situation that would most readily facilitate planning and anticipate potential problems is for a librarian to be sitting on the faculty committee charged with oversight of the curriculum. As is true of the faculty library committee, the ideal curriculum committee serves a vital communication function. It is much more than a courtesy for the library to have a seat on the committee; it is a logical and practical necessity.

STUDENTS

Of course, the largest population served by the library is the students. Looking at all colleges and universities collectively, it is readily apparent that instruction—teaching and learning—is certainly the most far-reaching segment of institutional mission. All institutions are involved in instruction and, for most, instruction is far and away their single most important activity. Because of the universality of instruction, libraries at most institutions must exist to a great extent to facilitate teaching and learning. What does this effectively mean for the library? In a fairly straightforward sense, it means building collections and structuring services that enhance the instructional process. Delving a little deeper, we see that a clear and complete understanding of the curriculum is essential to devising a cogent plan for the development of collections and access programs. It is imperative that librarians comprehend what is being taught on campus. In addition, it is extremely helpful to understand *how* content is being taught so that information and information services can most fully assist with education.

The foregoing seems simple and has been a part of the rhetoric of academic librarianship for many years. However, the effectiveness of libraries in supporting instruction has varied considerably from institution to institution. In the most ineffectual settings the library is passive; it waits until someone else, presumably the faculty, tells it what it needs to do. In such settings, the prevailing attitude appears to be to wait patiently until a request is made. In the poorest situation, the request has to conform to existing service structures and collections or it won't be fulfilled. It is difficult to conceive of a healthy relationship between library and institutional mission when the position of the library is reluctantly reactive. On the other hand, the effective library embraces an active role in the learning of the students. Services are designed that center on the student and how the act of learning can be facilitated. For instance, a simple service that is not uncommon in academic libraries is a term paper consultation service. When it works best, such a service is aimed at connecting the content of the student's assignment (linked to his or her thinking on the subject) with the record that has already been created by researchers, critics, and commentators. The purpose is to help the student create knowledge, not simply to show that others have written about a topic. An active stance by the library necessitates reaching out to students to demonstrate to them that the library can be integral to learning. This is by no means a simple matter; for one thing, the idea of an active library may seem less-than-readily apparent to students.

The typical student probably has an existing notion of how instruction works, a notion that has been reinforced over the years. This notion may include a process of lecture and recitation that was a mainstay of the university for the first several hundred years of its existence. As is true of the library, this notion (to the extent that it is accurate) reflects education in its most ineffectual state. In fact, the ineffectual states of the library and education are related, especially insofar as they add to the student's already formed notion of what a college or university can accomplish. Many teachers are more demanding of their students, however. They may work to foster the critical skills of independent thought and analysis. They may structure courses so that students have to take substantial responsibility for learning. They may attempt to connect the theories propounded in their disciplines with application in practice so that students can evaluate theory more readily. The difference between the two educational standpoints is primarily that one relies on authoritative, objective presentation and the other relies on exploration and evaluation on the student's part. An active role adopted by the library in conjunction with the active participation of students in the educational process has the potential to lead to the student's creation of knowledge.

It should not be forgotten that there really is no such thing as a "typical" student. The student body on most campuses is a diverse group. As noted in chapter 1, there cannot be an assumption that students are 18 to 22 years old, white, and middle class. Those students who do not conform to a narrow, preconceived notion may have particular needs that can be met by the institution and the library. There has been a tendency within higher education to refer to these students as nontraditional. This is an unfortunate term because it can imply a privileging of "traditional" students. Carol Hammond examined the needs of a group of students who didn't fit the customary model and found that they "indicate a stronger enthusiasm for and comfort with using electronic systems and more confidence in their ability to use the library than was expected. . . . Services that save time, as well as instruction designed for and marketed to women and part-time students, should be welcomed" (1994, 339). The services offered by the library also may have an impact on the recruitment and retention of students who are not of the majority population. As Camila Alire and Frederick Stielow wrote,

> most libraries can and should insure that their collection policies reflect and champion a minority presence. Librarians also have a cultural stewardship. They need to deal with the symbolic and practical roles of their institution as they relate to the socialization and recruitment for a new minority-conscious academy. Indeed, increasing staff diversity and developing the potential for minority students to excel within the key traditional symbol of the university should be trumpeted (1995, 516).

What becomes clear is that the library must be sensitive to diversity among students and make that sensitivity real through its collections and services.

The diversity of the student body is likely to be magnified by distance education programs. An institution is likely to be educating students of all ages, from all walks of life, and in all circumstances. Many individuals with full-time jobs may avail themselves of educational opportunities. Although technically not distance education, colleges and universities also are expanding evening and weekend course offerings. The needs of students in such courses mirror those of distant students in that they do not have ready access to the library's physical collection or on-site services. The electronically available materials and services can reach students across town or across the world. This kind of information is complex in content and in format. Students may need assistance to make the fullest use of available information. Distance education programs have proliferated greatly in the past several years, by both the entry of many traditional colleges and universities and the presence of for-profit institutions. Connectivity is a major reason for the growth (institutions investing in infrastructure and the availability of cable, DSL, or other high-speed connections in people's homes). As Smiti Gandhi (2003) pointed out, libraries and librarians are faced with the challenge of transforming services and access to meet the needs of distant students. Part of the challenge requires close collaboration with the faculty as they develop courses for online or other types of delivery. As librarians in some states are discovering, consortia can help with the delivery of materials to distant students. For example, only one university in a state may offer a course on a particular topic. A student in a location 100 miles away from that university may have ready access to another institution, so materials can be delivered from one library to the other. It is likely that academic libraries also will find themselves working more closely with public libraries as part of the demands of distance education. The shape, content, and delivery mechanisms of distance education can vary considerably. The library and librarians must be flexible in assisting, or even in helping to create, offerings that best fit the institution and its students. This includes being aware of the opportunities and restrictions of the Technology, Education, and Copyright Harmonization (TEACH) Act of 2002 (Lipinski 2003).

To serve both local and distant students, libraries are constructing and expanding Web-based tutorials and finding aids to help students navigate through the information maze more effectively. The University of California, Berkeley, is one institution that has developed online assistance aimed at students. (See http://www.lib.berkeley. edu/Instruction/.) E-mail-based services, sometimes called ask-a-librarian services, connect students with librarians so that questions can be answered in as timely a manner as possible. Also, more libraries are developing online information literacy programs to further enhance students' experience.

INFORMATION LITERACY

In the first edition of this book, this section heading was "Library Instruction." The name change is not merely cosmetic; it indicates the potential for a shift in focus and a quite different pedagogical and cognitive approach. "Information literacy" is a term that has been mentioned occasionally in the past; more common terms have been library instruction, bibliographic instruction, or information proficiency. Recent initiatives by ACRL have served to solidify (some might say reify) use of the term. The programs offered by libraries have tended, and to some extent still tend, to share some common goals. It should be noted that the literature on library instruction and information literacy is large and diverse; I don't intend to review the entirety of that literature here. (See Grassian and Kaplowitz 2001 for an extensive treatment of the topic and an excellent bibliography).

This section presents what has been some of the seemingly consensual thinking about library instruction, as it is reflected in the literature. As we will see, regardless of the focus or emphasis of individual writers, there is at least some commonality of approach to the instructional challenge. This commonality begins with the essential goals and objectives and extends to methods and means of instruction. The commonality that exists is certainly not absolute, though; there is some variance of purpose and method. We should examine both commonality and difference and then explore a way of thinking about library instruction.

Purpose of Instruction

Although instructional programs have existed for many years, they began to grow in numbers (both in terms of institutions adopting programs and numbers of students reached) and sophistication in the 1970s. In part, attention on instructional programs constituted a response to growing enrollments, expanding curricula, and increasing complexity within higher education. The role of the student was being transformed, and the library was seeking ways to enable students to cope with an exploding information base and the incorporation of information into their studies. Libraries began to inquire into the instructional process, seeking ways to improve instruction. A key event occurred in 1981, with the ACRL/Bibliographic Instruction Section Preconference on Library Instruction. At that time, there was a coalescing of contemporary thought and practice as well as a pointing to the future. The look ahead included the integration of library instruction into the profession of librarianship and higher education and the adoption of emerging technologies into instruction. That event spurred even more thought and work on the conception and delivery of instructional programs. It has served as something of a foundation on which much subsequent work has been based.

Over time, the perceived purpose of library instruction has been articulated. At times, it is more implicit than explicit. For instance, several years ago Constance Mellon (1982) wrote about problem solving in instructional programs, implying that a goal is to help students become better problem solvers. More specifically, she suggested that information problem solving involves identifying problems, determining desired outcomes, selecting strategies, implementing strategies, and evaluating outcomes, with the process being an iterative one allowing for revision at each stage (1982, 77–78). Cerise Oberman and Rebecca Linton (1982) integrated ideas of problem solving into a working instructional program. This fundamentally systems-based approach to instruction can be quite useful as a means of stating a programmatic goal and as a tool for students to use in handling their own needs, particularly those needs that spring from course assignments. However, a problem-solving approach poses certain difficulties. This way of thinking is based on the assumption that the user/student is aware of a particular need or problem and also can conceive of a solution to it. When a student is given an explicit assignment, such an assumption may be reasonable. When a task or need is not so explicit, the initial problem is not so easily defined, nor is the outcome. When both problem and desired outcome are not obvious, there is likely to be difficulty in arriving at a strategy for solving the problem.

The problem-solving approach, which borrows from systems-based thinking, tends to be linear. In fact, the steps of solving an information problem could be fitted into a flowchart. However, decisions are not always discrete; that is, it is not always clear that, given a particular circumstance, there is *an* appropriate choice that presents itself. In fact, the initial problem may not be easily articulated so as to extrapolate a definable desired outcome. The approach implicitly assumes that a considerable amount is known. The student knows enough to state the problem, state a desired outcome, define and select strategies, and evaluate the outcome at each stage of the process. This assumption is a cause for some concern. Librarians who adopt the approach may have expectations of students that cannot be fulfilled. Further, students may develop expectations of themselves that lead to difficulties. The latter is the greater concern. Students who are taught that information needs are analogous to other linear problems they may face may come to think of the library, and perhaps even the process of knowledge growth, as mechanistic and manipulable. If students experience frustration due to a seemingly insoluble problem, they may interpret the difficulty as residing with them—they did an inadequate job of stating the problem, defining an outcome, or selecting strategies. Although problem solving is a complex process, it may be too simplistic to serve well as a foundation for library instruction.

There is reason to believe that the goal of making students more adept at completing certain kinds of tasks is not an uncommon approach in library instruction programs. The program devised at Earlham College, mainly by Evan Farber, has influenced the design of a number of programs at other institutions.

A workbook of assignments is a part of this program, and workbooks also are used at many other colleges and universities. The assignments include searches of the library's catalog and of various secondary sources. Students are to respond to questions about specific parts of bibliographic entries, among other things (Farber 1993, 21–25). In other words, the students have to complete specific tasks. One feature of the program at Earlham is not so common at other institutions. At Earlham, library instruction is integrated into courses such as the first-year humanities course required of all students. The topics covered are placed in the context of the course, so students are grounded in the search for information relevant to the content of the course. The librarians work with teaching faculty to ensure full integration of all elements of the course. This approach appears to work at Earlham, but according to Farber, "we are not trying to export our program. . . . Do not try to adopt our program, but rather consider those aspects of it that could be useful for your situation" (1993, 13). At the heart of his advice is the realization that institutions have different missions and attempt to accomplish them by different means. A boilerplate approach cannot succeed.

It seems evident that the very terms used to define this service are indicative of the purpose it has had in many settings. To refer to "bibliographic instruction" or "library instruction" immediately suggests a task-based purpose. Stated or not, a primary goal is to enable students to navigate through tools or through a place. Attention is paid to the structures of the tools—the kind of indexing, the nature of the thesaurus, and so on. Attention also is paid to the physical space of the library—the location of the tools and the reference desk, the classification scheme as a locating device or address, and so on. These elements of instruction are certainly necessary; students would be at a loss without a comprehension of the tools and the place. Do these constitute the beginning and terminus of instruction? This question is addressed a little later.

Content of Instruction

Given the purpose of instructional programs, what is taught to students? For one thing, librarians must help students understand some of the technical terms of the library and information providers. Success at the tasks associated with information problem solving or, indeed, with effective library use, no matter how that might be conceived, can be enhanced when students are aware of the meaning of a bit of the language librarians use. As stated above, students' competence with regard to completing essential tasks is of concern in library instruction. Success, then, depends to a considerable extent on students' understanding of the vocabulary that is central to libraries. Rachael Naismith and Joan Stein showed that students are unlikely to have a full comprehension of the language used by librarians. Students are bringing experiences to bear on their interpretation of terminology that is separate from the context of libraries. They wrote, "Librarians cannot rely on the patrons to decipher a meaning from the context. Patrons rely on their existing schemas to help them interpret an unfamiliar term. If these schemas are lacking or incorrect, communication will be unsuccessful" (1989, 551). The instructional program seems an ideal locus for an introduction to the vocabularies used in the library and information worlds.

Beyond the comprehension of words used in libraries, some language-based aspects of library and information use are relevant to instruction. For instance, Paul Doty (1995) wrote of the importance of understanding the rhetorical side of indexing and abstracting. He illustrated that many abstracts are imprecise in their use of language, occasionally inadequate at providing a context for a reading of the article, and less than useful at describing whether the article is a research report or something else. His warning is well taken; very often the abstract is written by someone other than the author of the article. The creator of the abstract may not have a full understanding of the content of the article and thus might be almost purposely imprecise, perhaps in an effort at avoiding misleading the reader. What may not be realized is that the imprecision of the language of the abstract may itself be misleading. The linguistic difficulties presented by the nature of indexing and abstracting necessitate a critical reading of these secondary bits of information in order to achieve the relevancy goals that the information seeker has. The challenge of critical reading is affected by the use of such things as networked information. Doty pointed out that users, especially students, may have an expectation of immediacy (that is, that relevant information is provided immediately) and equality of output (that is, all of the hits resulting from a search are equally relevant). Doty wrote,

> Focusing on reading automated bibliographic tools acknowledges that interpreting text on a computer is a unique experience. . . . Students who get search sets in the dozens, hundreds, or even thousands from a keyword search are likely to start making arbitrary choices: the first five, publication year, and other limiters that are not critical. Further, it is important to remember that if students have had training for interpreting computer screens it comes from watching television. Watching television is a definitely passive experience. This does not suit well for making decisions about information (1995, 127).

Raymond McInnis (1982) adopted a similar stance regarding the importance of linguistic elements in library instruction. One point he made is that both the bibliographic citations and abstracts are metaphors for the contents of articles. As such, an entity such as an abstract is a representation of the article. By this, I mean that the abstract is linked to the article both conceptually and physically. Ideally, it is designed to include the essential concepts of the article and, along with the bibliographic citation, intended to provide a physical connection (usually interpreted in libraries as physical access provided by the abstract of the article). One important implication of the linking thus described for library instruction is helping students understand that finding citations and abstracts does not constitute the culmination of the quest for information. Moreover, as McInnis stated, there are further metaphorical connections of a bibliographic and substantive nature. When a search yields results, the results are likely to provide structural links of two kinds: bibliographic links through co-citation (two or more articles cited together in a paper or papers) or bibliographic coupling (a paper or papers citing two or more previously published articles together). Some conceptual links result from one piece of work being substantively influenced by previous work. McInnis wrote, "Substantive information and bibliographic information, both with underlying structural characteristics, are the primary goals of research. . . . Depicted metaphorically, the abstract structural characteristics of literature networks become a focus for both teaching and inquiry. In particular, their structural characteristics can be presented more concretely by symbolically representing them as models" (1982, 67–68). The work of Doty and McInnis may seem dated, but recent coalescing of information sources into massive databases may emphasize the warning to pay attention to language. A global source, such as Academic Search Elite, contains information from many disciplines. Terminology may be used differently across disciplines, so a search might retrieve separate, even incommensurable, hits. A student might be confused and frustrated by such search results.

The works of Doty and McInnis indicate that there may be some shortcomings in library instruction as practiced in some libraries. As stated earlier, a noncontextual approach to instruction is doomed to failure; it amounts to imparting a skill without also telling students what the skill might help them accomplish or, in short, what good it might be. In a program that focuses on telling students about the surface aspects of bibliographic structure—where the title of the journal can be found, how to determine the date and pages of the article, and so on—the students may have little understanding about the substantive structure of literatures. Finding a particular citation might be the ultimate goal in such a program. In actuality, the finding of a citation is the beginning of a process of comprehending the content of specific work and the substantive connections it may have with other work. As Farber said, instruction separate from the content of some academic courses is unlikely to be fruitful. Taking this notion a step further, instruction that is aimed only at the mechanics of bibliographic structure does not help students see the intellectual and/or practical value of the content of information packages, such as journal articles. Library instruction objectives aimed at making students better at manipulating the bibliographic structure (in the generic sense), without including the substantive aspect, are incomplete.

The content of instruction also is affected by the theoretical stance librarians can adopt. Elizabeth McNeer (1991), among others, stressed the importance of an awareness of learning theory and its application to library instruction. Actually, "learning theory" may be misleading because there are many learning theories and not all of them are in agreement on the essential elements of learning. However, many concentrate on some cognitive aspects of learning. "Cognitive" here is used in a broad sense and is not intended to reflect a solely physicalist approach (or reduction of mental processes to physical, specifically neural ones). Research in psychology and cognition has helped us understand that there are differences in development rates among individuals and that cognition is affected by such factors as gender, race, cultural background, and others. (See, for instance, Belensky et al. 1986). It has been observed that knowledge has a strong social element, so the social situation of the learner can be an important element to consider. These are some useful features to keep in mind, but we also must remember that there is no single recipe for effective learning; the variability in cognitive ability and in cognitive background precludes any checklist approach from being entirely effective. Of course, the challenge to all of teaching is the employment of multiple methods and content as an effort to reach as many members of a class as possible.

Some methods of instruction may allow for a concentration on content. Active learning is one such method that relies on engaging the student in the process to foster a better understanding of an ultimate aim of instruction—the awareness that a search for information is content based and not an end in itself. Eileen Allen stressed the involvement of students as active participants in learning *and* the active role of the teacher in stimulating student involvement. She suggested some strategies that might assist learning: brainstorming by students to open discussion, small group work to ensure cooperation and exploration, peer teaching to enable students to learn from one another, and writing to stimulate reflection on the subject matter (1995, 97–98). The thinking expressed by Allen embodies the assumption that participation will be a stronger reinforcement and will allow students to take more control of the learning process than is possible in a passive environment. Active learning might be facilitated in some instances through librarian and faculty cooperation in instruction. This may facilitate student participation through focus on a particular subject area. As Charlotte Cohen (1995) observed, such cooperation offers the opportunity to link content with the strategic necessities involved in exploring how to get to the content. We have to remember that active learning is an ideal in all educational situations; it may not be achieved if the students doesn't or can't participate.

Melissa Gross (1999) offered an extremely valuable focus in her inquiry. Much of library services and instruction tacitly assume that the student initiates the search for information. That assumption, in itself, is challenging because the study of information-seeking behavior tells us that it is an iterative process; information seekers begin from some position of ignorance (for lack of a better word) and begin to understand more throughout the process. Sometimes understanding is enhanced by finding information *not* related to the initial query. That is, connections that are genuine may be located while a person is searching on a different topic or comes upon the information accidentally. What Gross made clear is that some, probably many, queries do not initiate with the student but, rather, are imposed. If a teacher tells a student, "Go to the library to find out who directed the first production of *Oedipus Rex*," the teacher may intend for the student to discover the dynamics of Greek play festivals. The student, unaware of that intent, is likely to ask a seemingly direct question and assume there is an equally direct answer. "Answer learning" with these kinds of imposed queries can be problematic.

A *Literacy-based* Approach

What follows is reflective of the shift to information literacy and presents an idea for an instruction program. I should emphasize that this is only one conception and that some might disagree with it. Also, this conception is an ideal; any program in a library is undertaken with full awareness that resources are limited and there may be obstacles. I offer this conception as a way of educating that, with information literacy and almost all library services, we begin with the most fully formed goal before compromises are made, rather than beginning with an expedient alternative. In many ways, it builds on the progression from library instruction to information literacy detailed by Lorna Peterson (2001). Also, what is presented here is not entirely unique; numerous libraries have been revising their instructional programs in meaningful ways. The first concern is—or should be—the purpose of a program. As a goal, the instruction program should strive to enable students to assimilate information from diverse, complex sources and to integrate it into the context of a specific need. There are strategies and conceptual steps to reaching this goal. A model that begins with the formation of a question could help shape a literacy program. From question formation, a student can progress through awareness of what would be entailed in answering a question, including an understanding of information retrieval. The critical apprehension necessary to assess retrieved information also would be a part of the programmatic model, and the process would culminate in the student's ability to relate information to possible answers to the question, along with a reappraisal of the question itself. In other words, the model admits to an iterative process of learning.

This model illustrates a conceptual progression based on the essential character of the question. First comes awareness that a question exists, then we move through a clearer understanding of the meaning of the question to a comprehension that information related to the question can be found, on the way to a meshing of question and information and, ultimately, finding an answer. Such a notion of information literacy is, implicitly, less founded on the mechanics of specific sources of information than on a search for meaning. By this, I do not refer to a search for meaning *in* information sources but, rather, as an individual quest to form meaning. This conceptual framework also could be seen in terms of the growth of knowledge. A student, in the ideal, seeks to enhance his or her knowledge base and uses existing information as an aid to increasing his or her knowledge. Whether seen as centered on answers to a question, meaning, or knowledge, this model does not view dexterity in the use of secondary information sources as an end; rather, it is a means to the larger end, which is at the heart of the program.

The goals illustrated in the model, and the progression inherent in it, are consistent with ACRL's recently developed standards for information literacy. Perhaps most important, the standards recognize that information literacy has "broader implications for the individual, the educational system, and for society" (ACRL 2000). Further, the standards establish a set of goals that transcend a focus on the mechanics of manipulating databases and information sources (print or electronic). The goals are geared to enable a student to:

- Determine the extent of information needed
- Access the needed information effectively and efficiently
- Evaluate information and its sources critically
- Incorporate selected information into one's knowledge base
- Use information effectively to accomplish a specific purpose
- Understand the economic, legal, and social issues surrounding the use of information, and access and use information ethically and legally

These goals are ambitious but represent nothing less than should be offered to students so that their educations can be as complete as possible.

This model also suggests that a single experience, whether in a library-based course or integrated into another academic course, is not sufficient to achieve the goal. The ideal presented here is fairly involved and elaborate in that it mirrors, to some extent, the overall goal of a student's entire course of study. The ideal for an information literacy program founded along these lines is a series of tiered experiences that may even extend to the graduate level. The first tier of the program could create a foundation for freshmen students that will use active learning to foster a critical approach to information needs and to information structure, including the library. This experience is best offered as a formal, credit course, to both organize the content and communicate to students the importance of information proficiency. The focus at this tier would not be on information sources, although some essential tools would be used to translate the ideas of question formation into tangible sources of information.

The second tier of the program could have two parts. One incorporates education for information proficiency into academic programs. This part may involve integration of the critical approach and very specific information resources into existing or developing courses in individual academic departments. The librarian/educator could work with the instructor of a course to meld the information proficiency goals into the instructional design. The other part might be a formal course of one semester hour that could be offered in the broad clusters of disciplines: humanities, social sciences, sciences. This course would take the critical approach of the first tier a step further and focus on the more specific questions of the target disciplines and their more specific information resources. There could be attention to question formation at this level also, but with more emphasis on applying the critical approach to the complex information structures of the subject information sources.

The third tier would focus on graduate education. At times, there is a tacit assumption that students who have earned bachelor's degrees are information proficient. Those who respond to these students' needs in libraries know that this assumption is not necessarily correct. Librarians could work with the academic departments so that the education of graduate students about information sources can be at their intensive level of study. This graduate experience might be incorporated into those courses that introduce graduate students to inquiry in their disciplines because this level of proficiency is inseparable from formal inquiry.

To reiterate, not all will agree with this proposal and it is not offered here as the only means of information literacy. This model is presented to encourage thought and consideration of both the purpose of an instruction program and the means to accomplish program goals. I hope it can serve to stimulate a lively discussion. I've spent so much time on information literacy because the information universe faced by students (and faculty, for that matter) is becoming increasingly complex. It would be bordering on irresponsibility for academic libraries not to address the need for students to gain knowledge of that complexity if they are to succeed academically. Instruction is likely to become an even more essential service than it already is. Further, instruction will be complicated by other trends in higher education, such as increasing distance education offerings. The instruction program of the future will have to take such trends into account as planning for the evolution of instruction progresses.

GRADUATE STUDENTS

Given what has been said about faculty and students, there is little new to be added regarding graduate students. In some ways, their needs are akin to those of undergraduate students; in other ways, they are more similar to faculty. It is important to remember that they are students, which means that some of their information needs are strongly influenced by the academic calendar. For purposes of writing papers and completing course requirements, some of the information needs of graduate students are immediate and pressing. Further, as just stated, graduate students may not necessarily be proficient in the use of complex information sources. What can be said is that their level of knowledge of the content of their disciplines is likely to be quite sophisticated. Even with a fairly high level of knowledge, they are still students and still learning. Part of their learning may well include the structure of literature and information in their discipline. The full socialization of the student aspect of graduate students influences that part of the foregoing information literacy proposal dealing with instruction at the graduate level.

When the graduate student reaches the stage of writing a thesis or dissertation, individual information need may more closely emulate that of faculty. For one thing, the project undertaken is of considerable size and scope. In this way, it is somewhat similar to a large-scale faculty project, such as a book. The massiveness of the undertaking includes a large responsibility for the student to be aware of, and be able to assimilate, a wide-ranging literature on the subject. I should emphasize both aspects of the preceding statement—an awareness *and* an assimilation of a literature. Librarians may need to communicate to graduate students the rhetorical and metaphorical functions of secondary sources of information. Another similarity of a thesis or dissertation with faculty scholarship is that it is not so tied to the calendar that it must be completed in a single semester. Because of the less stringent time constraint, the graduate student can take advantage of library services whose benefits can take some time. This may include traditional services, such as interlibrary loan or document delivery, or other services aimed at instruction and/or consultation.

The one thing to remember is that graduate students present unique challenges to the library. They are not faculty, even though they may be conducting research and even teaching. They are not undergraduates; they have generally reached a more sophisticated level of knowledge. In those universities with active graduate programs, the library should heed the needs of this particular segment of the community. This may well entail examining this group in order better to understand its uniqueness.

SUMMARY

The library would have no reason for being if it weren't for the academic community (but then neither would the college or university). On every campus there is some level of diversity in the community. On some campuses the level of diversity is considerable. This diversity is manifest in a number of ways. There are substantial differences among undergraduate students, graduate students, and faculty; there are differences among the various academic disciplines that affect instruction, research, and knowledge growth; there can be differences by gender, age, race, and cultural background among faculty and students. The first two of the listed differences tend to be widely accepted and, at least to some degree, understood within the institution. There is some awareness of the last set of differences, but the implications of these differences regarding learning, acculturation, and success within the academic environment, and, subsequently, for library services, may be less well understood.

We return again to the importance of the culture, or multiple cultures, of the college or university. Each segment of the academic community comprises a culture, which includes subcultures. The culture includes elements of academic and nonacademic life. Effective services offered by the library will likely include a comprehension of the dynamics of the many cultures and incorporate such comprehension into communication with the various segments of the community. Let's turn to some questions relating to the library's community:

> How can the library contribute to teaching within a college
> or university?
>
> Can libraries play an active role in faculty research?
>
> Should the library begin an instruction program with
> the student's first semester?
>
> Can and should librarians and faculty work together on
> an information literacy program?
>
> What role should faculty play in library governance?
>
> Is the library basically passive in its service stance, and
> should it be?

Chapter II

The Academic Librarian

The preceding chapters have focused primarily on the organization of which the library is a part, the organization of the library itself, materials and access provided by the library, and the community for which the library exists. It would be a disservice in a book such as this if we didn't turn our attention to the librarians, without whom the services, collections, and mediation would be impossible. To understand the position of academic librarians at this point in our history, we have to examine the education that may be most appropriate, the relationships among the people performing the various functions of the library, the way librarians deal with the content of the library, the librarian and management, and the status of academic librarians within their institutions. This is a lot of ground to cover; we'll center our attention on the core elements of these aspects of the academic librarian. At the beginning of this book, it was noted that the academic library has much in common with libraries in other environments, but also that much about the academic library is unique. The same can be said with regard to a comparison of academic librarians with librarians in other environments. The differences are of special interest here.

THE EDUCATION OF ACADEMIC LIBRARIANS

Education for librarianship (in general) has been perceived in the past as too focused on the vocational side, with skills emphasized at the expense of principles. The first major critique of library education was written by Charles C. Williamson (1923). Among other things, Williamson suggested that education

248

be elevated to the graduate level so that it could build on a valid undergraduate base and that the programs be extended to two years. Ralph Munn (1936) echoed much of Williamson's critique and emphasized that the academic library demanded an enhanced attention to scholarship. Others through the years have been in agreement with assessments of a number of decades ago. The consistency of their critiques should prompt some questions: Are these assessments off base or misguided? Has there been no change in education since the 1920s? Are educators loath to change the system of education? Do the opinions of writers who agree with Williamson reflect the majority of practitioners? These are some provocative questions; some of them may be unanswerable, but some can be addressed.

Let's begin with the question of whether the many writers whose comments were similar to those of Williamson are reflective of others. This is actually a difficult question to answer for a complex set of reasons. One reason is that those who wrote on the topic were in the distinct minority, so there isn't a clear statement of majority opinion on the matter. It is a well-recognized shortcoming to accept anything on the basis of arguments from silence. Just because there seems to be consistency in public evaluations does not mean that agreement with those evaluations was universal, or even widespread. It is possible that there could be disagreement on the substance of the critiques. This matter is further complicated by the realization that people change their minds over the course of time. It may be that students in, and very recent graduates of, library and information science (LIS) programs are, of necessity, focused on the skills that will help them become employable or succeed in a first professional position. It is impossible to make sweeping generalizations about this or any other population, but the concerns of some at that stage of their careers may be more fixed on the technical aspects of library and information work and may see underlying principles or theories as being of secondary importance. Others at different stages in their careers may hold different views. Furthermore, professionals in different organizational positions may have certain views of the content of educational programs. A library director may have a different opinion from a reference or cataloging librarian. And, as is most likely, even with specific organizational roles there may not be complete agreement. One last point relating to this question: some individuals may articulate certain opinions because they believe that is what others want to hear, so the audience of formal communication may affect the content of the communication. All these factors make the task of interpreting opinion difficult.

What we are fundamentally left with is interpretation based on the formal communication itself. As suggested above, there may be some conflict between stated and unstated opinions and there may even be some inherent contradiction between statements regarding education. Some employers may say they believe in a strong need for technical training of potential professionals in their libraries. At times, this may extend to the desire for knowledge of, or experience with, specific library automation products, operating systems, software, purchasing or payment structures, or other facets of a position in a particular organization. I am not saying there is no need for technical proficiency. Someone who is a candidate for a cataloging position in a university library should have an understanding of MARC format and how to construct a bibliographic record. A candidate for a reference position should be aware of the workings of commonly used electronic reference sources. All librarians need to have an understanding of the general structure and content (shifting though it may be) of Web-based information. However, not every candidate should be expected to have the skills to be a network administrator. There is little agreement on where the line should be drawn regarding technical skill and who should be ensuring that librarians have needed skills. Undoubtedly, LIS programs are responsible to some extent for seeing to it that graduates attain some level of proficiency. Moreover, each library has some responsibility for enhancing the skills of its staff. Beyond that, however, the issue is moot.

To return to formal communication, we can see that almost a genealogy of thought illustrates the necessity for the communication of foundational principles in an educational program. Pierce Butler wrote of this many years ago: librarianship entails a science dealing with the properties of materials, a technology involving the processes necessary for the use of the materials, and a humanity that deals with "the motives, reasons, purposes, or ends for which the science has been accumulated and the technology invented" (1951, 240–41). Butler's notion was reexamined more recently by Lester Asheim, who said that education should combine "first, understanding of the underlying discipline; then, introduction to the mechanisms derived from it that lead to present practices; finally, analysis of how the skills and attitudes emerging from the discipline and the operational devices are applied in practice" (1977, 137). Very recently, some observers have emphasized the need for an understanding of fundamental principles. The Association for Library Collections and Technical Services (ALCTS) of ALA has drafted an "Educational Policy Statement." In this statement is written that, "The task of all those involved in educating librarians and other information professionals is to teach principles. These principles include the values of the profession and the reasons for their existence. Principles from other disciplines can be applied to librarianship as well" (1995, 7). Further, the ALCTS statement suggests that LIS programs "must ensure that their curricula provide a solid foundation for library and information science professionals by teaching basic values of the profession, stressing theory over practice, stressing professional decision making over performance of specific duties, stressing service to the user of the information, and preparing librarians with a plan for continuing education. Curricula must be continuously updated" (1995, 8).

Some individuals have stressed the need for academic librarians to be attuned to the nature of the academic institution and the work it exists for. Edward Holley (1970) has been a strong proponent of instilling in LIS students an awareness of some essential aspects of academe. He said that academic librarians should have "some background in the history and development of higher education . . . and appreciation for the history of scholarship and learning and the way knowledge is obtained in various disciplines . . . (and) the ability to evaluate research findings" (1970, 227–28). More recently, Raymond McInnis urged that focus on teaching for academic librarianship be on an understanding of academic cultures, which would introduce "students to concepts associated with scholarly discourse: that inquiry is a social system; that knowledge is socially constructed; that members of discourse communities share assumptions about what are appropriate skills members should possess" (1995, 144–45). It is probably obvious that by writing a book such as this, I believe there are unique elements of academic librarianship and of education for the academic environment. This book is itself an illustration of many of these elements. To succeed in the college or university culture, the librarian needs to have a clear comprehension of the environment. As I wrote several years ago, "The academic library exists to provide a variety of services (to aid research and teaching) to the community of students and scholars. The nature of this academic community, regardless of its size, effectively defines the backgrounds of its members. Academic librarians, as both members of the community and facilitators of the work of the community, should be prepared for the roles they are expected to assume (Budd 1984, 22).

LIS education has, to some extent at least, responded to the concerns that have been expressed by many. Some programs have revised their curricula to emphasize the theoretical foundations of library and information science. Some, such as the programs at the University of Arizona, the University of Tennessee, and Florida State University, have enhanced some undergraduate course offerings so as to provide more students with an awareness of the complexities of information work and to assist with recruiting students into the graduate program. Some programs, such as those at the University of Michigan and Indiana University, have essentially reinvented themselves. The need for critical examination of the purpose of LIS education and of the programs' curricula is not going unnoticed. A group of deans and directors discussed just these points and openly admitted the need for review of curricula ("Dean's List" 1994). There is little doubt that curricula will be reviewed continuously as the state of the profession evolves and as technology has an ever-increasing impact on libraries.

We have not discussed some other elements of education for academic librarianship that are somewhat problematic. For instance, it is almost a de facto requirement that academic librarians have or earn additional graduate degrees in subject areas. William Robinson (1993) examined 433 position announcements for collection development and management librarians and found that in 18 percent of them an additional graduate degree was required and in 42 percent it was desired. Some have disagreed with this requirement; Joe Rader wrote, "To say to librarians that, to get a job in the first place or to achieve career advancement within the profession, one must have a subject master's is to say that the library degree, ipso facto, is of little value. Apparently to be treated as a real professional, one must obtain a real advanced degree" (1978, 29). This issue might not be simple, though. In many academic library positions, librarians are called on not just to mediate between users and information structure, but also between users and information content. Some positions carry the designation "subject specialist." If such a position is integral to the college or university library, what should be the knowledge base of the person in that position and how is that knowledge acquired? This issue transcends education for academic librarianship and is a matter of potential discussion within all of the profession.

In fact, concerns regarding education have recently captured the attention of the ALA. Two Congresses for Professional Education, the first held in 1999 and the second in 2000, brought together representatives of many professional associations as well as individuals not affiliated with a particular group to discuss the educational needs of professionals now and into the future. These meetings resulted in a set of recommendations for education in general:

1. Define the Scope, Content and Values of the Profession;
2. Establish and Apply Standards for Accreditation;
3. Enable Credentialing and Continuing Education;
4. Position Librarianship as the 21st Century Profession;
5. Continue the Dialogue between Library and Information Studies Educators and Practitioners;
6. Recruit, Educate and Place Students from Diverse Populations (Congress for Professional Education 1999).

Mary Reichel, the representative from ACRL, issued a statement prior to the meeting that outlined the more specific concerns of the academic library community. Her statement focused on particular matters, including study and research in academic librarianship, information literacy, distance learning, and preparation for scholarly work (Reichel 1999). It may be that educational issues will continue to be a focus of attention in professional associations for some time to come.

At this time, there may be a question about the professional degree itself. To find some answers from the academic library community, we can turn to ARL SPEC Kit 257 (ARL 2000). That publication reports the results of a survey of ARL members, in which they were asked if the master's degree is required for all librarian positions. Seventy-three respondents (or 66%) said yes. This result is in contrast to a 1995 ARL survey in which 59 percent of the respondents answered in the affirmative. Even with such results in favor of the required degree, the Executive Summary of the SPEC Kit stated, "However, as libraries create new types of positions, especially for those with significant technology components, library directors and personnel officers have begin to question whether the M.L.S. degree is as necessary as other degrees or experience" (http: // www. arl.org/spec/257sum.html). James Matarazzo (2001) questioned the preceding statement in light of the survey results and wondered about the appropriateness of beginning the summary with something (seemingly stemming from the results) that is potentially misleading. The ARL is not the universe, but if its survey results are an indicator of hiring practices, the first professional degree remains vital to the profession.

ACADEMIC LIBRARIANS AND THE FUNCTIONS OF A LIBRARY

For several decades, since libraries reached a nebulous size threshold, the academic library has tended to be divided along functional lines. The organization of the academic library was discussed in chapter 6; the concern here is the impact of functional organization on academic librarians. With the division came, almost inevitably, some kind of organizational identity. Librarians became reference librarians, catalogers, serials librarians, and so on. Of course, this kind of specialization has some relationship to education. An individual with a fairly focused career goal may take courses centered on, for instance, cataloging, organization of information, and management of technical services. With the accompanying deeper knowledge of that library function, such an individual may be employable in a number of settings. A question that might arise is, As an individual specializes (both in a degree program and at work in a library), does he or she lose sight of the overall purpose of the library and how the particular function fits into that purpose? This is a rhetorical question. The answer, if there is an answer, is as variable as the people with functional specializations in libraries. Some have developed a kind of tunnel vision and can't see beyond the narrow tasks they perform. Others seek to integrate their work into the mission of meeting the information needs of students and faculty. It should go without saying, but we'll acknowledge the latter as unquestionably preferable.

Some of the concern about how individuals fit into library organizations centers on the traditional and functional divisions. Lois Buttlar and Rajinder Garcha (1992) surveyed some academic libraries and received ninety-three responses to a questionnaire on organizational patterns and changes to the traditional structure. Most of the libraries responding reported that their organizations are still bifurcated, although there is some evidence of a trend to integrate public and technical services. Respondents to the survey gave no indication of a move to a large-scale reorganization. This is not to say that some libraries have attempted sweeping organizational change (refer to the changes at the University of Arizona, reported in chapter 6), but those libraries are in the distinct minority. The survey by Buttlar and Garcha further indicates that where there is some functional crossover in academic libraries, it is most common for catalogers to work at the reference desk. There may well be some advantages to catalogers working with users: catalogers may increase their knowledge of searching behavior and the use of the library's catalog; they may gain an appreciation for the ways users approach subject access; and they may be able to see how reference librarians mediate between users and the bibliographic structure. These can lead to definite benefits, especially when these factors constitute the reasons for the crossover of catalogers to reference work.

There are other possibilities for multiple assignments for academic librarians. One possibility is for catalogers, reference librarians, and others to engage in selection activities. In some libraries, a functional division is responsible for selection and collection development and management. This division may comprise a coordinator and a number of subject specialists. Those affiliated with such a division may spend all their time doing collection management work. In other libraries, there may have been the realization that there are not sufficient staff resources (and won't be in the future) to allow for such specialization. As a response to resource constraints, some libraries have dispersed collection management duties throughout the library staff. An individual may be, for example, a cataloger and a specialist in psychology. Another might be a reference librarian and a specialist in history. As specialists, librarians may be responsible for selecting materials in subject areas, overseeing and/or evaluating segments of approval plans, and assessing journal subscriptions. Such an organizational structure is sufficiently widespread that the Collection Development and Evaluation Section of the Reference and User Services Association of ALA includes a Dual Assignments Discussion Group, which consistently attracts librarians who share and compare the elements of fulfilling multiple assignments. Another important aspect of multiple assignments is liaison work with faculty. This responsibility demands that librarians be able to communicate with faculty about their instructional and research concerns. It should be emphasized that such work necessitates two-way communication. The librarian must be prepared to listen to faculty and comprehend their subject needs and to convey information to them about budgets, approval plans, selection aids, and so on. Liaison work can be demanding on librarians but also can be personally and professionally rewarding.

The possibility of the electronic, or virtual, library has prompted something of a revisiting of the technical/public services dichotomy. Perhaps because some electronic media are not selected and acquired in the same way that print materials are, the distinctions between technical and public services are less clear. In part, the blurring of lines may lead to organizational change, but further integration of electronic information may be necessary before academic libraries reorganize. In the meantime (however long this period may be), there is exploration of the media themselves and how they may meet the information needs of users. This exploration is engaged in by librarians. By this, I mean that academic librarians must assume responsibility for understanding the potential of various media, understanding the needs of users and potential users and reaching some way to meld the two together. In the interim period of exploration, there may be some crossing of organizational lines or at least some cooperation among librarians from various functional divisions. Janet McCue (1994) claimed that technical services librarians can play a vital role in augmenting the value of the electronic library for the user through the kinds of organizational and descriptive activities that have been integral to technical services for a long time. This vision seems to assume that functional divisions, and even functional purposes, will persist. Even though McCue may be correct in her assessment, the assumption underlying the vision should be questioned; perhaps a different functional organization can accomplish the goals she wrote of and add still more to the use of information. Peter Wei He and Michael Knee (1995) didn't seem to assume quite so persistent an organizational structure. They maintained that electronic information could help to decentralize libraries and their management. The result may be fewer differences between public services and technical services.

A fairly recent move in academic libraries has resulted from, and contributed to, a different idea of the cataloger and cataloging. I am speaking of the outsourcing of cataloging. The word "outsourcing" is borrowed from recent activity in business, especially in manufacturing. In libraries, it refers to contracting with an outside party for certain services. As Carmel Bush, Margo Sasse, and Patricia Smith observed,

> Outsourcing for technical services and collection development is, of course, not a new concept in libraries. . . . Approval plans replace extensive title-by-title ordering and conveniently gather books on specified subjects for selectors to review. Book jobbers assist ordering

in libraries by verifying prices and availability of books, leading some libraries to eliminate this step in preorder searching. Claiming, reporting status from publishers, and cancelling are other areas where acquisitions processes merge with those of jobbers. Centralized processing, moreover, is common in corporate, school, or public libraries and has been tried with varying success among consortia for academic libraries (1994, 398).

The primary question is, what does outsourcing portend for the librarian? How might it change not only the job, but also the concept of the professional librarian in the academic library? Daniel CannCasciato offered one possibility: "By concentrating more of our time on enhancing existing records (through upgrades, supplying subject access that wasn't there, supplying classification that wasn't there, etc.) and contributing original records, we utilize ourselves and our staff to greater ends than we are currently doing" (1994, 6). If CannCasciato is correct, outsourcing could serve to remove some of the routine responsibilities from the librarian's work and could allow for a greater level of professional discretion. This certainly would be the ideal outcome of outsourcing. The existence of enterprises that can supply services and products to academic libraries does not automatically mean that the ideal will be a reality.

Outsourcing is not limited to cataloging, and the services provided by other external sources also have implications for academic librarians. Approval plans, which have been offered by vendors and jobbers for a few decades, exist to facilitate the selection and acquisition of library materials. The purpose of most approval plans is to ensure that the library gets those items for which selection criteria are most clear and straightforward or emanate from sources not readily apparent to librarians. The academic librarian's responsibility is to construct the most effective profile possible so that what should be included and excluded is readily evident. Further, the librarian must monitor and evaluate the plan to ensure that it is effective over time. An emerging service from jobbers and vendors is the purchase plan. This is a variation of the approval plan; materials received through a purchase plan cannot be returned. A purchase plan places an even heavier burden on librarians to construct the details of the plan and to evaluate performance. However, the front-end burden probably is wise in many instances, especially as libraries face personnel shortages. Bush, Sasse, and Smith recognized that a number of important questions are attendant to expanding outsourcing possibilities:

> Will collection development librarians choose to articulate collection needs to jobbers who will then take the systematic process for materials from that point? Will librarians demand full contracting services

for collections, from definition of user needs via marketing to selection, collection building, collection management, and cooperative efforts? Or will librarians emphasize selection and collection building as in the past and only selectively use jobber services? (1994, 408)

Claire-Lise Bénaud and Sever Bordeianu (1998) offered a useful list of questions and concerns relating to outsourcing. The list is intended as a guide for libraries looking critically at their own operations and alternative ways to accomplish their objectives.

ACADEMIC LIBRARIANS, USERS, AND CONTENT

Previous chapters have examined the academic library's community and the variety of the information environment. Now it's time to turn attention to the librarian's relationship with these external forces. No one would deny the service imperative at the heart of academic (as well all other) libraries. How is service manifest in the library? In part, service is a function of the collections and bibliographic apparatus of the library. In large part, it is a function of communication, both direct and indirect, between librarian and user. Indirect communication may come about through the library's catalog, its classification, its physical layout, and its signage. Further, indirect communication arises out of the selection decisions made by librarians, and this communication indicates what has been deemed sufficiently important to acquire, as well as what has not been acquired. Most who think about the library's collection would immediately be aware of the former but may not realize the communication of the latter. Also, the arrangement of the library's interior can communicate not only where certain information can be located (for instance, placement of the catalog, including OPAC terminals; the reference department; etc.), but also the privileging of some services over others. It may be obvious where circulation and reference are; is it equally obvious where someone might go for interlibrary loan service?

Much of the communication that occurs in a library is of the interpersonal type. A considerable amount has been written about the reference interview, for example. Much of the thought on the communication process inherent in the interview emphasizes the dynamic nature of the process. James Rettig (1978) devised a descriptive model of the complexities of the process. His model includes a dynamic feedback loop, indicating that the communication is not merely a linear list of instructions. The feedback component is recognition that communication may be ambiguous and that there needs to be a way to reduce ambiguity and enhance understanding. Although Rettig's model is very useful in its insistence on the iterative process of the reference transaction, it falls a bit short of grasping the problematic nature of communication. The librarian needs to be aware of the lurking, perhaps tacit, possibility that

> There is an almost ontological assumption at work; there is, in the user's mind, a true question that is completely understood and there is also a true answer to the question. This is frequently not the case. In many such transactions the library user is essentially attempting to express what he or she does not know. It is, of course, difficult for a person to relate what is not known. The feedback mechanism depends on fidelity, just as is true of a technical communication system. Given that, does the response, "I don't know," constitute feedback? It is probably useful only in that it effectively eliminates one tack for questioning. Nonetheless, feedback is necessary and invaluable in librarian-user communication (Budd 1992, 117).

Earlier with regard to library instruction, we saw from the work of Naismith and Stein that difficulties are likely to occur with word comprehension and lexical interpretation, given the technical or specialized language frequently used in librarianship. Sharon Mutter and Shahin Hashtroudi (1987) performed some experiments dealing with the effects of word frequency on understanding. They found that words that are less familiar to the hearer and occur infrequently require greater cognitive effort and processing than do words that are more familiar and occur more frequently in the course of communication. The greater frequency of occurrence provides the hearer with more contextual possibilities and facilitates interpretation, even of unfamiliar words. To be an effective communicator (that is, to be understood by the user), an academic librarian needs to be aware that there are some inherent semantic challenges to librarian–user communication because "meanings do not seem to be stable but to depend upon speakers, hearers and context" (Palmer 1981, 7). Perhaps especially important in the academic setting is that there also are cognitive aspects to the understanding of communication and that the user is employing cognitive protocols (not simply verbal protocols) in attempting to comprehend what the librarian is saying. "Being able to understand the word's 'call number' will help the library user locate a particular item in a library. Being able to understand the concept of classification will assist that user in making connections among containers of like content" (Budd 1992, 125). Perhaps most important, librarians should be aware of the integral role that understanding of purpose plays in communication.

One recent communicative stance has some obvious implications for the mission of academic libraries. Of late, a number of writers have advocated that librarians view library users as customers. Such a view received considerable institutional impetus when then-ALA president Hardy Franklin chose to stress customer service during his presidency. He said, "The term customer emphasizes the correlation between our work and the satisfaction of the person for whom it is carried out" (1993, 677). Others have adopted the word "customer" into their discourse. For example, Janet Dagenais Brown wrote, "The organization must be customer-driven—it should identify its customers and strive to meet their needs, ... It is useful to understand more about the service interaction and what it is that makes 'buying' and evaluating a service (such as reference service) different for the customer than 'buying' and evaluating a material product" (1994, 213). Brown's statement seems to embody a paradox; if something like reference service is different from the purchase of a material product, how does the concept of customer apply? In some cases, writers simply accept "customer" as a synonym for "user," as did Christopher Millson-Martula and Vanaja Menon (1995). Others, such as Charles Robinson, have been more explicit in their equation of library users with customers. He maintained that the library should be engaged in "merchandising," that it should aspire to be "the McDonald's of information and materials distribution" (1989, 152).

The view of users as customers is potentially problematic for librarians. If the library has customers, is it necessarily a business? If the library is marketing a product to an audience, it may be excluding some "market" for which there is no definable profit. Are collections, access, and information services the end or the means for the library? If the library's model is McDonald's, is its product disposable? Millson-Martula and Menon, among others, included customer satisfaction as one of the focal points of the library. It is difficult, though, to grasp what, precisely, is meant by satisfaction. It is conceivable that a satisfied customer in an academic library might be an undergraduate student for whom a librarian suggests a term paper topic, offers a thesis for the paper, compiles relevant secondary works, synopsizes those works, and provides an outline for the paper. Is that the kind of satisfaction librarians should strive for? Very few librarians would consider going quite so far as the above example. Sarah Pritchard said that assessment might include such things as "information literacy, success in graduate school, success in job seeking, faculty research productivity (as should by grants and publications), and the library's success as a department in attracting gifts and external funding to the campus" (1996, 591). Even Pritchard's list appears to focus on instrumental outcomes, perhaps because evaluation of a deeper sort is extremely difficult and elusive. The primary point here is that the discourse we employ is not neutral; it is likely to influence the way we think about ourselves and what we do and could affect the perceptions librarians have regarding themselves and the services that libraries offer.

Also implied by the customer service point of view is that information is a commodity. It can be bought and sold in the same way other commodities are.

Dan Schiller (1994) reviewed the stance that information is a commodity in several disciplines, including information science. Looking at information as a commodity may be encouraged by some outside LIS. Peter Drucker, whose work has been influential in this and many other fields, explicitly adopted a position of commodification of information, saying that "The basic economic resource—'the means of production,' to use the economist's term—is no longer capital, nor natural resources (the economist's 'land'), nor 'labor.' It is and will be knowledge" (1993, 8). This statement doesn't seem so startling until Drucker begins to define terms: "What we mean by knowledge is information effective in action, information focused on results" (1993, 46).

Commodification is likely to present something of a dilemma for librarians. There could be conflict between economic influences that we have dealt with (including the pricing of information and access) and the ideal of library service as a public good. This might well have some practical application in the academic library. Suppose the library has a long-standing policy stating that faculty are not charged for interlibrary loan services, but mandating that undergraduate students must pay any charges levied by the lending library. Why is there a differential charging policy for different segments of the community? Is the difference economically motivated? Is it motivated by the nature of the service? What does commodification imply for the role of the academic librarian? In particular, can there be unification, or at least reconciliation, between the role of a marketer or broker and that of a member of the academic community? It should be noted that there is some disagreement with the view of information as commodity. Stephen Elliott argued that "information does not work well as a commodity—not in definitional terms or in any other way. Information is subjectively valued, leaky, shareable, substitutable, etc." (1992, 362). The perspectives mentioned here deserve considerable attention by academic librarians before they are accepted uncritically. A key is looking carefully at the language we use to describe our mission and our communities; language is not neutral and may ultimately affect action in ways not originally intended (Budd 1997).

ACADEMIC LIBRARIANS AS MANAGERS

To reiterate a statement from an earlier chapter, this is not a management text. At this point, the focus of the presentation will not be on management so much as it will be on managers. Of necessity, some of the discussion centers on directors of libraries, but the management activities of others in the organization also need to be addressed. Almost every professional librarian in an academic library has to perform some managerial tasks. At times, these tasks include supervision of student workers. At the very least, these activities entail scheduling students' time, outlining their duties, and assessing their performance. At a higher level, this also includes training students so that they not only can be proficient at their assigned tasks, but also can function in situations that are not so routine. Full accomplishment of the managerial task means detailing what, precisely, is routine and how to identify nonroutine situations and where their own discretion lies. In other words, there should be an anticipation of anomalous occurrences and planning for responses when the unforeseen happens. Formal evaluation of students may be required. Even when it isn't, the librarian should assess students' performance, providing positive, negative, and constructive feedback as needed. It may be necessary, on occasion, to terminate a student's employment. The supervisor should make it clear what kind of behavior will result in termination and communicate to the students some assessment of their performance. Firing someone is never an easy thing to do, but sometimes it is necessary and every supervisor has to be prepared to face such an eventuality. Department heads and others in management positions should work with librarians to prepare them for the less pleasant aspects of their positions.

Librarians who aren't in formal management positions also may exercise managerial responsibility through the structure of the library. Many, if not most, academic libraries employ committees for a number of purposes. Some committees are designed to assist with decision making. Perhaps the most commonly occurring decision-based committee is the search committee. It is certainly possible that a librarian with no formal management duties associated with his or her position would be called on to serve on such a committee. He or she may even be placed in the position of committee chair. Because academic libraries rely to such an extent on committees, it is essential that the committees function well. Functioning well means no unnecessary delays regarding meeting, assigning tasks, accomplishing tasks, communicating, and reaching a decision, as well as exercising fairness in all deliberations. Stress probably should be on "unnecessary." By their nature, committees take time; there will be reviews of the committee's charge, documentation related to the task, reports to complete, and so on. The committee's success depends on two principal factors: commitment by all members to an outcome that is best for the library, and a committee chair who will facilitate communication and keep the committee focused on its charge. The work of the chair sounds simple, but most people are not trained in the effective operation of committees. If some committee members resist the chair's authority, the likelihood of successful completion of the charge is diminished substantially. Conversely, a chair who doesn't allow each member a voice is doing an organizational disservice. Each librarian on the committee should pay attention to the reason for its existence and resist conflict that can arise from personal differences and differences resulting from cultural variances in the organization. Also, committees probably should be used only when a clear charge can be stated and participation from various levels of the organization is necessary and welcome at the highest level.

Many libraries, as is true of many professional organizations, are committed, at least rhetorically, to participation by the members of the organization. What does this mean for reference librarians and catalogers, for example? There is no practical way to answer this question because the participation can be defined in a number of ways and the degree of participation by staff can be defined as being on a continuum that extends from minimal to substantive. Moreover, in most organizations, including libraries, participation is not uniform by all members. Some may choose or desire to participate in decision making as fully as possible; others may want to concentrate on the activities and decisions of one segment of the organization; still others may not want to participate in governance at all. As might be expected, the varying levels of participation can be the source of some tension. Those who prefer not to become involved may resent those who do, and vice versa. Part of the professional responsibility of librarians is to perform in a manner that is most beneficial to the library. That said, the reality of the library is that it is a human organization, subject to all the foibles of human beings. Each individual has to balance the ideal with the actual. In general, though, the academic library tends to function better if communication lines in all directions are open. One scenario that can lead to dysfunction is the statement that participation is welcome and encouraged, while efforts by librarians to participate in decision making are either stymied or ignored. It might be more humane for administrators to admit that the particular library is not a participation organization.

So we come to those in charge of the academic library. Before addressing the qualities of library directors, we should take a look at what, in some influential people's minds at least, characterizes leadership in any organization. First, it is widely acknowledged that leadership can arise from any organizational level. In reality, however, some leading that emerges from the lower levels may be squelched at higher levels. The organization that sets itself apart—be it a manufacturing company or some other type of firm, or a library—tends to be led in addition to being managed. It may seem obvious to say so, but leadership is not common; its rarity is part of what sets it apart from its absence. One thing that almost always sets leaders apart is their personal commitment. There are other characteristics that are recognized as applying to leaders. Warren Bennis and Burt Nanus (1985) observed some acknowledged leaders in a variety of fields and found that all seemed to follow a set of four strategies: attention through vision (creating a focus for all in the organization); meaning through communication (the ability to convey a clear image of where the leader wants to take the organization); trust through positioning (leaders make their positions clear and generate trust through their openness); and the deployment of self through positive self-regard (which involves acknowledging uncertainty, accepting error on the path to learning, and conveying those traits to others). These characteristics are independent of type of organization; they apply universally. Because Bennis and Nanus observed the traits in people, this is not a completely abstract ideal. On the other hand, any number of organizational forces can inhibit leadership in environments such as higher education.

What makes higher education a problematic environment? For one thing, a college or university is not a completely self-determining entity. As we have seen, governing boards and state legislatures influence the management of the institution. For the library, the situation is further complicated by the fact that it is only one unit on campus and is answerable to institutional administrators. The library director cannot simply create a vision for the library and work to bring it about; the library is part of an interrelated (albeit sometimes loose) confederation of academic units. Chapter 5 on governance, I mentioned the ambiguity of higher education (especially as experienced by the college president), as observed by Michael Cohen and James March. It is time to revisit Cohen and March, because they addressed some of the dilemmas that a college president faces in an ambiguous environment:

> The college president faces four fundamental ambiguities. The first is the ambiguity of purpose. In what terms can action be justified? What are the goals of the organization? The second is the ambiguity of power. How powerful is the president? What can he (sic) accomplish? The third is the ambiguity of experience. What is to be learned from the events of the presidency? How does the president make inferences about his experience? The fourth is the ambiguity of success. When is a president successful? How does he assess his pleasures? (1986, 195)

The ambiguities, and the questions posed by Cohen and March, apply as well to the academic library director. Because governance is dispersed in the college and university and because there are considerable external pressures on the institutions, goals can be less than clear. The lack of clarity affects the library and the library director, too. I suggest here, though, that there is a reason why the chief administrator of a library is called a "director"; it is that individual's job to provide direction for the library and all affiliated with it. The director's task is a complex one, as I have stated:

> The members of the library organization constitute a disparate group, an agglomeration of individuals with separate sets of experiences and beliefs. These individuals may also have differing notions

regarding the purpose of the library. What is shared is the confluence of professional ideals, principles, and premises. These are sufficient to suggest a certain amount of agreement among individuals, but it is neither a necessary nor a sufficient condition for complete agreement regarding specific organizational objectives within a library. It is highly (unlikely) that meaning can be shared throughout an organization to the extent that disagreement and dispute are eliminated. The leader's task is to provide direction to both agreement and disagreement so that the vision is not obscured and that personal and organizational goals can be seen to act in concert (Budd 1991, 113–14).

The complexity of the job is clearly evident in the results of a Delphi study conducted by Peter Hernon, Ronald Powell, and Arthur Young (2001 and 2002, summarized in 2003). They compiled a complex set of ideal attributes that the director of a research library should possess; the attributes underscore the demands that emerge from organizations that must respond to numerous communities and forces. The director's job is further complicated by the increasing need for him or her to be engaged in development and fund-raising activities, given the problematic nature of ongoing institutional support (Winston and Dunkley 2002).

In the face of the challenge facing the academic library, what kind of person emerges as director? Joanne Euster studied the role and function of the academic library director. She examined three key dimensions of activity or perception of the director: reputational effectiveness, management of organizational change, and leader activity. She observed that four types emerged more frequently than others.

Type I (HHH) may be called "the Energizer," based on the high levels of activity, change, and reputation enjoyed. Type III (HLH), "the Sustainer," enjoys a high reputation, is highly active, but heads a library experiencing relatively little organizational change. Type IV (HLL), in spite of low reader activity and low organizational change, is also reputationally effective and may be termed "the Politician." Finally, Type VIII (LLL) might best be called "the Retiree," as it appears that this director is relatively inactive as a leader, heads a fairly unchanging organization, and is not highly regarded—or perhaps is simply disregarded—by colleagues (1987, 90).

It seems obvious that individuals who fit Euster's types will respond differently to situations in libraries and, further, that as situations change, a response that was appropriate at one time in one set of circumstances may not be appropriate at other times in other circumstances. Euster's suggestion to library directors appears to take into account the writings of Bennis and Cohen and March. She urges academic library directors to:

> Understand the meaning-creating role of the library director
>
> Learn to focus energy and activities toward internal library operations and staff and the university as a whole
>
> Recognize that different stages in the organization's life cycle will require different emphases
>
> Accept the idea that the same person may not be the appropriate leader for all organizational circumstances
>
> Utilize the dual concept of management and leadership as essential and related functions, each of which requires different activities and focuses
>
> Learn methods of formulating goals and objectives for the library and consciously communicate this vision to the library and the university, frequently and consistently.

The above suggestions are very astute, and all academic librarians (not just directors) should heed them. The one thing missing, and is missing from most systems-based approaches, is the integral reality that libraries are human organizations. One of the purposes of this chapter is to emphasize that the library comprises a number of individuals. As we've already seen, any organization is made up of people who coalesce around a common set of beliefs and/or a common purpose. Additionally, agreement among the individuals will not be complete and perfect. One reason for the partial nature of agreement is that each person has personal beliefs and goals that may differ to varying extents with others. The library, then, is not a system in the same sense as a computer or a clock, or even in the same sense as a colony of ants (which is a fallacy of the reduction of human organization to the perceived principles of sociobiology). The constant challenge to both managers and leaders is the recognition that they are working with people, not with offices or positions. That said, the human side has to be tempered by the realization that there are some core organizational goals and purposes, and if some people don't fit those goals and purposes, they may be misplaced in the organization. In such instances, it's likely that both the individual and the organization would benefit from ending the connection.

LIBRARIANS AND STATUS

Almost everyone is aware of the stereotypical views of librarians that some people still adhere to. Although there is almost inevitably some grounding for stereotypes, there is always some measure of falseness to them as well. We usually think of stereotypes as popular misconceptions of groups; stereotypical thinking may enter the professional worlds, too. Such thinking can lead to organizational practices that affect status, types of work, relationships among organizational members, and salaries. I won't go deeply into it here, but stereotyping has had an impact on academic libraries for a long time. Perhaps an origin of certain thought and behavior patterns is the limited participation of librarians in the academic enterprise from the beginnings of American higher education well into the nineteenth century. Perhaps another origin has been the perception of education for librarianship as focused primarily on the clerical. Regardless of the source of thinking and action, academic librarians have been concerned about their place within colleges and universities for several decades. It may be that some of the concern about status has been mired in the venal, in concerns that don't depart from the financial and have little regard for the integral roles of library and librarian. The overwhelming concern, however, has centered on the recognition of the value of librarianship to higher education. One manifestation of the concern is the worry that the potential represented by librarians as academic professionals is being squandered. The following section looks at the nature of the status of academic librarians, the possible alternatives that exist, and the meaning of status concerns for the librarian.

Background

The literature on the status of academic librarians is voluminous. Most of it centers on the question of the appropriateness of a faculty status model. I will not review this literature at this time; however, some reviews do exist and can be used to get a picture of the history of, especially, the faculty status issue (Werrell and Sullivan 1987). More recently, Danielle Bodrero Hoggan (2003) examined the state of faculty status, including the benefits and the costs of such status and related responsibilities. There has been something of an institutional impetus behind faculty status as the preferred organizational role for librarians. Some years ago, ACRL proposed a set of standards for faculty status. These standards begin,

> Without the librarian, the quality of teaching, research, and public service in our colleges and universities would deteriorate seriously, and programs in many disciplines could no longer be performed. His (sic) contribution is intellectual in nature and is the product of considerable formal education, including professional training at the graduate level. Therefore, college and university librarians must be recognized as equal partners in the academic enterprise, and they

must be extended the rights and privileges which are not only commensurate with their contributions, but are necessary if they are to carry out their responsibilities (1970, 271).

A few years later, a statement on faculty status for librarians was drafted by representatives of ACRL, the Association of American Colleges (AAC), and the American Association of University Professors (AAUP). Parts of the statement echoed sections of the standards, but it attempted to elaborate on the rationale behind faculty status. Later, the statement was supplanted by a revised articulation of the place of academic librarians within their institutions ("Model Statement"). Throughout that statement, librarians are conjoined with other faculty through the language of the various segments of the statement. For instance, one passage reads, "The relationship between tenure and rank shall be the same for Library Faculty as for other faculty in the institution" (1987, 250). Very similar language is used in the section on appointment. The ACRL Committee on the Status of Academic Librarians was recently charged with re-examining faculty status. Recently approved guidelines for faculty status tend to emphasize equivalence of treatment and access to benefits with other academic personnel similar education and responsibilities ("Guidelines for Academic Status of College and University Libraries" 2001). No one has ever disputed that the activities mentioned in the statements constitute part of the role of the academic librarian, but these same activities have been the basis of both support and condemnation of faculty status, as we will see.

The more recent literature shows that there is little agreement even on how many institutions grant faculty status to librarians. For instance, John DePew (1983) estimated that 78.8 percent of academic librarians have faculty status; Ronald Rayman and Frank Goudy (1980) said the figure is 35 percent; Joyce Payne and Janet Wagner (1984) claimed the proportion is about 59 percent. Charles Lowry (1993) reported the results of a survey of 500 libraries. Of the 370 responding libraries, 67 percent said that librarians have faculty status (and another 7.3 percent) said librarians have academic status) (1993, 165). These findings are at odds with another survey of a similar population conducted by Betsy Park and Robert Riggs. They sent questionnaires to 469 libraries and received 304 responses. Of the respondents, 41.1 percent indicated that librarians have faculty status (1991, 279). It is evident that there is some discrepancy; but what is at the root of the differences?

What Is Faculty Status?

The differences in responses to questionnaires about faculty status may have something to do with the way questions are asked. Or, rather, responses may depend on how terms are defined. Suppose a surveyor of libraries asks whether librarians in a given library have faculty status, with faculty status defined as having the same ranks as teaching faculty, access to local funding for research, leaves equal to other faculty on campus, identical research and publication requirements, and academic-year contracts. It is likely that a small percentage of respondents would answer in the affirmative. Suppose the same respondent receives another questionnaire, with faculty status defined as ranks equivalent to those held by teaching faculty, the existence of some form of continuing appointment, and the requirement that librarians engage in some scholarly activity in order to earn a continuing appointment and/or promotion. The affirmative response may well be more frequent than in the first instance. If we look at only one factor—length of appointment period for librarians—we can see evidence of inconsistent practice regarding faculty status. In the survey reported on by Lowry, respondents were asked about appointment terms; a minority of librarians had nine-month contracts and a majority had twelve-month contracts (1993, 168). This immediately sets academic librarians apart from the majority of other faculty on their campuses.

A frequent sticking point regarding faculty status has to do with evidence of scholarship. I hasten to state at this point that well-conceived, well-executed scholarly activity is undoubtedly of benefit to individuals, institutions, and the profession. The question surrounding scholarship is not its potentially beneficial outcomes but, rather, the engagement of academic librarians in scholarly activity, including research and publication, at a level equal to that of other faculty at librarians' home institutions. The determination of some standard or target is not easy; there are disciplinary differences on each campus, with different productivity norms in operation (as has been discussed previously). Even within librarianship, there can be some variability of disciplinary approach to problems and questions. Further, some librarians may choose to engage in inquiry of a disciplinary nature, such as scholarship in history, economics, and so on. This variability can add to confusion about norms and kinds of evidence of scholarly activity. As William Black and Joan Leysen pointed out, a number of questions can arise, such as "What gets counted? How do published articles in journals compare with contributed papers, editorships, and poster sessions? How do we assess quality in the production of scholarship? What about the quality of the journal? How are contributions weighed? What about co-authored works? How much is enough?" (1994, 235).

The problem of what constitutes a scholarly contribution is also recognized by Charles Seavey and me. We speculated that "It may be that at some institutions anything in print—book reviews, reports of meetings, news notes, etc.— is seen as publication suitable for meeting promotion and tenure requirements," but added, "If this is true, it probably represents a departure from the requirements of the teaching faculty at these institutions" (1990, 469). Seavey and I examined a set of thirty-six journals over a five-year span and tracked both individual and institutional authorial responsibility. The institution that was most productive (that is, had more of its staff represented as authors) over the five years was the University of Illinois. Librarians there had a total of 88 credits (with sole authorship being one credit and coauthorship being a part of a credit, proportional to the number of authors). Translated to a per capita measure, the librarians at the University of Illinois had 0.693 credits each over the five-year period (Budd and Seavey 1990). In other words, on average, a librarian wrote less than an article in the thirty-six journals over a five-year period. Granted, this measure doesn't include publication in other journals or the publication of books or chapters of books, but these data do raise some questions about the scholarly activities of academic librarians.

Responses to Faculty Status

In addition to reviews of the literature and surveys on faculty status, there are analyses and position papers on the subject. The formal analyses are less numerous than other approaches, but they are instructive in some ways. For one thing, they are presentations of a discursive stance inasmuch as they begin with assumptions of their own and/or opposing starting points. One example is the article by Rachel Applegate. She began with what she saw as the fundamental assumptions of the faculty status model: "(1) that teaching faculty have certain roles and benefits, (2) that administrators or other college staff do not have these roles and benefits, and (3) that librarians who are not considered faculty will be considered administrators or staff and thus will not have these roles or benefits" (1993, 158). I am not going to refute or affirm the assumptions; they may be held by some but are probably not universal. Applegate's article is very useful in providing a compilation of some recent research on the phenomenon of faculty status, including matters of academic freedom, job satisfaction, attraction and retention of personnel, and institutional benefits.

One question that may arise in the course of considering the issue of faculty status for librarians is whether librarians who have some sort of faculty status are more satisfied in their positions than their counterparts. This was precisely the focus of Bonnie Horenstein's study. She distributed 1,500 questionnaires asking about such matters as the nature of status held, the level of participation in library governance, and satisfaction with the job. Based on 640 responses, she concluded that "Academic librarians with faculty status and rank are more satisfied than other librarians. . . . They have higher levels of overall satisfaction and are more satisfied with many of the aspects of their positions" (1993, 264). Because the response rate in her study was less than fifty percent, the results may be debatable, but they do present an opportunity for further investigation.

A recent study took a slightly different tack and focused on the specific issue of turnover and satisfaction of academic library directors. Michael Koenig, Ronald Morrison, and Linda Roberts articulated their expectations for the results of their inquiry: "Having to manage a library in which the library professional staff have tenure and faculty status increases the stress level of the director's position. More specifically, the thesis would be that the library director's position is functionally that of a classic line manager managing a service function in a complex, multifaceted environment, and, generally, is seen as such by his or her management" (1996, 297). The results of their study contradicted this expectation and showed that, especially, the existence of release time for professional staff to engage in scholarly activities correlated positively (and significantly) with the directors' job satisfaction. They further found that nominal faculty status (claiming that faculty status exists, but without the provision of release time) correlated negatively with directors' job satisfaction.

Some have suggested that some features of faculty status do not fit the academic librarian well. One recurring criticism is related to the notion of opportunity costs. The time and effort required to succeed at scholarly endeavors, such as publication, take away from the energy that can be focused on what is seen to be the primary responsibilities of librarianship. In some instances, a variation on faculty status is offered. Julie McGowan and Elizabeth Dow (1995) said that a clinical faculty model serves better than that of traditional teaching faculty. Clinical faculty spend more time on the individual needs of students and frequently do much of their work outside the classroom. McGowan and Dow maintained that such a model can result in greater institutional effectiveness and a higher level of fulfillment for librarians. Of course, many libraries reject faculty or academic status altogether and claim that librarians are academic professionals of a kind different from faculty. The effectiveness of any model depends on some integral factors: clear definition of rights and responsibilities of individuals, consistency in applying established criteria for success, fundamental recognition of the culture of higher education, and commitment to the academic mission of the institution. It may not be so important *what* status is adopted, but whether there is adherence to these essential elements of the academic librarian.

SUMMARY

One thing that becomes clear in the course of a close look at the role of the academic librarian is that it is a complex one. No single prescription of preparation, function, management style, or status fits everyone. There is too much individual and institutional variability for any prescription to be effective. The lack of any one way of behaving puts some pressure on academic librarians to be sensitive to some environmental condition. The librarian must be awake to the library's organization and operation. This means comprehending the communication patterns of the library, the structure of organization, the people of the library, and the openness and resistance that are likely to greet any event or proposal. This is not to say that the status quo cannot be changed, but the existing situation must be understood before any effort at change is undertaken. The librarian must be aware of the institution's structure, formal and informal. It is necessary to have a grasp on how decisions are made and who and what influences decision making. The librarian must have a clear understanding of the nature of the governance of the college or university. These conditions are essentially structural, political, and psychological. In addition to these factors, there is the important matter of the academic mission of the campus and how it is realized. The academic librarian cannot afford to make sweeping generalizations but, instead, must be sensitive simultaneously to the nature (perhaps idiosyncratic) of the local situation and to the ways other similar institutions act and react. For instance, the librarian should not assume that all campuses are adopting a private industry type of managerial stance just because the librarian's own institution is borrowing ideas from the private sector.

The above should suggest that the academic librarian is both a librarian and a citizen of the institution. It is a challenging role that will inevitably have its rewards and frustrations. It also suggests that there probably are more questions than answers regarding the role of the academic librarian. Here are a few questions to launch discussion:

> Should there be an academic library track in LIS education programs?
>
> Will the technical services/public services distinctions persist in an environment of electronic information?
>
> Can the academic librarian be effective in the absence of an understanding of information content?
>
> Is information a commodity?
>
> How does a leaderless library function?
>
> How would you construct an argument in favor of faculty status?
>
> Is there such a thing as opportunity costs related to faculty status?

Chapter 12

A Look Ahead

This final chapter affords us the opportunity to speculate on the future of academic libraries, mixed with reflections on the topics that form the rest of the book. It should be evident by now that the history and present state of college and university libraries indicate that libraries are not autonomous, are not isolated from their environment. Rather, they have developed in close conjunction with their parent institutions and have been affected by external forces such as social change, economic variability, and (especially) information production and dissemination. Some things have held constant over time: libraries have to be responsive to the needs of students and faculty; libraries have to be sensitive to the institution's curricula, including both content and means of delivery; libraries have to be aware of administrative emphases, both programmatic and managerial; libraries have to deal with the costs related to the provision of information services; and libraries have to realize that information content is produced externally to the library, in large part by college and university faculty. Although these factors provide constant challenges for libraries, the shape of the challenges is not fixed. The near-term future has inherent uncertainty attached to it, uncertainty that has social, political, economic, and technological roots. Some of the uncertainty must be addressed directly by the library. For instance, the question of how to pay for materials and access is inescapable. Other matters, such as the future of resident, extension, and other distance academic programs, may be determined outside the library. The remoteness of decision making doesn't eliminate the impact on the library, though. Let's take a look at some of the most pressing challenges.

THE FUTURE OF INSTRUCTION

Instruction on college and university campuses, as is true of just about every aspect of higher education, is being affected by technology. One manifestation of the impact is the incorporation of technology into on-campus instruction. At the most rudimentary level, this impact is affecting writing because word processing is ubiquitous. It is possible that the impact on writing will become more pronounced in the near future. The possibility now exists for the written work of students to transcend linear text. It may become relatively common for students to choose (or be required) to use multimedia authoring tools to enhance the presentation of their work. Faculty will likely become more accustomed to accepting combinations of text, photography, video images, and/or audio in fulfillment of class assignments. Some disciplines may gravitate to the use of media more readily than others. It is certainly not a stretch to imagine a student in a music course creating a multimedia presentation that integrates an analysis of a composer's work with audio clips from performances and, perhaps, video clips of an orchestra playing a particular composition. The proximity of the audio may well enhance the student's analysis of the composer's work. It is also conceivable that an architecture student will include multidimensional images of the exterior and interior of, say, a house design. In many disciplines, the image and the word may be used to convey a more complete understanding of particular subject matter.

Likewise, the teacher is able to use multimedia resources in classroom presentations. A political science faculty member can incorporate speeches by Richard Nixon, Henry Kissinger, and Abbie Hoffman into a class on the Vietnam War. An engineering professor might show students alternative designs that could be used in the construction of bridges. In the past, students and faculty may or may not have used the resources of the library or consulted a librarian when preparing assignments or presentations. On those campuses where the librarians are active in promoting the potential of library services, the likelihood is greater that members of the community turn to the library. In the near future, an active stance becomes even more imperative. The information universe, already huge, is expanding rapidly; faculty and students will benefit from librarians' knowledge and their willingness to contribute to instructional needs of the community. Of course, the success of a consultative stance will depend on librarians' ability to be constant learners. It has always been the case that successful librarians (that is, those who have been successful at providing effective service to students and faculty) have been eager to learn more about the content of the library's collection and about subject content generally. This kind of learning will not (or should not) diminish in the future, but it will be joined by the necessity to learn about the possibilities offered by evolving media. Just as student and teacher are challenged to explore new means of presentation and to be open to the learning and teaching changes accompanying the presentation, so, too, is the academic librarian.

Distance Education

A more far-reaching development looms for almost all colleges and universities. A combination of social and economic factors has progressively put more and more pressure on institutions to examine alternative ways to deliver instruction. It has always been true that not all people could afford, in time or money, to attend college on a full-time basis. In recent times, though, the national and global economies necessitate a level of preparedness that is unprecedented. The jobs and positions that offer the most in financial rewards, the greatest opportunities for advancement, and the highest level of personal challenge and satisfaction are likely to have accompanying high demands for skills, knowledge, and academic attainment. The shift to a postindustrial economy that began some time ago is reaching its mature stages. The result of the economic shift, along with the persistent economic pressures on many people, is a populace that needs the education that colleges and universities can offer, along with an alternative to the traditional resident setting. Many people can ill afford to forego any income for a four-year (plus) period. More are demanding other means of instructional delivery, including part-time opportunities (that may mean night and weekend offerings), extension offerings, and technology-based distance education.

One response by some institutions has been to enhance ongoing extension programs. This has led to increased numbers of courses offered away from the home campus, which, in turn, has meant faculty traveling to other locations to teach and the hiring of part-time adjunct faculty in other cities and towns. This means of instructing can take at least a couple of different forms. In some instances where specialized degree programs exist at one institution, there may be some interinstitutional cooperation that leads to courses sponsored by one campus being taught on another. Suppose a state university has the only program in social work in the state. That university may offer courses on the campuses of other state universities and colleges that lead to the degree in social work. When such a structure exists, it may be imperative for librarians at the various institutions to collaborate on ways to meet the information needs of the students who are taking the courses away from the degree-granting university.

In other instances, institutions may be offering courses in places where no other college or university exists. For instance, a regional state college may deliver instruction to towns in the region. Classes might meet in high schools or other public facilities. Where this kind of instruction exists, the challenge to meet students' information needs is even greater. Some libraries have expanded night and weekend hours to give people a chance to travel to the library. Some have enhanced interlibrary loan relationships with public libraries as a way to get materials to people. All libraries are looking to technological solutions to this problem. One way is the enhancement of remote access to the library's catalog and licensed databases (more and more of which are full text or full image) to accompany the catalog. However, there are limitations to providing such remote services. One is the level of connectivity the people in remote sites have. (We have to remember that this can be a financial, as well as a technical, challenge for students.) Another is the potential cost of license agreements if remote access is to be a feature of the configuration. Yet another limitation is the prohibition to remote access that copyright might entail. There is a good chance that print, as well as electronic, resources might be needed for course work and copyright will have to be taken into account when providing some information services. Libraries are constantly revisiting licensing agreements to ensure that students, wherever they live, can have access to the information the library offers (usually through proxy servers or other technological fixes).

The pressures felt by colleges and universities are increasingly leading to exploration of technological aids to distance education. Some quite large-scale efforts are being undertaken by the state of Maine and several western states. The simplest and least expensive solution to a distance education need is the production of videotaped courses that can be sold in multiple copies. A class presentation may be taped and then marketed to individuals or groups, along with a packet that provides class readings, or at least citations to readings. Although this is relatively inexpensive (and perhaps even profitable) for the institution, this is a passive medium. The student is unable to participate in class discussions unless the tapes are viewed by a group. Moreover, the student is unable to ask questions of the teacher when a question arises. Most would agree that this is not the ideal medium for distance education. An alternative is two-way interactive video. This medium has the advantage of real-time transmission, greater sensitivity to group dynamics, and the ability of students in remote locations to ask questions and offer comments and become involved in the class. This medium is not without its difficulties, too, including expenses. Streaming video over the Internet offers possibilities but, again, student access can be a limiting factor. Audio transmission, using available commercial products and Internet possibilities, can allow for class participation and accessibility, but cost can be an obstacle.

Other technological possibilities exist for distance education. One that is being used extensively is networking usually to provide Web-based instruction. That is, the potential of the Web and its hypertext capabilities is being used to deliver part or all of some courses. Commercially available tools, such as

Blackboard and WedCT, are used widely, as both the sole means of course delivery and a supplement to traditional instruction. Some institutions use software developed locally to deliver courses. An advantage of already developed tools is a saving in development time on the part of faculty or educational technology consultants. Another advantage can be consistency, so that both faculty and students can become familiar with the platform. Ideally, the tool becomes a facilitator of the instruction and interaction and not a barrier to learning and communication.

A course may incorporate Web-based elements to distribute common readings (with appropriate copyright restrictions), to present graphic and textual information to students, and to provide a mechanism for students to share their work and ideas. Electronic reserves can be an effective means of enabling students to have access to needed resources. Additionally, networking can be used to establish chat rooms wherein real-time interactive discussion can take place among students who are widely distributed geographically. The faculty member also may use networks to establish virtual office hours, enabling students to have real-time access at regularly scheduled times. Again, questions accompany this delivery mechanism. What is the optimum class size using Web-based instruction? (The answer undoubtedly will depend on course content.) Can, and should, the entirety of the course involve Web-based instruction? Should some personal contact with students and faculty be a part of the course? What part does information access play in the course? Can, and should, the library establish Web-based mediation for distance students? There is no doubt that distance education will grow rapidly in the near future. Librarians should have a voice in the structure of distance education programs and should examine, on each campus and across the profession, the goals and the possibilities related to information services in a distance program.

A substantial amount of rhetoric surrounds distance education. A good deal of it is based on a promise that was succinctly stated by John Seely Brown and Paul Duguid:

> for a large proportion of its clientele, education is an investment—a
> down payment on a career, social status, or, more immediately, just a
> job. Most students take the degrees they do to get the jobs they want,
> knowing or hoping that these jobs will repay the investment. For the
> vast majority, college implicitly provides a route into the general job
> "draft," much as it more explicitly prepares athletes for the NBA or
> NFL draft (1996, 11).

This premise begs the question, is knowledge effectively separate from the credential (the degree)? By this question I mean, does the employer want only evidence of some abstract credentialing in the form of a degree that has been awarded, or does the employer take the degree to be some form of evidence that the holder of the degree has acquired knowledge that is valuable through the degree program? A college or university that believes the former possibility is likely to have trouble succeeding according to the criteria of employability of its graduates. Also, an institution adhering to the former option is not likely to think it worthwhile to incorporate an information structure into the delivery of degree programs. With the latter possibility, there is no doubt that success has an instrumental character; the college or university attempts to enable students to acquire knowledge that employers value. If an information structure is seen to contribute to the instrumental goal, it will be valued.

Brown and Duguid offered a vision for one particular aspect of distance education that is not frequently stated, but may be widely shared. They said, "Communities of practice are, we think, essential and inevitable building blocks of society," but "we are not claiming, as communitarians do, that it would be useful to form communities and that universities are a good place to form them. Rather, we claim that communities, with all their strengths and shortcomings, grow inevitably and inescapably out of ongoing, shared practice. Learning a community's ways always requires access to that community and that practice" (1996, 13). For centuries, in fact since the founding of the first medieval universities, community has been seen as an essential element in the intellectual, social, and professional development of students. The idea of the resident college is based on such a belief and, for the past century or so, the library has fit into that idea. It is an open question, first, whether such a notion of community still inheres in the idea of the college or university. It also is an open question whether distance education can achieve and maintain a sense of community.

One of the realities of distance education is that it relies on an information base as part of teaching and learning (just as traditional instruction does). Such a reality creates some specific concerns. If some students will be receiving the instruction at a distance from the home campus, they will need access to some core information sources. The informational needs exist regardless of the means of delivery. If the chosen means is the Web, the information need is very widely dispersed. Present copyright restrictions may limit the ability of libraries to provide needed information sources for some time to come. Regardless of the means of delivery, instructors may require the assistance of librarians to help them structure at least a portion of the course presentation. Among other things, librarians can enable faculty to make optimal use of resources such as electronic reserves and other information tools. Distance education can be more time-consuming for both faculty and students for a number of reasons. The course is "always on," so students may work on it and be communicating at any time. Because communication among all of the participants can be asynchronous, effectiveness may necessitate frequent connection so that inter-action makes sense to everyone.

The success of distance education is dependent on this and other condi-tions. Howard Besser and Maria Bonn stated some of the conditions:

> If we can develop programs that relieve the financial pressure on our institutions of higher learning, if we can develop programs that open up the possibility of new and exciting teaching rather than exploiting faculty labor, and if we can design curricula that make wise use of the opportunities offered by distance independent media, then we will have begun to realize the educational potential of current informa-tion and communication technology (1996, 883).

The latter two of their conditions are indeed critical to the success of any dis-tance learning program. The technology can promise new and effective ways to enhance learning, and curricula should be reviewed to make use of that prom-ise. The first condition, however, is problematic. There is no available proof that effective use of technology for distance education saves an institution money. In fact, if an institution's goal is to save money (or to make money), any goal of effective teaching and learning may be in jeopardy (Noble 2003).

COPYRIGHT

Although the most recent revision of copyright law dates back only about twenty years, those two decades have seen such massive changes that the law is inadequate to address many questions. Once again, the challenges that face us with regard to the interpretation of copyright law are related to technology. Previous chapters have discussed how the world of communication can be al-tered by the use of network technology. This different way of functioning and thinking makes possible such things as electronic journals. The malleability of the medium renders written work unstable because it can potentially be altered many times by many people. As Karen Hersey observed, "When we ask what's different in the world of digitized information, the answer is, in a word—every-thing. Publishers and copyright holders who, like the libraries, were comfort-able in a world of print, now find themselves in a world of instant mass dissem-ination" (1995, 25). The magnitude of change renders invalid many of the assumptions we used to hold. Varying means of disseminating information call into question the nature of ownership of ideas and the control over them. This new reality is already having an impact on the academic world.

Let's create a scenario and take a look at what might happen with networked communication. Let's say a member of the chemistry department faculty is struck by an idea. Although it may not be fully developed, she decides to send her idea via e-mail to a colleague at another university. Her colleague is intrigued by the idea and forwards the e-mail to another colleague who has expertise in a specific area included in the author's idea. The third person copies the e-mail message in order to work on the facet of the idea that is of interest to him. This third chemist then presents the challenge to a graduate seminar he's teaching. By now, the authority of the first person, the one who had the original idea, is no longer connected to the text of her e-mail message. An unscrupulous doctoral student conducts a literature search and finds that the idea has not made it into the formal literature. The doctoral student appropriates the idea and publishes a paper based on it. The first chemist sees the paper in print and is angered and confused. Could someone have had the same idea? Could her idea have been stolen? If the latter is suspected, could it be proved? In this scenario, it may be possible to trace the transmission of the message and uncover the culprit. Suppose, though, that the original message has been passed on three or four more times and to multiple recipients each time. The challenge to protect and assign credit to intellectual property is a daunting one.

The difficulty of protecting copyright and intellectual property rights generally should not be an excuse for forsaking this essential legal and ethical right. Even with the difficulties presented by existing and emerging technologies, the purpose of copyright doesn't change. What does change, as Lawrence Lessig (2004) has pointed out so well, is the effective implementation of copyright. Because technology use creates a unique copy with the transmission of a file, each copy could be subject to designation as property and the copyright owner can conceivably treat the transmission activity as piracy. The challenge faced by all academics, librarians definitely included, in the realm of software may not be so much copyright as such, but the copyright protections that are part of the software code. It may be that in trying to render a product more usable, a librarian, a faculty member, or a student circumvents copyright protection and becomes liable for such an action. Knowledge may not be a commodity, but the packages through which recorded knowledge is transmitted are indeed bought and sold and have been for a long time. Perhaps it is the long-standing marketplace that is most threatened by technology. One reaction to the threat of the dissolution of familiar marketing activities is to restrict access in an effort to maximize income based on the control of dissemination. In some ways, the dilemma has been with us since the invention of the photocopier. When cheap photocopies became commonplace in libraries, the burgeoning photocopying activity may not have had a huge effect on sales of scholarly works. Students, and even faculty, probably didn't subscribe to large numbers of scholarly journals. The principal difference may have been in how students and faculty used the material that had already been provided by the library.

We (and I'm referring to the large "we" of society generally) are still groping for the best way to incorporate technology's possibility into the ideal of free exchange of ideas and unfettered growth of knowledge. From where we stand now, there is no way to predict what state will emerge or how we will get there. Copyright considerations present us with an effective cautionary tale. We have to keep reminding ourselves that technology helps us solve some kinds of problems but may present us with other kinds. Douglas Bennett summed up the challenge well:

> We need to recognize, however, that while the new technology inclines towards free inquiry and expression, it does not guarantee either. Broadly speaking, I believe there are two dangers. One is a rising tide of intolerance, active antagonism to art and intellect, and willful ignorance. . . . The other danger would be in relying too heavily on profit-making activities and institutions in shaping the electronic future (1995, 13).

SCHOLARLY COMMUNICATION

Earlier chapters have tackled many of the challenges faced by the scholarly communication system and what responses to those challenges may mean for libraries. At this point, we can take a brief look at what the future might bring. Some writers have proposed an overhaul of the system. Charles Schwartz rightly questioned the wisdom of the structural reform approach. As he convincingly pointed out, scholarly communication exhibits characteristics of a loosely coupled system. Because there is not necessarily a close and permanent relationship among the various components of scholarly communication (scholars themselves, their institutions, information producers, libraries), it is unlikely that a structural reconfiguration could be imposed. As Schwartz wrote, "Since the scholarly communication system includes a multitude of segmented groups, each with quite different interests, any realistic approach to reform of the system would have to anticipate in some detail the difficulties in strategy, plans, and sequences of action that inevitably would occur" (1994, 111). He was quick to point out that the challenge presented by loose coupling does *not* mean that change won't or shouldn't occur.

Historically, there has been resistance to large-scale changes in communication. In the fifteenth century, Angelo Poliziano decried the folly of printing, saying "The most stupid ideas can now in a moment be transferred into a thousand volumes and spread abroad" (Moorehead 1951, 60). No doubt Poliziano was correct that mountains of drivel have been printed, but printing transformed society nonetheless. No doubt virtual mountains of drivel are transmitted electronically today; will recognition of that state stop the spread of networked information? Findings reported in *University Libraries and Scholarly Communication* (Cummings et al. 1992) have been mentioned in this book.

What will be the future for scholarly communication? In the short term, we can expect to see more projects such as Project Muse and JSTOR, and an expansion of initiatives such as SPARC. These efforts have made substantive differences in the accessibility and use of information. There are still a number of unanswered questions regarding academic rewards, economics, copyright, access, and archiving of information. Until adequate responses to those questions are proposed, there is likely to be cautious progress in transforming the formal communication structure from print to electronic media. The authors of *University Libraries and Scholarly Communication* offer one vision of the future:

> It is extremely unlikely—we would say almost inconceivable—that any alternative model will completely supplant the existing one at any point in the foreseeable future. Rather, we envision a situation where we also argue, however, that it is equally inconceivable that there will not eventually be a more-or-less complete transformation of scholarly communication. The new technologies are too powerful and their advantages too clear for current practices to continue indefinitely. However one might regard present technological developments, no amount of nostalgic longing for traditional practices, in our view, will serve to forestall the application of the new technologies to scholarly communication (Cummings et al. 1992, 165).

Although the work of faculty today and the administrations' evaluation of faculty are not substantively different from the past, the means, purposes, and outcomes of scholarly communication may be subject to revolutionary change. Harold Billings (2003), for example, speculated that the coming decade may be subject to punctuated equilibrium; some current practices will remain while unforeseen alterations will also come about. How transforming will changes in access to information be? As Philip Davis (2003) pointed out, the open-access movement, which is garnering considerable attention and has many merits, has costs associated with it and sometimes authors are required to pay fees to offset them. It is undetermined at this time whether the movement can succeed, especially outside the natural sciences, if authors are asked to pay the freight for access. Some claim that open access will not reduce prices, but that opinion is disputed. As we have seen previously, open access is a potentially innovative solution, but we have to remember that the scholarly communication situation is complicated by high costs, budgetary challenges for libraries and institutions, and continuing administrative demands for greater faculty productivity.

Perhaps the only thing approaching a certainty is that all academic librarians (not just library directors) will have to contribute to a solution.

Any discussion of scholarly communication raises the question, what is the future for the scholarly book? We've seen how university presses are scaling back their publishing efforts; some are now ceasing to publish works in disciplines they were once committed to. Cathy Davidson has shown us that the publication of scholarly books is not profitable. This view is echoed by Lindsay Waters, who says, "We have financial records of publishing in the West since Gutenberg, and it is clear that books are a losing proposition. Widgets have been, and always will be, a surer bet. And the idea of milking the university presses—the poorest of all publishers—for cash is the equivalent of making church mice contribute to the upkeep of the church" (2004, 5). The answer, perhaps, is a break with the administrative maelstrom of demanding ever-greater numbers of "stuff." To thrive as a system, scholarly communication has to be composed of meaningful communication. Because technology allows for the production of more, faster, there should not be a causal link to producing more for its own sake. Meaningful communication is invaluable; meaningless products in quantity are not. Waters puts his finger on the problem in the humanities: "The humanities are in a crisis right now because many of the presuppositions about what counts—which is, not to be too cute about it, counting—are absolutely inimical to the humanities. When books cease being complex media and become rather objects to quantify, then it follows that all other media that the humanities study lose value" (2004, 6).

ACADEMIC LIBRARY SERVICES

Some might consider it heresy to say that libraries should be reactive in planning services to their communities. There is a great deal of rhetoric urging an active role for libraries on their campuses. I would propose that action and reaction need not occur (actually *cannot* occur) in isolation from one another. Yes, it's true that libraries and librarians must actively seek to know more about their communities, explore alternative means of providing information services, and influence the production of scholarly information. On what should that action be based? Well, before any action is taken, librarians have to examine the factors that could have effects on decisions. Let's take a look at an example. The official and actual stance of the library of a university is to ensure all students full and open access to the library's collections and services. The university administrators decide to launch an aggressive program of distance education, consisting of courses being offered at off-campus locations and the use of interactive video and the Web. The library's stance is active, but it now must react to the decision to engage in distance education. It must explore ways to ensure electronic access to its catalog, to licensed databases, and to librarians. It must seek creative ways to meet the information needs of the students who are not on-site and the faculty who are preparing the courses. All of these can be seen as active responses to a situation that is not of the library's creation. If we accept that Charles Schwartz is correct (and I do), there will constantly be decisions made by one player in the scholarly communication system that will affect all the others. The library has to be sensitive to the moves made by the other organizations and entities with whom they are loosely coupled.

The services offered by libraries are ineluctably affected by technology. New possibilities are created by technological developments that the library has to consider, in light of the work of students and faculty. Some seem to take firm positions regarding the place of information technology in libraries. For example, Michael Harris and Stan Hannah (1996) emphasized the differences between core communication technologies and the book (not just physically, but as defining mechanisms for human communication) and strongly advocated an embrace of the digital communication environment. Their position is adopted with full awareness that a shift from print to electronic media represents an encompassing social and cultural change of great magnitude. Will such a shift be absolute? Should it be? How long will it take? How much of academic and intellectual life will it affect? These are questions that we all have to grapple with for some time to come. Some people believe they have some answers for us. Kenneth Dowlin wrote that "one of the greatest challenges facing librarians and other staff of libraries will be replacing the traditional skills learned in traditional library schools, such as book acquisition, cataloging, and reference work in graphic records, with a whole new set of skills" (1995, 416). I would suggest that Dowlin, and others who make similar statements (although correct about a transformation of skills needed), are missing an important point. Preparedness for the future (whatever it holds) is not dependent so much on acquiring a set of skills as it is on understanding why we need to do certain things. Dowlin seems to assume that skills are separate from the intellectual activity related to practicing the skills. If a beginning professional academic librarian is proficient at working with a particular computer operating system, but has no idea what kinds of information are important to students and faculty and how they might use the information, his or her proficiency will be transient and may contribute little to the achievement of the library's goals.

There are some aspects of service that we have to accept; some of them relate to information itself. Harlan Cleveland's examination of essential features of information has often been quoted, and it is useful to look at it now:

1. *Information is expandable.* . . . The ultimate "limits to growth" of knowledge and wisdom are time (available to human minds for

reflecting, analyzing, and integrating the information that will be "brought to life" by being used) and the capacity of people—individ ually and in groups—to analyze and think integratively. . . .

2. *Information is compressible.* Paradoxically, this infinitely expandable resource can be concentrated, integrated, summarized—miniaturized, if you will—for easier handling. . . .

3. *Information is substitutable.* It can and increasingly does replace land, labor, and capital. . . .

4. *Information is transportable*—at the speed of light and, perhaps, through telepathy, faster than that. . . .

5. *Information is diffusive.* It tends to leak; the more it leaks the more we have and the more of us have it. . . .

6. *Information is shareable.* . . . Things are exchanged; if I give you a flower or sell you my automobile, you have it and I don't. But if a sell you you an idea, we both have it (1985, 29–33).

Information, then, is not a thing in the sense that a book or a computer is a thing. This has always been true but, as we'll see in a moment, we've tended to forget it.

Peter Ingwersen took the relation of information to communication (inherent in Cleveland) a step further:

1. Viewed from the perspective of the recipient, information is a potential until perceived;

2. Viewed from the perspective of the generator, recipients are also simply receivers potential;

3. When a recipient accesses potential information in a "state of uncertainty," it becomes data which may become information if perceived;

4. If not perceived the potential information remains data for the particular recipient and potential information for other recipients and generators;

5. Perception is controlled by the knowledge structures (K(S)) in the recipient's state of knowledge and problem space;

6. Information (dl) may infer (support) the uncertainty state and transform the problem space and the state of knowledge, causing considerations, decisions, actions, intentions, changes of values or other effects;

7. Information is a transformation of knowledge structures (1995, 96).

Carla Stoffle and others (2003) stated that newly created, customizable services developed by academic libraries would result in a lesser demand for intermediation, freeing staff to accomplish other objectives. The complexity that

Ingswersen described, however, suggests that customization may not be simple for information seekers. Rather, it could be that libraries will have to have a broader and deeper understanding of the cognitive and epistemic dimensions of questioning, informing, considering, and concluding. Intermediation may be even more essential than ever.

One final word about services in the future. Although we construct ideals for services, those ideals may be confounded by the realities associated with information sources and information users. The first reality has been defined, in part, as a problem of overload; too much is out there to be assimilated in any sort of timely manner. The second reality is frequently seen as users' selective incorporation of information into their work. Patrick Wilson presented an analysis that we may be reluctant to accept, but is nonetheless accurate:

> intellectual accessibility is a dominant feature. An easy and quickly useable source will get priority over one whose use will be slow and difficult. . . . (W)e should think of this as a question of the relative costs and benefits of different uses of time. The cost of acquiring information from difficult sources is higher than the cost of acquiring information from accessible sources. . . . We should see overload not as a problem to be solved, but rather as a condition in which we unavoidably live. . . . Work is done, conclusions are reached, theoretical and practical positions are adopted, all on the basis of imperfect and partial use of available relevant information. It cannot be avoided. There is not enough time (1995, 28, 31).

The challenge facing libraries and librarians is what to do in light of such a fundamental condition. First, realization that the condition exists enables us to adjust our thinking accordingly. Next, the services offered by libraries have to be based on the necessary selectivity that users require and create means by which the most relevant information can be selected. This imperative affects the bibliographic structure (library catalogs, indexes, and abstracting sources) as well as mediation services, such as reference. These effects should be kept in mind as libraries revisit traditional library operations, including replacing in-house cataloging with outsourcing and reconfiguring public services.

A WARNING

Through all of the reexaminations, reconsiderations, restructurings, and rethinking that are part of life in academic librarianship, there are a few things to be aware of. Altough we covered the principal purposes and functions of academic libraries and the workings of the scholarly communication system (including information production and use), we have to be wary of accepting certain particular views of information that could constrain and confine (as well as confound) us. I mentioned some of these views in chapter 11, but this matter deserves a bit deeper treatment. The first thing to be careful of is a very strong temptation to reify information and associated concepts. By this, I mean that there is a tendency, reflected in the literatures of our profession and other disciplines, to transform information into some material and objectified entity. For instance, there may be the equation of information packages—books, journals, electronic media—with the content of the packages. We have to remind ourselves continuously that the library exists not simply to preserve and store the packages of information, but also to ensure that the content is available to, and accessible by, those who want and need it. A similar reification tendency applies to knowledge. It's not uncommon in management literature, for example, to see references to knowledge industries, knowledge workers, and knowledge products. Objectifying the idea of knowledge in this way could lead to forgetting just what knowledge is. Cleveland's characteristics of information might help us resist the temptation to reify.

The reification of information and knowledge is made easier for us by a prevailing (in some circles at least) view of information as a commodity. Again, Cleveland's admonition is an attempt to counter such a view, but the urge to commodify information (and knowledge) is powerful. Information technology tends to feed that urge because technology breaks down some of the temporal and spatial constraints that can limit the commodification of information. As we see information more and more as a commodity, information (and the information services that are the essence of academic libraries) takes on, or is ascribed, value. Its value is not just expressed in economic, but also in social, terms.

I'm not offering a new insight; it dates back at least as far as Karl Marx, who wrote that "the productions of the human brain appear as independent beings endowed with life, and entering into relation both with one another and the human race. So it is in the world of commodities with the products of men's (sic) hands. This I call Fetishism which attaches itself to the products of labour, so soon as they are produced as commodities, and which is therefore inseparable from the production of commodities" (1995, 43–44). Marx further observed, "It is only by being exchanged that the products of labour acquire, as values, one uniform social status, distinct from their varied forms of existence as objects of utility" (1995, 44). When information is seen as a commodity, it is imbued with a certain kind of value, as is the information service provided by librarians and commercial organizations. Marx's notion of the fetishism of commodities is extended by Jean-François Lyotard (1984), who wrote,

> The relationship of suppliers and users of knowledge to the knowl-
> edge they supply and use is now tending, and will increasingly tend,

to assume the form already taken by the relationship of commodity producers and consumers to the commodities they produce and consume—that is, the form of value. Knowledge is and will be produced in order to be sold, it is and will be consumed in order to be valorized in a new production: in both cases, the goal is exchange. Knowledge ceases to be an end in itself, it loses its "use-value" (1984, 4–5).

Part of the nature of the warning I'm offering is a realization that one all-encompassing view of society probably does not serve the aims of higher education and of academic libraries. Though the temptation to avoid the matter is strong, all of us in higher education should scrutinize the place of consumerism in education. I do not mean that it has no place in education, but it is not appropriate as a defining force. For one thing, as David Hawkes noted, "In the consumer societies of the late twentieth century, exchange-value (a purely symbolic form) has become more real, more objective, than use-value (a material phenomenon). Objects are conceived, designed and produced for the purpose of making money by selling them, rather than for reasons of practical utility" (1996, 169). Hawkes quoted Georg Lukacs, who examined the consumerism of capitalist society in terms of a reified consciousness that invades all aspects of that capitalist society: "Reification requires that society should learn to satisfy all its needs in terms of commodity exchange" (1971, 91); "the basic structure of reification can be found in all the social forms of modern capitalism" (1971, 171); "Reification is, then, the necessary, immediate reality of every person living in capitalist society" (1971, 197). Frank Webster (1995) told us that the process of reification and commodification in the "information society" can obscure the semantic nature of information (in the sense of informing), which is founded on the premise that information is meaningful. Obscuring this idea can lead us to think, as Theodore Roszak warned, that "information has come to denote whatever can be coded for transmission through a channel that connects a source with a receiver regardless of semantic content" (1986, 13).

As stated earlier, the place and power of technology in our society may foster commodification and enforce reification. Just as printing was an agent of change on a grand scale in the fifteenth and sixteenth centuries, information technology is an agent of change today. The change is potentially of considerable breadth and depth. Neil Postman reminded us that "New technologies alter the structure of our interests: the things we think about. They alter the character of our symbols: the things we think with. And they alter the nature of community: the arena in which thoughts develop" (1992, 20). Does this mean that technologies *determine* how we think, what we will think about, and how we will live? It would be an error to impart that much power to technology; it is, after all, a human creation, and is used by humans. Technology is contextual;

it is a product and a part of our society. As such, it springs from the minds of people and is part of what we might see as a social envelope. Michael Smith saw the contextual side of technology and said, "About technological determinism we could also argue that the issue is not really technology at all but rather a curious cultural and political fetishism whereby artifacts stand in for technology, and technology in turn signifies national progress" (1994, 39). As technology becomes a part of society, though, it can, as Postman insisted, transform society in seemingly subtle, but nonetheless profound, ways. Technology, then, can be seen as a paradox—an effect of societal change and a cause of a transformed conception of both society and self.

The nature of this warning may make one think that I'm antitechnology. That's not so, as is evident from the recognition elsewhere in this book of the numerous possibilities afforded by technology. What I do see as dangerous is an uncritical acceptance of all things technological. Information technology does indeed help us serve academic communities in ways that were not possible just a few years ago. It may be best to keep in mind a framework for thinking about technology provided by Carl Mitcham (1994). His framework is based on four ways of thinking about technology (which may or may not occur together and may or may not be altogether positive): technology as object (that is, technology as part of the world, but separate from ourselves); technology as activity (technology has its uses, but it also has an influencing force); technology as knowledge (this is much more than awareness of how technology works and extends to a notion of technology as challenging that includes both revealing and concealing); and technology as volition (there is a will and purpose behind the creation of technology, and this will may be focused on control). Mitcham's framework illustrates the complexity of this warning and of the challenge that faces academic librarianship.

SUMMARY

It's obvious that the world of higher education is changing and will continue to change. The pace of change, in some regards (such as the academic rewards structure, curricula, the scholarly communication system), is not rapid at the present time. The impetus for change, however, is strong and, at least for now, unrelenting. So, we can expect a somewhat volatile environment for some time to come. In the near term, we are likely to see very lively debate about the alternatives facing higher education. For instance, although distance education is growing and diversifying, there is no consensus on the direction it should take, the magnitude it should reach, or the institutions that should be principally responsible for undertaking it. Debates surround other aspects of higher education as well. In all likelihood, we'll see some colleges and universities move on with some actions, such as the elimination of traditional tenure for faculty, while the debates continue. Higher education has tended to be conservative in the past (in that it has been reluctant to overhaul operations quickly or completely), but that conservatism is coming under fire both from within and without. There is no way to predict what the college or university of the year 2020 will look like, and it would be futile to attempt such a prediction.

The academic library is likewise subject to the forces of change. The transformation of the present institution will undoubtedly leave its mark on the library. The library and librarians will have to respond to alterations of purpose and operation because the library exists to provide optimum service to its community (which itself is subject to change). In addition to the institutional transformations that will take place, the library will be affected by other forces as well. Technological developments are not limited to the world of higher education but certainly have an impact on the storage and retrieval of information. As we've seen, there also may be organizational change in libraries, springing from an effort to be able to provide more effective service to the community and to be better equipped to handle a dynamic information production environment. The changes we've already seen signal that libraries are not adopting a static stance with regard to their work but, rather, are actively exploring ways to respond to increasing, and changing, demands. The active stance of librarians has to continue if the services and the organizations of libraries are to be vital components of the educational enterprise.

BIBLIOGRAPHY

Adams, Mike S. *Welcome to the Ivory Tower of Babel: Confessions of a Conservative College Professor*. Augusta, Ga.: Harbor House, 2004.

Alghamdi, Faleh A. "The Collegial Model: Its Applications and Implications for Academic Libraries." *Library Administration & Management* 8 (winter 1994): 15–20.

Alire, Camila A., and Frederick J. Stielow. "Minorities and the Symbolic Potential of the Academic Library: Reinventing Tradition." *College & Research Libraries* 56 (Nov. 1995): 509–17.

Allen, Bryce. "Information Services in Electronic Communities." In *The Role and Impact of the Internet on Library and Information Services*. Edited by Lewis-Guodo Liu, pp. 119–43. Westport, Conn.: Greenwood Pr., 2001.

Allen, Eileen E. "Active Learning and Teaching: Improving Postsecondary Library Instruction." *Reference Librarian,* no. 51/52 (1995): 89–103.

Anders, Vicki, Colleen Cook, and Roberta Pitts. "A Glimpse into a Crystal Ball: Academic Libraries in the Year 2000." *Wilson Library Bulletin* 67 (Oct. 1992): 36–40.

Antelman, Kristin. "Do Open Access Articles have Greater Research Impact?" *College & Research Libraries* 65 (Sept. 2004): 372–82.

Applegate, Rachel. "Deconstructing Faculty Status: Research and Assumptions." *Journal of Academic Librarianship* 19 (July 1993): 158–64.

Aronowitz, Stanley. *The Knowledge Factory: Dismantling the Corporate University and Creating True Higher Learning*. Boston: Beacon Pr., 2000.

Asheim, Lester. "Education for Future Academic Librarians." In *Academic Libraries by the Year 2000: Essays Honoring Jerrold Orne*. Edited by Herbert Poole, pp. 128–38. New York: Bowker, 1977.

Association for Library Collections and Technical Services. "Educational Policy Statement." *ALCTS Newsletter* 7, no. 1 (1995): 7–10.

Association of College and Research Libraries. "Standards for Faculty Status for College and University Librarians." Chicago: ALA, 2001.

———. "Standards for Faculty Status for College and University Librarians." *College & Research Libraries News* 31 (Oct. 1970): 271–72.

Association of Research Libraries. "The M.L.S. Hiring Requirement." ARL SPEC Kit 257 (June 2000). Available at http://www. arl.org/spec/257sum.html.

Atkins, Stephen E. *The Academic Library in the American University.* Chicago: ALA, 1991.

Atkinson, Ross. "Managing Traditional Materials in an Online Environment: Some Definitions and Distinctions for a Future Collection Management." *Library Resources & Technical Services* 42 (Jan. 1998): 7–20.

———. "A Rationale for the Redesign of Scholarly Information Exchange." *Library Resources & Technical Services* 44 (Apr. 2000): 59–69.

———. "Old Forms, New Forms: The Challenge of Collection Development." *College & Research Libraries* 50 (September 1992): 507–20.

Avdjieva, Maria, and Marie Wilson. "Exploring the Development of Quality in Higher Education." *Managing Service Quality* 12, no. 6 (2002): 372–83.

Beagle, Donald. "Conceptualizing an Information Commons." *Journal of Academic Librarianship* 25 (Mar. 1999): 82–89.

Beetham, David. *Bureaucracy*, 2nd Edition. Minneapolis: University of Minnesota Pr., 1996.

Belensky, Mary Field, Blythe McVicker Clinchy, Nancy Rule Goldberger, and Jill Mattuck Tarule. *Women's Ways of Knowing: The Development of Self, Voice and Mind.* New York: Basic Books, 1986.

Bénaud, Claire-Lise, and Sever Bordeianu. *Outsourcing Library Operations in Academic Libraries: An Overview of Issues and Outcomes.* Englewood, Colo.: Libraries Unlimited, 1998.

Bennett, Douglas C. "Fair Use in an Electronic Age: A View from Scholars and Scholarly Societies." In *Copyright, Public Policy, and the Scholarly Community.* Edited by Michael Matthews and Patricia Brennan, pp. 7–15. Washington, D.C.: ARL, 1995.

Bennis, Warren, and Burt Nanus. *Leaders: The Strategies for Taking Charge.* New York: Harper & Row, 1985.

Bensman, Stephen J., and Stanley J. Wilder. "Scientific and Technical Serials Holdings Optimization: A LSU Serials Redesign Project Exercise." *Library Resources & Technical Services* 42 (July 1998): 147–242.

Berardo, Felix. "The Publication Process: An Editor's Perspective." *Journal of Marriage and the Family* 38, no. 4 (1981): 771–79.

Bérubé, Michael. "Discipline and Theory." In *Wild Orchids and Trotsky.* Edited by Mark Edmundson, pp. 173–92. New York: Penguin, 1993.

Besser, Howard, and Maria Bonn. "Impact of Distance Independent Education." *Journal of the American Society for Information Science* 47 (Nov. 1996): 880–83.

Beyer, Janice M. "Editorial Policies and Practices among Leading Journals in Four Scientific Fields." *Sociological Quarterly* 19 (winter 1978): 68–88.

Biderman, B. "Proposal for a University of Toronto 'Information Commons': Information Technology Made Visible and Accessible." Toronto: University of Toronto Instructional Research Computing, 1992.

Billings, Harold. "The Wild-Card Academic Library in 2013." *College & Research Libraries* 64 (Mar. 2003): 105–9.

Birnbaum, Robert. *How Colleges Work: The Cybernetics of Academic Organization and Leadership.* San Francisco: Jossey-Bass, 1988.

Black, William K., and Joan M. Leysen. "Scholarship and the Academic Library." *College & Research Libraries* 55 (May 1994): 229–41.

Bloom, Allan. *The Closing of the American Mind: How Higher Education Has Failed Democracy and Impoverished the Soul of Today's Students.* New York: Simon and Schuster, 1987.

Bloom, Harold. *The Western Canon: The Books and School of the Ages.* New York: Harcourt Brace & Co., 1994.

Bok, Derek. *Higher Learning.* Cambridge, Mass.: Harvard University Pr., 1986.

———. *Universities in the Marketplace: The Commercialization of Higher Education.* Princeton, N.J.: Princeton University Pr., 2003.

Bolman, Lee G., and Terrence E. Deal. *Modern Approaches to Understanding and Managing Organizations,* 3rd Edition. San Francisco: Jossey-Bass, 2003.

Book Industry Study Group, Inc. *Book Industry Trends, 2004.* New York: BISG, 2004.

Bowker Annual and Library and Book Trade Almanac, 2003. Medford, N.J.: Information Today, 2003.

Brancolini, Kristine R. "Use and User Studies for Collection Evaluation." In *Collection Management for the 1990s.* Edited by Joseph J. Branin, pp. 63–94. Chicago: ALA, 1992.

Braxton, John M., and Alan E. Bayer. "Assessing Faculty Scholarly Performance." In *Measuring Faculty Research Performance.* Edited by John W. Cresswell, pp. 25–42. *New Directions for Institutional Research* no. 50 (June 1986).

Broad, William, and Nicholas Wade. *Betrayers of the Truth: Fraud and Deceit in the Halls of Science.* New York: Simon and Schuster, 1982.

Brockman, William S. 2001. *Scholarly Work in the Humanities and the Evolving Information Environment.* Washington, D.C.: Digital Library Federation and Council on Library and Information Resources.

Brown, Gary J. "The Business of Scholarly Journal Publishing." In *Understanding the Business of Library Acquisitions.* Edited by Karen A. Schmidt, pp. 33–48. Chicago: ALA, 1990.

Brown, Janet Dagenais. "Using Quality Concepts to Improve Reference Services." *College & Research Libraries* 55 (May 1994): 211–19.

Brown, John Seely, and Paul Duguid. "Universities in the Digital Age." *Change* 28 (July–August 1996): 10–19.

Buckland, Michael. *Information and Information Systems*. New York: Praeger, 1991.

———. *Redesigning Library Services: A Manifesto*. Chicago: ALA, 1992.

———. "What Will Collection Developers Do?" *Information Technology and Libraries* 14 (Sept. 1995): 155–59.

Budd, John M. "Academic Libraries: Institutional Support and Internal Expenditures." *Library Administration & Management* 4 (Summer 1990): 154-58.

Budd, John M. "A Critique of Customer and Commodity." *College & Research Libraries* 58 (July 1997): 310–21.

———. "The Education of Academic Librarians." *College & Research Libraries* 45 (Jan. 1984): 15–24.

———. "Faculty Publishing Productivity: An Institutional Analysis and Comparison with Library and Other Measures." *College & Research Libraries* 56 (Nov. 1995): 547–54.

———. "Humanities Journals Ten Years Later: Practices in 1989." *Scholarly Publishing* 22 (July 1991): 200–216.

———. "Increases in Faculty Publishing Activity: An Analysis of ARL and ACRL Institutions." *College & Research Libraries* 60 (July 1999): 308–15.

———. "Keepers of the Gate or Demons in a Jar?" In *A Service Profession, a Service Commitment: A Festschrift in Honor of Charles D. Patterson*. Edited by Connie Van Fleet and Dannie P. Wallace, pp. 42–69. Metuchen, N.J.: Scarecrow Pr., 1992.

———. "Leading through Meaning: Elements of a Communication Process." In *Library Communication: The Language of Leadership*. Edited by Donald E. Riggs, pp. 108–17. Chicago: ALA, 1991.

———. *The Library and Its Users: The Communication Process*. Westport, Conn.: Greenwood Pr., 1992.

———. "Scholarly Communication and Libraries: Contemporary and Future." In *For the Good of the Order: Essays in Honor of Edward G. Holley*. Edited by Delmus E. Williams et al., pp. 191–204. Greenwich, Conn.: JAI Pr., 1994.

———. "Serials Prices and Subscriptions in the Social Sciences." *Journal of Scholarly Publishing* 33 (Jan. 2002): 90–101.

Budd, John M., and Corrie Christensen. "Social Sciences Literature and Electronic Information." *portal: Libraries and the Academy* 3 (Oct. 2003): 643–51.

Budd, John M., and Charles A. Seavey. "Characteristics of Journal Authorship by Academic Librarians." *College & Research Libraries* 51 (Sept. 1990): 463–70.

Budd, John M., and Ellen R. Urton. "University Press Publishing and Academic Library Holdings." *Publishing Research Quarterly* 19 (summer 2003): 5–13.

Bush, Carmel, Margo Sasse, and Patricia Smith. "Toward a New World Order: A Survey of Outsourcing Capabilities of Vendors for Acquisitions, Cataloging and

Collection Development Services." *Library Acquisitions: Practice and Theory* 18, no. 4 (1994): 397–416.

Butler, Pierce. "Librarianship as a Profession." *Library Quarterly* 41 (Oct. 1951): 235–47.

Buttlar, Lois J., and Rajinder Garcha. "Organizational Structuring in Academic Libraries." *Journal of Library Administration* 17, no. 3 (1992): 1–21.

CannCasciato, Daniel. "Tepid Water for Everyone? The Future OLUC, Catalogers, and Outsourcing." *OCLC Systems and Services* 10 (spring 1994): 5–8.

Casserly, Mary F. "Collection Development in College and University Libraries: A Comparison." In *Collection Development in College Libraries*. Edited by Joanne Schneider Hill, William E. Hannaford Jr., and Ronald H. Epp, pp. 3–14. Chicago: ALA, 1991.

Chronister, Jay L. "Institutional Culture and the New Professoriate." *Academe* 77 (Sept.–Oct. 1991): 22–25.

Cleveland, Harlan. *The Knowledge Executive: Leadership in an Information Society.* New York: Dutton, 1985.

Cohen, Charlotte. "Faculty Liaison: A Cooperative Venture in Bibliographic Instruction." *Reference Librarian* no. 51/52 (1995): 161–69.

Cohen, Michael D., and James G. March. *Leadership and Ambiguity: The American College President*, 2nd Edition. Boston: Harvard Business School Pr., 1986.

Cole, Jonathan R. "Balancing Acts: Dilemmas of Choice Facing Research Universities." In *The Research University in a Time of Discontent*. Edited by Jonathan R. Cole, Elinor G. Barber, and Stephen R. Graubard, pp. 1–36. Baltimore: Johns Hopkins University Press, 1993.

Congress for Professional Education. "Recommendations—Congress for Professional Education." 1999. Available online at http://www.ala.org/ala/hrdrbucket/2nd congressonpro/2ndcongressprofessionaleducationfinal.htm#recs.

Cook, Colleen, Fred M. Heath, and Bruce Thompson. "'Zones of Tolerance' in Perceptions of library Service Quality: A LibQUAL+™ Study." *portal* 3 (January 2003): 112–23.

Crawford, Walt, and Michael Gorman. *Future Libraries: Dreams, Madness, & Reality.* Chicago: ALA, 1995.

Creth, Sheila D. "Creating a Virtual Information Organization: Collaborative Relationships between Libraries and Computing Centers." *Journal of Library Administration* 19, nos. 3/4 (1993): 111–32.

Culliton, Barbara J. "Harvard Tackles the Rush to Publication." *Science* 241 (July 29, 1988): 525.

Cummings, Anthony M., et al. *University Libraries and Scholarly Communication.* Washington, D.C.: Association of Research Libraries for the Andrew W. Mellon Foundation, 1992.

Darnton, Robert. "The New Age of the Book." *New York Review of* Books 46 (Mar. 19, 1999): 5–7.

Davidson, Cathy N. "The Futures of Scholarly Publishing." *Journal of Scholarly Publishing* (Apr. 2004): 129–42.

Davis, C. Roger. "No Difference But Dollars: Collection Development in College versus University Libraries." In *Collection Development in College Libraries.* Edited by Joanne Schneider Hill, William E. Hannaford Jr., and Ronald H. Epp, pp. 24–34. Chicago: ALA, 1991.

Davis, Philip M. "Tragedy of the Commons Revisited: Librarians, Publishers, Faculty and the Demise of a Public Resource." *portal: Libraries and the Academy* 3 (Oct. 2003): 547–62.

"Dean's List: 10 School Heads Debate the Future of Library Education." *Library Journal* 119 (April 1, 1994): 60–64.

Dempsey, John R. "An Essay: Reflections of a College President." *Community College Review* 20 (Fall 1992): 45–49.

DePew, John N. "The ACRL Standards for Faculty Status: Panacea or Placebo?" *College & Research Libraries* 44 (Nov. 1983): 407–13.

Dewey, Barbara I. "Personnel Costs and Patterns in Libraries." *Library Trends* 42 (winter 1994): 537–46.

Diaz, Joseph R., and Chestalene Pintozzi. "Helping Teams Work: Lessons Learned from the University of Arizona Library Reorganization." *Library Administration & Management* 13 (Winter 1999): 27–36.

Dill, David D. "The Management of Academic Culture: Notes on the Management of Meaning and Social Integration." *Higher Education* 11 (1982): 303–20.

———. "Research as a Scholarly Activity: Context and Culture." *Measuring Faculty Research Performance, New Directions for Institutional Research* no. 50 (June 1986): 7-23.

Dilmore, Donald H. "Librarian/Faculty Interaction at Nine New England Colleges." *College & Research Libraries* 57 (May 1996): 274–84.

Dimond, John G. "Faculty Involvement in Institutional Budgeting." *New Direction for Higher Education* no. 75 (fall 1991): 63–78.

Dingley, Brenda. "U.S. Periodical Prices—2003." *Library & Technical Resources* 47 (Oct. 2003): 192–207.

Dominguez, Patricia Buck, and Luke Swindler. "Cooperative Collection Development Work." *College & Research Libraries* 54 (Nov. 1993): 470–96.

Dooris, Michael J., and James S. Fairweather. "Structure and Culture in Faculty Work: Implications for Technology Transfer." *Review of Higher Education* 17 (winter 1994): 161–77.

Dougherty, Richard M., and Fred J. Heinritz. *Scientific Management of Library Operations*, 2nd Edition. Metuchen, N.J.: Scarecrow Pr., 1982.

Dougherty, Richard M., and Lisa McClure. "Repositioning Campus Information Units in the Era of Digital Libraries." In *Restructuring Academic Libraries: Organizational Development in the Wake of Technological Change.* Edited by Charles A Schwartz, pp. 67–80. Chicago: ACRL, 1997.

Doty, Paul. "How Index-Learning Turns No Student Pale: An Essay on Rhetoric and Bibliographic Instruction." *Reference Librarian* no. 51/52 (1995): 121–29.

Dowd, Sheila T. "Library Cooperation: Methods, Models to Aid Information Access." *Journal of Library Administration* 12 (1990): 63–81.

Dowell, David R., and Jack A. Scott. "What Community Colleges Need from Their Libraries." In *Academic Libraries: Their Rationale and Role in American Higher Education.* Edited by Gerard B. McCabe and Ruth J. Person, pp. 15–27. Westport, Conn.: Greenwood Pr., 1995.

Dowlin, Kenneth. "Distribution in an Electronic Environment, or Will There Be Libraries as We Know Them in the Internet World." *Library Trends* 43 (winter 1995): 409–17.

Doyle, Helen J. "The Public Library of Science: Open Access from the Ground Up." *College & Research Libraries News* 65 (Mar. 2004): 134–36, 152.

Drucker, Peter F. *Post-Capitalist Society.* New York: Harper Business, 1993.

D'Souza, Dinesh. *Illiberal Education: The Politics of Race and Sex on Campus.* New York: Free Pr., 1991.

Duderstadt, James J. *A University for the 21st Century.* Ann Arbor: University of Michigan Pr., 2000.

Dugger, Ronnie. "Introduction: The Struggle That Matters the Most." In *Campus, Inc.: Corporate Power in the Ivory Tower.* Edited by Geoffrey D. White, with Flannery C. Hauck, pp. 17–26. Amherst, N.Y.: Prometheus Books, 2000.

Eagleton, Terry. *Ideology: An Introduction.* London: Verso, 1991.

Edmundson, Mark. "Introduction: The Academy Writes Back." In *Wild Orchids and Trotsky*, pp. 3–28. New York: Penguin, 1993.

Eisenstein, Elizabeth L. *The Printing Press as an Agent of Change: Communications and Cultural Transformation in Early-Modern Europe*, volumes 1 and 2. Cambridge: Cambridge University Pr., 1979.

Elliott, Stephen. "Better Than Golde: Libraries and the New Information Economy." *Canadian Library Journal* 49 (Oct. 1992): 361–64.

Esposito, Joseph J. "The Devil You Don't Know: The Unexpected Future of Open Access Publishing." *First Monday.* 2004. Available online at http://www.firstmonday.org/issues/issue9_8/esposito/index.html.

Etzioni, Amitai. "Compliance, Goals, and Effectiveness." In *Classics of Organization Theory*, 2nd Edition. Edited by Jay M. Shafritz and J. Steven Ott, pp. 177–87. Chicago: Dorsey Pr., 1987.

Euster, Joanne R. *The Academic Library Director: Management Activities and Effectiveness.* Westport, Conn.: Greenwood Pr., 1987.

Faerman, Sue R. "Organizational Change and Leadership Styles." *Journal of Library Administration* 19, nos. 3/4 (1993): 55–79.

Farber, Evan. "Bibliographic Instruction at Earlham College." In *Bibliographic Instruction in Practice: A Tribute to the Legacy of Evan Ira Farber.* Edited by Larry Hardesty, Jamie Hastreiter, and David Henderson, pp. 1–25. Ann Arbor, Mich.: Pierian Pr., 1993.

"The Fate of the Undergraduate Library." *Library Journal* 125 (Nov. 1, 2000): 38–41.

Fayol, Henri. "General Principles of Management." In *Organization Theory: Selected Readings.* Edited by D. S. Pugh, pp. 101–23. Harmondsworth: Penguin, 1971.

Flexner, Abraham. *Medical Education in the United States and Canada.* New York: Carnegie Foundation for the Advancement of Teaching, 1910.

———. *Universities: American, English, German.* New York: Oxford University Pr., 1930.

Foucault, Michel. "Fantasia of the Library." In *Language, Counter-Memory, Practice: Selected Essays and Interviews.* Edited by Donald F. Bouchard, translated by Donald F. Bouchard and Sherry Simon, pp. 87–109. Ithaca, N.Y.: Cornell University Pr., 1977.

Frank, Donald G., Gregory K. Raschke, Julie Wood, and Julie Z. Ying. "Information Consulting: The Key to Success in Academic Libraries." *Journal of Academic Librarianship* 27 (Mar. 2001): 90–96.

Franklin, Hardy R. "Customer Service: The Heart of the Library." *American Libraries* 24 (July/August 1993): 677.

Franklin, Phyllis. "Scholars, Librarians, and the Future of Primary Records." *College & Research Libraries* 54 (Sept. 1993): 397–406.

Frazier, Kenneth. "The Librarian's Dilemma: Contemplating the Costs of the 'Big Deal' Computer File." *D-Lib Magazine* 7 (March 2001). Available at http://www.dlib.org/dlib.html.

Friday, William. "The Future of the American Research University." In *For the Good of the Order: Essays in Honor of Edward G. Holley.* Edited by Delmus E. Williams et al., pp. 31–36. Greenwich, Conn.: JAI Pr., 1994.

Galloway, Ann-Christe. "Grants and Acquisitions." *College & Research Libraries News* 65 (Apr. 2004): 228–29.

Gandhi, Smiti. "Academic Librarians and Distance Education." *Reference & User Services Quarterly* 43 (winter 2003): 138–54.

Gapen, D. Kaye. "The Campus Context." In *Leadership for Research Libraries: A Festschrift for Robert M. Hayes.* Edited by Anne Woodsworth and Barbara von Wahlde, pp. 41–66. Metuchen, N.J.: Scarecrow Pr., 1988.

Geiger, Roger L. *To Advance Knowledge: The Growth of American Research Universities, 1900–1940.* New York: Oxford University Pr., 1986.

Getman, Julius. *In the Company of Scholars: The Struggle for the Soul of Higher Education.* Austin: University of Texas Pr., 1992.

Getz, Malcolm. "Analysis and Library Management." In *Academic Libraries: Research Perspectives.* Edited by Mary Jo Lynch and Arthur Young, pp. 192–214. Chicago: ALA, 1990.

Giesecke, Joan R. "Reorganizations: An Interview with Staff from the University of Arizona Libraries." *Library Administration & Management* 8 (fall 1994): 196–99.

Goudy, Frank W. "Academic Libraries and the Six Percent Solution: A Twenty-year Financial Overview." *Journal of Academic Librarianship* 19 (Sept. 1993): 212–15.

Graham, Peter S. "Requirements for the Digital Research Library." *College & Research Libraries* 56 (July 1995): 331–39.

Grant, Joan. "Approval Plans: The Vendor as Preselector." In *Understanding the Business of Library Acquisitions.* Edited by Karen A. Schmidt, pp. 153–64. Chicago: ALA, 1990.

Grassian, Esther S., and Joan R. Kaplowitz. *Information Literacy Instruction: Practice and Theory.* New York: Neal-Schuman, 2001.

Gratch-Lindauer, Bonnie. "Comparing the Regional Accreditation Standards: Outcomes Assessment and Other Trends." *Journal of Academic Librarianship*, 28 (Jan.–Feb. 2002): 14–25.

Griffith, Belver C. "Understanding Science: Studies of Communication and Information." In *Scholarly Communication and Bibliometrics.* Edited by Christine L. Borgman. Newbury Park, Calif.: Sage, 1990.

Gross, Melissa. "Imposed versus Self-generated Questions: Implications for Reference Practice." *Reference & User Services Quarterly* 39 (fall 1999): 53–61.

"Guidelines for Academic Status of College and University Libraries." *College & Research Libraries News* 62 (Oct. 2001): 920–21.

Guterman, Lila. "The Promise and Peril of 'Open Access.'" *Chronicle of Higher Education* 50 (Jan. 30, 2004): A10–A14.

Hage, Jerald, and Michael Aiken. "Program Change and Organizational Properties: A Comparative Analysis." *American Journal of Sociology* 72 (Mar. 1967): 503–9.

Hamaker, Charles A. "Management Data for Selection Decisions in Building Library Collections." *Journal of Library Administration* 17, no. 2 (1992): 71–97.6

Hamlin, Arthur T. *The University Library in the United States: Its Origins and Development.* Philadelphia: University of Pennsylvania Pr., 1981.

Hammond, Carol. "Nontraditional Students and the Library: Opinions, Preferences, and Behaviors." *College & Research Libraries* 55 (July 1994): 323–41.

Harding, Thomas S. *College Literary Societies: Their Contribution to Higher Education in the United States 1815–1876.* New York: Pageant Pr. International, 1971.

Harloe, Bart, and John M. Budd. "Collection Development and Scholarly Communication in the Era of Electronic Access." *Journal of Academic Librarianship* 20 (May 1994): 83–87.

Harris, Michael H., and Stan A. Hannah. "The Treason of Libraries: Core Communication Technology and Opportunity Costs in the Information Era." *Journal of Academic Librarianship* 22 (Jan. 1996): 3–8.

Harrison, Teresa M., and Timothy D. Stephen. "The Electronic Journal as the Heart of an Online Scholarly Community." *Library Trends* 43 (spring 1995): 592–608.

Harvey, William B., et al. "The Impending Crisis in University Publishing." *Scholarly Publishing* 3 (Apr. 1972): 195–207.

Haskins, Charles Homer. *The Rise of the Universities.* Ithaca, N.Y.: Cornell University Press, 1957.

Hawkes, David. *Ideology.* London: Routledge, 1996.

Hayes, Robert M. *Strategic Management for Academic Libraries: A Handbook.* Westport, Conn.: Greenwood Pr., 1993.

———. "Strategic Management of Libraries and Information Resources." In *Collection Management for the 1990s.* Edited by Joseph J. Branin, pp. 16–38. Chicago: ALA 1993.

Hayes, Sherman, and Don Brown. "The Library as a Business: Mapping the Pervasiveness of Financial Relationships in Today's Library." *Library Trends* 42 (winter 1994): 404–19.

Hazen, Dan C. "Collection Development Policies in the Information Age." *College & Research Libraries* 56 (Jan. 1995): 29–31.

He, Peter Wei, and Michael Knee. "The Challenge of Electronic Services Librarianship." *RSR: Reference Services Review* 23, no. 4 (1995): 7–12.

Henderson, Albert. "Letter to the Editor." *College & Research Libraries* 57 (May 1996): 301–2.

Hernon, Peter, Ronald R. Powell, and Arthur P. Young. "Association of Research Libraries: The Next Generation, Part One." *College & Research Libraries* 62 (Mar. 2001): 116–45.

———. *The Next Library Leadership: Attributes of Academic and Public Library Leaders.* Westport, Conn.: Libraries Unlimited, 2003.

———. "University Library Directors in the Association of Research Libraries: The Next Generation, Part Two." *College & Research Libraries* 63 (Jan. 2002): 73–90.

Hersey, Karen. "Coping with Copyright and Beyond: New Challenges as the Library Goes Digital." In *Copyright, Public Policy, and the Scholarly Community.* Edited by Michael Matthews and Patricia Brennan, pp. 23–32. Washington, D.C.: ARL, 1995.

Hildenbrand, Suzanne. "Ambiguous Authority and Aborted Ambition: Gender, Professions, and the Rise of the Welfare State." *Library Trends* 34 (fall 1985): 185–98.

Hill, Michael R. "Creative Journals and Destructive Decisions: A Comment on Singer's 'Academic Crisis.'" *Sociological Inquiry* 60 (summer 1990): 298–300.

Hirsch, E. D., Jr. *Cultural Literacy: What Every American Needs to Know*. New York: Vintage Books, 1988.

Hoadley, Irene B. "Customer Service? Not Really." *College & Research Libraries News* 56 (Mar. 1995): 175–76.

Hoggan, Danielle Bodrero. "Faculty Status for Librarians in Higher Education." *portal: Libraries and the Academy* 3 (July 2003): 431–45.

Holleman, Curt. "Electronic Resources: Are Basic Criteria for the Selection of Materials Changing?" *Library Trends* 48 (spring 2000): 694–710.

Holley, Edward G. "The Librarian Speaks: What the Modern Library Expects of the New Graduate." *Southeastern Librarian* 20 (winter 1970): 222–31.

Hoon, Peggy. "Who Woke the Sleeping Giant?" *Change* 35 (November/December 2003): 28–33.

Horenstein, Bonnie. "Job Satisfaction of Academic Librarians: An Examination of the Relationships between Satisfaction, Faculty Status, and Participation." *College & Research Libraries* 54 (May 1993): 255–69.

Houghton, Bernard. *Scientific Periodicals: Their Historical Development, Characteristics and Control*. Hamden, Conn.: Linnet Books, 1975.

Howze, Philip C. "Collegiality, Collegial Management, and Academic Libraries. *Journal of Academic Librarianship* 29 (Jan. 2003): 40–43.

Hummel, Ralph P. *The Bureaucratic Experience*, 4th Edition. New York: St. Martin's Pr., 1994.

"Information Literacy Competency Standards for Higher Education." Chicago: ACRL, 2000. Available online at http://www.ala.org/acrl/acrl/acrlstandards/information literacycompetency.htm.

Ingwersen, Peter. "Information and Information Science in Context." In *Information Science: From the Development of the Discipline to Social Interaction*. Edited by Johan Olaisen, Erland Munch-Pederson, and Patrick Wilson, pp. 69–111. Oslo: Scandinavian University Pr., 1995.

James, William. "The Ph.D. Octopus." *Harvard Monthly* 36 (1903): 1–9.

Johnson, Corey M. "Online Chat Reference: Survey Results from Affiliates of Two Universities." *Reference & User Services Quarterly* 43 (spring 2004): 237–47.

Johnson, Benjamin, Patrick Kavanaugh, and Kevin Mattson. *Steal This University*. New York: Routledge, 2003.

Jones, Phillip J. "Individual Accountability and Individual Authority: The Missing Links." *Library Administration & Management* 14 (summer 2000): 135–45.

Katz, Daniel, and Robert L. Kahn. "Organizations and the System Concept." In *Classics of Organization Theory*, 2nd Edition. Edited by Jay M. Shafritz and J. Steven Ott, pp. 250–62. Chicago: Dorsey Pr., 1987.

Keller, George. *Academic Strategy: The Management Revolution in American Higher Education*. Baltimore: Johns Hopkins University Pr., 1983.

Keller, Michael A. "Moving toward Concrete Solutions Based in Fundamental Values." *Journal of Academic Librarianship* 18 (Mar. 1992): 7–8.

Kerr, Clark. *The Uses of the University*, 5th edition. Cambridge, Mass.: Harvard University Pr., 2001.

Kevil, Hunter S. "The Approval Plan of Smaller Scope." *Library Acquisitions: Practice and Theory* 9 (1985): 13–20.

Kirp, David L. *Shakespeare, Einstein, and the Bottom Line: The Marketing of Higher Education.* Cambridge, Mass.: Harvard University Pr., 2003.

Kling, Rob, and Roberta Lamb. "Analyzing Alternate Visions of Electronic Publishing and Digital Libraries." In *Scholarly Publishing: The Electronic Frontier.* Edited by Robin P. Peek and Gregory B. Newby, pp. 17–54. Cambridge, Mass.: MIT Pr., 1996.

Kochan, Carol Ann, and John M. Budd. "The Persistence of Fraud in the Literature: The Darsee Case." *Journal of the American Society for Information Science* 47 (Aug. 1992): 488–93.

Koenig, Michael, Ronald Morrison, and Linda Roberts. "Faculty Status for Library Professionals: Its Effect on Job Turnover and Job Satisfaction among University Research Library Directors." *College & Research Libraries* 57 (May 1996): 295–300.

Kyrillidou, Martha. "Research Library Trends: ARL Statistics." *Journal of Academic Librarianship* 26 (November 2000): 427–36.

LaFollette, Marcel C. *Stealing into Print: Fraud, Plagiarism, and Misconduct in Scientific Publishing.* Berkeley: University of California Pr., 1992.

Lam, K. D., Frank D. Watson, and Stephen R. Schmidt. *Total Quality: A Textbook of Strategic Quality Leadership and Planning.* Colorado Springs, Colo.: Air Academy Pr., 1991.

Lanham, Richard A. *The Electronic Word: Democracy, Technology, and the Arts.* Chicago: University of Chicago Pr., 1993.

Leach, Ronald G., and Judith E. Tribble. "Electronic Document Delivery: New Options for Libraries." *Journal of Academic Librarianship* 18 (Jan. 1993): 359–64.

Lee, Susan. "Organizational Change in the Harvard College Library: A Continued Struggle for Redefinition and Renewal." *Journal of Academic Librarianship* 19 (Sept. 1993): 225–30.

Lehmann, Stephen, and Patricia Renfro. "Humanists and Electronic Information Services: Acceptance and Resistance." *College & Research Libraries* 52 (Sept. 1991): 409–13.

Lessig, Lawrence. *Free Culture: How Big Media Uses Technology and the Law to Lock Down Culture and Control Creativity.* New York: Penguin, 2004.

Levi, Edward H. *Point of View: Talks on Education.* Chicago: University of Chicago Pr., 1969.

Lewis, David W. "Economics of the Scholarly Journal." *College & Research Libraries* 50 (Nov. 1989): 674–88.

Library Statistics of College and Universities, 1976 Institutional Data. Urbana–Champaign, Ill.: University of Illinois, Graduate School of Library Science, 1979.

Library Statistics of Colleges and Universities: 1979 Institutional Data. Washington, D.C.: National Center for Education Statistics, 1981.

Library Statistics of Colleges and Universities, 1982 Institutional Data. Chicago: ACRL, 1984.

Library Statistics of Colleges and Universities, 1985. Chicago: ACRL, 1987.

Lipinski, Tomas A. "The Climate of Distance Education in the 21st Century: Understanding and Surviving the Changes Brought about by the TEACH (Technology, Education, and Copyright Harmonization) Act of 2002." *Journal of Academic Librarianship* 29 (Nov. 2003): 362–74.

Louis, Mary Reis. "Organizations as Culture-bearing Milieux." In *Classics of Organization Theory*, 2nd Edition. Edited by Jay M. Shafritz and J. Steven Ott, pp. 421–32. Chicago: Dorsey Pr., 1987.

Lowry, Charles B. "The Status of Faculty Status for Academic Librarians: A Twenty-year Perspective." *College & Research Libraries* 54 (Mar. 1993): 163–72.

Lucas, Christopher J. *Crisis in the Academy: Rethinking Higher Education in America.* New York: St. Martin's Pr., 1996.

Lukacs, Georg. *History and Class Consciousness: Studies in Marxist Dialectics.* Translated by Rodney Livingstone. Cambridge, Mass.: MIT Pr., 1971.

Lynch, Beverly P. "Changes in Library Organization." In *Leadership for Research Libraries: A Festschrift for Robert M. Hayes.* Edited by Anne Woodsworth and Barbara von Wahlde, pp. 67–78. Metuchen, N.J.: Scarecrow Pr., 1988.

Lynch, Clifford A. "Institutional Repositories: Essential Infrastructure for Scholarship in the Digital Age." *portal: Libraries and the Academy* 3 (Apr. 2003): 327–36.

Lynch, Mary Jo. *Alternative Sources of Revenue in Academic Libraries.* Chicago: ALA, 1991.

Lyotard, Jean-François. *The Postmodern Condition: A Report on Knowledge.* Translated by Geoff Bennington and Brian Massumi. Minneapolis: University of Minnesota Pr., 1984.

MacWhinnie, Laurie A. "The Information Commons: The Library of the Future." *portal: Libraries and the Academy* 3 (Apr. 2003): 241–57.

Magner, Denise K. "Brigham Young U. Professors Must Prove Spiritually Worthy." *Chronicle of Higher Education* 42 (Feb. 23, 1996): A17.

Marchant, Maurice. 1985. "The Library as an Open System." In *Management Strategies for Libraries: A Basic Reader*, edited by Beverly P. Lynch, 151–66. New York: Neal-Schuman.

Martell, Charles R., Jr. *The Client-centered Academic Library: An Organizational Model.* Westport, Conn.: Greenwood Pr., 1983.

Martin, Joanne, and Caren Siehl. 1983. "Organizational Culture and Counterculture: An Uneasy Symbiosis." *Organizational Dynamics* 12 (autumn): 52–64.

Marx, Karl. *Capital*, an abridged edition. Edited by David McLellan. Oxford: Oxford University Pr., 1995.

Matarazzo, James M. "The M.L.S. Hiring Requirement: A Tremendous Vote of Confidence." *Journal of Academic Librarianship* 27 (July 2001): 253–54.

McCabe, Mark J. "The Impact of Publisher Mergers on Journal Prices: Theory and Evidence." In *Making Waves, New Serials Landscapes in a Sea of Change*. Edited by Joseph C. Harmon and P. Michelle Fiander, pp. 157–66. New York: Haworth Pr., 2001.

McCue, Janet. "Technical Services and the Electronic Library: Defining Our Roles and Divining the Partnership." *Library Hi-Tech* 12, no. 3 (1994): 63–70.

McDonald, Kim A. "Scientists Urged to Help Resolve Library 'Crisis' by Shunning High-Cost, Low-Quality Journals." *Chronicle of Higher Education* 36 (Feb. 28, 1990): A6.

McGowan, Julie J, and Elizabeth H. Dow. "Faculty Status and Academic Librarianship: Transformation to a Clinical Model." *Journal of Academic Librarianship* 21 (Sept. 1995): 345–50.

McInnis, Raymond. "Do Metaphors Make Good Sense in Teaching Research Strategy?" In *Theories of Bibliographic Education: Designs for Teaching*. Edited by Cerise Oberman and Katina Strauch, pp. 47–74. New York: Bowker, 1982.

———. "Why Library Schools Need to Change Their Curriculums." In *Russian–American Seminar on Critical Thinking and the Library*. Edited by Cerise Oberman and Dennis Kimmage, pp. 127—50. Occasional Papers of the Graduate School of Library and Information Science, University of Illinois at Urbana–Champaign, Nos. 200/201, 1995.

McMurray, Adela. 2003. "The Relationship between Organizational Climate and Organizational Culture." *Journal of the American Academy of Business* 3, no. 1: 1–15.

McNeer, Elizabeth J. "Learning Theories and Library Instruction." *Journal of Academic Librarianship* 17 (Nov. 1991): 294–97.

Mele, Domenec. "Organizational Humanizing Culture." *Journal of Business Ethics* 45 (June 2003): 3–14.

Mellon, Constance A. "Information Problem-solving: A Developmental Approach to Library Instruction." In *Theories of Bibliographic Education: Designs for Teaching*. Edited by Cerise Oberman and Katina Strauch, pp. 75–89. New York: Bowker, 1982.

Melville, Annette. *Resource Strategies in the '90s: Trends in ARL University Libraries*. Washington, D.C.: ARL, 1994.

Mermin, N. David. *Boojums All the Way Through: Communicating Science in a Prosaic Age*. Cambridge: Cambridge University Pr., 1990.

Millson-Martula, Christopher, and Vanaja Menon. "Customer Expectations: Concepts and Reality for Academic Library Services." *College & Research Libraries* 56 (Jan. 1995): 33–47.

Mintzberg, Henry. *Mintzberg on Management: Inside Our Strange World of Organizations*. New York: Free Pr., 1989.

"Model Statement of Criteria and Procedures for Appointment, Promotion in Academic Rank, and Tenure for College and University Librarians." *College & Research Libraries News* 48 (May 1987): 247–54.

Mitcham, Carl. *Thinking through Technology: The Path between Engineering and Philosophy*. Chicago: University of Chicago Pr., 1994.

Molyneux, Robert E. "Growth at ARL Member Libraries, 1962/63 to 1983/84." *Journal of Academic Librarianship* 12 (Sept. 1986a): 211–16.

———. "More Hortatory Than Factual: Fremont Rider's Exponential Growth Hypothesis and the Concept of Exponentialism." In *For the Good of the Order: Essays in Honor of Edward G. Holley*. Edited by Delmus E. Williams et al., pp. 85–117. Greenwich, Conn.: JAI Pr., 1994.

———. "Patterns, Processes of Growth, and the Projection of Library Size: A Critical Review of the Literature on Academic Library Growth." *Library & Information Science Research* 8 (Jan.–Mar. 1986b): 5–28.

Moorehead, Alan. "The Angel in May." *New Yorker* 27 (Feb. 24, 1951): 34–65.

Morgan, Gareth. *Images of Organization*. Beverly Hills, Calif.: Sage, 1986.

MU Research: Summary of Grant and Contract Activity, Fiscal Year 1996. Columbia, Mo.: Office of Research, University of Missouri-Columbia, 1996.

Muller, Steven. "Presidential Leadership." In *The Research University in a Time of Discontent*. Edited by Jonathan R. Cole, Elinor G. Barber, and Stephen R. Graubard, pp. 115–30. Baltimore: Johns Hopkins University Pr., 1994.

Munn, Ralph. *Conditions and Trends in Education for Librarians*. New York: Carnegie Corporation, 1936.

Mutter, Sharon A., and Shahin Hashtroubi. "Cognitive Effort and the Word Frequency Effect in Recognition and Lexical Decision." *American Journal of Psychology* 100 (spring 1987): 93–116.

Naismith, Rachael, and Joan Stein. "Library Jargon: Student Comprehension of Technical Language Used by Librarians." *College & Research Libraries* 50 (Sept. 1989): 543–52.

National Center for Education Statistics. *Digest of Education Statistics, 1995*. Washington, D.C.: U.S. Department of Education, Office of Educational Research and Improvement, 1995.

———. *Digest of Education Statistics, 2003*. Washington, D.C.: U.S. Department of Education, Office of Educational Research and Improvement, 2003.

National Enquiry into Scholarly Communication. 1979. *Scholarly Communication: The Report of the National Enquiry*. Baltimore: Johns Hopkins University Press.

Neal, James G., and Patricia A. Steele. "Empowerment, Organization and Structure: The Experience of the Indiana University Libraries." *Journal of Library Administration* 19, nos. 3/4 (1993): 81–96.

Negroponte, Nicholas. *Being Digital.* New York: Knopf, 1995.

Nelson, Cary, and Michael Bérubé. "Introduction: A Report from the Front." In *Higher Education under Fire: Politics, Economics, and the Crisis of the Humanities.* Edited by Michael Berube and Cary Nelson, pp. 1–32. New York: Routledge, 1995.

Nisonger, Thomas E. *Management of Serials in Libraries.* Englewood, Colo.: Libraries Unlimited, 1998.

Nixon, Will. "University Presses: Highs and Lows." *Publishers Weekly* 236 (Sept. 22, 1989): 18–24.

Noble, David F. *Digital Diploma Mills: The Automation of Higher Education.* New York: Monthly Review Pr., 2003.

Noll, Roger, and W. Edward Steinmueller. "An Economic Analysis of Scientific Journal Prices: Preliminary Results." *Serials Review* 18 (spring–summer 1992): 32–37.

Oberman, Cerise, and Rebecca A. Linton. "Guided Design: Teaching Library Research as Problem-solving." In *Theories of Bibliographic Education: Designs for Teaching.* Edited by Cerise Oberman and Katina Strauch, pp. 111–34. New York: Bowker, 1982.

O'Donnell, Michael J. "Electronic Journals: Scholarly Invariants in a Changing Medium." *Journal of Scholarly Publishing* 26 (Apr. 1995): 183–99.

Oswick, Cliff, Peter Anthony, Tom Keenoy, and Iain L. Mangham. "A Dialogic Analysis of Organizational Learning." *Journal of Management Studies* 37 (Sept. 2000): 887–901.

Palmer, F. R. *Semantics,* 2nd Edition. Cambridge: Cambridge University Pr., 1981.

Park, Betsy, and Robert Riggs. "Status of the Profession: A 1989 National Survey of Tenure and Promotion Policies for Academic Librarians." *College & Research Libraries* 52 (May 1991): 75–89.

Patterson, Samuel C., and Shannon K. Smithey. "Monitoring Scholarly Journal Publication in Political Science: The Role of the ASPR." *PS* 23 (Dec. 1990): 647–56.

Payne, Joyce, and Janet Wagner. "Librarians, Publication, and Tenure." *College & Research Libraries* 45 (Mar. 1984): 133–39.

"The Payoff for Publication Leaders." *Change* 23 (Mar.–Apr. 1991): 27–30.

Pelikan, Jaroslav. *The Idea of the University: A Reexamination.* New Haven, Conn.: Yale University Pr., 1992.

Perkins, F. B. "On Professorships of Books and Reading." In *Public Libraries in the United States of America: Their History, Condition, and Management,* pp. 230–39. Washington, D.C.: Government Printing Office, 1876.

Peterson, Lorna. "The Transition of Traditional Bibliographic Instruction to Information Literacy." In *International Yearbook of Library and Information Management, 2001–2002.* Edited by G. E. Gorman, pp. 279–97. London: Library Association Publishing, 2001.

Peterson, Marvin W., and Theodore H. White. "Faculty and Administrator Perceptions of Their Environments: Different Views or Different Models of Organization?" *Research in Higher Education* 33 (Apr. 1992): 177–204.

Pfeffer, Jeffrey. *Organizations and Organization Theory.* Boston: Pitman, 1982.

Philipson, Morris. "Intrinsic Value versus Market Value." In *Publishers and Librarians: A Foundation for Dialogue.* Edited by Mary Biggs, pp. 13–20. Chicago: University of Chicago Pr., 1984.

Phipps, Shelley E. "Transforming Libraries into Learning Organizations: The Challenge for Leadership." *Journal of Library Administration* 18, nos. 3/4 (1993): 19–37.

Postman, Neil. *Technopoly: The Surrender of Culture to Technology.* New York: Knopf, 1992.

Praeger, Frederick A. "Librarians, Publishers, and Scholars, Common Interests, Different Views: The View of an Independent Scholarly Publisher." In *Publishers and Librarians: A Foundation for Dialogue.* Edited by Mary Biggs, pp. 21–29. Chicago: University of Chicago Pr., 1984.

Pritchard, Sarah M. "Determining Quality in Academic Libraries." *Library Trends* 44 (Winter 1996): 572–94.

Prosser, David. "Institutional Repositories and Open Access: The Future of Scholarly Communication." *Information Services & Use* 23 (2003): 167–70.

Rader, Joe. "The Second Master's—Some Personal Views." *Tennessee Librarian* 30 (fall 1978): 29–31.

Radford, Gary P. "Positivism, Foucault, and the Fantasia of the Library: Conceptions of Knowledge and the Modern Library Experience." *Library Quarterly* 62 (Oct. 1992): 408–24.

Rayman, Ronald, and Frank W. Goudy. "Research and Publication Requirements in University Libraries." *College & Research Libraries* 41 (Jan. 1980): 43–48.

Readings, Bill. *The University in Ruins.* Cambridge, Mass.: Harvard University Pr., 1996.

Reichel, Mary. "Statement for Congress on Professional Education: Issues in Higher Education and Library and Information Studies Education." 1999. Available online at http://www.ala.org/ala/ hrdrbucket/1stcongressonpro/1stcongress association.htm.

Rettig, James. "A Theoretical Model and Definition of the Reference Process." *RQ* 18 (fall 1978): 19–29.

Rhodes, Frank H. T. *The Creation of the Future.* Ithaca, N.Y.: Cornell University Pr., 2001.

Rider, Fremont. *The Scholar and the Future of the Research Library: A Problem and Its Solution.* New York: Hadham Pr., 1944.

Robinson, Charles. "Can We Save the Public's Library?" *Library Journal* 114 (Sept. 1, 1989): 147–52.

Robinson, William C. "Academic Library Collection Development and Management Positions: Announcements in *College & Research Libraries News* from 1980 through 1991." *Library Resources & Technical Services* 37 (Apr. 1993): 134–46.

Rosenzweig, Robert M. "Governing the Modern University." In *The Research University in a Time of Discontent*. Edited by Jonathan R. Cole, Elinor G. Barber, and Stephen R. Graubard, pp. 299–308. Baltimore: Johns Hopkins University Pr., 1994.

———. *The Political University: Policy, Politics, and Presidential Leadership in the American Research University*. Baltimore: Johns Hopkins University Pr., 2001.

Roszak, Theodore. *The Cult of Information*. Berkeley: University of California Pr., 1986.

Rudolph, Frederick. *The American College and University: A History*. New York: Vintage Books, 1962.

Sannwald, William. "Understanding Organizational Culture." *Library Administration & Management* 14 (winter 2000): 8–14.

Schein, Edgar H. "Defining Organizational Culture." In *Classics of Organization Theory*, 2nd Edition. Edited by Jay M. Shafritz and J. Steven Ott, pp. 381–95. Chicago: Dorsey Pr., 1987.

———. "Three Culture of Management: The Key to Organizational Learning." *Sloan Management Review* 38 (fall 1996): 9–20.

Schiller, Dan. "From Culture to Information and Back Again: Commodification as a Route to Knowledge." *Critical Studies in Mass Communication* 11 (Mar. 1994): 93–115.

Scholarly Communication: The Report of the National Enquiry. Baltimore: Johns Hopkins University Pr., 1979.

Schwartz, Charles A. "Scholarly Communication as a Loosely Coupled System: Reassessing Prospects for Structural Reform." *College & Research Libraries* 55 (Mar. 1994): 101–17.

Scudder, Mary C., and John R. Scudder Jr. "Faculty Involvement in College Library Collection Development." In *Collection Development in College Libraries*. Edited by Joanne Schneider Hill, William E. Hannaford Jr., and Ronald H. Epp, pp. 140–49. Chicago: ALA, 1991.

Self, Jim. "Using Data to Make Choices: The Balanced Scorecard at the University of Virginia." *ARL* 230/231 (Oct./Dec. 2003): 28–29.

Senge, Peter M. *The Fifth Discipline: The Art & Practice of the Learning Organization*. New York: Doubleday, 1990.

Shafritz, Jay M., and J. Steven Ott. *Classics of Organization Theory*, 2nd Edition. Chicago: Dorsey Pr., 1987.

Shapiro, Ben. *Brainwashed: How Universities Indoctrinate America's Youth*. Nashville, Tenn.: WND Books, 2004.

Shaughnessy, Thomas W. "Benchmarking, Total Quality Management, and Libraries." *Library Administration & Management* 7 (winter 1993): 7–12.

Shiflett, Orvin Lee. *Origins of American Academic Librarianship*. Norwood, N.J.: Ablex, 1981.

Shils, Edward. *The Calling of Education*. Chicago: University of Chicago Pr., 1997.

Shores, Louis. *Origins of the American College Library, 1638–1800*. Hamden, Conn.: Shoe String Press, 1966.

Singer, Benjamin D. "The Criterial Crisis of the Academic World." *Sociological Inquiry* 59 (May 1989): 127–43.

Slaughter, Sheila, and Larry L. Leslie. *Academic Capitalism: Politics, Policies, and the Entrepreneurial University*. Baltimore: Johns Hopkins University Pr., 1997.

Smith, Eldred. *The Librarian, the Scholar, and the Future of the Research Library*. Westport, Conn.: Greenwood Pr., 1990.

Smith, Eldred, and Peggy Johnson. "How to Survive the Present While Preparing for the Future: A Research Library Strategy." *College & Research Libraries* 54 (Sept. 1993): 389–96.

Smith, Michael L. "Recourse of Empire: Landscapes of Progress in Technological America." In *Does Technology Drive History? The Dilemma of Technological Determinism*. Edited by Merritt Roe Smith and Leo Marx, pp. 37–52. Cambridge: Mass.: MIT Pr., 1994.

Solomon, Robert, and Jon Solomon. *Up the University: Re-Creating Higher Education in America*. Reading, Mass.: Addison-Wesley, 1993.

Southern Association of Colleges and Schools. *Principles of Accreditation: Foundations for Quality Enhancement*. Decatur, Ga.: SACS, 2001.

"Standards for Faculty Status for College and University Librarians, 2001." Available online at http://www.ala.org/ala/acrl/standards/standardsfaculty.htm.

"State Legislators Examine Funding for Public Higher Ed." *Spectrum* 28 (Oct. 2001): 3.

Stein, Robert G., and Gifford Pinchot. "Building an Intelligent Organization." *Association Management* 47 (Nov. 1995): 32–39+.

Stelter, Nicole Z. "Gender Differences in Leadership: Current Social Issues and Future Organizational Implications." *Journal of Leadership Studies* 8, no. 4 (2002): 88–99.

Stoffle, Carla J., Barbara Allen, David Morden, and Krisellen Maloney. "Continuing to Build the Future: Academic Libraries and Their Challenges." *portal: Libraries and the Academy* 3 (July 2003): 363–80.

Stoffle, Carla J., and Kathleen Weibel. "Funding Academic Libraries." In *Academic Libraries: Their Rationale and Role in American Higher Education*. Edited by Gerard B. McCabe and Ruth J. Person, pp. 125–48. Westport, Conn.: Greenwood Pr., 1995.

Stoll, Clifford. *Silicon Snake Oil: Second Thoughts on the Information Highway*. New York: Doubleday, 1995.

Stoller, Michael A., Robert Christopherson, and Michael Miranda. "The Economics of Professional Journal Pricing." *College & Research Libraries* 57 (Jan. 1996): 9–21.

Strauch, Katina. "Don't Get Mired in It: Make Some Bricks." *Journal of Academic Librarianship* 18 (Mar. 1992): 12–13.

Stueart, Robert D., and Barbara B. Moran. *Library and Information Center Management*, 4th Edition. Englewood, Colo.: Libraries Unlimited, 1993.

Sykes, Charles J. *ProfScam: Professors and the Demise of Higher Education*. New York: St. Martin's Pr., 1988.

Taylor, Frederick Winslow. "The Principles of Scientific Management." In *Classics of Organization Theory*, 2nd Edition. Edited by Jay M. Shafritz and J. Steven Ott, pp. 66–81. Chicago: Dorsey Pr., 1987.

Terenzini, Patrick T. "On the Nature of Institutional Research and the Knowledge and Skills It Requires." *Research in Higher Education* 34 (Feb. 1993): 1–10.

Thatcher, Sanford. "Scholarly Monographs May Be the Ultimate Victims of the Upheavals in Trade Publishing." *Chronicle of Higher Education* 37 (Oct. 10, 1990): B2–B3.

Thompson, Ann. "Getting into a Cooperative Mode: Making Cooperative Collection Development Work." In *Collection Management for the 1990s*. Edited by Joseph J. Branin, pp. 127–34. Chicago: ALA, 1993.

Thorne, Rosemary, and Jo Bell Whitlatch. "Patron Online Catalog Success." *College & Research Libraries* 55 (Nov. 1994): 479–97.

Tierney, William G. "Academic Work and Institutional Culture: Constructing Knowledge." *Review of Higher Education* 14 (winter 1991): 199–216.

———. "Organizational Culture in Higher Education." *Journal of Higher Education* 59 (Jan.–Feb. 1988): 2–21.

Tighe, Thomas J. *Who's in Charge of America's Research Universities? A Blueprint for Reform*. Albany: State University of New York Pr., 2003.

Townley, Charles T. "Designing Effective Library Organizations." In *Academic Libraries: Their Rationale and Role in American Higher Education*. Edited by Gerard B. McCabe and Ruth J. Person. Westport, Conn.: Greenwood Pr., 1995.

Van House, Nancy A., Beth T. Weil, and Charles R. McClure. *Measuring Academic Library Performance: A Practical Approach*. Chicago: ALA, 1990.

Veaner, Allen B. "Paradigm Lost, Paradigm Regained? A Persistent Personnel Issue in Academic Librarianship, II." *College & Research Libraries* 55 (Sept. 1994): 389–402.

Veblen, Thorstein. *The Higher Learning in America: A Memorandum on the Conduct of Universities by Business Men*. New York: Hill and Wang, 1957.

Veysey, Laurence R. *The Emergence of the American University*. Chicago: University of Chicago Pr., 1965.

Von Ungern-Sternberg, Sara, and Mats G. Lindquist. "The Impact of Electronic Journals on Library Functions." *Journal of Information Science* 21, no. 5 (1995): 396–401.

Wagner, Colette A., and Augusta S. Kappner. "The Academic Library and the Non-Traditional Student." In *Libraries and the Search for Academic Excellence.* Edited by Patricia Senn Breivik and Robert Wedgeworth, pp. 43–56. Metuchen, N.J.: Scarecrow Pr., 1988.

Waters, Lindsay. *Enemies of Promise: Publishing, Perishing, and the Eclipse of Scholarship.* Chicago: Prickly Paradigm Pr., 2004.

Watts, Emily Stipes. "Governing beyond the Individual Campus." *Academe* 77 (Sept.–Oct. 1991): 28–30, 32–33.

Webster, Frank. *Theories of the Information Society.* London: Routledge, 1995.

Weick, Karl E. "Administering Education in Loosely Coupled Schools." *Phi Delta Kappan* 63 (June 1982): 673–76.

———. "Educational Organizations as Loosely Coupled Systems." *Administrative Science Quarterly* 21 (Mar. 1976): 1–19.

Werrell, Emily, and Laura Sullivan. "Faculty Status for Academic Librarians: A Review of the Literature." *College & Research Libraries* 48 (Mar. 1987): 95–103.

Williamson, Charles C. *Training for Library Service.* New York: D. B. Updike, 1923.

Willilnsky, John. "The Nine Flavours of Open Access Scholarly Publishing." *Journal of Postgraduate Medicine* 49, no. 3 (2003): 263–67.

Wilshire, Bruce. *The Moral Collapse of the University: Professionalism, Purity, and Alienation.* Albany: State University of New York Pr., 1990.

Wilson, Karen A. "Outsourcing Copy Cataloging and Physical Processing: A Review of Blackwell's Outsourcing Services for the J. Hugh Jackson Library at Stanford University." *Library Resources & Technical Services* 39 (Oct. 1995): 359–83.

Wilson, Louis Round, and Maurice F. Tauber. *The University Library: Its Organization, Administration, and Functions.* Chicago: University of Chicago Pr., 1945.

Wilson, Patrick. "Some Consequences of Information Overload and Rapid Conceptual Change." In *Information Science: From the Development of the Discipline to Social Interaction.* Edited by Johan Olaisen, Erland Munch-Pedersen, and Patrick Wilson, pp. 21–34. Oslo: Scandinavian University Pr., 1995.

Wilson, Robin. "Faculty Salaries Rise 2.1%, the Lowest Increase in 30 Years." *Chronicle of Higher Education* 50 (Apr. 23, 2004): A12–A13.

———. "A Higher Bar for Earning Tenure." *Chronicle of Higher Education* 47 (Jan. 15, 2001): A12–A14.

———. "Innovation or Ruin?" *Chronicle of Higher Education* 40 (Nov. 30, 1994): A19–A21.

Winston, Mark D., and Lisa Dunkley. "Leadership Competencies for Academic Librarians: The Importance of Development and Fund-raising." *College & Research Libraries* 63 (Mar. 2002): 171–82.

Wolpert, Ann J. "The Future of Electronic Data." *Nature* 420 (Nov. 7, 2002): 17–18.

Zanetti, Lisa A., and Guy B. Adams. "In Service of the Leviathan: Democracy, Ethics and the Potential for Administrative Evil in the New Public Management." *Administrative Theory & Praxis* 22, no. 3 (2000): 534–54.

INDEX

B

Bayer, Alan, 75
Beagle, Donald, 153
Beetham, David, 136
Bénaud, Claire-Lise, 257
Bennett, Douglas, 280
Bennington College, 111
Bennis, Warren, 262–263
Berardo, Felix, 79
Bernal, J. D., 80
Bertalanffy, Ludwig von, 37
Bérubé, Michael, 99, 106
Besser, Howard, 278
Billings, Harold, 281
Birnbaum, Robert, 109, 123
Black, William, 268
Blackboard, 276
Bloom, Allan, 91–92
Bloom, Harold, 95–96
Bodley, Thomas, 15
Bok, Derek, 100, 171
Bolman, Lee, 36, 38–39
Bologna university library, 14
Bonn, Maria, 278
Book publishing, 69–71, 73, 183–184
Books/monographs, 181–185
Bordeianu, Sever, 257
Brancolini, Kristine, 200
Braxton, John, 75
Brigham Young University, 111
Broad, William, 74
Brown, Don, 154–155
Brown, Gary, 184
Brown, Janet Dagenais, 259
Brown, John Seely, 276–277
Buckland, Michael, 150, 205–206, 221–223
Budget growth, 163–164, 171–176. *See also* Financial support
Bureaucracies, 136–140
Bush, Carmel, 255–257
Business model vs. learning model
    costs and, 87–88
    criticisms of, 99–101
    historical aspects of, 24
Business models
    criticisms of, 145
    governance and, 119–122
    management issues and, 154–155
Butler, Nicholas Murray, 24
Butler, Pierce, 250
Buttlar, Lois, 254

C

California trusteeships, 112
Campus, Inc., 99
CannCasciato, Daniel, 256
Carnegie Foundation for the Advancement of Teaching, 64, 94
Casserly, Mary, 194–195
Cataloging & Classification Quarterly, 189
Cataloging materials
    and allocation of monies, 172–173
    librarian education for, 250
    outsourcing of, 255–256
Centralization, 8–9
Christopherson, Robert, 189
Chronister, Jay, 46
Civil War era colleges, 22–25
Classical school approach, 36–37
Cleveland, Harlan, 283–284
Codex volume
Coeducation, 20
Cognitive science
    across disciplines, 11
    faculty and, 49–50
    as faculty influence, 86–87
    of information literacy, 242
Cohen, Charlotte, 242
Cohen, Michael, 263
Collaboration of services, 148, 216–217
Collection departments
    curriculum planning and, 234
    fluidity of, 150–151
    historically, 180–181
    holistic service views and, 11
    organizational culture and, 55–56
    selection authority and, 92
    student recruitment and, 235
Collection Development and Evaluation Section (CODES), 196
Collections
    books, 181–184
    development of, 193–200
    environment and, 191–193, 202
    outsourcing and, 256–257
    physical space and, 191–193
    serials, 184–188
    serials pricing and, 188–191
Colonial colleges, 16–18
Columbia University, 18–19, 25
Commercialization of higher education, 100
Communication. *See also* Evaluations
    bureaucracies and, 137–138

organizational culture and, 47–48
term paper consultation service and, 234
Kochan, Carol, 76

L

Land Grant College Act of 1862, 22–23
Lanham, Richard, 224–225
Leadership, 155, 157–158. *See also* Management
Lehmann, Stephen, 231
Lehrgreiheit/lernfreiheit, 23
Leslie, Larry, 74
Lessig, Lawrence, 279
Leysen, Joan, 268
Lib-License, 212
LibQUAL+^{TM}, 146
Librarians. *See also* Faculty
  education of, 248–253
  and functions of academic library, 253–257
  as managers, 261–265
  status of, 265–270
  users/content and, 257–260
Library and Information Center Management, 114
Library director
  authority and, 2
  leadership and, 262–265
  management issues and, 154
  in structure of governance, 130–131
Library instruction. *See* Information literacy
Library Journal, 62
Library of Congress (LC), 82
Lindquist, Mats, 213
Linton, Rebecca, 238
Literacy. *See* Information literacy
Literacy-based approaches, 243–246
Literary society libraries, 21
Loosely coupled system of governance, 127–129
Louisiana State University (LSU), 22, 112, 190,
  200–201
Lowry, Charles, 267–268
Lucas, Christopher, 98
Lukacs, Georg, 287
Lynch, Clifford, 82
Lyotard, Jean-François, 286–287

M

Magner, Denise, 111
Management. *See also* Organization of
  academic libraries; Organizational culture
  decision making and, 114–115
  importance of leadership alignment with,
    44–45

librarians in, 261–265
Weber on, 34
March, James, 263
Martell, Charles, 145
Matarazzo, James, 253
Mattson, Kevin, 120
McCabe, Mark, 190
McClure, Lisa, 148
McCue, Janet, 255
McGowan, Julie, 270
McInnus, Raymond, 240–241
McMurray, Adela, 44
McNeer, Elizabeth, 242
Measuring Academic Library Performance,
  143–144
Mechanics' Magazine, 62
Mediation, 221
Medieval libraries, 14–16
Mellon, Constance, 237–238
Menon, Vanaja, 144, 259
Mermin, David, 230
Millson-Martula, Christopher, 144, 259
Mintzberg, Henry, 154
Miranda, Michael, 189
Mitcham, Carl, 288
MOBIUS, 204
Modern Language Association, 26, 75
Molyneux, Robert, 28
Moran, Barbara, 114
Morgan, Gareth, 40
Morrill, Justin, 22
Morrison, Ronald, 270
Muller, Steven, 120–121, 123

N

Naismith, Rachel, 239–240
Nanus, Burt, 262–263
National Center for Education Statistics, 166
National Enquiry into Scholarly
  Communication, 68
National Library of Medicine, 217
Neal, James, 140–141
Negroponte, Nicholas, 206
Nelson, Cary, 106
Networked information, 207, 214–217, 275–276
Newman, John Henry Cardinal, 98
Nisonger, Thomas, 201
NLRB v. Yeshiva University, 124
Noll, Roger, 189
Nontraditional students, 6–7, 9–12
North Carolina (volume size of 1900), 25